Beyond Auteurism
New Directions in Authorial Film Practices in France, Italy and Spain since the 1980s

Beyond Auteurism
New Directions in Authorial Film Practices in France, Italy and Spain since the 1980s

Rosanna Maule

intellect Bristol, UK / Chicago, USA

First Published in the UK in 2008 by
Intellect Books, The Mill, Parnall Road, Fishponds, Bristol, BS16 3JG, UK

First published in the USA in 2008 by
Intellect Books, The University of Chicago Press, 1427 E. 60th Street, Chicago,
IL 60637, USA

A catalogue record for this book is available from the British Library.

Cover Design: Gabriel Solomons
Copy Editor: Holly Spradling
Typesetting: Mac Style, Nafferton, E. Yorkshire

ISBN 978-1-84150-204-5

Printed and bound by Gutenberg Press, Malta.

CONTENTS

LIST OF ILLUSTRATIONS

Cover: Olivier Assayas

LIST OF TABLES

ACKNOWLEDGMENTS

In the academy, I am first of all grateful to Dudley Andrew, my dissertation advisor, for his mentorship and inspiration, as well as to the members of my dissertation committee, Rick Altman, Kathleen Newman, Lauren Rabinovitz, and Louis G. Schwartz, whose comments have been crucial for the strengthening of my arguments. A special thanks goes to my colleague Catherine Russell, for her precious advice and constant support during the development of my thesis into a book. I would also like to thank Nataša Durovicová, Flavia Laviosa, and Martin Lefebvre, from whose expertise I have benefited at different stages of my writing. I also thank Anna Antonini, Ana Brígido Corachán, Stephanie Dennison, Eduardo Guízar Álvarez, Susan Hayward, Song Hwee Lim, and Phil Powrie for their comments on earlier versions of parts of this study, which have been crucial for improving the present manuscript.

I am grateful to Olivier Assayas and Gabriele Salvatores for their generous collaboration during interviews. Thanks also to staff members of the Bibliothèque du Film in Paris, especially those who work in the Iconothèque section of the library, as well as to the personnel of various institutions in France, Italy, and Spain where I have done research over the past six years.

The agencies and the institutions that have provided financial support for this book, including the Fonds Québecois de la Recherche sur la Société et la Culture, the Social Science and Humanities Research Council of Canada, the Fine Arts Faculty at Concordia University in Montreal, and the Research Group on the Inception and Formation of Cinematographic & Theatrical Institutions, should receive special acknowledgment.

A very special thanks to my research assistants, Zoë Constantinides and Bruno Dequen, who have been with me from the very beginning, for their wonderful collaboration and their patience. Their insightful comments have contributed immensely to improving this book. Many thanks also to Van Ha and Valérie Lefebvre, who put in long hours editing and formatting, as well as to Sylvain Duguay, Emmet Henchey, Nicky Park, and Cheryl Williams, for their technical support and their availability.

I am also particularly thankful to May Yao and Melanie Harrison at Intellect, for their punctual and skilful assistance throughout the editorial process. Thanks to Holly Spradling for her wonderful editorial work and patience throughout the process.

At Concordia, I would like to thank Catherine MacKenzie, Richard Kerr, and Tom Waugh for their support as chairs of the Cinema Department, as well as Amely Jurgenliemk, Marielle Nitoslawka, Eric Prince, Peter Rist, and Donato Totaro, whose friendship has helped me during my years as junior faculty.

Parts of chapters 1, 5, 6, and 8 appear in Antonini, A., (ed.). 2003. *Il film e i suoi multipli/Film and its Multiples*. (Udine: Forum, pp. 241–50); Guízar Álvarez, E. and A. Brígido Corachán (eds). 2000. *Lugares Sin Limites: Cinema of the 80s and 90s in Latin America, Spain, and Portugal*. *Torre de Papel* Spec. Issue 10.1 (Spring), pp. 65–76; 'Spanishness' in the Spanish Novel and Cinema of the 20th-21st Century, ed. Cristina Sánchez-Conejero, Cambridge, 2007: 107–20; Hayward, S. and P. Powrie. (eds). 2006. *The Films of Luc Besson: Master of Spectacle*. (Manchester: Manchester University Press, pp. 23–41); and Dennison, S. and S. Hwee Lee, (eds). 2006. *Remapping World Cinema: Identity, Culture and Politics in Film*. (London and New York: Wallflower Press, pp. 73–85).

The friendship of Chiara, Eleonora, Jennifer, Narcisa and James, Romaric and Yves, Guylaine, Rodrigue, Chiara and Dario, and Sandra has sustained me throughout the writing of this book.

Finally, and above all, I am indebted to my family in Italy, who have always encouraged me, and whose love and support have made my entire academic career possible. To them, and to the memory of Monte, this book is dedicated.

INTRODUCTION

In western modern culture, the idea of authorship is associated with various theoretical approaches and sociocultural contexts to designate not only the person at the origin of an aesthetic manufacture, but also the unifying principle in the production, interpretation, and the reception of an artwork. As such, the author has been defined as a unifying element or a deep structure within a corpus or a text pointing to an ideological discourse, a philosophy, or a world-view. The concept of authorship emerged parallel to that of subjectivity and marked the recognition of individual agency and intentionality in the production of artworks. As Michel Foucault argued in his essay 'What Is an Author?' originally published in 1967, the author 'is an ideological figure by which one marks the manner in which we fear the proliferation of meaning' and 'since the eighteenth century [...] has played the role of the regulator of the fictive, a role quite characteristic of our era of industrial and bourgeois society, of individualism and private property' (Rabinow 1984: 119). The figure of the author consolidated especially within Romanticism, through the idea that art is the expression of individual genius and of an artist's struggle to maintain creative originality and personal autonomy within the ideological and economic forces of middle-class society.

The conflict between the notion of individual expression, on the one hand, and the status of cinema as a social practice based on collective and commercial activities, on the other hand, has often confined theoretical discussions of the film author to a conceptual impasse. Indeed, the figure of the author was not widely in use in relation to cinema until the second half of the twentieth century. The term became internationally established through the attribution of aesthetic value to the work of some film directors, including those traditionally regarded as 'artisans' of the Hollywood studio system, by a small group of film critics and cinéphiles gravitating to Parisian film journals and cine-clubs. The 1950s French notion of 'auteur' connoted a film-maker with an original *temperament*; that is, a personality capable of conveying individual perspectives through thematic motifs and stylistic markers (Hillier 1985: 5–6). Despite its inception as a discrete case in intellectual history, this critical approach generated a breed of followers in film criticism and theory, especially in Europe and North America. Since then, in film discourse the author mainly indicates an aesthetic and promotional category through which film theorists, critics, and spectators attribute coherence and value to the corpus of a professional figure generally identified with the film director.

The figure of the author is also coterminous with an idea of film-making as an artistic and intellectual practice, whose methods and goals are juxtaposed to those of mainstream cinema, Hollywood in particular. In this respect, within the framework of national cinemas, the film author is generally identified with an indigenous film culture and a discrete niche of film production meant for domestic as well as international distribution. This is particularly the case with European cinemas, where 'author film' superseded 'art film' as a distinguishing category for culturally oriented film projects. Constituted in the cultural climate of the New Wave styles and film-making methods, the film author in European national cinemas brings together the romantic model of the artist as original creator and the counter-hegemonic agenda of the New Wave independent film director. Another common characteristic of the European film author is an affiliation to a *cinéphile* culture promoted at cine-clubs, film archives, art house film theatres, and film festivals during the 1950s and 1960s, and documented by a young generation of film critics and the foundation of new film magazines.

This book reconfigures the sociocultural function of the film author and advocates a historicized view of this category with regard to modes of film production and reception developed in Western European cinemas since the 1980s. Western Europe is here assumed as a geo-political area belonging to the European Community and which has common economic interests in the European Economic Community (E.E.C.). The overall premise is that since the mid-1950s the European film author represents a symbolic figure associated with modes of film production and reception as well as discursive formations that view cinema as a cultural practice and an important sector of the cultural patrimony. In the countries belonging to the E.E.C., author cinema conventionally refers to a specific sector of the film industry, mainly funded through state subsidies or independent film producers, circulating in small and specialized circuits of exhibition for an informed and educated film audience, and almost exclusively discussed in film journals and magazines. The survival of this category of 'author cinema' was put at risk by the economic crisis that hit the Western European film industry in the 1970s and lasted for more than two decades, provoking the decline of theatrical film distribution and exhibition and the disappearance of the art house circuit. The main contention here is that since the 1980s the practices and discourses associated with author cinema in this geo-political area epitomize the various ways in which governments, film systems, and cultural institutions, as well as film practitioners, critics, and theorists responded to this crisis. These strategies loosely coalesced in two, rather opposite agendas, one supporting the film author as the emblem of Europe's culturally oriented cinema, funded through public institutions and government subsidies conceived outside the economic imperatives of the film industry and the new audio-visual system; the other promoting the film author as a marketing figure for niche theatrical distribution mediating between cultural and commercial interests. Especially since the 1990s, the second line prevailed, with significant repercussions for the production modes and systems readily associated with the film author.

This book views the film author as a sociology-of-production and a discursive function of sociocultural practices related to cinema within specific periods and contexts, from within a post-auteur oriented framework of analysis (Staiger 2003b: 40–43; 49–52). Within the film industries and cultures here examined, as well as in current approaches to the film author in international circuits of film promotion and reception, the figure of the film author is mostly identified with that of the film director. While acknowledging the prevalence of an equation originally stipulated within auteur-oriented criticism, this study does not view the film author from an auteur-informed perspective; that is, as a creative force and individuality traceable in a film director's corpus. Likewise, the methodology here proposed avoids the type of hermeneutics common in auteur theory, which entails textual, intertextual, and contextual analyses of a film director's oeuvre and approach to film-making to point out underlying motifs and stylistic elements that justify her/his authorial status. Quite the opposite, the new directions in authorial film practice described in this book signal either a rejection or a radical reconceptualization of this model of authorship. Film directors appear as case studies because the figure of the film-director-as-author, even outside of auteur-informed film modes and practices of reception, is still a relevant category in the critical evaluation of films, and, more importantly, it is tied to a specific mode of film production and marketing. The film-director-as-author is, therefore, a crucial topic of discussion and debate in cultural policy and discourses about cinema. In this respect, the illustration of film directors' approach to film-making and film aesthetic is not meant to delineate their authorial personality but, instead, to describe the sociocultural context within which these film-makers operate and are associated with discussions about their films that constitute them, using Foucault's expression, as author-functions (Foucault 1981: 284–89). By the same token, writings, declarations, or interviews by or with these film directors are not used to confer authorial authority, but instead to draw out film-making practices and ideas about cinema that reconfigure the role of the film director in Western European cinema with respect to the traditional concept of the auteur. Examination of these testimonies points to new ways of addressing the question of authorship in present-day cinema.

This investigation of new authorial practices has a temporal and geo-political delimitation that reflects its methodological orientation: the aim is not to provide a general definition of authorship in the cinema, an endeavour that Gianni Rondolino estimates to be 'as difficult to discuss as film history as a whole' (1995: 170). Rondolino encourages historical approaches that appraise the social and cultural dimension of film authorship (ibid.). This book moves in that direction. The focus is on three national cinemas from Western European countries that are part of the geo-political and economic area belonging to the European Community: France, Italy, and Spain. Although the decision to concentrate on these national contexts is to a certain extent arbitrary and reflects a personal interest in the cinematic production of these countries, there are specific reasons for privileging a national approach and for selecting these over other European film systems and cultures. To be sure, the act of film-making is indissolubly intertwined with industrial, commercial, and aesthetic activities that operate at a global and trans-national level. Yet, as Victoria de Grazia reminds us, during the post-World War II period the E.C. nations 'pursued no common cultural politics [yet] carried forward policies that had ample cultural implications,' especially for the cinema, through the integration of 'Europe on a societal level around a common material culture' that at the same time maintained each state's autonomy against US hegemony (1998: 27). According to de Grazia, Europe's 'materialist' approach to cultural unity had a fourfold purpose with regard to the film industry: facilitating trade among the six countries of the E.C.; securing the European film industries through protectionist laws and subsidies; concentrating state ownership and monopolies in television and letting the national film industries develop into an open and competitive market; and, finally, encouraging a cross-European standard for production values (ibid.). A fundamental tenet in this study is that within Western European film systems and cultures author cinema represents a mode of film production and reception supported by government policies, public institutions, and filmic traditions that are the result of the E.C. cultural policies described above. In this respect, author cinema in Western Europe is nationally over-determined, although variously interfaced with the trans-European and global dimensions of film and audio-visual practices.

As for the choice of these three national film systems (besides their prominence, only comparable within Western Europe to those of Germany and the U.K.), French, Italian, and Spanish cinema are especially representative because of the central role the author plays in these countries' efforts to maintain culturally oriented film production despite the constraints of an audio-visual industry becoming more and more standardized and a film market dominated by large corporate media monopolies and Hollywood films. Especially during the 1980s, author cinema in these film systems became the symbol of a mode of production to be safeguarded through special laws and initiatives. Cases in point were the reinforcement of import quotas and special subsidies (the *avance sur recettes* in France, the *articolo* 28 in Italy, and the Miró Law in Spain) for implementing the production of culturally oriented films, as well as the investment of state television networks in projects developed within authorial modes of production. Also remarkable in these national cinemas is the discrete space given to author cinema by major film production and distribution companies (such as Gaumont in France, in particular under the direction of Daniel Toscan du Plantier; the Cecchi Gori group/Tiger Cinematografica and, during the 1980s and the 1990s, the producer Angelo Rizzoli the Lucky Red and Filmauro in Italy; and Sogecine and its distribution branch Sogepaq in Spain), as well as by national television networks Radio Televisione Italiana (RAI in Italy and Spain's national television networks [RTVE] and regional television networks), and pay television channels (France's Canal+ and Canal+ España in Spain). Another significant contribution, especially starting from the 1990s, comes from major players within these national film industries committed to author cinema, including independent film producers and film directors such as Bruno Pesery and Marin Karmitz (the latter also the founder of the Paris-based chain of art house film theatres MK2) in France; film directors who have established their own film productions such as Nanni Moretti, Pupi Avati, and Gabriele Salvatores in Italy and Pedro Almodóvar in Spain; and veteran film directors who have acted as mentors and executive producers for emerging film authors such as the aforementioned Moretti and Almodóvar, as well as Fernando Trueba, Fernando Colomo, and José Luis Cuerda in Spain.[1] These initiatives are all the more noteworthy because they are closely intertwined with public debates about these countries' film systems and traditions that involve not only film critics and theorists, but also politicians and major players in the film industry.

In addition to the above, since the 1990s French, Italian, and Spanish cinema offer the most significant examples of a radical departure from the authorial model that emerged during the

1950s and 1960s and was reinforced by government subsidies and import quotas during the 1980s. This shift is in part the result of a change in subsidy policies and an effort to address a vaster audience within the culturally oriented sector of film production and distribution. Furthermore, the film directors here discussed represent a diffuse trend among the latest generation of film-makers working within this area: a refusal to be affiliated with the authorial tradition established in the 1950s and fortified through the 1980s. Finally, the cultural and cinematic traditions that for years informed the aesthetic and the reception of authorial cinema in these countries have been superseded by interests in various forms and styles of audio-visual expression, also drawing on new media technologies.

This book is in three sections, each one dealing with a specific aspect of the professional and cultural redefinition of authorship in Western European cinemas since the 1980s. Part one illustrates the consolidation and the crisis of the authorial mode of production depending on state subsidies and institutions. Part two concentrates on the repositioning of the film author as a professional and symbolic figure within the audio-visual context and culture of the past twenty years. Part three considers the redefinition of subjectivity and agency in authorial discourse associated with women film-makers who dismiss the idea of a feminine or feminist perspective. Each part is developed in individual chapters in relation to film directors that have been associated with the idea of authorship within their respective national film systems, as well as in the international context of reception: the French Olivier Assayas, Luc Besson, Claire Denis, and Maurice Pialat; the Italian Gianni Amelio, Francesca Archibugi, and Gabriele Salvatores; and the Spanish Alejandro Amenábar and Víctor Erice. These film-makers are the most significant examples of Western Europe's efforts to reposition the film director as author outside of the circuits of film production and reception established by art house and auteur-informed cinematic traditions. They also typify new directions in Western European author cinema, including the exploration of different film forms and genres, and a more cosmopolitan, not primarily western- or European-centred, cultural horizon.

The chapters in the first two sections of this book inquire into the changing status of the film author in the audio-visual industry over the past three decades, a period characterized by cinema's transition to a multi-media platform and a global film market. In these parts the concept of authorship is discussed in relation to film directors who have made their débuts between the late 1960s and the early 1970s (Víctor Erice, Maurice Pialat, and Gianni Amelio), others who started during the 1980s (in chronological order, Gabriele Salvatores, Luc Besson, and Olivier Assayas), and, finally, Alejandro Amenábar, who made his first feature film in the mid-1990s. To varying degrees, these film-makers exemplify a reaction to the institutional figure of the author financed mainly through government subsidies, aid programmes for culturally oriented films, and national television networks, and characterized by slow production processes, small budgets, and poor or no theatrical distribution. The detachment from traditional and institutional models of author cinema allowed these film directors to maintain control over their film projects and especially to gain increased visibility in the film market. Their working methods conform to those associated with the idea of the Western European auteur, including individual control over all phases of the film-making process, independent systems of production (in some cases linked with the author's own production company), and recurring collaborations with particular casts and crews. At the same time, they negotiate tensions between the intentionality and agency connected with the idea of authorship and the industrial and commercial constraints of the new audio-visual system.

Chapter 1 illustrates the genealogy of the film author in the three national film systems selected as an institutional mode of film production and reception and explains the ways in which, particularly throughout the 1980s, film critics and practitioners framed the interplay between the author and the new audio-visual industry in terms of conflict. Chapter 2 further examines this question in relation to directors Maurice Pialat, Gianni Amelio, and Víctor Erice, whose professional trajectories (spanning three decades of authorial film, from the 1960s onwards) epitomize the changes in the discursive construction of the Western European film author as a creative and professional agent. Chapter 3 investigates the heritage of France's auteur-oriented film criticism and of the *nouvelle vague* model of the film auteur. The chapter concentrates on film director and former *Cahiers du Cinéma* film critic Olivier Assayas, who is often identified with France's auteurist tradition, although his approach to film-making and his view of contemporary cinema result from a stern rejection of this legacy, and his practices actually suggest a new conception of authorial film.

Part two opens with chapter 4, which addresses the relations of author cinema to various circuits of film production and distribution. A case in point is Gabriele Salvatores, a socially and politically engaged film director whose predilection for genre films and hybrid aesthetics makes him an outsider vis-à-vis Italy's authorial tradition. Chapter 5 examines the most recent amongst the case studies discussed in this book, the Spanish Alejandro Amenábar, whose authorial status is linked to an audio-visual culture that blends classical cinephilia with new aesthetics and the Spanish auteur tradition with classical Hollywood film. Part two, chapter 6, closes with Luc Besson, whose atypical role within France's film system blurs the boundaries between mainstream and author cinema. He engages forthrightly with diverse film modes, regardless of pre-established parameters of cultural value, and with the birth of his own studio, Europa Corp., in 2000, Besson's activities as a film producer and distributor have provided a viable source of financing and distribution for French and international film authors. His professional position, as well as his critical stance towards France's policy of 'cultural exception,' calls into question the ideological ambiguity implicit in France's definition of its national film production as mainly culturally oriented.

The final section of this book is devoted to questions of authorship in Western European women's cinema. This section considers female film directors' position from within a post-feminist context intended both as a discursive formation following the impasse of feminism as a sociocultural praxis and as a feminine aesthetics conceived in terms of post-subjective expression. Chapter 7 lays out the conceptual questions involved in approaching female authorial film practices in the three countries here examined from a feminist point of view, after the waning of the Women's Movement and within a post-feminist cultural framework. The fact that most female film directors active in these national contexts (as well as in Western Europe in general), including those that film critics regard as film authors, dismiss feminist and even gender-specific labels or classifications of their works is the main concern here. Chapters 8 and 9 offer two instances of women film directors whose authorial discourse is predicated upon a refusal of a specifically feminine subject position: Claire Denis in France (chapter 8) and Francesca Archibugi in Italy (chapter 9). The discussion of their roles as female film authors draws on current directions in feminist film theory and criticism that view female authorship either in terms of an assertion of personal agency within specific sociocultural milieus (especially in the chapter devoted to Archibugi) or of post-subjective conceptions of filmic representation which disavow the feminist theorization of feminine expression and identity informed by psychoanalytic notions of the gendered subject (particularly in relation to Denis). These chapters propose that the films of Denis and Archibugi provide a post-feminist version of women's cinema in which women's authorial agency is no longer related to the enunciating standpoint of a gendered subject, but is instead a negotiation of personal subject positions vis-à-vis various types of identity politics and cultural formations.

The discussion of individual case studies intersects with, and supplements, concepts or theoretical frameworks that have been important in authorial discourse or, conversely, have not primarily been addressed in relation to authorship (such as, for instance, André Bazin's definition of impure cinema or post-colonial theory) and are even at odds with the notion of authorship (like, for instance, Julio García Espinosa's concept of imperfect cinema and post-subjective theories of film inspired by Gilles Deleuze's philosophy). These varied – and not necessarily linked – theoretical frameworks help situate the topic of this book within the larger framework of film discourse, with particular attention given to recent developments and current discussions on the role of cinema within a postmodern context of production and reception.

Auteurism and beyond

Launched at the French film magazine *Cahiers du Cinéma* in the mid-1950s, *la politique des auteurs* waged war against hierarchical conceptions of art in film discourse not just by arguing that aesthetic value may be found in genres or cinematic modes generally disdained by film critics such as the comedy or the Hollywood studio system, respectively, but also by distinguishing the film author from authorship recognized in other arts, most notably literature and theatre (Corrigan 1991; Crofts 1998; de Baecque 1991; Durovicová 1994; Pescatore 2006: 59–75). From this perspective, *la politique des auteurs* opposed a national typology of auteur cinema to the *Cinéma de qualité* at the time dominant in France. The *Cinéma de qualité* ('Tradition of Quality') emerged during the interval between the two world wars and became particularly prevalent in the post-World War II period as a studio-dependent type of film-making based on high production values and adaptations of canonical works of French literature. This type of cinema was conceived to offer a competitive alternative to Hollywood films.

As Alan Williams explains, '"Quality" meant, first of all, that the films could not be inferior to the best American products, either technically (smoothness of editing, glitchless camera movements) or materially (eye-catching, expensive costumes and sets, appealing stars, "seeing the money on the screen")' (1992: 278). Williams also notes that in the post-war period, the Tradition of Quality went back to contemporary themes and social issues, as had been the case with earlier films produced within this tradition, especially during the 1930s. Yet, he emphasizes, 'the cinema of quality never fully regained the strong sense of contact with everyday life that had characterized many of the best works of the 1930s' (ibid.: 280). The purpose of the article that launched the auteur as a critical figure at *Cahiers du Cinéma*, François Truffaut's 'Une certaine tendance du cinéma français' (1954), was to counter this mode of production, endorsed by a cultural tradition that gave authorial credit to the screenwriter and considered the script (especially the adaptation of a canonical literary work) the element that determined a film's artistic quality (Truffaut 1954). In opposition, auteur cinema placed authorial creativity in the film-making process itself and in particular in the activities involved in producing the *mise-en-scène*. As well as the above, the *politique des auteurs* consolidated two practices, screenwriting and *mise-en-scène*, that had remained distinct since the development of film as a narrative form. Regardless of whether a film director was also responsible for the script (which could be anything from an idea, a treatment, a drafted script, a fully developed screenplay, or the adaptation of a literary text), her/his authorship resided in the process of translating this material into a film. Hence, the insistence upon the film director as auteur (to be distinguished from a *metteur en scène*, that is, a film director who just transposes a script into film) indicated the intention to link authorship in the cinema less with a specific professional role than with a conceptual and practical approach to film-making.

The *politique des auteurs* prompted debate from its very incipience: the senior editors at *Cahiers du Cinéma* disagreed with the contingent of young film critics who promulgated the editorial policy, the so-called *Jeunes Turcs* (Truffaut, Claude Chabrol, Jean-Luc Godard, Jacques Rivette, and Eric Rohmer) and even set apart the latter and their mentor, film critic André Bazin (Caughie 1991: 44–46; Crofts 1998a: 313; de Baecque 1991). In particular, Bazin objected to the polemical and aesthetic nature the *politique des auteurs*, considering the distinction between auteur and *metteur en scène* arbitrary and the focus on the auteur a loss of overall perspective about a film. In the same years, another fierce diatribe opposed the two auteur-oriented film magazines based in Paris, *Cahiers du Cinéma* and *Positif* (established in 1952), the latter having developed a partisanship for some left-wing-oriented Hollywood auteurs (de Baecque 2003: 211–13).

Predicated upon the recognition of the film director as the personality responsible for the aesthetic and artistic coherence of a film, the French concept of auteur bespeaks an idealistic and essentialist view of cinema, of which the ideological and conceptual downsides have been the object of many debates in film studies (Caughie 1981: 2–3; Crofts 1998a: 315). The *politique des auteurs* attributed aesthetic uniqueness and expressive control to the films of certain Hollywood film directors, as well as of those working in art-oriented film modes (de Baecque 1991 and 1998; Darke 1993; Hillier 1985). Yet, by and large, the approach combined conservative and apolitical notions of art with rebellious intentions that were actually drawn from traditional aesthetics (McCabe 1985: 4–5). As Nataša Durovicová has pointed out, the *politique des auteurs* had the double-edged effect of highlighting 'the compatibility of cinema's aesthetic powers with those of twentieth-century arts and literature [while] freeing [the medium] from earlier, more idealist notions of what it ought to be like if it was to be "really art"' (1994: 5). In this respect, Durovicová underlines how authorial cinema undermines, rather than reinforces, the 'spectral antagonism' that opposes European 'art' cinema to Hollywood 'commercial' cinema (ibid.).

In spite of its ideological and conceptual flaws, the idea of the film auteur had a strong impact on film discourse and practices throughout the 1960s and 1970s and also informed a specific niche of film production and distribution circulating within art house or specialized circuits of theatrical film exhibition, film archives, and film clubs. The notion of auteur was first developed into auteur theory during the 1960s, notably at the British film magazine *Movie* and by the US film critic Andrew Sarris. By and large, *Movie* embraced the assumption that the film director is the author of a film. However, similarly to André Bazin, the magazine did not exclusively identify the auteur with the film director, on the one hand noting that other professional figures such as the screenwriter or the director of photography could be considered as auteurs, on the other hand taking issue with the rigid distinction between auteur and *metteur en scène* (Caughie 1991: 48–60; Crofts 1998a, 314). Quite the opposite, the US film critic Sarris further consolidated the correspondence film director-author, although, like *Movie*, he dismissed the idea that bad directors could never be considered authors and adopted more flexible and varied criteria to identify authorship in films (Caughie 1991: 63–65; Crofts 1998a: 314). He thus identified a set of key premises to assess authorial value in film, which included technical competence, distinguishable personality, and interior meaning (Caughie 1991: 61–63; Crofts 1998a: 314).

The auteur remained an important reference in film discourse for another decade and was adopted by different approaches to film (Caughie 1991: 122–195; Crofts 1998a: 315–318; Pescatore 2006: 59–106). During the 1960s, the notion of auteur appeared in textual analyses informed by anthropological structuralism, Marxist-inspired analysis, and semiotics (Caughie 1981: 9–120; Corrigan 1991; de Baecque 1991; Hillier 1985; Pescatore 2006: 59–71). Within these theoretical frameworks, the auteur became de-personalized, a pointer to deep structures present in a given culture or ideology (ibid.). With the emergence of radical politics and Marxist-structuralist theory, the concept of auteur was either heavily attacked or reformulated as a symptom of deep structures in a film text pointing to ideological conflicts within a given sociocultural context.[2] The most direct attack on the bourgeois underpinnings of auteurism came with the 1968 movement. Throughout the early 1970s, film critics and directors formed production collectives and wrote political manifestos and editorial programmes that rejected the concept of authorship as an expression of the compromise between art and commerce in bourgeois culture. In a 1969 article for *Cinétique* (one of France's most radical film journals in those years), Gérard Leblanc opines:

> The opposition art/commerce at work in authorial discourse is after all of no other use but that of justifying commerce by means of creating within itself a domain reserved for personal expression [...]. Commercial cinema/authorial cinema, cinema for the masses/ cinema for the elites, these pairs of oppositions do nothing but come together in the same ignorance of the ideology that determines them. (1969: 1, my translation)[3]

During these years, the discourse on authorship was obscured by an emerging concern with the socio-political dimension of films and the development of counter-cinema as an anti-aestheticizing and anti-bourgeois approach to film-making. Some of the most established film authors embraced counter-cinematic practices, often connected to extreme-left parties and revolutionary political positions. In France, radical film activists included the Dziga Vertov collective with Jean-Luc Godard and Jean-Pierre Gorin, Chris Marker's SLON (later Groupe Medvedkine), and the couple Jean-Marie Straub and Danièle Huillet. In Italy, politically active film-makers included the Taviani brothers and Valerio Orsini (who also formed a collective), Vittorio De Seta, Marco Bellocchio, and Pier Paolo Pasolini· In the same years, Western European counter-cinema generated a conspicuous body of feminist film work and academic studies, although concentrated only in some countries, most notably Italy, France, the U.K., and the former German Democratic Republic. In the U.K., feminist film theory dominated the Marxist-oriented and psychoanalytic/structuralist theoretical paradigm proposed by the film journal *Screen* and the work of film-makers and critics related to that journal, a paradigm that influenced and had a lasting fortune in North American academe.[4]

The notion of authorship and more specifically the French-based idea of the auteur produced effects of gender bias in film discourse. In the first place, auteurism disparaged women because of their typically subordinate roles in film history, in which the figure of the female film director was a rare exception. Furthermore, this critical framework posed ideological problems to feminist scholars because of its gender-blind, if not misogynist, underpinnings, based on a male-centered model of subjectivity and agency (de Lauretis 1987; Flitterman-Lewis 1996; Mayne 1990; Vincendeau 1998). Such exclusion reinforced the idea of female authorship as a marker of difference, defined in relation to male authorial models of representation. As such, most feminist studies of female authorship consist of symptomatic readings of films by male directors that unconsciously assert female agency or analyses of films by women film-makers operating in mainstream cinema that show a gender-specific viewpoint and style (Mayne 1990 and 1994; Penley 1988). Feminist film theory contributed to the portrayal of women's authorship as an oppositional type of expression found in avant-garde, experimental, documentary, and New Wave cinemas (Bruno 1993; Flitterman-Lewis 1996; Mayne 1990; Mellencamp 1994; Minh-Ha 1991; Penley 1988; and Rabinovitz 1991). The theorization of female authorship in terms of radical alterity or oppositional practices reflects a more general problem in feminist film discourse: how to account for female subjectivity in cultural and theoretical contexts where the female subject has no position or voice and where femininity is inflected by the concept of 'otherness.' As Teresa de Lauretis notes, trying to identify 'formal, stylistic, or thematic markers that point to a female presence behind a camera [...] finally only means complying, accepting a certain definition of art, cinema, and culture and obligingly showing how women can and do "contribute," pay their tribute, to "society"' (1987: 131). Recent approaches to women's film authorship concentrate on gender roles in terms of professional politics of self-assertion and, in this respect, partake in a more general discussion of authorial practices as tactics of personal orientation that depend on contextually specific and variable circumstances (Crofts 1998b; Gerstner and Staiger 2003; Wright Wexman 2003).

The concept of author as textual construct pointing to an individual personality was definitively set aside with the advent of post-structuralism, deconstruction theory, and cultural studies in film discourse (Crofts 1998a: 318–322). According to Seán Burke (1992), the beginning of the anti-authorial enterprise resides in the rise of structural linguistics, which informed the de-subjectivized discourse of structuralism, post-structuralism, and deconstruction theory. Yet he argues that the belief that 'subjectivity was something to be annihilated' and that 'the removal of the authorial subject [was] not to be seen as a strategy, a means toward an end, but as a primary claim in itself' (Burke 1992: 14–15). Indeed, one of the attacks on the concept of authorship, Michel Foucault's notion of the author-name as embedded in and produced through discourse (Foucault 1981), was in the end very influential for later reconsiderations of the author in film discourse. By the same token, sociological and Marxist-inspired examinations of labour organization developed within the framework of cultural studies also proved important for the elaboration of a different notion of authorship in film as a sociology-of-production (Staiger 2003b: 40–41).

Especially since the 1980s, with the blurring of anti-dominant ideologies and film systems into global patterns of cultural consumerism, the dialectic between film author and the cinema industry progressively changed. So, if the author as a sociology-of-production linked with independent film companies and public systems of financing is still a marginal figure in the larger picture of the film industry, most film directors recognized as authors now work with more diversified systems of film production and distribution, not excluding those identified with mainstream cinema. The promotion of authorship for a larger audience – evident already in the attention that French magazines and newspapers gave to the nouvelle vague auteurs – is a prominent strategy for monitoring the median range of international spectatorship once defined by the art house circuit of film distribution and exhibition. As Timothy Corrigan notes, '[I]f, in conjunction with the so-called international art cinema of the sixties and seventies, the auteur had been absorbed as a phantom presence within a text, he or she has rematerialized in the eighties and nineties as a commercial performance of "the business of being an auteur"' (1991: 104).[5]

The author is among the many categories and approaches that have been under theoretical and historical scrutiny in meta-theoretical film studies discussions since the 1990s. As John Caughie suggests in the introduction to an anthology on authorial approaches published in 1981, the positive contributions of auteur theories to film criticism include their potential to develop critical approaches to film which focus on the intersection of cultural production and meaning (Caughie 1981: 14–15). The reconceptualization of auteurism prompted a variety of articles, books, and special issues of film journals and magazines during the past fifteen years (Andrew 1993; Corrigan 1991; Crofts 1993 and 1998; Esquenazi 2002; Gerstner and Staiger 2003a, 2003b; Pescatore 2006; Wright Wexman 2003). In an article contributing to this revisionist trend, Dudley Andrew welcomes these analyses as a return to authorial concerns after two decades of proscription from the discipline, beginning with the rise of ideological criticism and reinforced during the shift to post-structuralism and cultural studies (1993). Timothy Corrigan gave one of the most convincing reconsiderations of auteurism in a chapter of his 1991 book, A Cinema without Walls: Movies and Culture after Vietnam (1991). Using three case studies (Francis Ford Coppola, Alexander Kluge, and Raoul Ruiz), each working within disparate film modes and contexts of film production and distribution, he approaches their authorship in terms of a sociology-of-production in post-classical cinema (Corrigan 1991). Corrigan describes the resurfacing of the auteur in post-Hollywood and post-New Wave European cinemas as the result of self-conditioned circumstances of production and reception, as well as of the technological environment of media society (Corrigan 1991: 104). As he explains, although 'since the early 1970s, the commercial conditioning of this figure [the author] has successfully evacuated it of most of its expressive power and intellectual coherence,' the same conditioning has also 'renewed attention to the layered pressures of auteurism as an agency that establishes different modes of identification with its audiences' (1991: 135–36).

More recent publications situate auteurism within the framework of the 1950s and 1960s *cinéphile* culture and art house exhibition circuit (de Baecque 1991 and 2003) or else verify the viability of auteurism in contemporary frameworks of discourse and various film modes (Esquenazi 2002; Gerstner and Staiger 2003; Pescatore 2006; Polan 2000; Wright Wexman 2003). Film scholars are also revising the auteur-informed equivalence between film director and film author, arguing either that other professional figures (markedly the producer, the screenwriter, and the actor) can also occupy an integral creative role (Boschi and Manzoli 1995) or that a collaborative model of authorship is more appropriate for examining the film author as a sociology-of-production (Crofts 1998a; Gaut 1997; Staiger 2003b: 43). The most recent discussions of authorship regard its pertinence to postmodern discourse. Many scholars working within a postmodern critical framework remain skeptical of the possibility of applying the subject-informed concept of the author to an approach and aesthetics based on a decentred and fragmented idea of subjectivity; others consider the postmodern author an index of cultural performance which may provide resistant tactics of orientation in the global and local structures of film production and reception (Maule 1998; Staiger 2004).

The terms auteur and author and their respective derivatives were interchangeable in film studies for as long as auteurism remained a prominent approach in film discourse. Within a post-auteurist framework of analysis the author no longer refers to an individual artist through whom we infer textual coherence in films; it is instead the result of reading or reception strategies conditioned by cinema's sociocultural and industrial structures and practices, a function of extra-textual discourses in a given sociocultural context, or else of an instance of sociocultural production in historical examinations of film modes and systems (Corrigan 1991; Crofts 1998a: 321–322; Gerstner and Staiger 2003; Wright Wexman 2003). However, the distinction between auteur-informed and authorial approaches remains blurred even in our post-auteurist era. The film author is still a synonym of individual signature in the promotion and the reception of film directors within national and international art house theatrical circuits, film archives, and film festivals, as well as in academic publications and curricula (Corrigan 1991; Crofts 1998a: 321–322). In this respect, the term auteur appears in most historical and theoretical analyses of European national cinemas, even those that reject generalizing equivalences between European and art or culturally oriented film practices and films. This is the case with Anne Jäckel's overview of European film industries, where the expression 'auteur cinema' refers to 'a production trend, arguably, the European film genre par excellence' (2003: 28). Similarly, Ginette Vincendeau argues that the 'canon of "great auteurs"' reflects a dominant critical construction of the European tradition along with the theorization of authorship in art and literary history (a link that explains the disregard for popular cinema and film directors in auteur-based film discourse) (1998: 445).

The auteur, as well as auteurist and post-auteurist approaches to film and are objects of inquiry in this study. Yet *Beyond Auteurism* does not assume auteurism as a synecdoche for all authorial approaches and practices in film. Quite the opposite, this book stresses the scarce applicability of the term auteur and of auteur-informed analysis to current modes of film production and reception. The terms 'auteur' or 'auteur cinema' appear with reference to French-based models of authorship or auteur-related approaches to European cinema. Beyond these contexts, the terms 'author,' 'author cinema,' and 'authorial film practices' will be preferred. The point is not just to substitute the historically determined and ideologically charged notion of auteur with a more neutral term, now more readily accepted in film discourse. The word author subsumes an epistemological transition to a post-auteur framework of discussion encompassing the practices of and discourses about film consolidated during the past two decades.

The intention is to propose European film authorship as a form of cultural production and reception and as a discursive approach to film that mediates among different aspects and levels of the cinema. This approach foregrounds the cultural specificity of film authorship in relation to the international film system from within a national framework of discourse and practices.

Notes

1. These and other specific examples will be illustrated further in the following chapters. Data related to film production, distribution, and exhibition in Europe and particularly in France, Italy, and Spain appear in some of the appended tables.
2. On the ideological constitution of the subject in western aesthetics, see Eagleton (1990) and Young (1990).
3. 'L'opposition art/commerce à l'oeuvre dans le discours des 'auteurs' ne sert en fin de compte qu'à justifier le commerce en créant en son sein un domaine réservé à l'expression personnelle ... Cinéma commercial/cinéma d'auteurs, cinéma pour le grand public/cinéma pour les élites, ces couples d'opposition s'unissent dans la même ignorance de l'idéologie qui les détermine.'
4. On the historical and cultural shortcomings of feminist film practices in the three countries here considered, see, for France, Vincendeau (1987 and 1998) and Hayward (1993a: 228–331); for Italy, Bruno and Nadotti (1988); for Spain, Jordan and Morgan-Tamosunas, particularly part three, titled 'Gender and Sexuality in Post-Franco Cinema' (1998: 61–111).
5. Italics appear in the original text.

References

Andrew, D. 1993. The Unauthorized Auteur Today. (*In* Collins, J., Radner, H. and Preacher Collins, A., (eds). *Film Theory Goes to the Movies.* New York–London: Routledge, pp. 77–85.)

Boschi, A. And Manzoli, G. (eds). 1995. *Oltre l'autore I. Fotogenia*, 2.

Brunetta, G. P. 1998. *Storia del cinema italiano. Dal miracolo economico agli anni novanta. 1963–1993.* Roma: Editori Riuniti.

Burke, S. 1992. *Death and Return of the Author: Criticism and Subjectivity in Barthes, Foucault and Derrida.* Edinburgh: Edinburgh University Press.

Caughie, J. (ed.). 1981. *Theories of Authorship.* London and New York: Routledge and Kegan Paul.

Corrigan, T. 1991. *A Cinema without Walls: Movies and Culture after Vietnam.* New Brunswick, New Jersey: Rutgers University Press, pp. 101–36.

Crofts, S. 1993. Reconceptualizing national cinemas. *Quarterly Review of Film and Video*, 14(3): 49–68.

—. 1998a. Authorship and Hollywood. (*In* Hill, J. and Church Gibson P., (eds). *The Oxford Guide to Film Studies*. Oxford: Oxford University Press, pp. 310–24.)

—. 1998b. Concepts of National Cinema. (*In* Hill, J. and Church Gibson P., (eds). *The Oxford Guide to Film Studies*. Oxford: Oxford University Press, pp. 385–94.)

Darke, C. 1993. Rupture, Continuity and Diversification: *Cahiers du Cinéma* in the 1980s. *Screen*, 34.4: 362–79.

De Baecque, A. 1991. *Histoire d'une revue. Tome 1: Les Cahiers à l'assault du cinéma: 1951–1959*. Paris: Cahiers du cinéma.

—. 1998. *La nouvelle vague: portrait d'une jeunesse*. Paris: Flammarion.

—. 2003. *La Cinéphilie: Invention d'un regard, histoire d'une culture. 1944–1968*. Paris: Fayard.

De Grazia, V. 1998. European cinema and the idea of Europe: 1925–95. (*In* Nowell-Smith G. and Ricci, S., (eds). *Hollywood and Europe: Economics, Culture, National Identity: 1945–95*. London: BFI, pp. 19–33.)

De Lauretis, T. 1987. *Technologies of Gender: Essays on Theory, Film, and Fiction*. Bloomington and Indianapolis: Indiana University Press.

Dibie, J-N. 1993. *Aid for Cinematographic and Audio-visual Production in Europe*. London: John Libbey.

Durovicová, N. 1994. Some Thoughts at an Intersection. *Velvet Light Trap*, 34: 3–9.

Esquenazi, J.-P. (ed.). 2002. *Politique des auteurs et théories du cinéma*. Paris: L'Harmattan.

Finney, Angus. *The State of European Cinema: A New Dose of Reality*. London: Cassel, 1996.

Flitterman-Lewis, S. 1996. *To Desire Differently: Feminism and the French Cinema*. Urbana: University of Illinois Press.

Foucault, M. 1981. What Is an Author? [1969] (*In* CAUGHIE, J., (ed.). *Theories of Authorship*. London and New York: Routledge, pp. 282–91.)

Gerstner, D. and Staiger, J. (eds). 2003. *Authorship and Film*. New York: Routledge.

Hayward, S. 1993a. *French National Cinema*. London and New York: Routledge.

—. 1993b. State, Culture, and the Cinema: Jack Lang's Strategies for the French Film Industry. *Screen*, 34(4): 380–91.

Hillier, J. (ed.). 1985. *Cahiers du Cinéma. Volume 1: The 1950s, Neorealism, Hollywood, the New Wave*. London: RKP/BFI.

Hopewell, J. 1986. *Out of the Past: Spanish Cinema after Franco*. London: BFI.

—. 1991. Art and a Lack of Money: The Crises of the Spanish Film Industry: 1977–1990. *Quarterly Review of Film and Video*, 14 (4): 113–122.

Jäckel, A. 2003. *European Film Industries*, London, BFI.

Kinder, M. 1993. *Blood Cinema: The Reconstruction of National Identity in Spain*. Berkeley: University of California Press.

—, (ed.). 1997. *Refiguring Spain: Cinema/Media/Representation*. Durham and London: Duke University Press.

Lagny, M., Ropars, M-C. and Pierre, Sorlin, P. (eds) 1990. *L'état d'auteur* Spec. issue of *Hors Cadre* 8: printemps.

Leblanc, G. 1969. La notion de production: producteurs/produits. *Cinéthique*, 4: 1.

Martin-Márquez, S. 1999. *Feminist Discourse and Spanish Cinema: Sight Unseen*. Oxford: Oxford University Press.

Maule. R. 1998. De-authorizing the Auteur: Postmodern Politics of Interpellation in Contemporary European Cinema. *Postmodernism in the Cinema*. (In Degli-Esposti, C., (ed.). Oxford: Berghahn Books, pP. 140–62).

Mayne, J. 1990. *The Woman at the Keyhole*. Bloomington and Indianapolis: Indiana University Press.

—. 1994. *Directed By Dorothy Arzner*. Bloomington, Ill. and Indiana, In.: Indiana University Press.

McCabe, C. 1985. *Theoretical Essays: Film, Linguistics, Literature*. Manchester: Manchester University Press.

Mellencamp, P. 1994. *Indiscretions: Avant-Garde Film, Video, and Feminism*. Bloomington and Indianapolis: Indiana University Press.

Minh-Ha, T. T. 1991. *When the Moon Waxes Red: Representation, Gender, and Cultural Politics*. New York and London, Routledge.

Penley, C. (ed.). 1988. *Feminism and Film Theory*. New York: Routledge, 1988.

Pescatore, G. 2006. *L'ombra dell'autore: teoria e storia dell'autore cinematografico*. Roma: Carrocci.

Petrie, D. (ed.). 1992. *Screening Europe: Image and Identity in Contemporary European Cinema*. London: BFI.

Polan, D. 2001. Auteur Desire. *Screening the Past*. [Online]. Available: http://www.latrobe.edu.au/screeningthepast/firstrelease/fr0301/dpfr12a.htm.

Powrie, P. 1990. *Contemporary French Fiction by Women: Feminist Perspectives*. Manchester: Manchester University Press.

Puttnam, D. 1997. *The Undeclared War: The Struggle of the World's Film Industry*. London: Harper Collins.

Rabinovitz, L. 1991. *Points of Resistance: Women, Power and Politics in the New York Avant-garde Cinema, 1943–71*. Urbana and Chicago: University of Illinois Press.

Rabinow, P. 1984. *The Foucault Reader*. New York: Pantheon Books.

Rondolino, G. 1995. A Film History without Authors? (In Boschi, A. and Manzoli, G., (eds). Oltre l'autore I. *Fotogenia*, 2.)

Staiger, J., 2003. Authorship Approaches. (In Gerstner, D. and Staiger, J. (eds). *Authorship and Film*. New York: Routledge, pp. 27–57.

—. Authorship Studies and Gus Van Sant. *Film Criticism* 29.1: 1–22 (Fall).

Talens J. and Zunzunegui, S. 1998. *Modes of Representation in Spanish Cinema*. Minneapolis, MN: University of Minnesota Press.

Truffaut, F. 1954. Une certaine tendance du cinéma français. Cahiers du Cinéma, 31: 15–28, janvier.

Vincendeau, G. 1987. Women's Cinema, Film Theory, and Feminism in France. *Screen*, 28(4): 4–18.

—. 1996. *The Companion to French Cinema*. London: Cassell.

—. 1998. Issues in European Cinema. (In Hill, J. and Church Gibson P. (eds). *The Oxford Guide to Film Studies*. Oxford: Oxford University Press, pp. 440–48.)

Williams, A. 1992. *Republic of Images: A History of French Film-making*. Harvard: Harvard University Press.

Wilson, E. 1999. *French Cinema Since 1950: Personal Histories*. Lanham, MD/Boulder, CO/New York, NY: Rowman & Littlefield Publishers.

Wright Wexman, V. (ed.). 2003. *Film and Authorship*. New Brunswick: Rutgers University Press.

PART ONE: THE 'DEATH OF CINEMA' AND THE INSTITUTIONALIZATION OF THE AUTHOR

1

THE FILM AUTHOR AND THE SURVIVAL OF EUROPEAN CINEMA

Besides identifying subjectivity in films as a source of expression and signification traceable via aesthetic and thematic motifs, the notion of authorship in the cinema signals an attempt to demarcate individual agency and orientation within the plurality of practices related to film production, distribution, and reception. In this respect, the establishment of the film auteur as a prominent category in film points to not only what Dana Polan describes as an irrepressible 'desire' for differentiating films and to categorize them through criteria borrowed from the other arts (2001), but also, as Timothy Corrigan appropriately observes, 'a commercial strategy for organizing audience reception, a critical concept bound to distribution and marketing aims that identify and address the potential cult status of an auteur' (1991: 103). Corrigan highlights some of the circumstances that consolidated the film auteur as an aesthetic and promotional category within the contemporary film industry. One such factor is the 1950s and 1960s expansion of production and distribution systems and initiatives as fostered by the advent of lightweight equipment and 'the desire and demand of an industry to generate an artistic (and specifically Romantic) aura during a period when the industry as such needed to distinguish itself from other, less elevated, forms of mass media (most notably, television)' (ibid.: 102).

In Western Europe, film authorship emerged as a marketing value at various times and in different circumstances. In its 1950s heyday, the art film directors consolidated European cinema's prestige within the international art house circuit. At the end of the decade, the author had become not only an important approach to film because of auteur criticism, but also a cinematic mode and a promotional category of its own, endorsed by government subsidies and public institutions aiming at maintaining a distinctive niche in the art house film circuit. From this perspective, author cinema in Western Europe represents more than just an aesthetic concept and is strictly intertwined with the industrial, economic, and cultural interests of the film systems, as well as the national and transnational priorities of the Member States of the European Community.

The national specificity of film authorship

In Western European cinema the figure of the film author as a sociology-of-production resulted from the interplay of cultural politics and economic structures in national film systems. The precursor of the film author in Western Europe is the Italian neo-realist film-maker, a socially committed intellectual with a strong hold on the practical aspects of film-making. Georges Sadoul summarizes the defining characteristics of neo-realist cinema as such: location shooting, lengthy takes, unobtrusive editing, natural lighting, non-professional cast, contemporary subjects, low-class protagonists, and vernacular dialogue (Marcus 1986: 21–22).[1] Neo-realism was also the result of historical circumstances that brought film production outside the closed-down studios of a dismembered film industry, into spontaneous sets and locations (Cannella 1973). Indeed, many Italian neo-realist film directors who had an ethical urgency to report on the tragic events of their time had had their early professional experiences in the film industry of the fascist regime. Because of the anti-fascist pressure of the resistance and of the post-war period, these film directors became exclusively identified with an ethical agenda: that of bearing witness to the country's conditions after the hardship of the long conflict and especially the dramatic situation following the 1943 Armistice.

In many ways, the same motivations that constituted the convictions of neo-realist cinema informed the new aesthetics emerging in France, Italy, and Spain throughout the 1950s and 1960s, although in quite different political and economic circumstances. As in Italian neo-realism, the limited budgets and the unavailability of professional sets also determined the aesthetic of the New Wave film authors and their penchant toward on-location settings, realist representation, and contemporary themes. At the same time, the New Wave film-making methods in France, Italy, and Spain reflected a generational reactions against, respectively, the conservative, outdated, or oppressive hegemonic formations of these three countries. Hence, the nouvelle vague auteurs moved away from the academic culture of the Cinéma de qualité. The Italian young intellectuals of the nuovo cinema movement cut loose from both the institutional cinema identified with the studios of Cinecittá and the political influence of the Christian-Democratic government on Italian culture. The realist Spanish film-makers of the nuevo cine movement opposed the ideological and aesthetic limitations of a censorship-ridden and politically structured film industry by resorting to film forms and aesthetic styles borrowed both from realist and Hollywood cinemas.

In each of the national film systems here considered, the film author as a sociology-of-production finds origin in systems of film production derived from government policies and state institutions for the promotion of culturally oriented film projects existing since before World War II and further implemented in the post-war period. In France, a fundamental establishment in this sense is the Institut de Hautes Etudes Cinématographiques (I.D.H.E.C.), a national school for the professional training of film-makers, film technicians, and film actors, founded in 1943 by the film director Marcel l'Herbier and in a fascist context, under the Vichy government. The institution was 'rehabilitated' after the end of World War II, in conjunction with the opening of a private institution subsidized by the state, the Cinémathèque Française. In 1946 the French government created the Centre National de la Cinématographie (C.N.C.), in place of the Comité d'Organisation de l'Industrie Cinématographique (C.O.I.C.), established during the

German occupation period to co-ordinate the French film industry. Since 1948 the C.N.C. has controlled the system of government film funds, the *Compte de soutien*, collected from a combination of tax receipts, bank supports, and state grants. Once the most immediate priorities of reconstructing the production and exhibition structures were met, the *Compte de soutien* focused more on subsidizing film projects. In 1959 and 1960 two forms of financing were introduced: the *Soutien automatique*, aimed at the film industry in general and based on box office receipts; and the *Aide sélective*, better known as *avance sur recettes*, based on the selective funding (20 per cent of films made) and privileging of culturally oriented films (Hayward 1993a: 46–47). In 1981 the Minister of Culture, Jack Lang, promoted a significant increase in the advance funds, instituting also a financial company with the purpose of advancing capital to producers and film-makers, the Société de Financement des Industries Cinématographiques et Audiovisuelles (S.O.F.I.C.A., 'Society for the Financing of Cinema and the Audio-visual') (Hayward 1993b: 384). Unlike in Italy – where financial aids exerted a strong political and censorship supervision – in France state contributions to the film industry took more of a purely economic direction. This explains why in France the struggle for the control of film distribution has often allied the government with the film industry and has considered its worst enemy the new audio-visual apparatus *per se* and not, as in Italy, the political structure behind it. As René Prédal remarks, film authors in France would claim a sense of their artistic identity depending on the medium they would be working with, so that '[t]he filmmaker calls himself artist and treats the television director as an artisan. The first talks creation and the second profession, one expresses himself through film and the other impressed tape, the latter makes a living out of his work, while the other starves for his art' (Hennebelle and Prédal 1987: 15, my translation).[2]

In France as much as in Italy, educational film institutions remained the main points of reference for film-makers seeking professional training. Yet many other venues were offered to aspiring film authors through unofficial channels of apprenticeship. First the film industry and later the television networks provided for the professional development of most emerging film-makers in the 1960s and 1970s. The Parisian-based tradition of *cinéphilisme* (cinephilia) and film criticism is largely responsible for the cultural shaping of French film authorship (de Baecque 2003). This scene, in turn, arguably was influenced by the cultural climate of post-World War II Parisian intelligentsia, most notably the figures of Jean-Paul Sartre and André Malraux (de Baecque 1991 and 1998).[8] To be sure, French auteurism tried to disengage itself from these cultural links. However, as Antoine de Baecque notes, the *Jeunes Turcs* of *Cahiers du Cinéma* both betrayed and continued this critical tradition, embodied by the father figures of André Bazin and Jean Georges Auriol and hosted in the *Revue du cinéma*. If Truffaut and colleagues moved away from the literary style of the *Revue du cinéma* and eventually freed themselves from their Oedipal complexes, they nevertheless retained some of the critical approaches and perspectives of both, including their interest in literature and their use of film to explore contemporary reality (de Baecque 1991: 15–16). De Baecque (1991: 16) argues that insofar as the critics of *Cahiers du Cinéma* considered cinema at the level of any other art, their aesthetic agenda was very much in line with Bazin and Auriol's philosophical and critical positions. However, he also points out that

Because it was founded on a heritage, but at the same time took issue against it, *Cahiers du cinéma*, took upon itself the suspicions of betrayal, from the beginning. The 'fidelity' of its followers is constantly trapped in a reading where the syndrome of betrayal and the abandon of critical values fluctuate. (Ibid., my translation)[3]

In other words, if the *politique des auteurs* succeeded in getting rid of the climate of *engagement* that was pending in French art cinema and produced a new type of film discourse with the *nouvelle vague*, it certainly failed to expunge from other film critics of *Cahiers du Cinéma* and other film journals the commitment to a 'high cultural' literary tradition and to an idea of criticism as an expression of personal views and beliefs.

The figure of the film author in Italian cinema is linked to both professional training and intellectual education. These apparently antithetical lineages have a historical common foundation, institutionalized by the fascist regime during the 1930s reorganization of the Italian film industry. As mentioned earlier on, Italian film-makers and critics have long overlooked this genealogy for ideological reasons. Their interpretation of neo-realism came from an anti-fascist perspective that inspired many Italian film-makers to claim their derivation from neo-realism, down to the present generation of film-makers. Gian Piero Brunetta identifies the origin of this ideological lineage in neo-realism, also noting that 'neo-realist poetic [was] founded on the myth of spontaneity and immediacy and on the celebration of the Work and of the Author' (Brunetta 1998: 263, my translation).[4] Brunetta inserts this comment in a chapter about post-World War II screenwriters, who, according to him, represented 'the production element removed from such poetics, in order to maintain its image of immediacy' (ibid., my translation). Especially since the 1970s, many historians have promoted a revisionist approach to neo-realism by underlining the continuity between the film authors and styles of the regime and those of the neo-realist renaissance.[5] The descent of neo-realism from the 1940s vogue of realism in film and literature (both mediated by North American 'realist' literature and cinema as well as Soviet socialist cinema) and the former careers of neo-realist masters in the fascist film industry is fundamental for understanding one of the most distinctive traits in Italy's authorial film practices: the frequent combination of opposite aesthetics and ideologies.[6] The peculiarity of Italian film authorship also derives from another tradition in the national film industry: the involvement of famous intellectuals and artists. Since the early 1910s, these figures brought an aura of cultural prestige to Italian cinema and contributed to the representation of European cinema as the homeland of art film.

The reorganization of the Italian film industry under the fascist regime institutionalized this national cultural heritage and put it at the service of a sophisticated strategy of popular appeal. This effort was evident in the fascist creation of film institutions, schools, and associations on the one hand and the diffusion of film culture through academic organizations and local associations on the other. The institutions that became centres of formation and discussion for film authors were the Centro Sperimentale di Cinematografia and the Venice International Film Festival. Founded during the fascist regime, the two institutions were closed down during the war and both reopened in 1946. In the years immediately following the end of World War II, the institutionalization of the Centro Sperimentale followed the strategies of the vice-secretary to the Prime Minister specifically in charge of film policies, Giulio Andreotti. A skilled politician and one of the most powerful men of the Christian Democratic Party, in 1949 Andreotti promoted two laws that introduced a system of indirect yet close control and censorship on the Italian film industry. He also appointed Christian Democratic figures at the direction of film production and distribution companies, of the Centro Sperimentale, and of the Venice Film Festival (Brunetta 1998: 59–81). These two were points of cultural reference also after the fall of the fascist regime and the end of World War II. A professional school for film technicians, directors, screenwriters, and actors/actresses seeking direct contact with the national film industry, the Centro Sperimentale became an international centre of film formation. In the 1960s, the school attracted students coming from Latin America who brought their experience in the New Wave and counter film movements that were developing in that area. At the Centro Sperimentale were the headquarters of Bianco e Nero, a film journal that shaped generations of critics in Italy. Bianco e Nero began publishing again after World War II, in 1947, first directed by the intellectual Umberto Barbaro. Soon after Andreotti was appointed vice-secretary of the Prime Minister, Barbaro was dismissed and a new cultural trend began.

The Centro Sperimentale di Cinematografia and the Venice Film Festival also took on a more pragmatic and mainstream direction. The Centro Sperimentale became a state institution, more oriented toward professionalism than artistic expression and experimentation. A fine intellectual, film teacher, and a film-maker himself, Francesco Pasinetti directed the Venice Film Festival from its re-opening in 1946 until his premature death in 1949. Under the direction of a Christian Democratic board, the festival lost its cultural prestige and was often at the centre of polemics and critiques (Brunetta 1998: 58–59). For this reason, the school promoted what still remains as a unique typology of film author: a film-maker with a strong professional training, as well as intellectually versatile.[7] The importance of the Centro Sperimentale faltered with the crisis of the film industry. Brunetta places the institutional decadence of the Centro Sperimentale even earlier, in the years immediately following World War II. According to Brunetta, the centrality of the film studios and cultural institutions in Rome was forever lost after the Liberation, in spite of – and probably because of – all state efforts to concentrate the entire audio-visual system in Rome. Brunetta views the consequences of this fragmentation in the creation of new centres for cultural film practices (Milan in particular). Many small and ephemeral film production companies were founded in the years following the end of World War II. Sometimes these companies were financed by local industrialists (as it was the case for the Industrie Cinematografiche e Teatrali (I.C.E.T.), established in 1946) or by film producers based in other cities than Rome (Brunetta 1998: 44–45).

The prestige of Cinecittá waned in the 1970s and 1980s. In those years, many aspiring Italian film-makers rather tried to make their début there by entering the film industry as assistant directors, 'ghost' screenwriters, film critics, or cultural promoters. However, getting access to film direction was more and more difficult in the Rome studios. Cinecittá offered lifelong humiliating positions as film directors in spaghetti westerns or soft-core productions. Film journals and film festivals highly contributed to the negative image of Cinecittá as the headquarters of the national film production, in the effort to encourage independent cinema and non-dominant film practices. Yet the lack of confidence in these structures was also the reflection of a nationwide distrust of public institutions and of the widespread assumption that they were run on the basis of political and personal recommendations. On the other hand, state television held out the meagre prospect of directing educational programmes. For these reasons, the 1970s and 1980s generations of Italian film-makers walked out of national and institutional structures and opted for more marginal yet more independent opportunities in local film schools and audio-visual structures (many of which primarily worked on video). The discussion of the crisis of cultural film production and the role of film schools had started in the 1970s. In 1974 the Venice Film Festival hosted a round table on the relationship between the new audio-visual industry and cultural film production. Former students of the Centro Sperimentale who had founded an independent film production company, the '2/K,' attended the meeting and discussed the role of film schools to face the crisis of art house cinema and the lack of independent film structures in Italy.

Spanish cinema went through a period of total cultural isolation soon after the end of World War II, especially with the break of relationships between the regime and the foreign powers from 1946 to 1950.[8] In these years, the government restructured the film system according to a strongly nationalist orientation. Part of this project was the creation of professional institutions and associations for the promotion of cultural cinema. In 1945 the Círculo de Escritores Cinematográficos (C.E.C.) was created, and two years later the first national film school was opened, the Instituto de Investigaciones y Experimentaciones Cinematográficas (I.I.E.C.).[9] The government's investment in the national film system included the structuring of a new censorship board in 1946, the Supreme Board of Film Orientation. This powerful instrument of production control paralleled an even stricter board, that of the Catholic Church, the National Board of Classification of Spectacles (Hopewell 1986: 40–41). As in France and Italy, in Spain, too, film journals, cultural institutions, and university circles determined the construction and diffusion of independent and often politically radical film forms. This was all the more true in a political situation where the state had absolute control on every aspect of Spanish cultural life. Strengthened by its renewed international endorsement (the 1950 cancellation of U.N. sanctions against Spain and the re-opening of French borders in response to diplomatic pressure by the US government), the regime consolidated its monopoly on the film industry through a stricter cultural control. In 1951 Franco created the Ministry of Tourism and Information, an agency that supervised every sector of Spain's culture, including cinema, and was also in charge of the censorship board. This move had a double and quite contradictory function: on the one hand, it intensified the prevention against a growing cultural opposition; on the other, it promoted a more 'liberal' image of Spain abroad. Authorial film practices in Spain assumed a dialectical position vis-à-vis the national film system. With respect to censorship, Spanish film-makers adopted highly symbolic or allegorical styles of representation. Two film models helped pave the way: Italian neo-realism and Hollywood cinema.[10] As Marsha Kinder argues, both models 'could be used to challenge the regime's monolithic hold over Spanish culture' (1993: 19). Neo-realism encouraged Spanish film-makers to depict contemporary society, in contrasts to the self-celebrating epics and the escapist folklorist melodramas that dominated Spanish screens. On the other hand, Hollywood films represented looser standards of morality and offered a variety of understated modes of representation (Higginbotham 1988; Hopewell 1991; Kinder 1993).

In Francoist Spain, trying to open a breach toward new aesthetics and types of production was up to individual initiatives, including those of cultural promoters who occupied key positions in the regime's main institutions. José María García Escudero, a military officer twice appointed as head of the censorship board, was a progressive intellectual whose personal defence of some films cost him the post in 1952.[11] Escudero also mediated between the government and the neo-realist-oriented film-makers and critics at the 1955 Salamanca Congress. Another central figure for the development of Spanish film authorship was Carlos Serrano de Osma, who was the main organizer of the national film school established by Franco in Madrid. Although strictly controlled by the state, Spain's national film school allowed many aspiring film-makers to make important connections. Luis García Berlanga and Juan Antonio Bardem Bardem (the most representative directors of the 1950s anti-regime film authors) met there. Madrid and Barcelona were the two main centres of cultural film production in Spain. Madrid was more institutionalized and linked to state financing, Barcelona more experimental and based on independent film companies. Serrano de Osma was also the promoter of the *Telúricos* movement, an aesthetically committed group that preceded the creation of the Barcelona School, the Catalan counterpart to the Madrid-based *nuevo cine*. His directorial début, *Abel Sánchez* (1946), betrays this aesthetic concern (Hopewell 1986: 40). In the mid-1960s, Vicente Aranda and the film critic Román Gubern, among others, founded the *Escola de Barcelona* film movement. Film journals represented another vanguard in the battle against the regime and its censorship board, even before the official mobilizing of Spanish directors and cultural operators at the Salamanca Congress.

Film criticism offered another point of reference for the cultural resistance against Spain's regime's cinema. Right after the Spanish Civil War two new film magazines opened, *Cine Experimental* (1940–1946) and the more popular *Otro Cine* and *Revista Internacional del Cine*. Many of the film journals and magazines published from the mid-1950s to the mid-1970s took a Marxist orientation (often derived from the examples of Italian journals such as Guido Aristarco's *Cinema Nuovo*). Their political position made them the target of the government's action. Hence, *Objetivo* (1953–1956), which supported Italian neo-realism, *Documentos Cinematográficos* (1960–1963), openly related to *Cinema Nuovo*, and the scholarly journal *Cinema Universitario* (1955–1963), which continued along the same lines as *Objectivo*, all had short lives.[12] The latter two introduced a type of film criticism that took after French auteurism and the *nouvelle vague*, a direction also followed by the initially Marxist-oriented *Nuestro Cine* (established in 1961 by Serrano de Osma) and modelled on the Italian leftist film magazine *Cinema Nuovo* and by *Film Ideal* (1956–1970), a moderate journal that grew militant in the 1960s.[13]

Among the initiatives that revealed new film currents and styles to Spanish film-makers were the Italian Cinema Weeks at the Institute of Italian Culture in Madrid in 1949 and 1951. During these occasions, several neo-realist films were shown and presented by Italian film-makers and screenwriters, thanks also to the illegal imports channelled through diplomatic pouches.[14] The consolidation of university film clubs promoting the new film aesthetics from Italy and France started right after the end of World War II, led by a cultural association based in Saragossa. During the 1950s, these film clubs provided the only channels for the distribution of film classics from the national archive of the Filmoteca Nacional. It was the Saragossa film group and its university network that promoted the Salamanca Congress in 1955. This national film congress was organized by the Salamanca University Film Club, publisher of the university journal *Cine Universitario*. The event brought few concrete results for Spanish cultural film production, but its manifesto gave new directions to Spanish film-makers. Quite rhetorical in its formulation and abstract in its programme, this manifesto transposed one, fundamental purpose: using Spain's realist tradition to depict its contemporary society. Besides re-appropriating Spanish cinema of its national cultural heritage, the film-makers of the Salamanca Congress waged war against the government's allotment of subsidies according to topics of national interest, which in fact was a strategy to fail every project not complying with the criteria of the censorship board.[15] Eventually, the Salamanca Congress boosted a spirit of collaboration and innovation against state film practices and government censorship that remained as the constitutive mark of Spanish film authors of the *nuevo cine*, including, among others, Juan Antonio Bardem, Luis García Berlanga, Luis Buñuel, Víctor Erice, and Carlos Saura.

Film authorship and the crisis of European cinema

Starting from the 1970s, the crisis of the film industry and theatrical film exhibition circuit progressively hindered the marketing viability of Western European film authors in domestic and foreign film markets. The closing of film theatres left the exhibition circuit diminished by more than a third of the capacity it had in the 1950s and 1960s. Furthermore, film exhibition came to be monopolized by Hollywood blockbusters and popular genre films, mainly produced for the domestic market, such as erotic comedies and soft-core films. The spread of red-light movie theatres was a prevalent phenomenon during this period. Throughout the 1970s, European film producers and distributors tried to maintain the promotional value of established European film authors by presenting them in European and Euro-American co-productions featuring international stars and high production values. In part, this development in authorial film practices coincided with the phenomenon Peter Lev identifies as the 'Euro-American film' in his book *The Euro-American Cinema* (1993). According to Lev, the main characteristics of the Euro-American film are prominent use of the English language; presence of some native English-speaking actors; involvement of a European film director; periodization (1945–present); larger budgets and better production values; cast and crew from two or more countries; use of qualities characteristic of the European art film (such as ambiguity, originality, personal style, character-focused narrative, and artistic links); use of qualities typical of the US entertainment film (stars, genres, pre-sold subjects, spectacle, and action); and subject matter addressing encounters between European and American cultures (1993: 30–32). Lev sets the emergence of this type of film all the way back in the 1950s, with the production of films directed by Italian art film-makers of the calibre of Federico Fellini and Michelangelo Antonioni. These productions were backed by international co-production companies and featured international casts. What distinguishes this earlier trend from the shift seen in the 1970s is that, as Lev acknowledges, American financial participation in the 1950s was primarily related to distribution rather than production. The limited investment in distribution limited the potentiality of the Euro-American author film to reach the normal circuit of national and international film exhibition.

By the late 1970s, Europe's author cinema had become the symbol of an endangered mode of production, laid down by an industrial and commercial film system lacking a coordinated arrangement of production and distribution resources and infrastructures and surviving only through government subsidies and television productions. During the 1980s the pre-acquisition of TV programming rights and government quotas for TV networks to co-produce with cinema and for national TV networks to programme domestic and European films almost completely replaced the art house cinema's dying companies of independent distribution and exhibition. Yet these new types of financing also had a negative effect on authorial film practices: they established a sort of 'welfare' system, often blamed for its bureaucratic slowness and aesthetic indiscrimination and did not help film authors regain popularity with the audience.

In France, during his two terms as Minister of Culture (from 1981 to 1986 and from 1988 to 1993), Jack Lang promoted big-budget films and intensified the domestic exhibition and international distribution of French films through the creation of new exhibition circuits and advanced funds. Lang's policies also imposed strong limitations on film and video monopolies and promoted independent and regional channels of distribution and exhibition against the Hollywood conglomerate, as well as the national corporation Gaumont-Pathé (Hayward 1993b). These measures soon revealed their inability to overcome the progressive disaffection for the stylistic trend of 'quality films' and the inflationary policy of national distribution of French films. In Italy, although not formally promoted by a change in government direction, state subsidies began in 1978 with the law on state contributions to cultural production. This law encouraged an endless series of authorial débuts, hardly ever concretized into further achievements and seldom adequately promoted or even released in the domestic film market.[16] In 1983, Spain's 'General Director of Cinema,' film-maker Pilar Miró, introduced new quotas on imported films and with those receipts financed culturally committed projects meant to re-instate the prestige of Spanish cinema. Yet her effort to increase government subsidies even worsened the situation of Spanish film production. These funds swelled cultural film production and even individual films' budgets, without finding correspondence in box office receipts. Miró had established advance subsidies up to 50 per cent of a film's budget that, as Hopewell remarks, were 'repayable only through further subsidies calculated as percentages of subsequent box office takings [...] 25% more for "Special Quality' films"' (in Kinder 1997: 117). Television productions have been more effective in boosting film production, through different regulations in each national context.[17] In France, television has surpassed the government formula of *avance sur recettes* with the pre-acquisition of films rights for programming. In Italy, the phenomenon involved both the RAI and the private networks of Fininvest, Berlusconi's audio-visual corporation (Sesti 1996: 207). As René Prédal remarks, in France the percentage of films produced by television moved from 11 per cent in 1986 to 20 per cent in 1990, doubling in the year between 1986 and 1987.

Since the 1980s, television networks in Western Europe acquire broadcasting rights to two-third of the films annually produced within a country before the films are actually made. Canal+ provides 40 per cent of French television's total investments in film (in Aprá and Turigliatto, 1996: 75). In Italy, state television began to invest on quality cinema and film authors since the 1970s and is still a major source of funding for author cinema. Since the mid-1980s, Fininvest has been making large investments in film production (40 per cent of total TV investments in 1985).[18] During the past ten years, television networks' purchasing of broadcasting rights has for the most part replaced the financing system known as 'minimum percentages guarantees,' through which the Italian government used receipts to anticipate money to film producers. Television's support of author cinema has been a relief for the traditionally scarce popularity of this type of cinema in Spain and has slightly jolted a film industry troubled by a chronic crisis.

Despite all efforts from Europe's national film industries and television systems, the project of creating alternative circuits of theatrical film exhibition through the marketing of film authors also encountered many obstacles. To begin with, the shift from movie theatrical attendance to home viewing systems made the promotion of film authors even more difficult. Challenged by increasingly affordable electronic equipment (which added up to the advantages of viewing films at home), both Hollywood and the national film industries attracted spectators back in the movie theatres by producing spectacular formulaic films. This move automatically affected the middle and small ranges of film production and exhibition. Author cinema moved either to larger structures of film production and distribution or remained confined to small, independent film companies, whose films had almost no impact on the film market. Either way, the global dimension of mainstream film distribution left hardly any room for theatrical or videotape distribution of author films. European national film industries used popular subgenres to counteract the prominence of Hollywood blockbusters in their domestic markets. Red-light cinemas monopolized the exhibition circuit and replaced many art house and parochial movie theatres. Comedies and soft-porn films became dominant subgenres. The social infrastructures and cultural contexts that once distributed art house films in selective and alternative circuits of film exhibition were supplanted by various types of audio-visual distribution and exhibition. Since the 1970s, television programming and videotape release, not art house movie theatres, control the marketing of author films, in what would seem an increase in accessibility. However, if state and private television programming assured some circulation to authors' films, they were hardly effectual to their development in a competitive European film market and instead increased their distance from film audiences (Dibie 1993: 3; Ilott 1996: 2). Television programming of author films hardly ever produced high shares in France, Italy or Spain, in spite of the markedly cultural orientation of these countries' state television networks. Author cinema's low success in French, Italian, and Spanish television include discriminating programming strategies that gave priority to popular types of programmes during prime time in order to compete with private commercial networks (the Berlusconian networks Canale 5 and Retequattro above all). Similarly, author films have always constituted a small percentage of the videotape output and circulation and their presence is significant only in special circuits of film distribution or else in non-profit, cultural, and public institutions, such as libraries, schools, and cine-clubs.

Overall, the massive involvement of governments, state televisions, and national television networks in film practices increased the extant tension between aesthetic autonomy and institutional control of the film author. Thomas Elsaesser (1989) stresses this point in his discussion of the German autorenfilm. In this mode of production the film author is a state employee determined by the structures and infrastructures of national cultural production and, as self-employed, 's/he is an "artist" in the conventional bourgeois sense, and a producer in the pre-capitalist sense' (1989: 3–4). The new audio-visual systems also prompted critical responses and initiatives, including promotional campaigns for movie theatre exhibition in film journals, newspapers, cultural magazines, academic circles, and non-profit screenings and events.[19] The struggle to contain the progressive decline of art house film practices in the public sphere also engaged political and economic antagonists. Film distribution and exhibition mainly turned to television programming, creating competition between private or public networks or between television programming and videotape circulation.

A highly debated point was the allocation of film programming on television, which juxtaposed initially public and private networks and, especially in the 1990s, also involved pay channels and networks' alliances for satellite broadcasting. Each country dealt with these issues according to national orientations, government directions, and local interests. In France, the government maintained and even reinvigorated film exhibition, by monitoring private television networks and balancing the number of films on the air, so as not to disadvantage movie theatre releases. In Italy, the question concerned less an attempt to re-launch film exhibition in movie theatre circuits (already monopolized by domestic exploitation of popular subgenres), than the necessity of regulating the ratio between the films produced and those actually distributed in movie theatres and videotape circuits. In Spain, the struggle for film distribution had yet another focus. One the one hand, there was the effort of the government to maintain central control, after the dismantling of the regime's production monopoly and censorship board.[20] On the other hand, there was the phenomenon of global deregulation, which brought international financial groups and production or distribution corporations to invest in Spain's local and regional networks (Kinder 1993: 388–94).

Since the mid-1990s, the situation has slightly changed: film practices associated with film authors are involved in more diversified modes of film production and distribution, especially since film admissions for domestic films have been slightly increasing. On the one hand, author cinema has re-established its relations with private forms of financing and freelance film production companies, slowly recuperating from a long phase of economic depression. On the other hand, the recognition that some film authors received at international film festivals and awards has drawn the attention of corporate companies of audio-visual distribution and exhibition and television networks.

Since the early 1990s, television networks and independent film companies have enhanced the number of national productions and international co-productions in Western Europe, often backed by European trans-national subsidies. These initiatives have re-established authorial film practices in the international market, ultimately provoking the response of Hollywood and its entrance in the art house circuit of film distribution.[21] During the past decade the role of film author as a sociology-of-production has been changing, adapting to various sectors of the audio-visual industry. These modifications gave rise to new authorial figures, most notably that of the author-producer, who seeks new margins of autonomy through the management of all sectors of film production and distribution. Many of these author-producers establish their own production companies and promote other authorial projects; others work in different audio-visual media, transferring not only modes of production and techniques of representation but also entire production structures from one medium to another. The most radically independent category of author-producer is almost exclusively operative in video production and often linked to co-operatives.

Reception practices linked with film authors, once identified with specialized forms of distribution and exhibition (art house movie theatres, cine-clubs, and state television) now extend to a larger sector of the audio-visual market (tables 1–5). With the early 1990s attempts of European cinema at reinforcing the distribution of its quality films in the domestic and international markets, authors' films have in part broken their long banning from movie theatre exhibition (table 6), particularly in the three national film contexts here considered (tables 7–9). The promotion of film authors found new niches in the diversifying structures of the audio-visual exhibition sector, occasionally venturing in mainstream circuits and multiplex movie theatres.[22] 'Commercial' authors would typically combine technological sophistication and production values, with results that often raised questions about how their films were different from Hollywood blockbusters. The phenomenon began in the mid-1980s in France, especially with the *cinéma du look* and its film-makers Luc Besson, Jean-Jacques Beineix, and Leos Carax. Film authorship also became involved in distribution strategies that combine theatrical distribution and television programming. The European author films pitched an increasing middle-range section of movie theatre audience by using E.C. subsidies, committees, and agencies that promote the

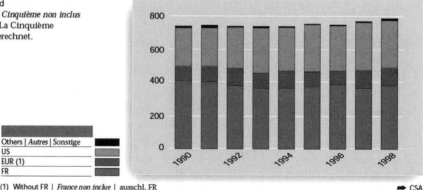

G.1.FR

Number and origin of feature films broadcast by French unencrypted TV channels | 1990-1998

Nombre et origine des films diffusés par les chaînes françaises « en clair » | 1990-1998

Zahl und Herkunft der von den französischen unverschlüsselten Fernsehdiensten gesendeten Filme | 1990-1998

| ARTE and La Cinquième not included
ARTE et La Cinquième non inclus
ARTE und La Cinquième nicht eingerechnet.

Others | *Autres* | Sonstige
US
EUR (1)
FR

(1) Without FR | *France non inclue* | ausschl. FR   ➡ CSA

Table 1: Lange, 'Les films européens sur les chaînes européennes de television.' (04/2000) France. European Audiovisual Observatory Report, http://www.obs.coe.int/online_publication/reports/films_in_tv.pdf.en.

G.1.IT

Number and origin of broadcasts of films on Italian broadcasters | 1995-1998
Nombre et origine de diffusion de films par les diffuseurs italiennes | 1995-1998
Anzahl und Herkunft von Filmsendungen bei italianischen Veranstaltern | 1995-1998

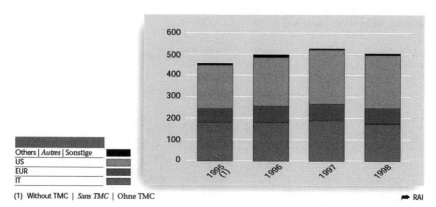

(1) Without TMC | *Sans TMC* | Ohne TMC ➡ RAI

Table 2: Lange, 'Les films européens sur les chaînes européennes de television.' (04/2000). Italy. European Audiovisual Observatory Report, http://www.obs.coe.int/online_publication/reports/films_in_tv.pdf.en.

collaboration among different national film systems and occasionally include US partnerships for local and international distribution. The renewed interest of Hollywood in European author films in fact led to the acquisition of independent art house film distributors by Hollywood corporations, including Miramax, Fine Line, Goldwyn, and Sony Pictures Classics. Tino Balio identifies a second wave of art film marketing in the 1990s (the first was in the 1970s, with the Hollywood 'mini-majors' Orion and Dino De Laurentiis Entertainment) (1998: 63–73). Equally important for reviving the interest in European art films in North America was the creation of Hollywood subsidiaries by European-based audio-visual corporations. Yet the problem that European film companies have to face is how to monitor the US film distribution and enter its market (table 10). Most attempts at establishing a network of distribution in the United States are local or have short life. A case in point is the Italian distribution company Penta America, created in 1989 by the Berlusconian group Fininvest through its film production branch Reteitalia and with the partnership of another audio-visual Italian corporation, the Cecchi Gori Group. Penta-America closed down after five years of activity.[23]

The multiple commitments of the film author

French auteurism proposed a cinematic model informed by art-derived metaphors that equated the camera to the pen. This authorial model suggests a modern version of the Romantic artist: a genius with expressive talent and an idiosyncratic perception of the world. Nevertheless, as parlayed by the *Jeunes Turcs*, the film auteur is also closely connected with industrial and commercial contexts of film production. In fact, proponents of the *politique des auteurs* were especially impressed by individual film-makers who conveyed their personal

G.1.ES
Number of feature films broadcast by Spanish television channels (rebroadcast not included) | 1995 and 1998

Nombre de films diffusés par les chaînes de télévision espagnoles (rediffusions non incluses) | 1995 and 1998

Anzahl der von den spanischen Fersehdiensten gesendeten Spielfilme (ausschl. Wiederholungen) | 1995 und 1998

| Channels with national coverage
Chaînes à couverture nationale
Dienste mit nationaler Ausstahlung

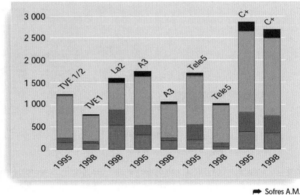

Others | *Autres* | Sonstige
US
EUR
ES

➡ Sofres A.M.

Tables 3 and 4: Lange, 'Les films européens sur les chaînes européennes de television.' (04/2000). Spain. European Audiovisual Observatory Report, http://www.obs.coe.int/online_publication/reports/films_in_tv.pdf.en.

| Channels of the Autonomic Communities
Chaînes des communautés autonomiques
Dienste der autonomen Gemeinschaften

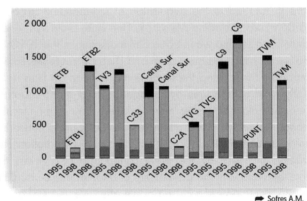

Others | *Autres* | Sonstige
US
EUR
ES

➡ Sofres A.M.

visions and original styles from within the confines of mainstream cinema's institutionalized conformity. Having dismissed the cultural pretensions of the French *Cinéma de qualité*, the auteur-oriented film critics set out to individuate 'personalities' from film modes and contexts that, until that time, had been overlooked or dismissed as commercial by film criticism and cultural discourse. Furthermore, some of the founders of the *politique des auteurs* who later became prominent representatives of the French *nouvelle vague* – as well as many film-

Ranked by operating revenue in EUR thousand.
Revenue from activities other than theatrical distribution (such as production, video distribution, trade in rights, Pay-TV, video games and consoles etc.) may be included in operating revenue for some companies.

	Company	Country	2001	2002	2003	2004	2005	2005 / 2004
1	Metropolitan Filmexport	FR	150 483	145 089	181 513	190 012	190 421	0,2%
2	Entertainment Film Distributors Ltd	GB	127 845	182 287	187 747	181 225	~	–
3	Pathé Distribution	FR	50 393	120 789	86 563	260 941	180 367	-30,9%
4	Medusa Film S.P.A.	IT	83 341	~	~	147 140	110 929	-24,6%
5	Nordisk Film AS	DK	1 861	6 824	117 873	101 080	109 620	8,4%
6	01 Distribution	IT	11 700	36 461	37 664	44 232	93 667	111,8%
7	Eagle Pictures S.P.A.	IT	62 765	77 916	86 869	97 778	89 937	-8,0%
8	AB Svensk Filmindustri	SE	63 584	90 817	99 081	94 188	87 474	-7,1%
9	Sociedad General de Derechos Audiovisuales S.A. (Filmax)	ES	62 541	76 579	72 005	81 391	~	–
10	Société nouvelle de distribution (SND)	FR	12 021	15 193	59 195	55 935	56 173	0,4%

Source: European Audiovisual Observatory

Table 5: 'Film Distribution Companies in Europe.' European Audiovisual Observatory Report, 5 February 2007, http://www.obs.coe.int/about/oea/pr/distributionreport.html.

makers connected to the New Wave film movements that proliferated in Europe in the 1950s – used classical Hollywood-inspired generic conventions and formulas in their films. Within Europe, Hollywood's most significant impact on New Wave film authors is found in France, Germany, the United Kingdom, and Spain.[24] Hollywood cinema forms an important intertext with respect to the three national contexts considered in this book, particularly for French and Spanish film authors. Most of the auteur-oriented critics of the 1950s Cahiers du Cinéma testify to the influence of Hollywood films on the film-makers of the nouvelle vague. For example, references to Hollywood films are prominent in the early films of Jean-Luc Godard and form a consistent subtext to the works of François Truffaut and Claude Chabrol. Beginning in the 1950s, Spanish film authors used these films as a fundamental source of inspiration that could also ease their efforts to cope with the regime's censorship policies (Kinder 1993 and 1997). Despite the fact that the pristine model of the auteur established by the politique des auteurs was based on mainstream film production, that the films of the New Wave auteur generation presented a strong Hollywood intertext, and that both commercial and artistic interests motivated the emergence of European film authorship as a promotional category in international film markets, many film critics and academics have traditionally overlooked the actual implications of authorial film practices in industrial, commercial, and technological aspects of cinema. This is especially true with regard to the discussion of the European author film. Such oversight, shared by industry players and film critics, reflects a more general tendency: that of considering European cinema primarily as a culturally oriented film system and market. From this perspective, film discourse has largely treated the European film author's relationship to the industry in terms of conflict. This bias is deeply rooted in the institutional and cultural treatment of the film author during the 1980s.

At end of the 1980s, Jacques Aumont concludes his book L'oeil interminable. Cinéma et peinture, on the relations between cinema and painting, with a post-script in which he discusses the death of cinema within the framework of the new media. He notes:

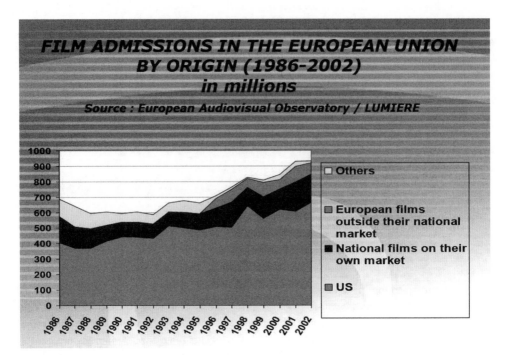

Table 6: 'The Fragmented Universe of Film Distribution Companies in Europe.' European Audiovisual Observatory, Contribution to the Workshop 'Distribution of European Films' (Venezia, 29–31 August 2003). European Film Distributors. http://www.obs.coe.int/online_publication/expert/filmdistcompanies. pdf.en.

This is written in 1988. A view from now and here: France, Paris, the situation on the side of cinema is despairing, but not bad. Cinema dies, cinema is dead, they keep repeating everywhere and every day. Yet cinema does not seem to be doing that bad at all [...] At the present time, there is no new art standing at the horizon that would come and replace or even simply substitute the agonizing sound cinema. The emerging products, in their still a bit swarming diversity, difficult to tell apart, at least have this much in common: that they all say not to care about art, that their consumer circuits, their networks of pleasure and imagination, are not the same, nor do they have pretensions of entering museums. (Aumont 1989: 249, my translation)[25]

The 1980s marked by the definitive stagnation of Western European cinema's production and the struggle to maintain the culturally oriented sector of its film industry alive through institutional and state interventions aiming at containing the monopoly of new Hollywood blockbusters and domestic soft-porn and erotic comedy subgenres in the national film markets. Contributing to the downsizing of theatrical exhibition was the circulation of mainstream and pornographic films in video stores and of Hollywood films on private television networks. During this decade, questions about the fate of European art cinema and the position of European film authors within the global audio-visual system were at the centre of attention in film journals and magazines within the three national contexts here considered. One of the most contentious points was whether cinema would benefit or suffer from a strengthening association with other media, first through the emergence of television as a source of production and exhibition and the growth of the video rental market, then with the expansion of pay TV and cable as alternative forms of exhibition.

Another important locus of debate concerned the impact of new technologies (from high-definition television to digital effects and cameras) on film aesthetics and film-making techniques. At its most conservative, the discussion stressed the allegiance of film authors with cultural objectives struggling against the increasing commercialization and technological focus of the film industry. One of the most contested issues in this respect was how new media would affect the distribution and exhibition of films; predictably so since the crisis of the theatre circuit had hit the cultural sector of the film industry particularly hard. Authors' films were poorly distributed not only in movie theatres, but also in the video rental market and they did not constitute a significant share of television programming, especially with the emergence of private and commercial TV networks.[26] Dario Formisano (1994) has examined the 'micro-economy of the audio-visual media,' mainly with reference to the Italian film context (which is however comparable to that of other European countries). He argues that the proliferation of more diversified exhibition systems (including multiplex movie theatres, free TV, pay and pay-per-view television, home video, CD-ROMs, and global networks) exceeds both social demands and production needs. More importantly, the growth of new viewing systems had virtually no impact on either the average film market, which wasn't very interested in expensive new technologies, or on the cinema advertising industry, whose main concern was promoting theatrical films. Formisano argues that the ramifications of this imbalance have been neglected, especially during the 1980s themselves (1994: 203–04).

In the 1980s, auteur and art-oriented film-makers and film critics also denounced the disproportion of films produced to those actually screened or programmed on television. They also criticized the selection criteria for video releases and questioned the aesthetic appropriateness of watching a film on a video monitor. Finally, these detractors deplored the late programming schedules and the commercial disruptions of television networks. In an article whose title plays on the word 'clip' and the French word for the clapping board ('Le clip et le clap ou l'esthétique publicitaire'), published in a 1987 special issue of CinémAction about the influence of television on cinema, Gérard Leblanc notes how TV commercials influence film aesthetics and narrative structures. He terms this 'l'effet de grille' (the timetable effect) – that is, a mode of representation conceived of as inserted between the 'grilles' (TV time slots) of television programming (Leblanc 1987: 101). In France, scholars and intellectuals led the discussion about audio-visual media in film journals and magazines, academic publications, and state institutions such as the Institut National de la Communication Audiovisuelle ('National Institution of Audio-visual Communication'), established in 1982.

In the aforementioned special issue of CinémAction, Daniel Serceau presented a brief survey conducted with French directors working in both television and film, titled 'Tourner pour la télé ou pour le cinéma: des réalisateurs parlent' (1987: 106–11). He interviewed film directors Jean

Evolution des entrées des films français dans l'Union européenne, en Europe et aux Etats-Unis 1996-2001

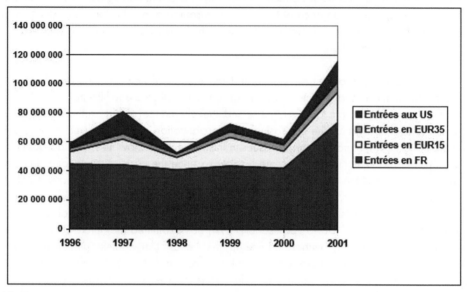

Table 7

Evolution des entrées des films italiens dans l'Union européenne, en Europe et aux Etats-Unis 1996-2001

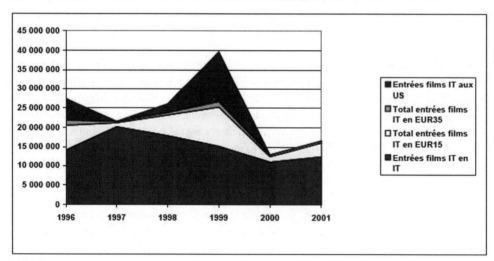

Table 8

Tables 7–9: Newman-Baudais, S. 'The distribution of European Union films in Europe outside national markets.' European Audiovisual Observatory Report (11/2002), http://www.obs.coe.int/online_publication/expert/disfilms_ue.pdf.en.

Evolution des entrées des films espagnols dans l'Union européenne, en Europe et aux Etats-Unis 1996-2001

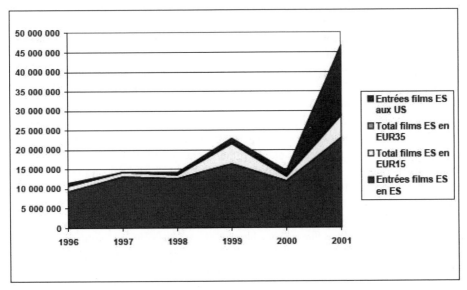

Table 9

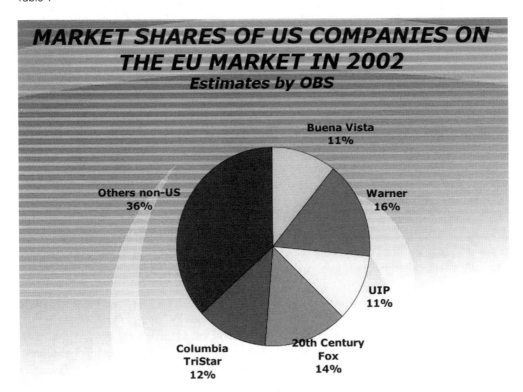

Table 10: 'The Fragmented Universe of Film Distribution Companies in Europe.' European Audiovisual Observatory, Contribution to the Workshop 'Distribution of European Films' (Venezia, 29–31 August 2003). US Share in European Markets. http://www.obs.coe.int/online_publication/expert/filmdistcompanies.pdf.en.

Marbœuf, Michel Soutter, Paul Vecchiali, Benoît Jacquot, and André Téchiné; television director and union representative Raoul Rossi; film critic Jean Collet; and René Bonnell, an executive from the television network Canal+, the French pay-television channel launched in 1984 with a strong involvement in film production. Serceau's short survey focuses on two, interrelated concerns: stylistic specificity and exchange among audio-visual media (for example, editing, subject matter, and techniques); and the professional requirements involved in switching from one medium to the other. Serceau's introduction refers to Roberto Rossellini and Alain Tanner as the two poles of the authorial position vis-à-vis television (1987: 107). Starting in the 1960s, while working at French and Italian state television organizations, Rossellini foresaw the potential of the medium and of the newly emerging video industry for promoting direct vision and creating audio-visual archives. Tanner, on the contrary, believes that a film director has only one option in the era of communication industries: that of 'radicalizing his/her position, resisting, and holding true to his/her singularity' (1987: 106–07).[27]

In Italy, the issue of the place of author cinema within the new audio-visual system was more politically charged and divided film-makers, film critics, and film scholars along two main axes. One involved the so-called 'militant' film critics participating at various levels in the cultural politics of the national film industry. Some of them wrote film columns in national and local newspapers, others promoted film events and series at cine-clubs and art movie theatres or organized symposia and debates at film festivals such as those at Pesaro, Salsomaggiore, Rimini, and Porretta Terme. The second axis combined film scholars and critics affiliated with academic institutions and scholarly publications that were engaged in more systematic and scientific analyses of authorial discourse. The 1974 edition of the Venice Film Festival promoted a 'Convegno Internazionale Progettuale' ('International Planning Meeting') to discuss the crisis of culturally oriented film production and the festival's negotiating power within the audio-visual industry. The contributions centred on two questions: the ideological position of film-makers and critics in relation to the new audio-visual system and the orientation of the film author in regard to the growing power and involvement of television entities in film production and exhibition. In Italy, this issue split the Associazione Nazionale Autori Cinematografici (A.N.A.C., 'National Association of Cinematographic Authors') into two factions: the Cinema Democratico ('Democratic Cinema'), led by film director Nanni Loy, which looked favourably upon cinema's integration in the audio-visual industry; and the A.N.A.C. Unitario ('Unitary A.N.A.C.'), which rejected new media as a system that operated in the interests of a capitalist film industry. The points on which the associations most diverged concerned media institutions involved in film production (e.g. national and private television networks) and the progressive assimilation of culturally oriented film practices into government-funded systems of production.[28]

In Spain, discussions over the position of authorial film practices within the new audio-visual context coincided with a crucial period of transition in the country's history following the death of Franco in 1975. The Spanish film industry had remained isolated from the international film scene for almost 40 years and needed to reconfigure and integrate itself within an international context. The main priority for Spain was to upgrade its film industry to the levels of the other European countries. Another significant concern was the global and multi-media dimension of the international film market. For its part, the Spanish government, particularly since the Socialist Party won the elections in 1982, strongly promoted cultural film projects through the creation of national and regional aid systems and through television network production (see the Introduction for an examination of these measures and the Miró Law). Some of the many film journals and magazines inaugurated during this period – including *Dirigido por*, *Fotogramas*, and *Revista Internacional del Cine* – adopted an authorial perspective aligned with the government's cultural policies, which also involved endorsing Spanish film authors. At the opposite end of the spectrum, film critics and film-makers interested in cultural and media hybridity and the aesthetic cross-contamination of film styles and genres developed a very different approach to film. This countercultural position first emerged as a reaction to the restrictions imposed by the dictatorship and was led by *Movida*, the Madrid-based underground movement within which Pedro Almodóvar made his cinematic début. This campaign also included regional film groups and institutions, especially in Catalonia, whose development had been either limited or crushed in the past by the regime (see the Introduction). The film magazine that dealt the most with these issues was *Contracampo*, a newly founded publication in 1977 that, until the mid-1980s, had a section on the condition of film production in Spain. This segment included reviews of films aired on Spanish television and criticism regarding the paltry appeal of some author films for Spanish audiences.[29] Starting in the mid-1980s, with the fading of the *Movida* and the failure of Spain's authorial film policies, some film-makers and film critics, especially of the new generation, jumped on board in opposing state- and television-funded authorial films.

On a pragmatic level, considering author cinema in juxtaposition to the new audio-visual system proved to be an untenable position in the heterogeneous reality of Western European film industries, especially as more film-makers and film critics were becoming interested in the cinematic possibilities of other media and new technologies. Almost a decade after Rossellini's ventures into television, internationally celebrated art house film-makers such as Michelangelo Antonioni, Bernardo Bertolucci, Jean-Luc Godard, and Wim Wenders became involved in exploring the medium's expressive potential. The film authors' forays into television production resulted in both expectations and disappointments, especially with respect to their use of the innovative technology available in this medium. Some of the earliest debates about experimenting with new audio-visual forms and techniques took place in Italy, first when Michelangelo Antonioni adopted electronic colouring processes for a film conceived for television, *Il mistero di Oberwald/The Mystery of Oberwald* (1980), and, some years later, when the emerging film-maker Peter Del Monte shot *Giulia e Giulia/Julia and Julia* (1987) on high-definition television, with the collaboration of the prestigious director of photography Giuseppe Rotunno. Whereas Antonioni used electronic special effects (a 625-line definition camera), Del Monte avoided them, opting for a more 'realistic' style. He was the first director worldwide to make a film on High Definition System magnetic tape (1225 lines of definition), which was then reversed onto 35mm Eastmancolor film for theatrical release. (Neither of these systems has been widely adopted commercially due to cumbersome and costly equipment and poor image quality.) Both films had mixed receptions. Antonioni was either accused of betraying the realist tradition of Italian cinema or, conversely, praised for his courage in facing a new challenge that extended his career-long research on 'material realism' (Alemanno 1993: 180–81). On the other hand, hopes that *Giulia e Giulia* would inaugurate a new era of technological innovation in cinema were soon frustrated: the film fared poorly both with critics and the box office and received only limited international distribution. Furthermore, the high costs of image processing served to discourage further investigations into this expensive technology (Montini 1988: 76–77).

In the 1980s, European governments launched new laws and programmes with the purpose of protecting film authorship against the monopoly of Hollywood products in the European exhibition circuit. These initiatives had little impact on the circulation and commercial performance of authorial films, both on the national and international levels, and paradoxically, contributed to marginalizing art house films even further. In particular, foreign distribution of authorial films was not adequately organized and wagered upon the random fortune of individual films at international film festivals. The international viability of European film authors in this decade was mainly entrusted to European distribution networks and was hardly concerned with the North American market at all.[30] The failure of these policies was mainly due to the privilege given to the creative process, which encouraged film-makers to explore thematic and stylistic choices that showed very little concern for audiences' tastes.

In 1984, the Italian film journal *Filmcritica* published a survey of some Italian independent producers, including Antonio Avati, Claudio Biondi, Giuliani G. De Negri, Mario Gallo, Gianni Hecht Lucari, Flavio Lucisano, Gianni Minervini, Luciano Perugia, Gianfranco Piccioli, and Luigi Rovere (1984: 136–58). The survey asked the producers to testify to the condition of the Italian system of film production and to express their opinions about Italy's film industry, with a specific focus on state subsidies, television productions, and new audio-visual media. All participants expressed their dissatisfaction with the national production system and especially with public forms of financing. Many of them showed an interest in new audio-visual technologies, which they considered to be an inevitable development in the field, yet remained quite ambivalent regarding the possibility of personally adopting any of the new devices.

Europe's financial endorsement of authorial cinema was mostly concentrated in production and did not resolve a fundamental issue for European cinema: the viability of authorial cinema within the theatrical, as well as the video and broadcasting circuits of film exhibition. The cases of France, Italy, and Spain are particularly significant in this respect. In France, Jack Lang increased the allowance for the *Avance sur recettes*, the government's selective aid mechanism aimed at authorial film production. In 1983, Spain promulgated new legislation for film production (the Miró Law) that was clearly oriented toward art and authorial films. Pilar Miró's new policies had minimal impact on Spanish audience's attendance of Spanish films: quite to the contrary, they contributed to further alienating Spanish film spectators from culturally oriented films. In Italy, the 1990 Mammí Law intervened in the regulation of film broadcasting on private and public TV networks and, in 1994, the government revised *Articolo 28*, Italy's aid system for film production, in place since 1965, by putting particular emphasis on the financial endorsement of young film authors. Claudio Zanchi critically summarizes the history of Italy's selective aid system from its inception in 1965 to its revision in 1994. The 1994 update sought to ameliorate the criteria of selection and attract more capital but instead produced the opposite effect due to a mistrust of private investors and a lack of collaboration with European-based funds (Zanchi 1996).[31]

The representation of the French film auteur as a symbol of Europe's response to Hollywood cinema was incongruous with some of the political and industrial initiatives that France and other European nations were adopting in those years to counter the American monolith. France is the homeland of European art house cinema's 'mystique', sustaining a type of cinema diametrically opposed to Hollywood's production and distribution agenda. Throughout the 1980s and 1990s, the country reinforced domestic production and authorial cinema in particular by applying exhibition quotas on French films and protectionist policies on foreign films (a policy not applied by other European countries, most notably the United Kingdom). Yet, at the same time, France's largest film companies were merging their distribution circuits with US majors (Gaumont with Buena Vista International in 1993 and U.G.C. with Twentieth Century Fox in 1995). As much as these commercial strategies were profitable for the development of French cinema abroad through international co-productions, they obviously clashed with the country's emphasis on cultural distinction from Hollywood.

Chris Darke stresses the anti-Americanism underlying the strategies adopted by Jack Lang, France's twice-appointed minister of culture – a title he held during the first mandate, whereas for his second mandate from 1988 to 1993 he was nominated Minister of Culture and Communications – to endorse French cinema against Hollywood's monopoly (1993: 372). In the same issue of Screen in which Darke's article appears, Susan Hayward (1993b) also discusses Lang's 1980s and 1990s film policies. Hayward highlights the interventional and centralized nature of Lang's measures, which were aimed at developing two key concepts: 'l'état culturel' (the cultural state) and the 'industrie culturelle' (the cultural industry) (Hayward 1993b: 381). The most radical reforms for protecting the French market from American domination were adopted during Lang's second mandate, notably by incrementing budget allocations and quotas to assure French films greater distribution within the theatrical, as well as video, market (ibid.: 388). However, Hayward notes that Lang's imposition on independent and mainstream film distributors and television networks to show auteur films had the boomerang effect of undermining the potential of 'art' and 'essai' theatres to be competitive. Furthermore, the increasing popularity of pay-TV network Canal+ made it a main competitor to these theatres and encouraged French film audiences to attend theatrical screenings of US films (Hayward 1993b: 389–90).

Towards the devolution: the local/global interface of film authorship

Especially since the 1990s, European governments and cinema institutions have been adopting marketing strategies more in step with the commercial and marketing directions of the international film system, mostly due to new alliances among private, independent, and corporate film companies, and also because of new professional incentives and programmes offered by the E.C.[32] Spain has been holding true to an internationally oriented conception of authorial film production and distribution, especially in relation to Latin American countries. Spanish authorial cinema has kept its export interests up, carefully combining domestic and international strategies of promotion. In addition to Pedro Almodóvar, a number of other 1980s and 1990s film-makers have gained international renown: José-Luis Bigas Luna, Vicente Aranda, Fernando Trueba, and, representing a new generation, Alejandro Amenábar and Julio Medem. These film-makers have succeeded by exploiting a mix of traditional and innovative themes and styles. Particularly in the

1990s, promotional strategies have paved the way for younger directors to reach international distribution circuits (Heredero 1999; Jordan and Morgan-Tamosunas 1998: 107–10).

Over the past decade, Western European governments have been promoting a series of measures to encourage film production and distribution within domestic, as well as international contexts, both in the private and public sectors. These initiatives include incentives for financial institutions to develop credit facilities for film production: guaranteed funds (such as the European Guarantee Fund); implementations of support systems (for example, grants, advances against box office receipts, tax concessions, awards); tax shelter schemes; and automatic or selective aid mechanisms. France, Italy, and Spain have issued new policies on film production and the import of foreign films. Following up on the position it held at the 1993 edition of the General Agreement on Tariffs and Trade (G.A.T.T.) meeting, France increased its quotas on imports in 1995. After years of proposals and political debates, the Italian government approved a new law on cinema in 1994 that did not, however, effectively achieve its main goal of increasing industrial support to cinema and selective aid for quality films. Spain introduced a new automatic subsidy scheme in 1995, replacing the previous project-by-project system, and increased the pre-existing grant from Instituto de la Cinematografía y de las Artes Audiovisvas (I.C.A.A.) the Spanish Film Institute to new directors and experimental films by 700 million pesetas per year (more than $5 million US).

Most importantly, state, regional, and private television networks, as well as cable broadcasters, digital and satellite television providers, pay-TV companies (most notably Canal+) and transnational cultural channels (above all, the Franco-German ARTE) have become major sources of film financing. Finally, the European Council has prompted a relatively more integrated and profitable context for the production and distribution of European films, both within Europe and abroad, through the establishment of special funds (Eurimage, funded by the European Council in 1988) and development plans for the support of pan-European film structures, film-making projects (the MEDIA and MEDIA Plus programmes) and film exhibition circuits (the EUROPA CINEMAS circuit, part of the MEDIA programme).[33] Independent film companies, media corporations, and TV networks also took steps in this direction. Within this new context of film production and distribution, the figure of the film author has regained a domestic and international profile and found a new marketing niche in selected film theatres and, more importantly, in the growing home market of DVD distribution and cable and satellite television programming. During the past decade, author cinema has consolidated a discrete position as a promotional strategy in alternative forms of film distribution and exhibition, including cable and pay-TV's packages, DVD rentals or purchases (especially through online sale companies), and Internet downloads or video blogs. The commercialization of the film-maker-author is now a prominent issue outside of Europe as well and is prompting new debates on the actual autonomy of North American 'Indie' cinema. Hollywood distributors, the majors, and international distribution companies based in the US (Miramax above all) have lately appropriated the independent cinema movement by monitoring the circuit of film festivals and art houses in North America for films to buy and distribute within the national and international theatrical exhibition circuit.

The following chapters outline the genealogy and the crisis of the institutional and discursive function of authorship in the three national cinemas examined.

Notes

1. The list originally appeared in an anthology on neo-realist cinema edited by Carlo Verdone and is quoted by Marcus in the introduction to her *Italian Film in the Light of Neorealism*.

2. 'Le cinéaste se dit artiste et traite le téléaste d'artisan. Le premier parle *création* et le second *profession*, l'un s'exprime par la pellicule et l'autre imprime de la bande, le second vivant de son métier tandis que l'autre crève de son art.' Prédal's note appears in his introduction to a special issue of *CinémAction* on the influence of television on cinema, edited with Guy Hennebelle (Hennebelle and Prédal 1987).

3. Malraux was appointed Minister of Culture during Charles de Gaulle's second government, from 1960 to 1969. Malraux's role in France's film culture will be further discussed in this book.

4. 'Dès leurs début, les *Cahiers du cinéma*, en se fondant sur un héritage, mais en le mettant en cause dans le même temps, se sont attiré les suspicions de trahison. La 'fidélité' des continuateurs est constamment prise au piège d'une lecture où plane le syndrome de la trahison, de l'abandon des valeurs critiques.' The punctuation in French is as it appears in the original text.

5. 'La poetica neorealista, fondata sul mito della spontaneitá e dell'immediatezza e sulla celebrazione dell'Opera e dell'Autore.'

6. A vast literature exists on this issue, some selections of which I include in my bibliography. In English, a good outline of the cultural and ideological genealogy of neo-realism appears in Millicent Marcus' introduction in her book *Italian Film in the Light of Neorealism* (Marcus 1986). Also important is a 1973 special issue of *Screen*, entirely devoted to the critical and historical reconsideration of neo-realism, particularly Mario Cannella's long contribution, titled 'Ideology and Aesthetic Hypotheses in the Criticism of Neo-Realism' (Cannella 1973).

7. Italian film journals have tackled these issues especially throughout the 1970s. Now a given, the new academic perspective on Italian neo-realism had started to develop in the Anglo-American in the early 1970s (as the aforementioned 1973 issue of *Screen* illustrates).

8. Arguably, both the French I.D.H.E.C. and the Spanish national film institute, the I.I.E.C. were more scholarly and culturally oriented, although both represented the national film schools and thus provided a privileged channel of access to the film industry.

9. In 1946 the U.N. rejected Spain's application for membership, and France closed its borders to Spain. In the same year, the U.N. recommended that all foreign countries withdraw their ambassadors in Madrid (Molina-Fox 1977: 8).

10. In 1962 the school took the name of Escuela Oficial de Cinematografía (E.O.C.).

11. Many scholars (including John Hopewell, Miriam Higginbotham, and Marsha Kinder) and Spanish film authors underline the influence of Hollywood cinema on 1950s and 1960s Spanish *nuevo cine*.

12. As mentioned before, the occasion was his 1952 defense of *Surcos*. Ten years later, in 1962, Escudero was restored to the same position and kept it for six years.

13. The journal was a spin-off of the literary magazine *Índice de Artes y Letras*, since 1951 published by the progressive Juan Fernández Figueroa.

14. In 1965, José Miguel Baviera, Román Gubern, Iván Tubau, Antonio Castro, José Léon, Alfonso Guerra, Julián Marcos, and José Antonio Páramo attempted at reviving the journal, publishing a special issue on New Spanish Cinema (Tubau 1983: 50).

15. Higginbotham (1988: 25–26) dates the episode 1951.
16. In 1952 the government had issued a new law on state subsidies. De facto, this law mainly created a powerful Board of Classification that penalized any film not aligned with the regime's ideological perspective (Molina-Fox 1977: 11–12).
17. The main political shifts took place in the early 1980s, with the 1981 and 1982 installation of socialist governments respectively in France and Spain and their contributions to the development of the national film industry through the reinforcement of protection laws and the increase of production subsidies.
18. On television film production, see in France, Williams (1992: 394–95) and Hennebelle and Prédal 1987; in Italy, Brunetta 1998a and Bondanella 1993; and in Spain, Kinder 1993.
19. These data appear in an article by Albio Pedroia about the impact of Berlusconi's private networks on Italian film production, titled 'Italie: la combinazione de Sua Emittenza' (Hennebelle and Prédal 1987: 213).
20. About the debates and initiatives promoted to prevent the 'death of cinema' in France, see the special issue of *CinumAction* on cinema and television (especially Prédal's introduction in Hennebelle and Prédal 1987: 14–16). For Italy, Brunetta has devoted an entire chapter to the role that cine-clubs, cultural associations, city councils, and universities had in promoting art house film practices (1998: 565–79). In Spain the situation was different, as the country had not consolidated a national discourse and a specific market for art house cinema. The main efforts to promote art house exhibition circuits came from universities, film archives, and cultural associations.
21. Hopewell argues that 1980s government-subsidized art house cinema in Spain produced a type of 'liberal film-making' (1986: 119).
22. Tino Balio (1998) refers to Hollywood's early 1990s engagement in the art film circuit in his article 'The art film market in the new Hollywood.'
23. On the distribution of European films in the USA, see the periodical reports and publications on film distribution issued by the European Audiovisual Observatory, established in 1992 and part of the Council of Europe (Conseil d'Europe). The reports are available online at http://www.obs.co e.int/. The tables included in this chapter come from data available on the European Audiovisual Observatory's website.
24. In the 1980s, Penta-America distributed many films by emerging Italian directors in the United States. Some titles include Gabriele Salvatores' *Turnè* (1990), the Academy Award winner *Mediterraneo* (1991), and *Puerto Escondido* (1992), which will be discussed in this book. The Berlusconi group is active in the international distribution and co-production market, especially in Europe, through a new production company, Mediaset, and the revived distribution company Medusa. It is worth mentioning that because of some illicit operations done by Medusa, Berlusconi (head of the Italian coalition Forza Italia, now reconstituted as Partito delle Libertá [PDL], Italy's prime minister in the mid-late 1990s, re-appointed in April 2008) was charged with illegal financing, money recycling, and political bribery.
25. On this topic, see, among others, Lev 1993 and Nowell-Smith and Ricci 1998.
26. 'Ceci est écrit en 1988. Vue de maintenant, et d'ici: la France, Paris, la situation sur le front du cinéma est désespérée, mais pas mauvaise. Le cinéma se meurt, le cinéma est mort, on nous le répète partout et tous les jours. Il ne semble pas se porter plus mal pour autant [...] À présent, nul art nouveau à l'horizon qui viendrait remplacer, ou même simplement vicarier le ciné-parlant à l'agonie. Les produits qui emergent, dans leur diversité encore un peu grouillante, difficile à démêler, ont au moins ceci de commun: qu'ils disent tous se soucier de l'art comme d'une guigne, que leur circuits de

consommation, leur réseaux de jouissance et d'imaginaire, ne sont plus les mêmes, ni non plus leur prétention, à entre au musée.'

27. On the debate regarding the television programming of films, see Brunetta (1998: 504–17) and Hennebelle and Prédal 1987.

28. '[...] de radicaliser sa position, de résister, de s'en tenir fermement à sa propre singularité.'

29. A detailed account of the internal struggle among Italian film authors in those years appears in an anthology by Roberto Alemanno (1993) that collects the articles the film critic published in the left-leaning film journal *Cinema Nuovo* and in *Il quotidiano dei lavoratori* (*The Workers' Daily*).

30. On *Contracampo*, see Asier Aranzubia Cob's 'Contracampo y el cine español' (Cob 2002), an article that examines the history of the film magazine in relation to post-Francoist cinema. The article appeared in an issue of the online film journal *Otrocampo* dedicated to film criticism.

31. For a more complete discussion of this phenomenon within Europe, see Jäckel 2003, particularly chapters 2 and 3.

32. On the problems related to Jack Lang's initiatives, see Susan Hayward's article 'State, Culture and the Cinema: Jack Lang's strategies for the French Film Industry 1981–93' (1993b). On the Mammí Law, see, among others, Fania Petrocchi's study on the relations between Italy's public and private television networks and the film industry, *Il cinema della televisione italiana: La produzione cinematografica di RAI e Fininvest (1976/1994)* (1996). On the Italian legislation for selective aid (*Articolo 28*) and on Italy's public funding sources for film production – RAI, the national television system, and the Istituto Luce, an institution founded during the fascist regime for the development of culturally relevant film projects – see Torri (1996) and Zanchi (1996). On the problems related to Miró's policies, see Hopewell 1991.

33. On Europe's changing forms of film distribution within Europe and in North America during the 1990s, see Jäckel (2003: 91–115).

References

1989. *Per una nuova critica: i convegni pesaresi 1965–1967*. Venezia: Marsilio Editori.

Pratica economica e pratica politica. Questionario. 1984. *Filmcritica*, 343–344: 136–58.

Alemanno, R. 1993. *Segnali di fumo. Per una verifica della crisi. Teoria e prassi di politica cinematografica*. Roma: Edizioni Associate.

Aprá, A. & Turigliatto, R. (eds). 1996. *Giovinezza del cinema francese*, Venezia: Marsilio.

Aumont, J. and MARIE, M. 1988. *L'analyse des films*. Paris: Nathan.

Aumont, J. 1989. *L'oeil interminable. Cinéma et peinture*. Paris: Librairie Séguier.

Austin, G. 1996. *Contemporary French Cinema: An Introduction*. Manchester and London: Manchester University Press.

Balio, T. 1998. The art film market in the new Hollywood. (*In* Nowell-Smith G. and Ricci, S. (eds). *Hollywood and Europe: Economics, Culture, National Identity: 1945–95*. London: BFI, pp. 63–73).

Brunetta, G. P. 1998. *Storia del cinema italiano. Dal miracolo economico agli anni novanta. 1963–1993*. Roma: Editori Riuniti.

Cannella, M. 1973. Ideology and Aesthetic Hypotheses in the Criticism of Neo-Realism. *Screen*, 73–74: 5–60.

Cob, A. A. 2002. *Contracampo y el cine español*, *Otrocampo*. [Online]. Available: http://www.otrocampo.com.

Corrigant, T. 1991. *A Cinema without Walls: Movies and Culture after Vietnam*. New Brunswick, NJ: Rutgers University Press.

Darke, C. 1993. Rupture, Continuity and Diversification: *Cahiers du Cinéma* in the 1980s. *Screen*, 34.4: 362–79.

De Baecque, A. 1991. *Cahiers du cinema: Histoire d'une revue. Tome 1: Les Cahiers à l'assault du cinema: 1951–1959*. Paris: Cahiers du cinéma.

Dibie, J. N. 1993. *Aid for Cinematographic and Audio-visual Production in Europe*. London: John Libbey.

Elsaesser, T. 1989. *New German Cinema: A History*. New Brunswick, NJ: Rutgers University Press.

— and Hoffman, K. (eds). 1998. *Cinema Futures: Cain, Abel, or Cable?* Amsterdam: Amsterdam University Press.

Finney, A. 1996. *The State of European Cinema: A New Dose of Reality*. London: Cassel.

Formisano, D. 1996. Il grande imbroglio. Produzione e finanziamento nel cinema italiano degli anni Novanta. (*In* Sesti, M. (ed.). *La 'scuola' italiana: storia, strutture e immaginario di un altro cinema (1988–1996)*. Venezia: Marsilio, pp. 203–11.)

Hayward, S. 1993b. State, Culture, and the Cinema: Jack Lang's Strategies for the French Film Industry. *Screen*, 34 (4): 380–91.

Hennebelle, G. and PRÉDAL, R. (eds). 1987. L'influence de la télévision sur le cinéma. *CinémAction*, 44.

Heredero, C. F. 1999. Cine español: nueva generacion. *Dirigido*: 49–67, abril.

Hewitt, N. (ed.). 1989. *The Culture of Reconstruction: European Literature, Thought, and Film, 1945–50*. New York: St. Martin's Press.

Higginbotham, V. 1988. *Spanish Film Under Franco*. Austin: University of Texas Press.

Hopewell, J. 1991. Art and a Lack of Money: The Crises of the Spanish Film Industry: 1977–1990. *Quarterly Review of Film and Video*, 14(4): 113–122.

Ilott, T. 1996. *Budgets and Markets: A Study of the Budgeting of European Film*. London and New York: Routledge.

Jäckel, A. 2003. *European Film Industries*. London: BFI.

Jordan, B., Morgan-Tamosunas, R. 1998. *Contemporary Spanish Cinema*. Manchester: Manchester University Press.

Kinder, M. 1993. *Blood Cinema: The Reconstruction of National Identity in Spain*, Berkeley: University of California Press.

—, (ed.). 1997. *Refiguring Spain: Cinema/Media/Representation*, Durham and London: Duke University Press.

Leblanc, G. 1987. Le clip et le clap ou l'esthétique publicitaire. (*In* Hennebelle, G. and Prédal, R. (eds). L'influence de la télévision sur le cinéma. *CinémAction*, 44: 98–103).

Lev, P. 1993. *The Euro-American Cinema*. Austin: University of Texas Press.

Marcus, M. 1986. *Italian Film in the Light of Neorealism*. Princeton, NJ: Princeton University Press.

Molina-Fox, V. 1977. *New Cinema in Spain*. London: British Film Institute.

Montini, F. (ed.). 1988a. *Una generazione in cinema: esordi ed esordienti italiani.1976–1988*. Venezia: Marsilio Editori.

Nowell-Smith, G., RICCI, S. (eds). 1998. *Hollywood and Europe: Economics, Culture, National Identity: 1945–95*. London: British Film Institute.

Petrocchi, F. 1996. *Il cinema della televisione italiana: La produzione cinematografica di RAI e Fininvest (1976/1994)*. Roma: RAI ERI.

Pinto, F., Barzoletti, G. and Salizzato, C. (eds). 1988. *La televisione presenta: la produzione cinematografica della RAI 1965-1975*. Venezia: Marsilio Editori.

Polan, D. 2001. Auteur Desire. *Screening the Past*. [Online.] Available: http://www.latrobe.edu.au/ screeningthepast/firstrelease/fr0301/dpfr12a.htm.

Prédal, R. 1988. *900 cinéastes français d'aujourd'hui*. Paris: Cerf.

Rainbow, P. (ed.). 1984. *The Foucault Reader*. New York: Pantheon Books.

Serceau, D. 1987. Tourner pour la Télé ou pour le cinéma: des réalisateurs parlent. (*In* Hennebelle, G. and Prédal, R. (eds). L'influence de la télévision sur le cinéma. *CinémAction*, 44: 106-11.)

Sesti, M. (ed.). 1996. *La « scuola » italiana. Storia, strutture e immaginario di un altro cinema (1988-1996)*. Venezia: Marsilio Editori.

Torri, B. 1996. Un po' di luce. Limiti e prospettive dell'intervento dello stato nella produzione e nella distribuzione. (*In* Sesti, M. (ed.). *La « scuola » italiana. Storia, strutture e immaginario di un altro cinema (1988-1996)*. Venezia: Marsilio Editori, pp. 213-17).

Tubau, I. 1983. *Crítica cinematográfica española: Bazin contra Aristarco, la gran controversia de los años sesenta*. Barcelona: Edicions Universitat de Barcelona.

Vernon, K. 1997. Reading Hollywood in/and Spanish Cinema: From Trade Wars to Transculturation. (*In* Kinder, M. (ed.). *Refiguring Spain: Cinema/Media/Representation*. Durham and London: Duke University Press, pp. 35-64.)

Zanchi, C. 1996. La lenta eutanasia di un articolo. Archeologia e disavventure del '28'. (*In* Sesti, M. (ed.). *La « scuola » italiana. Storia, strutture e immaginario di un altro cinema (1988-1996)*. Venezia: Marsilio Editori, pp. 219-37.)

2

THE MIDDLE GENERATION: MAURICE PIALAT, GIANNI AMELIO, AND VÍCTOR ERICE

Since the 1980s, the film modes and practices associated with the concept of authorship emerged in French, Italian, and Spanish cinemas signal an attempt to move out of the shadow cast by the pre-eminently art-oriented reputation of European cinema and the auteur-informed reception of European film-makers associated with the New Wave movements. This effort underlies both the desire to update the conceptual definition of film authorship established during the 1950s and 1960s and the need to extricate the professional status of the film author from state-funded systems of film production investing in art- and culturally oriented types of film projects. In both instances, the purpose was to disavow a 'politics of authorship' (to paraphrase the *Cahiers du Cinéma*'s 1950s editorial policy, the *politique des auteurs*) exerted over certain niches of film production and reception relying on government subsidies, national television networks and cultural institutions such as national television channels, film festivals, film archives, film clubs, and film magazines.

This chapter illustrates the attempts to move beyond an institutional model of authorship by examining three film directors, Maurice Pialat (France), Gianni Amelio (Italy), and Víctor Erice (Spain) who distanced themselves from the 'politics of authorship' while maintaining a distinctly authorial approach to film-making. The careers of these film-makers span three generations of authorial film practices. First, the generation associated with the New Wave movements of each national cinema here examined (the *nouvelle vague* in France; the *nuovo cinema* in Italy; and the *nuevo cine* in Spain). Second, the post-New Wave generation that emerged during the crisis of the European film industry, one marked by culturally specific political changes such as left-wing radicalism in France and Italy and the progressive loosening of Franco's dictatorship in Spain. Third, the generation of film-makers that began their careers since the 1980s and experienced the transition of cinema to a new audio-visual system, on which this book mainly concentrates.

Maurice Pialat

Although Pialat, Amelio, and Erice's works are contemporaneous with the New Wave film-makers of their respective countries, their débuts in feature film-making came much later than their colleagues. Maurice Pialat (1925–2003) was born halfway between the oldest (Eric Rohmer, born in 1920) and the youngest (François Truffaut, born in 1932) of the *nouvelle vague* auteurs issued from the editorial staff of *Cahiers du Cinéma*.[1] He made documentary films and shorts for years before directing his first feature, *L'Enfance nue/Naked Childhood* (1968), released at the end of the *nouvelle vague* movement. The film's plot, about an unruly ten-year-old boy who is rejected by his mother and ends up moving from foster home to foster home, curiously recalls one of the movement's first hits, Truffaut's début film, *Les 400 coups/The 400 Blows* (1960). Pialat continued to make films throughout the 1970s but was not internationally acknowledged as a major film author until the 1980s. Gianni Amelio, who was born in 1945, is roughly the same age as the two most prestigious film-makers of Italy's post-neo-realist New Wave, Bernardo Bertolucci (born in 1945) and Marco Bellocchio (born in 1939). Yet, like Pialat, Amelio also had a late start as a feature film-maker after a long apprenticeship first as a provincial *cinuphile* film critic, then as an assistant director, and eventually as a film director of TV movies and documentaries for the Italian state television networks' cultural programmes. Of the three film directors, Víctor Erice (born in 1940) is the only one who was directly involved in the New Wave movement of his country, Spain's *nuevo cine*. He started his directing career with a segment of *Los desafíos/The Challenges* (1969), an anthology film produced by Elías Querejeta, the most important producer of the Spanish New Wave.[2] Since then, Erice has been primarily associated with this film movement. However, as was the case for Pialat and Amelio, Erice arrived at film-making towards the end of the New Wave cinema's golden era. After graduating from Instituto de Investigaciones y Experiencias Cinematográficas in Madrid in 1960, he worked for almost a decade as a film critic and a screenwriter before Querejeta offered him the opportunity to get behind the camera for *Los Desafíos*. Querejeta later produced Erice's début feature film, the internationally acclaimed *El espíritu de la colmena/The Spirit of the Beehive* (1973). Since then, Erice's feature films have been few and far between; to date, he has only completed three feature films: the aforementioned *El espíritu de la colmena*, *El Sur/South* (1983), and the documentary film *El Sol del membrillo/ The Dream of Light* (1992).

The professional trajectories of Pialat, Amelio, and Erice are interconnected with Europe's dichotomous discourse on authorship, described by Anne Jäckel as such:

El sol del membrillo: the painter A. López García and the quince tree

> Developing from the intellectual climate of French film criticism in the 1950s, auteurism celebrates the centrality of the film director's vision. In Europe, this belief has had an enduring effect as directors continue to be either hailed as the greater strength of European cinema or keeping European cinema stuck in a rut of artistic indulgence. (2003: 28)

Throughout their careers, Pialat, Amelio, and Erice have worked within various systems of film production. Although highly critical of state institutions and the national film industry (which they blame for limiting authorial creativity), they have dealt with large production and distribution companies yet never made concessions to the commercial aspects of their profession, both on the level of personal artistic choices and production methods. Their attitude foreshadows that of the new generation of film directors/authors who are involved with multiple agents and interests of contemporary cinema and adopt a dialectical interchange with filmic traditions, aesthetic forms, production systems, and marketing niches traditionally associated with Europe's author cinema.

The multiple commitments of film authorship
Pialat, Amelio, and Erice have an idiosyncratic approach to film-making, one that involves paying meticulous attention to the organization of *mise-en-scène* and cinematography on the set. From this perspective, these film directors take the definition of the film author prevalent in

auteur-informed film criticism and reception (a film director whose approach to film-making and control of the *mise-en-scène* points to an individual world-view and a unique style) to the extreme. Their authorial status relies not just on the recognition of intentionality and genius to their creative work on the set, but of the scrupulous, almost maniacal nature of this work. Their projects take a long time to complete; even, as is the case with Erice, up to several years. Their rehearsal and shooting schedules require long hours or days of waiting on the part of the crew and the actors. These circumstances result in strained relationships between the director and the crew (especially technicians), and have caused numerous conflicts between director and crew (this was often the case for Pialat) and drastic divergences between director and producer (as with Erice), some of which will be further elucidated in this chapter. Yet it would be inaccurate to assume that these directors overlook the practical and economic implications of their profession. Though they do not always respect shooting schedules or contracts, they are very conscious of the commercial aspects of art house cinema, at times even betraying their original blueprints to make their films more amenable to popular consumption.

With the exception of *La gueule ouverte/The Mouth Agape* (1974), a somber drama about a woman dying of throat cancer and the pettiness that ensues between the family members caring for her on her deathbed, Maurice Pialat maintained in various interviews that his films never lost money. Rather, he attributed his problems with the film industry to his unwillingness to work with stars, who he avoided due to the constraints of their schedules, which tended to conflict with Pialat's long and unpredictable shoots (Carrère and Sineux 1984: 9). His reluctance to work with star actors significantly lowered his chances of receiving government funding since the *avance sur recettes* committee showed a preference for projects with box office friendly names. This lack of government support made it difficult for him to complete his films. He occasionally stopped production because he could not put his crew on hold any longer. Sometimes, he even was obliged to resume shooting with different technicians since the original employees had to move on to other projects. At times he made substantial changes to the narrative or cut part of the script because some actors could not be recalled to the set (Carrère and Sineux 1984: 4–5). Pialat's shooting deadlines and budgets cost him dearly throughout his career, but he always talked about these incidents, less polemically than analytically, as unavoidable aspects of his work and of film production in general.

Gianni Amelio is aware that his films are not for a large audience and does not expect them to be popular. Still, since the 1990s, most of his films have been relatively successful at the box office. Ultimately, the film-maker is quite pragmatic about the fact that cinema needs to entice the film spectator. He believes that ignoring the audience negates the meaning and function of cinema and that 'in the cinema the need for audience is necessary,' both for monetary and ethical reasons (Fofi 1994: 118). Amelio considers box office receipts a film-maker's primary concern because cinema involves costly and complex structures. For example, he thinks that a film-maker should accept the risk of losing money on a film and considers this risk a personal challenge and proof of the film-maker's commitment to his audience:

> I believe that risks and battles are part of the cinema; inside this struggle you must also put the affection or disaffection you have for the audience. Or else you must decide to

have or not have an audience; or again, wanting the largest possible audience. Your choices enliven or diminish your being as a filmmaker. (Ibid.: 119, my translation)[3]

Víctor Erice comments only sparingly on his approach to film-making. Like Pialat and Amelio, he takes for granted that his films will not have a large audience. Also, like the other two directors, he discusses the limitations imposed by the film industry and market as components inherent to his profession, with which he is willing to comply. Speaking about *El Sur*, for example, he once commented that he had 'tried to engage in a higher degree of communication with the spectator' because the film was meant for the major distribution circuit (Marías and Vega 1983: 60–1). For him, a film meant for regular circuits of distribution should retain a certain formal quality in which 'there may perhaps be contradictions, but never misunderstandings' (ibid.). This 'formal election,' as Erice describes it, is all the more necessary in contemporary cinema where classical conventions are no longer predominant (ibid.).

The personal backgrounds of these three film-makers are quite similar; they all come from the provinces and are very attached to their places of origin. Pialat was from the rural village of Cunlhat, in the Puy-de-Dôme province of the D'Ambert region, in central France. Amelio was raised in the poor and rustic village of San Pietro Magisano, in Calabria, a region in south-eastern Italy. Erice was born in the small town of Carranza, in the Basque province. All three began working as screenwriters or film critics and continued these activities parallel with their feature film-making. In the 1970s, Pialat made two TV commercials, one for a detergent and one for a pesticide company and directed a TV series about disabled people (Goldschmidt and Tonnerre 1983: 6). At the same time, Amelio was directing TV commercials to avoid the path of low-budget genre and exploitation films such as spaghetti westerns, soft porn, and horror films, that many of his colleagues took (Fofi 1994: 89). Amelio occasionally taught film courses at the prestigious national film school Centro Sperimentale di Cinematografia. Erice directed TV commercials and worked as a screenwriter for Spanish state television throughout his entire career (Schwartz 1987: 88). Since the 1960s he has also been writing several film articles and books.[4]

These film-makers took their first steps in film-making within the context of national television networks in their respective countries and then moved to independent production companies. Pialat directed the TV series *La maison du bois* (1971) in seven episodes, which depicted the life of a woodcutter and his wife in a small French town during World War I. The TV series was a French-Italian co-production between the Office de Radiodiffusion de Télévision Française (ORTF) and Radio Televisione Italiana (RAI). His following films, *Passe ton bac d'abord/ Graduate First* (1979), which focuses on the life of working-class teenagers, was co-produced by France3 (FR3) and the national subsidy institute Institut National de l'Audiovisuel. By and large, Pialat made most of his 1970s films with independent film companies, including the aforementioned *La gueule ouverte* and *Nous ne vieillierons pas ensemble/We Won't Grow Old Together* (1974), a largely autobiographical chronicle of the twisted relationship between a married film-maker and his young lover. In the 1980s, Pialat worked for Gaumont, France's largest film company, for ten years. At Gaumont he directed *Loulou* (1980), a love story involving a bourgeois woman and a petty crook, *À nos amours/To Our Loves* (1983), a family

Pialat shooting *Van Gogh*

drama featuring violent confrontations between relatives, *Police* (1985), a *polar* focusing on a detective's dangerous infatuation with a *femme fatale* under investigation, and *Sous le soleil de Satan/Under the Sun of Satan* (1987), an adaptation of the Georges Bernanos's 1926 drama about religious crisis. During this time, he worked with Gaumont's executive director, Daniel Toscan du Plantier, on many of his projects.[5] In the early 1990s, Pialat turned to state funding (Sofica, C.N.C.), Canal+, and the collaboration of independent film companies for his spectacular biopic *Van Gogh* (1991). The French television network France2 produced Pialat's last film, *Le garçu* (1995), which focused on the life of a young boy (played by his own son, Vincent) during his parents' separation.

Amelio spent most of the 1970s making some remarkable films through the Italian state television network RAI. *La fine del gioco* (1970) was a project conceived within the framework of RAI's experimental programming. The story concerns a television director's difficult relationship with an adolescent selected to help him with an inquiry into delinquent youth detention centres. *La città del sole* (1974) is a reflection on the life and work of the Italian philosopher Tommaso Campanella (1568–1639). *La morte al lavoro/Death at Work* (1978) is a psychological thriller inspired by the short story *The Spider* (Hanns H. Ewers 1915), in which a young man moves into a new apartment and becomes obsessed with the abandoned belongings of an actor who committed suicide there. *Il piccolo Archimede/The Little Archimedes* (1979) is an adaptation of Aldous Huxley's short story *The Young Archimedes* (1924), about an analphabetic peasant boy from Florence whose extraordinary talents for music and mathematics are discovered by a young English couple living in Italy. The last film Amelio directed for RAI was *I velieri* (1983), an adaptation of Italian writer Anna Banti's novel of the same title about an adolescent boy's relationship with his mother. In 1983, Amelio released *Colpire al cuore/Blow to the Heart*, with Jean-Louis Trintignant in the role of a university professor who befriends one of his students and is denounced to the police by his adolescent son when the son finds out the student is a member of a terrorist organization. This film was released in Italian in film theatres and was very well received by film critics, establishing Amelio as a major film author in Italy.

In the late 1980s Amelio started collaborating with independent producer and well-known former publisher Angelo Rizzoli and the film and television corporation Cecchi Gori Tiger Cinematografica, owned by Mario Cecchi Gori. Rizzoli produced Amelio's first international hit, *Porte aperte/Open Doors* (1990). The film, based on the short novel of the same title, was written by Leonardo Sciascia, a novelist whose stories about the Sicilian mafia, Italy's political corruption, and terrorism have been often adapted for the screen. Cecchi Gori produced Amelio's most internationally successful films to date, *Lamerica* (1994), a tragic epic about Albanians trying to illegally emigrate to Italy, and *Cosí ridevano/The Way We Laughed* (1998), a road movie set on a train about the traumatic stories of two brothers from southern Italy. Throughout the 1980s and 1990s, Amelio continued making films through the support of Italian television networks. In 1988 he directed *I ragazzi di via Panisperna* (1988), a TV film also meant for theatrical release for Radio Televisione Italiana (RAI). The film is about the life of a group of Italian physicists, which includes the Nobel Prize winner Enrico Fermi and Ettore Majorana, whose discoveries in nuclear energy eventually led to the development of the atomic bomb. A few years later, the Italian national network RAI2 co-produced – along with Canal+, several other film companies, and contributions from the European funding system Euroimages – another of Amelio's successful films, *Il ladro di bambini/The Stolen Children* (1992). The film features Enrico Lo Verso, the Sicilian actor who, in *Lamerica*, plays the character of the unscrupulous businessman who ends up living the same experience as the desperate Albanian workers he is trying to exploit. In *Il ladro di bambini*, Lo Verso plays his first cinematic leading

Gianni Amelio and the little protagonist of *Il ladro di bambini*

Lamerica (Enrico Lo Verso)

role as a police officer assigned to bring two siblings to an orphanage after their mother is convicted of trying to sell her daughter into prostitution.

For his two most recent films Amelio again opted for mixed-bag production financing from national and foreign television networks, Italian independent film companies, and Euroimages. *Le chiavi di casa/The Keys to the House* (2004) is a moving coming-of-age story about a father who meets his teenaged son, whom he abandoned at birth because of the boy's severe disability. The film is an international co-production with German and French television networks. His most recent film, *La stella che non c'è/The Missing Star* (2006), which premiered at the Venice Film Festival in August 2006, involved several Italian television networks and film companies from Italy and Switzerland, including the Italian Cattleya, which specializes in culturally oriented cinema. The film is about an Italian engineer who travels to China to reclaim an old, defective machine in the fear that it might cause the same fatal accident as the one in the factory where he used to work. The story brings to a global context the representation of poverty and labour exploitation in underdeveloped countries, which was also a predominant theme in *Lamerica*.

Erice worked for over twenty years with Elías Querejeta, one of the most prominent independent producers of the *nuevo cine*. Their professional relationship ended abruptly during the arduous making of *El Sur*. *El Sur* took a long time to finish mainly because Erice was anxious about tackling the theme of childhood, a subject that he was familiar with but felt was too often reduced to a cliché (Marías and Vega 1983: 60). Erice's working method, which is painstakingly speculative and usually only resolves at the moment of shooting, provoked Querejeta to intervene in the final cut. Querejeta took the early footage away from Erice before he could start the second part of the film and edited it without his consent. His actions raised objections from many film critics and intellectuals on behalf of Erice's authorial rights. At the Cannes presentation of the film, Erice remained evasive about his dramatic confrontation with Querejeta. Even though the film was acclaimed as a masterpiece and film critics from all across the world were voicing their indignation at Querejeta's intervention, Erice assumed a diplomatic and conciliatory position that, at times, seemed almost condescending (Fernandez-Santos 1983). When asked to comment on the film's troubled production history, he simply commented:

> I believe that unless one approaches one's own personal research with an open mind (although what one can know in advance is always little) nothing can happen. The initial ideas, in and of themselves, are not useful. What counts is how one puts the ideas into practice. On the other hand, certain aspects that can, in principle, appear as limitations, can turn out not to be such. (Marías and Vega 1983: 60, my translation)[6]

Rather than launching a defiant or resentful attack toward Querejeta, Erice's remarks instead offer a lucid and unbiased analysis of the author's situation in contemporary film. His next film, which he made almost ten years later, *El sol del membrillo*, is a documentary about realist painter Antonio López García and his project of capturing a quince tree from the same position in his backyard over a long period of time. For this film, Erice switched to the prominent production system in Spain's author cinema since the 1990s, one that combines deals with independent film companies and international co-productions among national television networks.

Each in his own way, Pialat, Amelio, and Erice, has been critical of state and television production systems, particularly regarding their excessive and inconsiderate allowance of economic support. For them, part of the author's compromise in the audio-visual industry involves buying into a welfare conception of cultural film production that encourages a self-contained mode of expression that undermines reception and lowers the quality of production, thus complying with the conservative orientation of government committees and TV networks. Refusing state and public financing means refusing to deal with lengthy bureaucratic procedures and low-quality standards due to budget restrictions. It also means refusing to be alienated from one's audience given that most subsidized projects and television productions are given little exposure in the theatrical circuit and no airtime.

Pialat made some cutting remarks about the French system of cultural film production and his comments became increasingly detached and cynical towards the end of his life. In the mid-1980s he described his production problems in a straightforward manner that acknowledged the temporal and financial constraints in this type of cinematic practice. Despite his disenchantment with the audio-visual market, he maintained that a film-maker should always keep his/her audience in mind. Amelio is more abrasive on the subject of national film production regulations. He asserts that 'not even a Fellini should be financed [just] because of the law' (Fofi 1994: 82). In a context where any and every proposed film was subsidized through *articolo 28* ('article 28', the Italian equivalent of the French *avance sur recettes*), going through the hardship of finding financial support elsewhere for a film became indicative of cultural distinction and commitment (Fofi 1994: 82–86).[7] Erice's opinion on systems of financing is aligned with that of Amelio and Pialat, but with different justifications. He considers commercial and cultural modes of film production to be distinct yet interrelated systems, neither of which corresponds to the contemporary film system. He believes that the relationship between cinema and its audience has changed accordingly, especially since homogeneous film conventions have lost their monitoring power and cinema, like its audience, has become more and more fragmented into a variety of audio-visual media and styles of representation (Marías and Vega 1983: 61).

As most European film directors since the 1980s, Pialat, Amelio, and Erice are involved in a mixed system of film production in which financing sources are diversified between public financing (the institutionalized mode of authorial cinema which was dominant in France, Italy, and Spain during the 1980s and classified author cinema in terms of artistic patrimony) and private financing (a specific sector of the national film industry, including both independent and large film companies of production and distribution). The authorial discourse associated with these three film directors is based not only on the acknowledgment of creative individuality or agency, but also (and most significantly) with the definition of a specific sociology-of-production within a national film system. In this respect, these film-makers' professional trajectories during the worst decade in the history of Western Europe's author cinema (mid-1970s to mid-1980s) foreshadow those dominant in the following two decades, which are at the centre of this book's analysis.

According to Timothy Corrigan, the film author since the 1980s self-reflectively interacts with an audio-visual culture fragmented and diversified by social and technological changes. Within a context of reception that Corrigan defines as a 'contemporary cinema without walls,' the film author self-reflectively interacts with audiences that 'remove images from their own authentic and authoritative place within culture and disperse their significance across the heterogeneous activity that now defines them' (Corrigan 1991: 6). Corrigan borrows this definition from André Malraux's description of the 'museum without walls' (Malraux 1978: 44), paraphrasing Malraux's concept as follows: 'a way of collecting art and the details of aesthetic culture not as separate and distinctive objects but as a family of photographs' (Corrigan 1991: 5). For Corrigan, the new author 'run[s] the commerce of the auteurist and autonomous self up against its textual expression in a way that shatters the coherence of both authorial expression and stardom' (ibid.: 107). Pialat, Amelio, and Erice's attitude vis-à-vis film-making foreshadows the author's self-conditioned assumption of her/his role in the new audio-visual industry and culture, an awareness that is fully assumed by the latest generation Western European film-makers.

Personal idiosyncrasies, authorial signatures
Arguably, experience with vastly different types of film production provided Pialat, Amelio, and Erice a greater authority in their profession and helped them overcome awkward situations in their careers, including those provoked by their idiosyncratic working methods. These film-makers are famous for their idiosyncratic working methods. Pialat had a reputation as the most

difficult film director in France, both on and off the set, amongst crews and film critics alike. His moods alternated from violent fits to long periods of aloofness. In a 1991 overview of French 1980s cinema published in a special issue of Cahiers du Cinéma, the presiding chief editor, Serge Toubiana, praised Pialat for being 'bitter, full of hate, but at least enraged, unsatisfied with cinema'[8] (1991: 48). Toubiana's commentary reflects the opinion of many French film critics toward a film-maker they have always unconditionally supported, despite the fact that each had taken issues with Pialat's brazen manner. The title of an article by Alain Bergala in a Cahiers du Cinéma tribute to Pialat described him as 'un marginal du centre' ('a marginal at the centre'), with reference to Pialat's ability to maintain a unique and an idiosyncratic approach to film-making while working during most of his career in public institutions (France television) and with France's largest film company (Gaumont) (Bergala 1983).[9] The most dramatic confrontation between Pialat and film critics took place at the 1987 Cannes awards ceremony when the director won the Palme d'Or for his adaptation of Bernanos's drama Sous le soleil de Satan. Pialat starred in the main role, beside two of his favourite actors, Gerard Depardieu and Sandrine Bonnaire. Accusing Pialat's film of aping the much-derided Cinéma de qualité ('Cinema of Quality') formula, French journalists welcomed him to the stage with a chorus of whistles, a sign of disapproval in Europe. Pialat reacted in line with his infamous temper, yelling back at them, 'Vous ne m'aimez pas, je ne vous aime pas non plus' ('You don't love me, I don't love you either'). This episode and the polemic that followed embittered Pialat to the point that he almost considered abandoning cinema altogether.[10] Indeed, Pialat was always a marginal figure in the French film industry. He worked at his own pace and occupied an unusual historical position in the national film circuit equidistant both from the tradition of the nouvelle vague and that of the Cinéma de qualité. Pialat himself neatly differentiated his filming style from the nouvelle vague, which he defined as 'easy-going' and 'amateurish.' As early as 1979, when he was not yet a renowned film auteur in France, he defiantly declared in an interview with Cahiers du Cinéma (where many nouvelle vague film-makers started their careers) that 'French cinema has not always been bad. I place its decline at the appearance of the nouvelle vague.' He boldly adds, 'I know you are not going to like my saying this, but I think Godard has done French cinema a big disfavour' (Amiel and Rabourdin: 63, my translation).[11]

Due to Pialat's contentious place in France's film industry, some critics choose to discuss his work in relation to his early experience as a painter, framing his cinematic style within the modernist aesthetic tradition of the 'gesture,' which reached its apotheosis in the 1950s with abstract and action painting. For instance, Pascal Bonitzer compares Pialat's film style in À nos amours to that of Robert Bresson, another film-maker with former training as a painter. According to Bonitzer, both Bresson and Pialat inject the art of portraiture into their films and while Bresson's portrait is classical, Pialat's is modern; it 'de-figures or treats violently the figure' (1983: 6). Bonitzer compares Pialat's mise-en-scène to Francis Bacon's 'marques libres' (free marks) which, in À nos amours, produce the 'paroxystic effects' Bonitzer considers to be the most remarkable element of the film (ibid.: 10).

Most film critics locate Pialat's authorial signature in his ability to retain the immediacy of the profilmic on film. However, Pialat's cinematic method is more consanguine with the representational rather than the figurative arts insofar as it expresses not merely an individual gesture but the fortuitous and contingent conditions of a collective process and performance. In this respect, Pialat's approach to film-making exemplifies the French notion of film auteur as a personality capable of conveying a unique view of reality through the work done in the *mise-en-scène*. At the same time, his film-making method also marked a point of no return for the romantic notion of auteur as an independent sociology-of-production and a mark of personal consciousness behind a film. Pialat's film-making method in fact does not comply with that established in auteur-informed film cinema, which denotes intentional expressiveness and control. Pialat's role on the set reconfigures and in many cases goes against any notion of authorial premeditation or control. His long pauses between takes, his abrupt changes of mind about lights or camera positions, the tendency of giving only generic directions to the cast and unethical habit to express subjective and often devastating comments on the actors' work on the set, his frequent tiffs with the technicians, and his unrestrained performances (off-screen and sometimes on-screen as an actor) are not just part of the maniacal ritual of a 'savage' film-maker, nor the product of spontaneous inspiration. They are the result of a methodical search for creative momentum during the process of film-making.

Amelio achieved international recognition in 1990 with his aforementioned film *Porte aperte*, an adaptation of Leonardo Sciascia's eponymous novel. His socio-economic status and cultural environment did not present him the same opportunities as his contemporaries, Bertolucci and Bellocchio, both of whom were born to upper-class families and educated in intellectually stimulating environments. While Bertolucci and Bellocchio financed their own first films right after graduating from the Centro Sperimentale di Cinematografia, Amelio had no formal education. He was a self-taught *cinuphile* and gained experience on the set of Vittorio De Seta's *Un uomo a metá/Almost A Man* (1965) as a volunteer assistant director (Sesti 1994: 30–40). De Seta took him under his wing and offered him a regular contract. Subsequently, Amelio was also assistant director to Gianni Puccini and Andrea Frezza, among others (ibid.). Amelio made his first feature film more than ten years after Bertolucci and Bellocchio got started and he gained international recognition more than twenty years after his two contemporaries had already become art house cinema stars. As Amelio has alluded, it was only by chance that he broke into film production as an assistant. In 1994, he declared:

> I have always done everything late. My cultural age now is that of a thirty-year-old. There was a period in my life that instead was the one that they have utilized and exploited to *act* – during which period I had to try and understand what to do and what strength I had to do this thing. The problem was – and still is – understanding, and I did not have the means to understand. I had only some confused occasions, occasions that I sought, but also occasions that I ran into and that I was all too happy to welcome, because they were sources of experience (Fofi 1994: 19–20, my translation).[12]

Exhibiting lucid and uncompromising introspection, Amelio admits to having to sublimate his inferiority complex. In many ways, Amelio's career runs parallel to that of another important director born in the 1940s, Ermanno Olmi. Raised in a modest family in the mountains of northeast Italy, Olmi also began his career as an amateur film-maker and bypassed formal training, eventually becoming a film teacher.[13] Another striking similarity between Olmi and

Amelio is that both directors developed styles that, while respectful of classical film rules, strive to erase any trace of artifice in order to develop a more realistic *mise-en-scène* and narrative. In this respect, Olmi and Amelio differ radically from Bertolucci and Bellocchio, whose unconventional techniques foreground cinematic and literary quotations and anti-naturalistic elements. Paradoxically, Bertolucci and Bellocchio were educated in a film school that cherished Italian neo-realism. Instead of following that tradition, they became the revolutionaries of the post-neo-realist era, drawing less from the films of Roberto Rossellini and Vittorio De Sica than from their *nouvelle vague* contemporaries and certain Hollywood studio directors who had been re-evaluated and reclaimed by the *politique des auteurs*. Conversely, Amelio and Olmi's authorial development outside the dominant tradition of national film schools ultimately led them to inherit the very styles and techniques championed by these institutions.

As the forerunner of the self-taught Italian film-makers of his generation, Amelio proves that institutional and professional constraints can be overcome without compromising creative integrity. Gian Piero Brunetta makes a distinction between film authors who, like Amelio and Olmi, began their careers in the 1970s and their predecessors:

> What distinguishes the 1970s authors from those of all previous generations is the division and multiplication of their voices and hypotheses, their lack of a common social context and common points of reference, along with their professional and operative mobility. Few of them consider themselves "born" directors; a good many of them came across a movie camera and decided to use it to test ideas they had so far expressed through other means. In this way, film is deprived of its aura as a definitive point of arrival in a professional trajectory and instead becomes an intermediate stage, a mere variation of the communicative medium (1998: 804, my translation).[14]

Amelio's first film, *La fine del gioco*, was a modest black-and-white 16mm project for quality television programming. The title, which translates as 'The End of the Game,' is a direct cinema documentary about commuting workers. It was shot on a train on a low budget (five million liras) with a minimal crew (nine people altogether). This film was arguably the kernel for his most acclaimed and mature works, which he made with big budgets while maintaining the rigour and social commitment of his early career. Though stylistically refined and intellectually sophisticated and steadfast, Amelio has avoided cultural snobbery. Yet he has not succumbed to the relativist pitfall of validating every type of film production. Regretful of not having a formal film-making education (he attended the Centro Sperimentale di Cinematografia for only a short time), Amelio accepted a teaching post in the early 1980s at Centro Sperimentale as an opportunity to refresh his knowledge. When he completed his residency, he declared that teaching helped him resolve his complex over not having studied film. It also allowed him to relax his obsession with stylistic perfection. Until then, the film director confesses, he had fallen victim to 'that *cinuphile* cult,' seduced by 'the senseless tracking shot, the absurd dolly, and that idea that the camera comes before the thing represented' (Amelio 1994: 7 – 8, my translation).[15] Amelio's 'coming of age' as a film author began when he learned that cinema must staunchly avoid gratuitous flourishes.

Amelio locates the very nature of cinema at the confluence of art and commerce and affirms that 'the film-enterprise' should engage in a 'dialectical struggle' involving not only author and producer, but also author and target audience. A film author, he concludes, should hold true to the motto 'rigour is my rule, compromise is my enemy' and not just treat it as an empty mantra. Having worked for many years in Italian television, often relying on government subsidies, Amelio is critical of the tradition of public institutions financing authorial film practices. He holds these programmes responsible for lowering the quality of Italian cinema and the attending loss of marketing power. For him, a film director should build a relationship with both producer and spectator and never make assumptions about financial success. In particular, a film-maker's relationship with a producer should be a mutual exchange wherein both come to understand each other's motivations (Fofi 1994: 82–87).

With a career spanning over 30 years, Erice is the most reclusive Spanish director of his generation. His discretion about his life and career has earned him a solid reputation as a loner. He is well known for avoiding interviews and he will only open up to a very select group of critics from specific film journals.[16] In these rare conversations he talks less about his work than about cinema in general, always filtering his own experiences as a film-maker through his views as a film critic and cinuphile. This elusiveness is a strategy for maintaining control over the media's representation of his work. Erice's diffidence makes it difficult to pin down his authorial identity, especially since the interview format is traditionally a main tool for constructing a single, unified subjectivity from a film-maker's often diverse activities. His role as a film author is further complicated because he has never focused exclusively on making films, despite the fact that he is widely considered an undisputed master of contemporary Spanish cinema. As he has declared several times, he considers his involvement in cinema accidental. He only intermittently directs feature films and alternates this activity with film criticism and TV production.

Like many film-makers of his generation, Erice has had difficulty financing his films, despite being backed for many years by Elías Querejeta, the most prominent Spanish producer of the nuevo cine.[17] His first film work was a short piece for an anthology film called Los desafíos (1969). In comparison to the other contributions, Erice's short film is considered by far the most nihilistic. The story follows an aging American G.I. who takes revenge on a doctor for sleeping with his lover. He blows himself up along with the doctor, his lover, and another woman, after picking them up on a desolate Spanish road. The piece is an audacious representation of social violence and serves as a political allegory for Spain's subordinate economic position in the North American capitalist model (Molina-Fox 1977: 34; Schwartz 1986: 89). Erice's first feature-length film, El espíritu de la colmena, won top prize at the San Sebastián Film Festival and screened at the Chicago Film Festival, receiving good overall reviews in Spain and abroad.[18] After this distinguished start, Erice was on the threshold of a prolific career along the lines of Carlos Saura, who also worked with producer Querejeta.[19] Instead, his momentum dissipated over the next ten years while he completed his next feature, El Sur. In the interim period between his first and second features, he worked as a screenwriter and director for Spanish television while occasionally making TV commercials (Schwartz 1988: 88–89). For Erice, making films is only one way to relate to cinema and not necessarily the end goal. Hence, he is not merely an intellectual film-maker who disregards the rules and the pace of the film industry. Instead, Erice applies his time and effort to establishing a dialectical exchange between different practices related to cinema. Like Godard, whom Erice greatly admires for his ability to reinvent his work, Erice thinks that one makes films not only by filming but also by thinking, writing about, and watching films (Marías and Vega 1983).

Erice's career choices hold true to this vision. He began making shorts in the early 1960s while still at the national film school in Madrid and continued working as a film critic for the Spanish journals *Nuestro Cine* and *Cuadernos de arte y pensamiento* for most of the decade.[20] During these years, he wrote essays on Luchino Visconti, Pier Paolo Pasolini, Kenji Mizoguchi, and Joseph von Sternberg using an auteur-oriented framework that was the dominant interpretive model for Spanish film journals at the time, especially *Nuestro Cine*.[21] Erice returned to criticism during the 1980s and, in 1986, he co-wrote a volume on Nicholas Ray with Jos Olivier.[22] Santos Zunzunegui underlines the importance of Erice's critical work in relation to his films making specific references to *El espíritu de la colmena*.[23] Many of the intertextual motifs and stylistic elements Zunzunegui identifies are borrowed from directors about whom Erice wrote, especially Pasolini and von Sternberg.[24] Ultimately, Erice's diverse engagement in film criticism and film-making coalesces in a unitary model of cinema and culture. Erice's film practice is a continuation of his discourse about film and either draws on the aesthetic and technical elements that Erice appreciates in the cinema or presents inter-textual references and homages to specific films. Erice quotes from classical Hollywood films, such as the footage from James Whale's 1931 horror masterpiece *Frankenstein* in *El espíritu de la colmena*, and pays homage to Spanish melodramas and Hollywood woman's films. *El Sur* is one of the most obvious examples of how Erice casts a wide intertextual net. In citing examples from classical Hollywood as well as art house cinema, Erice defines himself less as a film director than a *cineasta* (the Spanish equivalent of 'film-maker'), referring to a frame of mind in which, even when he's not directing, he relates to the world through cinema. His natural disposition as a *cinuphile* and film theoretician emerges even when he discusses his own films.

While Erice's films puzzle film critics because of their elliptical narrative and stylistic heterogeneity, they also inform Erice's authorial reputation as a sophisticated storyteller able to convey core themes of social and political oppression in Francoist Spain through a representational strategy that is both lyrical and mythical. This is particularly true of the critical reception of *El espíritu de la colmena*. Erice also received international acclaim as a film author for this film because of his expressive use of the *mise-en-scène*, dominated by the juxtaposition of 'warm' and 'cold' colours, infinite landscapes and confined interiors, long shots and close details, extremely bright and dark spaces. Another element that film critics considered as an authorial mark of artistic view and cinephilia is Erice's use of aesthetic and film styles that combined together naturalism with classical and expressionism, the psychological drama and the horror film. Ultimately, Erice has become an internationally appreciated author especially because of his refined use of film techniques, which included the use of grainy film stock, blurry extreme close-ups, difficult lighting set-ups and complex camera movements. These authorial marks were also present in Erice's next film, *El Sur*, and even further accentuated there to express notions of physical and figurative distance, including north and south, reality and filmic representation, past and present, image and vision, dark and light, inside and outside. Erice's latest feature film, *El sol del membrillo*, which won two awards at the 1992 Cannes Film Festival, is a subtle contemplation on the process and meaning of representation, as well as an affectionate portrayal of a painter's methods and views of art. The film, shot in a documentary style, articulates Antonio López García's process as he paints a quince tree over time from the same position in his backyard to capture the sunlight's changing reflection on the leaves and fruit from late summer to early winter.

In an interview that Erice made many years earlier with the Spanish film journal *Casablanca* on the occasion of the theatrical release of *El Sur*, Erice stressed the precariousness that characterizes modern cinema and the unpredictability of its reception. According to him, cinema is doomed because it no longer follows classical conventions, resulting in the loss of a common frame of reference for the spectator. For Erice, the crisis of representation and the takeover of television constitute the turning points for cinema after which any act of film-making is an act of survival. Yet Erice embraces the transition to new media: indeed, Erice's most recent work includes short films, as well as videos. Some of these pieces have been shown in an itinerant exhibition arranged by French film critic Alain Bergala and Spanish film critic Jorge Balló, inaugurated in Spain at the Centre de Cultura Contemporània de Barcelona in spring 2006 and which subsequently worked its way to La Casa Encendida in Madrid in summer 2006, eventually closing at the Centre Pompidou in Paris, where it stayed from February to April 2007. The exhibit contained photographs, drawings and video letters between Erice and the internationally renown Iranian film-maker Abbas Kiarostami. The videos were shot with mini-DV cameras and feature the two film directors (who have known each other and have been corresponding for some years) revisiting their own, as well as each other's works. In one video, Erice returns, fifteen years later, to the garden where he filmed *El sol del membrillo*. He also made a short film about Spanish schoolchildren in response to Kiarostami's 1987 film *Kane-ye doust kodjast/Where Is The Friend's Home?*. On his part, Kiarostami made a film about quinces, an homage to Erice's latest feature film.

The underlying purpose of the exhibition was to trace the parallel trajectories and similarities between the two film-makers' practices and conceptions of the cinema (Ehrlich 2006). One of the exhibit's curators, former chief editor of *Cahiers du Cinéma*, Alain Bergala, wrote an article published in the exhibition's catalogue and the online film magazine *Rouge*, titled 'Erice-Kiarostami: The Pathways of Creation.' In the piece, Bergala observes that both film-makers have left an imprint on their respective national cinemas, making films that indirectly record the histories and tragedies of their countries (Bergala 2006). One of Bergala's most salient commentaries about Erice and Kiarostami regards the compatibility of their respective attitudes about the commercial aspects of film-making. He writes:

> Today, in 2006, it seems obvious that in their lives as filmmakers these two men have made the same basic choices of never submitting to the laws of cinema as an industry and a market; of keeping all careerism fiercely at bay in order to bring their work to a successful conclusion with the sovereignty befitting an artist, even if both of them must put up with severe cutbacks in the financing without which no film can get made. (Bergala 2006)

Bergala's comments on Erice and Kiarostami's approach to the film industry and market could also perfectly apply to Pialat and Amelio. Indeed, Pialat, Amelio, and Erice's individual strategies of professional orientation within the new audio-visual industry, their uncompromising yet pragmatic attitudes towards the complex reality of film production and distribution are present, in varying degrees, in the case study explored in the next chapter, Olivier Assayas. As is the case for Pialat, Amelio, and Erice, Assayas has moved beyond the New Wave tradition of authorial discourse and rejected the institutional system of film production and reception that endorse this model of authorship in Western Europe.

Notes

1. For an overview of Europe's implementation of national film industries and transnational projects and institutions, see Jäckel (2003), which provides a synthetic yet accurate overview of Europe's systems of film production, distribution, and exhibition, with specific focus on the 1990s.
2. Of the other film-makers of this group, Jacques Rivette was born in 1928, Claude Chabrol in 1930, and Jean-Luc Godard in 1931.
3. The other film-makers on the project were Rafael Azcona, José Luis Egea, and Claudio Guerín. Querejeta has been widely acknowledged as one of the main promoters of Spanish New Cinema.
4. 'Ritengo che i rischi e le battaglie fanno parte del cinema; quindi all'interno di questa lotta devi metterci anche l'amore o il disamore che hai per il pubblico, o il fatto di sceglierti un pubblico o di non scegliertelo, il fatto di volerlo più ampio possibile. Le tue scelte alimentano o spengono il tuo essere uomo che fa cinema.'
5. A complete list of articles and film reviews written by Erice appears in Arocena (1996: 351–54).
6. Until 1982, Pathé-Gaumont controlled approximately 30 per cent of the French film market. The other two major distribution film companies were the U.G.C. France (originally state-owned and privatized in 1969); and Parafrance (linked to Paramount), which controlled, respectively, 20 per cent and 5 per cent of the market. The rest was divided among independent distributors and exhibitors (Hayward 1993a: 33). Jack Lang broke the Pathé-Gaumont monopoly through an anti-trust law that was approved in 1982 and reinforced independent, local, and regional exhibitors through a special programme of financial aid (Hayward 1993b: 382). In 1985, Parafrance was liquidated and left over 50 per cent of the market to U.G.C. and to the two companies born from the Pathé-Gaumont division, Pathé-Édeline and Gaumont.
7. 'Creo que si se trabaja dentro de una perspectiva abierta, de búsqueda personal, lo que de antemano se puede saber es siempre poco, acaso nada. Las ideas previas, por sí solas, no sirvien. Lo que cuenta es cómo se realizan. Por otro lado, ciertos aspectos que pueden, en principio, aparecer como una limitación, luego resulta que no lo son tanto.'
8. The *articolo 28* was created in 1934 by Italy's fascist government to advance quality film production and has since been a point of interest for discussions of Italian film authorship. The glut of subsidized projects in the 1980s started to thin out in the early 1990s. Since the 1993 approval of a new law on cinema (law 153), *articolo 28* has been almost discontinued, despite the new law's recommendation to finance fifteen to twenty films per year. Part of the reason the government financing system has been 'frozen' is that surplus production has flooded the market, a consequence of the 1980s abuse of article 28. Another reason government subsidies have declined is that many production companies have not paid back their loans with Italy's national bank.

9. 'Je pense à Pialat, amer, haineux, mais au moins rageur. Mécontent du cinema.'

10. The tribute was published soon after Pialat's À nos amours was awarded best film at the César Awards.

11. In an interview appearing in *Cahiers du Cinéma* 399 (Pialat 1987), Pialat defended the 'modernity' of this film.

12. 'Le cinéma français n'a pas toujours été mauvais. Je situe son déclin à l'apparition de la Nouvelle vague [...] je sais que je ne vais guère plaire à votre équipe, mais je pense que Godard a fait un tort énorme au cinéma français.' Capitalization has been retained from the original.

13. 'Io ho fatto sempre tutto in ritardo. L'età che ho adesso è l'età culturale di un trentenne. C'è stato un periodo molto lungo della mia vita-che è stato invece quello che loro hanno utilizzato e sfruttato per fare-in cui io ho dovuto cercare di *capire* cosa fare e quali forze avessi per fare questa cosa. Il problema era-ed è-capire, e io i mezzi per capire non li avevo, avevo confusamente delle occasioni, occasioni che mi cercavo, ma anche occasioni che mi capitavano e che io ero ben felice di accogliere perché erano fonti di esperienza.' Punctuation and italicization in the original.

14. Olmi made industrial documentaries for Montedison, a corporate company, for over ten years. He taught in an experimental film school that he founded with Paolo Valmarana, the 'Laboratorio del Cinema' (Laboratory of Cinema) in Bassano, a town in the province of Vicenza, Valmarana's home and near to Olmi's birthplace. Francesca Archibugi attended that school before going into feature film-making. Coincidentally, Valmarana was the television producer for *Colpire al cuore* and became a good friend of Amelio's, too. Until his premature death in the mid-1980s, Valmarana was one of the most appreciated executives of Italian state television.

15. 'Ció che distingue gli autori degli anni settanta da quelli di tutte le generazioni che li hanno preceduti è la disgregazione e moltiplicazione delle voci, delle ipotesi, la mancanza di un tessuto culturale e di punti di riferimento comuni, la mobilitá professionale e operativa. Ben pochi si considerano registi per vocazione: una buona parte incontra la macchina da presa e decide di usarla per verificare idee finora espresse con altri mezzi. La regia, destituita della sua aura di punto d'arrivo di un cursus professionale, diventa piuttosto un momento di passaggio, una semplice variazione del momento comunicativo.'

16. '[...] quel culto cinefilo [...] che mi portava spesso alla carrellata insensata, al dolly assurdo, a quell'idea della macchina da presa che viene prima della cosa rappresentata.'

17. One of Erice's few interviews was with Ronald Schwartz and was published with the screenplay for *El espíritu de la colmena* (Madrid, (ed.) Elías Querejeta 1976).

18. Querejeta has been widely acknowledged as a main promoter of the Spanish *nuevo cine* movement. He was formerly a renowned soccer player and has written the occasional screenplay. Since the 1960s, he has produced works by some of the most distinguished Spanish directors, including Carlos Saura's *La prima Angélica* (1973) and Ricardo Franco's *Pascual Duarte* (1976). Most recently, he has produced work from young film-makers, including his daughter Gracia's *El ultimo viaje de Robert Rylands* (1996) and *Cuando vuelvas a mi lado* (1999).

19. On the film's reception, see Paul Julian Smith's article 'Between Metaphysics and Scientism: Rehistoricizing Víctor Erice's *El Espíritu de la Colmena*' (Evans 1999: 91–114).

20. From the early 1960s, Saura has been the most prolific of the Spanish film authors. The director has made a film every two to three years since his 1962 début, *Los golfos*.

21. *Nuestro Cine* was founded in 1961 and published until 1970. It was characterized by a focus on realism and a radical perspective. As such, the journal took up the legacy of *Objectivo*, which was

forced to shut down operations in 1955. *Nuestro Cine* went through an intermediary phase, when it assumed a mellower and more theoretical tone, and a last phase, clearly informed by French auteurism (Tubau: 39–44).

22. For more about Spanish film journals, see chapter 1.

23. Santos Zunzunegui's comments on Erice's theoretical works in a narrative analysis of *El espíritu de la colmena* (Talens and Zunzunegui 1998: 128–54).

24. According to Zunzunegui, Erice's study of other film-makers' style provided him with fundamental sources to draw on for his own aesthetic. Zunzunegui identifies the influence of various film-makers in *El espíritu de la colmena*. For example, the figure of the protagonist, an amateur astronomer, recalls Prince Salina in Visconti's *Il Gattopardo* (1963); the use of metaphors and a particular type of realism is reminiscent of Pasolini's theoretical and aesthetic notion of 'cinema of poetry;' the focus on characters attempting to break their social constraints is characteristic of Mizoguchi's films; and the characters' difficulty in escaping their burdensome pasts is typical of von Sternberg's cinema (Talens and Zunzunegui 1998: 131–34).

References

Amelio, G. 1994. Autoritratto. (*In* Sesti, M. (ed.). *Nuovo cinema italiano. Gli autori, i film, le idee*. Roma-Napoli: Teoria, pp. 37–43.)

Amiel, M. and Raboudin, D. 1979. Entretien avec Maurice Pialat. *Cinéma*, 250: 60–64.

Argentieri, M. 1995. Cinema italiano: una grave crisi strutturale. *Cinemasessanta*, 1: 4–8, gennaio/febbraio.

Arocena, C. 1996. *Víctor Erice*. Madrid: Cátedra.

Bergala, A., Narboni, J. and Toubiana, S. 1983. Le chaudron de la création: Entretien avec Maurice Pialat. *Cahiers du Cinéma*, 354: 11–18, décembre.

Bergala, A. 1983. Maurice Pialat, le marginal du centre. *Cahiers du Cinéma*, 354: 20–21, décembre.

——. 2006. Erice-Kiarostami: The Pathways of Creation. Hammond, P. (trans.). *Rouge*. [Online]. Available: http://www.rouge.coom.au/9/erice-kiarostami.html.

Bonitzer, P. 1983. C'est vous qui êtes tristes. *Cahiers du Cinéma*, 354: 6–10, décembre.

Brunetta, G. P. 1998. *Storia del cinema italiano. Dal miracolo economico agli anni novanta. 1963–1993*. Roma, Editori Riuniti.

Carrère, E. and Sineux, M. 1984. Entretien avec Maurice Pialat. *Positif*, 275: 4–11, janvier.

Ehrlich, L. C. 2006. Letters to the World. Erice-Kiarostami: Correspondences. Curated by Alain Bergala and Jordi Balló. *Senses of cinema*, 41. [Online.] Available: http://www.sensesofcinema.com/contents/06/41/erice-kiarostami-correspondences.html#3.

Ehrlich, L. C. 2000. *An Open Window: The cinema of Víctor Erice*. Lanham, MD: Scarecrow Press.

Evans, P. W. (ed.). 1999. *Spanish Cinema: The Auteurist Tradition*. Oxford: Oxford University Press.

Fernandez-Santos, A. 1983. Treinta y tres preguntas eruditas sobre "El Sur." *Casablanca*, 31–32: 55–58, julio/agosto.

Fieschi, J. 1983. Tourner avec Pialat. *Cinématographe*, 94: 188–89, novembre.

Fofi, G. 1994. *Amelio secondo il cinema: conversazione con Goffredo Fofi*. Roma: Donzelli.

Goldschmidt, D. and Tonneterre, J. 1983. Entretien avec Maurice Pialat. *Cinématographe*, 94: 3–7, novembre.

Hayward, S. 1993a. *French National Cinema*. London and New York: Routledge.

—. 1993b. State, Culture, and the Cinema: Jack Lang's Strategies for the French Film Industry. *Screen*, 34(4): 380–91.

Hennebelle, G. and Predal, R. (eds). 1987. *L'influence de la télévision sur le cinéma*, CinémAction, Spec. Issue 44.

Ilott, T. 1996. *Budgets and Markets: A Study of the Budgeting of European Film*. London and New York: Routledge.

Jäckel, A. 2003. *European Film Industries*. London: BFI.

Marías, M. and Vega, F. 1983. En el camino del Sur. Una conversación con Víctor Erice. *Papeles de Cine Casablanca*, 31–32: 59–70, julio-agosto.

Molina-Fox, V. 1977. *New Cinema in Spain*. London: British Film Institute.

Montini, F. and Spila, P. 1990. Il cinema di Gianni Amelio. Intervista. *Cinecritica*, 19–20: 7–12, ottobre1990/marzo 1991.

Pialat, M. 1987. La ligne droite. Entretien avec Maurice Pialat. *Cahiers du cinéma*, 399: 6–7; 60–62, septembre.

Predal, R. 1988. *900 cinéastes français d'aujourd'hui*. Paris: Cerf.

Schwartz, R. 1986. *Spanish Film Directors (1950–1985): 21 Profiles*. Metuchenm N.J. and London: Scarecrow Press.

Sesti, M. (ed.). 1994. *Nuovo Cinema Italiano: gli autori, i film, le idee*. Roma-Napoli: Theoria.

—. 1996. *La « scuola" italiana. Storia, strutture e immaginario di un altro cinema (1988–1996)*. Venezia: Marsilio Editori.

Talens, J., and Zunzunegui, S. (eds). 1998. *Modes of Representation in Spanish Cinema*. Hispanic Issues, 16. Minneapolis-London: University of Minnesota Press.

Toffetti, S., and Tassone, A. (eds). 1992. *Maurice Pialat. L'enfant sauvage*. Torino: Lindau.

Toubiana, S. 1991. Trajectoire en 20 points. *Cahiers du Cinéma*, 443–444: 43–48.

Vincendeau, G. 1990. Therapeutic Realism: Maurice Pialat's A nos amours (1983). (*In* Hayward, S. and Vincendeau, G. (eds). *French Film: Texts and Contexts*. London and New York: Routledge, pp. 257–68.)

3

THE DIFFICULT LEGACY OF THE *NOUVELLE VAGUE*: OLIVIER ASSAYAS AND FRENCH FILM AUTHORS AT THE END OF AUTEURISM

Within the French film system and international film circuits such as film festivals and art house film theatres, Olivier Assayas is readily associated with France's auteur-oriented cinematic practices. Indeed, he belongs to the same Paris-based milieu in which auteur-oriented film criticism emerged in the mid-1950s and has since constituted an important framework for French film discourse. During the first half of the 1980s, he was a regular contributor to *Cahiers du Cinéma*, the French film magazine that inaugurated the critical policy known as the *politique des auteurs* on the basis of which auteurism developed as a specific type of film criticism and promotional strategy in France and elsewhere. Also like many of the film-makers associated with auteur-based film practices, Assayas switched from film criticism to feature film-making after having contributed for some years to the prestigious magazine. About thirty years earlier, the *Jeunes Turcs*, the group of film critics that launched the *politique des auteurs*, which included Claude Chabrol, Jean-Luc Godard, Jacques Rivette, Eric Rohmer, and François Truffaut, had made the move from film criticism to film-making. A number of subsequent *Cahiers* collaborators would make the same transition throughout the 1970s and the 1980s, such as Jean-Claude Biette, who expanded his career to include acting and directing; Pascal Bonitzer, a prolific screenwriter and occasional actor and director; Serge Toubiana, who was involved in a small number of motion-picture productions; and full-time film director Leos Carax. Assayas, then, is part of a long tradition within the film magazine. Furthermore, like many of his predecessors and colleagues at *Cahiers du Cinéma* (most notably Godard) he considers film criticism, screenwriting, and film-making to be complementary activities and in fact defines film-making as 'the path between theory and practice' (Peranson 2003: 37–39). Finally, his profile as a film-maker is ostensibly akin to the type of film authorship that emerged within the *nouvelle vague* movement. In perfect accordance with Michel Marie's definition of the *nouvelle vague* auteur's film-making method, Assayas writes and directs films following his original ideas and personal conception of the cinema, does not keep strictly to a pre-established storyboard, privileges natural settings and opts for direct sound and minimal additional lighting, utilizes non-professional and new actors whom he can direct more freely, and deploys a small but consistent production crew (Marie 1998: 63).

In spite of his connections with France's auteurist tradition and context of film production and reception, Assayas is very critical of this legacy and has always kept his distance from the *cinuphile* culture that informs French auteurism. His attitude exemplifies not only the establishment of post-auteur discourse on cinema in France during the 1980s, but also the abandonment of an idea of authorship modeled on the *nouvelle vague* auteur. His short experience as film critic at *Cahiers du Cinéma* during the 1980s is fundamental to place his attitude vis-à-vis France's auteur-informed discourse and cinema. Since the mid-1960s, *Cahiers du Cinéma* progressively abandoned its auteur-oriented policy in order to address the social and political determinants of film. When, almost two decades later, the film magazine reconsidered its position on film authorship, the cultural climate and the production context that had inspired the *politique des auteurs* had necessarily changed and cinema was part of the larger context of audio-visual industry. Assayas was among the most vocal among the French film critics working at *Cahiers du Cinéma* at the time who advocated a radical repositioning of French cinema vis-à-vis the new audio-visual industry and culture. At the same time, in those years Assayas disavowed the legacy of French author cinema based on the model of the *nouvelle vague* auteur, which he thought responsible for the aesthetic and production limitations afflicting French author cinema in the 1980s. The innovative ideas about cinema that he expressed as a film critic find logical continuation in his film-making practice.

A film critic in spite of himself: Assayas and French cinephilia

In France, auteur-oriented film criticism in the post-war period was closely associated with cinephilia. Antoine de Baecque, a *Cahiers du Cinéma* collaborator from 1984 until 1999 and the magazine's chief editor between 1996 and 1999, appropriately notes in his book *La Cinéphilie: Invention d'un regard, histoire d'une culture* (de Baecque 2003), that French cinephilia was a countercultural movement. This movement was characterized by two concomitant intellectual factors: academic erudition and discursive strategies informed by classical and humanistic culture. Together, these elements formed the basis of a militant political commitment to viewing films of all types, including those considered outside of the established 'artistic' or cultural milieu (de Baecque 2003: 18–23). Cinephilia as a movement was consolidated in Paris during the 1950s through the proliferation of new film magazines and the personal investment of Henri Langlois, the main curator at the Cinémathèque française.[1] Cinephilia was the driving force behind the film critics who championed the *politique des auteurs* approach to film-making before themselves becoming film auteurs within the context of the French *nouvelle vague*.

Olivier Assayas has often distanced himself from this tradition. In a 1995 interview, he commented on his attitude toward film criticism and French film culture in those years:

Olivier Assayas

Anyway, at that time cinephilia was not something essential, in the sense that what attracted me to the cinema was the possibility of finding a way to express the things I had inside, but did not pass at all through the indigestion of films and the fascination for the films of the past, which were very common among people of my generation who wanted to make films. (Fornara and Signorelli 1995: 28, my translation)[2]

Assayas's reservations about the penchant for cinephilia in French film culture should be considered within the framework of *Cahiers du Cinéma*'s general history and, in particular, the period during which Assayas was writing for the publication: 1980 to 1985. At this time, *Cahiers du Cinéma* was undergoing a dramatic change in direction. The conversion involved a progressive reconciliation of the magazine's editorial mandate with more moderate ideological positions including a return to aesthetic concerns and the re-assessment of the film medium in terms of its place within the international cinema market and an expanding array of audio-visual technologies. Chris Darke traces the phases of the auteur's comeback within the framework of the film magazine's editorial makeover in an article published in a 1993 special issue of *Screen* devoted to French cinema since the 1980s. In his piece, Darke remarks that *Cahiers du Cinéma* came to terms with two interrelated problems during this period: 'The first is the definition of its place in the audio-visual environment of 1980s France. The second, which dictates the first, concerns the journal's concerted attempt to come to terms with its own history, and in particular with the notion of the auteur' (Darke 1993: 362). Darke perceives an ideological continuity in *Cahiers du Cinéma*'s approach to auteurism, from its 1970s radical dissociation from the bourgeois conception of the auteur to the reformulation of the term in the 1980s according to the views of the magazine's new chief editor, Serge Daney. Daney identified two features of 1980s auteurism. First, he asserted that the word 'auteur', though meant to designate artistic singularity, had gradually grown so ubiquitous as to become standardized, impoverished, and nearly meaningless. Second, Daney proposed that in some cases a film's producer could also be considered an auteur. Daney's call to expand the signification of 'auteur' prefigures *Cahiers*' later emphasis on the institutional aspects of auteurism (Darke 1993: 327). In short, the magazine's post-auteurist, anti-bourgeois editorial stance of the 1970s and Daney's pragmatic and socio-political approach to the doctrine of the auteur are two sides of the same coin. Both positions call attention to the magazine's commitment to critical and historically informed discussions of film. According to Darke, *Cahiers du Cinéma*'s reconciliation with its auteurist past entailed endorsing France's culturally oriented cinema against the monopoly of Hollywood films in the domestic market. He notes:

The figuring of the 'blockbuster' subsequently became a touchstone presence in the 1980s Cahiers' reformulation of the auteur as an oppositional presence in 1980s French cinema. The 'return to cinema' in the 1980s, then, is a return to a critical object different in nature to that of the 1960s and 1970s (Darke 1993: 365).

This difference is a consequence of the fact that French cinema in the 1980s had become immersed in a considerably more complex and hybridized audio-visual industry than existed in the 1960s and 1970s. Ever since the 1980s, French film has been inextricably engaged in global media systems. Darke concludes that Cahiers du Cinéma set out to respond with a critical discourse that addressed new audio-visual systems and offered an alternative to the 'generalized babble, neither truly critical nor truly promotional, a bit of everything at once, in perfect allegiance with fashions and institutions' (ibid.: 366).

Cahiers du Cinéma's progressive detachment from auteurism had begun in the mid-1960s when the magazine shifted its focus from the social and political to the cultural aspects of film production. De Baecque's writing on Cahiers du Cinéma's deliberate abandonment of auteurist thought provides some edifying insights into the changes made during those years. He stresses that during the 1960s and 1970s a new editorial policy was promoted by the chief editor at the time, Jean-Luc Comolli, who headed the magazine from 1963 to 1973, and then taken up by Serge Daney from 1973 to 1981 (de Baecque 2003: 336). Daney had been involved with Cahiers du Cinéma since 1964 and had a personal investment in new national cinemas. He exhibited a deep fascination with non-western countries and cultures, an interest he cultivated with long and frequent trips. Significantly, de Baecque closes his study of French cinephilia with a discussion of Daney. He describes him as an anachronistic, albeit self-consciously so, cinuphile, totally absorbed in film at a moment when cinema was being 'vampirized' by the 'audio-visual universe of images' (de Baecque 2003: 376). Thus, de Baecque characterizes Daney as a 'melancholic' cinuphile, remarking that Daney was a 'ciné-fils' (a pun that translates literally as 'son of the cinema'). The neologism was coined by Daney himself to express the idea that, for the film critic, life and cinema are always indiscernibly intertwined (ibid.: 365–77). After Daney left Cahiers du Cinéma in 1981, he went on to write for the newspaper Libération. In 1991, he founded his own film magazine, Trafic, which he chaired until his untimely death in June 1992.

Indeed, Daney was the initiator of a new phase in French cinephilia and film culture, an era of which Assayas is one of the most significant representatives, both as a film critic and as a film-maker. This new period began in the years when Assayas was associated with Cahiers du Cinéma. In the late 1970s, the co-chief editors of the film magazine, Serge Daney and Serge Toubiana, were planning a generational turnover. With this in mind, they asked Assayas to join the editorial staff after having seen his first short film, Copyright (1979). Assayas was a perfect choice for Daney and Toubiana. He had no particular interest in the Parisian milieu of film criticism and cine-club culture and he did not engage in cinuphile activities with the same spirit as his fellow critics and film-makers. He is the son of screen and television writer Jacques Rémy, who worked on a number of European co-productions, mainly genre films, throughout the 1940s and 1950s. He began screenwriting when, as a teenager, his elderly father fell ill and he and his brother, Michka (who became a music critic and a writer), helped their father prepare scripts for the popular TV series *Le Commissaire Maigret* in the mid-1970s. In his twenties, Assayas was an amateur painter while studying literature at the university in Paris. He learned the basics of film-making by working as an assistant producer on French B-movies and international big-budget films including *The Prince and the Pauper* (Richard Fleischer, 1978) and *Superman* (Richard Donner, 1978).[3] During this period, he also wrote two short films, *Scopitone* (1977), directed by his friend Laurent Perrin, and *Nuit féline* (1978), directed by Gérard Marx. Prior to and during his collaboration with *Cahiers du Cinéma*, he also worked for other magazines as a freelance journalist, notably the alternative comic magazine *Métal hurlant* (1979–1981) and the music magazine *Rock & Folk* (1982–1988), for both of which he wrote film reviews. He also kept up with the countercultural punk music scene in London and the radical Situationist movement in Paris. The latter promoted cultural happenings and political actions in Paris throughout the 1970s, maintaining anti-capitalist positions (Assayas 2004).[4]

Assayas's film interests accommodated both the international scope that Daney had stressed throughout the 1970s and the need for a fresh and updated look at the emergent audio-visual scene that the new editorial board (under the direction of Toubiana since 1981) was hoping to get from young collaborators such as Leos Carax and Charles Tesson. In this respect, Assayas's affection for a broad range of cinematic modes, including independent as well as mainstream films and film-makers perfectly matched the film magazine's needs. His favourite film-makers covered the spectrum of international cinema: the American independents such as John Carpenter: in 1982 he co-wrote a special dossier on this film director, whom he considered one of the most audacious American film-makers of his generation (Assayas, Le Peron, and Toubiana 1982d). He also admired Clint Eastwood, (Assayas 1983b; Assayas and Tesson 1985), for his depiction of the southern United States, and George Lucas, whose cinema he defines as 'conceptual' (Assayas 1981b); New Hollywood and the 'brat generation,' as exemplified by George Lucas; he also includes in his top-lists films by the intellectual French film auteurs like Jean-Luc Godard, Philippe Garrel.

Assayas's most significant contributions to *Cahiers du Cinéma* include a four-part article on special effects in the cinema (Assayas 1980a, 1980b, 1980c, 1980d), two special issues on US cinema (Assayas et al. 1982a), and a co-edited book on Hong Kong cinema (Assayas and Tesson 1984).[5] He also introduced the Taiwanese New Wave film-makers, such as Hou Hsiao Hsien and Edward Yang, to French film audiences and festivals (Assayas 2004). In the mid-1980s, he personally invited and presented the work of Hsiao Hsien to the Nantes Film Festival. Years later, his interest in this particular director would culminate in the making of *HHH. Un portrait de Hou Hsiao-Hsien* (1997).[6] The documentary was made for 'Cinéma de notre temps,' a French TV series coordinated by Janine Bazin and André S. Labarthe, which features biographical portraits of important film directors (Assayas 2004). Most importantly, many of his articles tackled crucial questions regarding the place of cinema in general and French cinema in particular, within the context of the audio-visual landscape of the 1980s. In regard to French film directors, Assayas proposed a significant reconsideration of the undervalued comedic work of Jean-Pierre Mocky, whom he considers the best example of a 'commercial' auteur (see Assayas 1981a, 1982b, 1982c). He also 'discovered', and, as he has recently admitted, was influenced by, such 'post-*nouvelle vague*' auteurs as Robert Bresson, Jean Eustache and Philippe Garrel (Fornara and Signorelli 1995: 44; Peranson 2003: 39; Assayas 2004).

Assayas regards his work as a film critic as a temporary and almost accidental parenthesis in his professional trajectory that helped him solidify his knowledge of film and develop his innate vocation as a film director. In fact, while he was writing for *Cahiers du Cinéma*, he continued to make short films and to work as a screenwriter on other short and feature films. After *Copyright*, he directed three short films in which he combined the visual experimentation of his first film with songs by pop and rock music performers. *Rectangle, deux chansons de Jacno* (1982) is a proto-music video illustrating two songs by the pop singer Jacno; *Winston Tong en studio* (1984) is a musical documentary about the recording of Tuxedomoon's frontman and performance artist Winston Tong's first solo album; and *Laissé inachevé à Tokyo* (1982), an abstract noir film with a complex narrative structure, which Assayas shot in black-and-white 35mm. *Laissé inachevé à Tokyo* and, particularly, *Winston Tong en studio* are the only of his early works that Assayas still stands behind.[7] Assayas also began to write screenplays for feature films, notably Laurent Perrin's first feature film, *Passage secret* (1984), *Rendez-vous* (André Téchiné, 1985), *L'unique* (Jérôme Diamant-Berger, 1986), *Le lieu du crime/Scene of the Crime* (André Téchiné, 1986), and *Avril brisé* (Liria Begeja, 1987). The success of *Rendez-vous* prompted Assayas's decision to move to feature film-making (Assayas 2004).

Cahiers du Cinéma interviewed Assayas upon the release of his first feature film, *Désordre/Disorder* (1986). In the interview, he stressed that making films had been his first vocation and he described his collaboration with *Cahiers du Cinéma* as a form of apprenticeship for his future film-making practice, a sentiment in keeping with the tradition of the magazine:

> My privileged link with *Cahiers* is explained by the film magazine's tradition, which is more or less comprised of people who wanted to make films. It's the only place where writing about films does not contradict the desire to make them. And it's true; this period of reflection has been indispensable to my orientations. (Assayas 1986: 8, my translation)[8]

Despite his mildly dismissive attitude towards his experience as a film critic, Assayas was of the most original contributors to *Cahiers du Cinéma*. Following the customary path set by other film critics at the magazine, he wrote two books, both of which were published by the *Cahiers du Cinéma*'s press. The first, *Conversations avec Bergman* (1990), is a book of interviews with Ingmar Bergman that he conducted in collaboration with the Swedish film director Stig Björkman. The second, *Kenneth Anger: vraie et fausse magie au cinéma* (1999), is about the work of the experimental American film-maker. Even when he left the magazine to become a full-time film-maker, he continued to write intermittently about films. For example, he wrote prefatory essays for some of his published screenplays, including *Fin août, début septembre* (1998) and *Les destinées sentimentales* (2000), and the preface to an anthology of *Cahiers du Cinéma* articles written in the 1990s by Thierry Jousse, who was then chief editor (Assayas 2003). Recently, he completed an autobiographical book in which he describes his adolescence in Paris during the post-revolutionary 1970s (Assayas 2005b). These writings, as well as interviews conducted on the occasion of his films' releases and director's commentaries included in the DVD versions of his films, reveal his formation as a film critic and testifies his ability to cast a lucid and analytical gaze onto past and current directions in the cinema.[9]

If film criticism for Assayas is complementary to his work as a film-maker, then it is fundamentally important to consider his theoretical reflections on cinema and the new media society in order to understand his approach to film-making, perhaps even more so during the past few years. In his aforementioned preface to the collection of articles by Thierry Jousse, Assayas provides an overview of the magazine's trajectory over the past decade (Assayas 2003). In this short piece, he praises the innovative spirit that has always characterized *Cahiers du Cinéma* and congratulates Jousse for having been able to keep up with the constantly changing panorama of contemporary cinema (Assayas 2003). He also warns film theorists – that is, academics, film critics, and film-makers alike, against separating film theory from practice. In the final section of the preface, he asserts that cinema is a theoretical practice about which it is impossible to write or make films without remaining aware of the changes and movements of contemporary life:

> Nevertheless, I think that something of a real 'faith' in the cinema – in the sense of human experience that this word implies – is precisely located in this verification [of ideas with reality]. This verification is the geometric place through which a frontier passes, one that separates thought and practice. It is an old distinction, one which we know has been refuted by everything that has mattered in twentieth-century thought. We can even say that in every artistic epoch, modernity takes place in the negation of this frontier, in the fluidity, in the freedom of circulation from one side to the other, from one direction to the other, indifferently. (Assayas 2003: 9, my translation)[10]

Assayas perfectly applies this view of the cinema to his own film-making practice, from a perspective that disengages the film author from the institutional and cultural legacy of the *nouvelle vague* auteur.

Assayas and the difficult legacy of the *nouvelle vague*

Cahiers du Cinéma's re-evaluation of auteur-based positions during the 1980s followed a general trend in French film criticism that paralleled the efforts of the French government to endorse a primarily domestic niche of small- and middle-range film productions.[11] These productions were supported by the prestige of established film-makers and aimed at promoting new film-makers with specific aesthetic and cultural agendas. During the 1980s, reclaiming the importance of film authorship in France meant supporting national film practices that found little or no place within the circuits of film distribution and exhibition under the control of France's largest film studios and distribution companies: Gaumont, Pathé, and U.G.C.; and those variously integrated global media corporations such as U.G.C.'s partnership with Warner, Sony, and Fox, as well as Gaumont's partnership with Buena Vista International (Jäckel 2003: 109).

A turning point in the film magazine's revival of authorial discourse was a 1983 special issue dedicated to the critical situation of auteur-oriented cinema titled *Cinéma d'auteur: la côte d'alerte* (*Auteur Cinema: The Crisis Point*). The issue contained articles from the magazine's editors and collaborators including Alain Bergala, Pascal Bonitzer, Jean Narboni, Charles Tesson, and Serge Toubiana, as well as testimonies from French film distributors and publicists and the 'auteur-connected' director of photography Bruno Nuytten. As the title suggests, the issue proposed less a celebration than an alarmist overview of French authorial cinema. Most of the articles blamed the crisis on two interrelated phenomena: the French film audience's disaffection for auteur-oriented films, which were considered too far removed from the average product available in the mainstream circuit of film exhibition; and the inadequate distribution of French authorial films produced through government subsidies or institutions. State-funded films often did not make it to the theatrical circuit or even to television programming, in spite of the fact that the majority of them were co-produced by, or pre-sold to, national television networks.

In his contribution to this issue, an article titled 'Sur une politique' ('About a Politic') (Assayas 1983), Assayas opines that 1950s auteurism and the *nouvelle vague* movement inaugurated a negative trend in French cinema. In particular, he suggests that the premise of auteur-oriented cinema – that is, a subjective conception of cinema – has unfortunately inspired a generation of self-absorbed film-makers, alienated from film spectators and too comfortable in their reliance on public subsidies to worry about the reception of their films (Assayas 1983: 23–24). Assayas's solution is to dismiss the notion of auteur and instead re-evaluate the figure of the film-maker ('*cinéaste*') who may in fact consider him/herself an author but whose primary goal should be to remain aware of the context and the audience for which he/she is making films. He states:

> Being a film-maker is to be respectful of the contingencies by taking into account the economy and the public, whose presence in the discourse is still the best way of gauging one's epoch. If everyone willingly admits that the author exists before the work, then we can also assume the inverse: that the epoch exists before the author. (Assayas 1983: 25, my translation)[12]

In 1985, the final year of his regular collaboration with *Cahiers du Cinéma*, during which he was already preparing his first feature, Assayas wrote a piece on the different approaches to film scripts in North America and in France, an essay which contains some polemic views regarding the *nouvelle vague*. In the article, he differentiates between the North American use of the 'finished screenplay' and the French 'open screenplay' (Assayas 1985). He describes the open screenplay as the main achievement of the *nouvelle vague* film-makers insofar as it has encouraged creative and autonomous teamwork between screenwriters and directors and requires the continuous validation of the script on the set. He attributes the theorization of the open screenplay to the *Jeunes Turcs* and, especially, to François Truffaut's campaign against the literary scripts of the *Cinéma de qualité* which he launched in 1954 with the article 'Une certaine tendance du cinéma français' (Truffaut 1954). According to Assayas, the crusade against the *Cinéma de qualité* was less a criticism of a certain kind of cinematic practice than a proposal for a new one in which the auteur was a creative visionary and held sole responsibility for his/her films. 'The point was not Aurenche or Bost, not *Diary of a Country*

Priest or Bresson,' writes Assayas, '[t]he point was juxtaposing a screenwriter's screenplay to an author's film' (Assayas 1985: 8, my translation).[13]

However, the open screenplay has also left a problematic legacy. Star vehicles developed from barely sketched scripts that merely reproduce archetypal narrative structures are an unappealing alternative to the North American model of the finished screenplay, informed by 'an aesthetic of the accomplished work' (Assayas 1985: 8, my translation). The degeneration of the open screenplay, he adds, has given way to '[...] stumbling and nonsense that triumph under the auspices of self-absorbed and narcissistic stars, of their agents that encourage them, and of the distributors who, in the short term, find their profits' (ibid., my translation).[14] Assayas deduces the following:

> It is no surprise then if today we are immersed in a return to the values of craftsmanship, the well-made, polished, and finished product; that we are so repelled by meaning that we boast – shamelessly so – about the merits of advertisements and of their directors. Since we do not believe in anything any more, form is the only thing that remains. The object of all efforts, it has become an aim in itself. We sense very well today that the scenario is again folding in on itself. We feel the return of technical values, of completion – and the contempt for ourselves who bring them. (1985: 8, my translation)[15]

Assayas's article suggests that it is the marred legacy of the open screenplay that recently led French cinema to produce so many slick, 'well-made', if uninspired, films (ibid.).

In recent interviews, Assayas uses more conciliatory tones vis-à-vis the role of auteur-oriented film criticism and of the *nouvelle vague* in contemporary French cinema (Assayas 2004; Peranson 2003). Even back in the early 1980s, the point for him was not to set aside the figure of the film auteur or blame the legacy of the *nouvelle vague* for the crisis in French authorial cinema; rather, it was to denounce the degeneration of auteur-informed film practices into self-contained filmic forms and institutionalized systems of film production. More importantly, his polemic against auteur-derived cinema and his insistence on the film-maker's engagement with the economic and reception-based determinants of her/his practice is quite coherent with the special issue's effort to place the French film auteur in context. In this respect, Assayas's position against auteurism spelt out the obvious contradictions implied in French film criticism and the government's ambivalent position regarding the reception-related problems of authorial cinema.

Assayas discusses the challenge of making films in the vacuum left by the *nouvelle vague* and of staying in step with the fast-changing reality of contemporary society. He feels an affinity to the generation of film directors who emerged after the *nouvelle vague* (he mentions André Téchiné, Philippe Garrel, Jacques Doillon, Benoît Jacquot, Chantal Akerman, Jean Eustache, and Maurice Pialat), about whom he remarks:

> They are the ones who had to rebuild something. And whatever they rebuilt certainly benefited the following generation, meaning mine. [...] Those are the film-makers I feel

indebted to, those I have a dialogue with. They have been concerned with maintaining the dialogue that they couldn't have with their elders. I think they don't have the recognition they should have in terms of French film history, because they are the ones who reinvented French cinema, and somehow nothing of what came after would have been possible without them. What I'm saying is that they reattached the broken thread. (Peranson 2003: 39)

The 'thread' in question is the one that the *nouvelle vague* film directors had cut by moving away from classical cinema. The thread was left dangling because they were unable to envision the possibility of further development beyond post-classical or modern cinema. In Assayas's opinion, these film-makers have been forced to define their work in terms of 'post-cinema' and are unable to think of themselves in historical terms (Peranson 2003: 39).

Assayas's idiosyncratic relationship with the tradition of French cinema is hardly unusual within the generation of French film-makers who made their débuts in feature film-making in the 1980s. The decade was marked by the economic crisis of the European film industry, which was unable to counter the consolidation of a global film exhibition circuit that was monopolized by Hollywood blockbusters. As a result, France, like most Western European countries, became less and less interested in investing in author cinema. The goal became developing a transnational mainstream model of production and distribution through transnational systems of subsidies and special programmes; an effort that produced uneven results.[16] In this rapidly changing climate, enterprising film-makers had to find a way to make their pursuits viable without compromising their values.

The 1980s witnessed French film-makers' move away from art house and auteur-informed cinema, now considered to be out of touch with France's social reality and film industry. The film style that paved the way for the young generation's rejection of French art and authorial cinema is the *cinéma du look*. Ginette Vincendeau describes the *cinéma du look* as a typical example of 'mainstream co-optation' of 'avant-garde, artisanal, or auteur' cinema (1996: 14). In fact, most of the film-makers associated with the *cinéma du look* had some professional experience in the mainstream film industry or in television before moving to feature film-making: Jean-Jacques Beineix and the Jean-Pierre Jeunet/Marc Caro team worked in TV commercials and music videos; Leos Carax and Luc Besson learned about working with technologically sophisticated sets while observing technicians at work on big-budget shoots (Besson) and working as assistant producers in mainstream films (Carax). In line with *Cahiers du Cinéma's* editorial policy, which dismissed the trend because it is both heavily influenced by advertising aesthetics and an example of *"cinéphilie sans mémoire* (Bergala, quoted *in* Darke 1993: 375–76), Assayas was not interested in the *cinéma du look* and his films generally stand in contrast to the films of this style. One of the many differences between Assayas and the film-makers of the *cinéma du look* concerns the attitudes and approaches the two parties assumed in terms of new audio-visual technologies. The film-makers of the *cinéma du look* adopted video techniques and aesthetics derived from high-quality TV commercials and music videos and brought film crews back to the studios (deserted since the 1950s due to the emphasis on auteur-oriented cinema) and to big-budget productions. Conversely, at least until *L'Eau froide*, Assayas used techniques and styles more indebted to art house film than to new media forms, as well as borrowing from artistic disciplines such as painting and literature. Still, he shares with the *cinéma du look* film-makers a determination to challenge the limitations of the *nouvelle vague* paradigm and the *cinuphile* tradition. In spite of this stated position, both Assayas and his *cinéma du look* counterparts make use of some styles and methods reminiscent of the *nouvelle vague*.[17]

By and large, Assayas feels that he has no true interlocutors among his generation of film directors. From his feature film-making début to the present moment, he has considered himself isolated within the context of French cinema. Back in the 1980s, all of the emerging film-makers of the new generation were working within the style of *cinéma du look*, a path from which Assayas veered. Even Claire Denis, with whom Assayas would later find some affinity, was making a significantly different type of film in the 1980s (Assayas 2004). Indeed, the only French films Assayas remembers from that period are Alain Bergala and Jean-Pierre Limosin's *Faux fuyants/Subterfuge* (1983) and Limosin's second film, *Le Gardien de la nuit/Guardian of the Night* (1986), both films that Assayas considers quite distinct from his own approaches at the time. Instead, he finds he has deeper connections with art and independent cinema directors from other periods in the French tradition and from different geo-cultural areas altogether. As a film critic, he discovered the films of Robert Bresson and has ever since cited them as a major source of inspiration for his own work. Yet the film directors that left the strongest imprint on Assayas, including Ingmar Bergman, Andrei Tarkovsky, and John Cassavetes, come from outside of the French cinematic tradition. Additionally, Assayas claims to have no particular affection for classical cinema, another factor that separates him from the *nouvelle vague* film-makers. Since his years at *Cahiers du Cinéma*, he has had a preference for contemporary cinema based on pertinent stories from areas as diverse as North America, Hong Kong, and Taiwan. His own aesthetic models transcend even the sphere of contemporary cinema; Assayas considers modern painting and fictional narrative (*le romanesque*) to be the most important sources of inspiration for his films.

In a 2004 unpublished interview, Assayas recounts how he found his way into film-making only when he understood that he could combine two seemingly incompatible artistic trends: post-figurative modern painting and French post-experimental narrative literature. In relation to modern art, his films allude to the works of Balthus (1908–2001), Francis Bacon (1909–1992), Andy Warhol (1928–1987), and Pierre Bonnard (1867–1947). His primary literary references are French (or France-based) novelists François Mauriac (1885–1970), Julien Green (1900–1998), and Jacques Chardonne (1884–1968), whose novel *Les destinées sentimentales* he adapted for the screen in 2000.[18] (The script of the adaptation marks the only time Assayas has shared writing credits, with film critic and screenwriter Jacques Fieschi.)[19] Interestingly, Assayas's exploration of modern painting and narrative literature as a way to move beyond post-experimental art echoes the *nouvelle vague* film-makers' engagement with modern art and non-canonical literature, which was, in turn, a reaction to the realist style of the *Cinéma de qualité* and the practice of adapting prestigious French literary works. In this respect, Assayas adopts one of the most innovative aspects of *nouvelle vague* cinema, but from a perspective founded in contemporary society that contrasts with the cinephilia, intertextual references, and knowing winks typical of the *nouvelle vague* film-makers. For Assayas, art is a means of establishing a relationship with reality and perception. For the *nouvelle vague* film-makers, art is an intertextual component of film. In this respect, although some of Assayas's film-making practices seem quite similar to those introduced by the film directors of the *nouvelle vague*, his techniques in fact serve an entirely different purpose: that of being in sync with the fast paced and multi-layered context of contemporary audio-visual culture. Rather than following in the footsteps of the *nouvelle vague*, Olivier Assayas creates new avenues for addressing the crisis of representation brought about by postmodern and post-figurative aesthetics. In his films, he transcends the inherent limitations and shortsightedness of the *nouvelle vague* tradition by developing a figural conception and practice of the cinema.

Post-figuration: making films after auteurism

Olivier Assayas's concept of cinema as a modern art-inspired medium of plastic figuration and his preference for character-driven plots drawing on 1930s and 1940s French literature apply to collective narratives conform to what David Bordwell has recently defined 'network narratives,' that is, narratives involving many characters involved in intertwining plots, and may be 'strangers, slight acquaintances, friends, or kinfolk' (Bordwell and Thompson 2006). The film aims to show a larger pattern underlying their individual trajectories. His first film, *Désordre*, traces the downward trajectory of a group of young friends who play together in a rock band and are on the lam after one of them kills the owner of a music store while trying to steal new instruments. *L'Enfant de l'hiver/Winter's Child* (1989) and *Paris s'éveille/Paris Awakens* (1991) deal with the evasion of parental responsibility and the volatility of romantic obsession. *Une Nouvelle vie/A New Life* (1993) looks at the breakdown of a family due to a lack of communication between its members. *L'Eau froide* (1994) is an episode of the TV series *Tous les garçons et les filles de leur âge*. French state television commissioned episodes from a group of prominent film-makers working in France including Claire Denis and Chantal Akerman. Assayas's episode is set in the early 1970s and further develops the theme of family and miscommunication, this time from an adolescent's point of view.

L'Eau froide (Virginie Ledoyen and Cyprien Fouquet)

During the past ten years Assayas's films still concentrate on French-based situations and stories, more and more seen from the perspective of modern global society and culture. *Irma Vep* (1996) and *Fin août, début septembre/Late August, Early September* (1998) tackle the complex friendships and love relationships among adults in their mid-thirties from a reflexive and, at times, critical point of view. The former is a humorous yet honest account of a fictional moment in French authorial cinema history. It depicts the confused production of a remake of Louis

Feuillade's 1916 serial, *Les Vampires*, by a *nouvelle vague*-esque film director (ironically played by Jean-Pierre Léaud, the quintessential *nouvelle vague* actor). The latter film is a more pensive yet visually dazzling portrait of a group of friends coping with personal and professional struggles and their coming-of-age crises brought on by the death of a terminally ill member of their group. *Les destinées sentimentales/Les Destinées* (2000) is a saga that covers three decades in the life of a Presbyterian priest who comes from a wealthy family of porcelain manufacturers from Limoges. The film is Assayas's only period piece, and though it is set in the past, the film infuses vitality into its portrayal of early-twentieth-century French bourgeoisie by framing events within the contexts of contemporary social relations and character psychology. *Demonlover* is a grim representation of new media and post-capitalist society. The film portrays a group of executives working for rival companies who have no qualms about resorting to homicide in order to take over the international marketing of pornographic media. Assayas's next film, *Clean* (2004), is about the trials of an ex-heroin addict named Emily, who travels across North America and Europe to reconstruct her life after the drug overdose death of her husband (a rock musician), in an effort to regain custody of her son who has been living for years with her in-laws. (His latest feature film, *Boarding Gate* (2007), is a thriller set in an international context, featuring Asia Argento as the protagonist. The film had a poor reception both by film audiences and critics. In the same year, Assayas contributed to the omnibus film *Paris, je t'aime*.)

Demonlover

Assayas claims that in developing a film he aims at discovering through the characters what a scene contains, creating a real osmosis between the camera and the work of the actors (Fornara and Signorelli 1995: 76). He proceeds by constructing a story from an abstract idea, a mental image to which he gives shape first in the script and then in the filming process. Characters and stories find concrete manifestation in the *mise-en-scène* and through the individual input of actors and actresses (ibid.). In *Désordre*, Assayas conducts a progressive (trans)figuration of the characters, moving from something abstract, derived from the imagination, and making it concrete through the elements of film style and narrative.[20] Echoing the title, which in English means 'disorder', the film follows the gradual disintegration of a group of young friends after one of them accidentally kills a stranger. The film depicts the progressive disorientation of the characters as their friendships fall apart, epitomizing the uncertainties faced by young people who have yet to find a place in life and society (ibid.: 32). *L'Enfant de l'hiver* opens with images of a pregnant woman who has been abandoned by her partner, followed by her return some years later with her baby. Next are images of a young woman who, as we soon learn, is consumed by an impossible and desperate love. Throughout the film, Assayas weaves together and balances two elements: 'the sensation of performing acrobatics' and a 'scheme that would push [him] to be at the same time realist, and enigmatic and abstract' (ibid.: 76). The film was inspired by Ingmar Bergman, whom Assayas coincidentally interviewed for *Cahiers du Cinéma* soon after completing the film's shoot (ibid.: 49). The original idea for *Paris s'éveille* was based on the metaphorical figure of the 'explosion,' which Assayas envisions as the energy and movement of the young protagonist who is still defining her role in society; she is not yet, as the director puts it, closed off and settled in her chosen 'place, neighbourhood, social class, values' (ibid.: 80). The same metaphor could apply to *Fin août, début septembre* wherein the restlessness of the characters reveals their unwillingness to find their place within society.

According to Assayas, the relationship of the author to his/her film must be direct, unmediated by reflection, common sense, or reason. This relationship entails a personal struggle with the matter of creation, a struggle that may or may not produce an outcome. Assayas finds this creative struggle exemplarily manifested in the works of Francis Bacon who he considers the most important painter and also the greatest image-thinker of our times. In Bacon, Assayas perceives 'this idea of fighting with a thing that is present, that is about to take shape or that won't, but which has a meaning for him' (ibid.: 85). Assayas's figural approach to film-making is best exemplified in *L'Eau froide*, a little-seen film that was recently re-released in a French DVD box set. *L'Eau froide* recounts the vicissitudes of two adolescents, Christine and Gilles, over a short period of time. Set in the early 1970s, the years of Assayas's youth, the film uses a variety of popular music and rock tunes to re-create the era. In what is the longest – comprising almost a third of the film's length – and most significant sequence of the film, the young protagonists and their friends end up in the ruins of an abandoned house in the countryside. Filmed on the last day of shooting in one long take, the sequence has nearly no dialogue. The group spends the entire night in the desolate yet suggestive landscape, playing music, drinking, smoking pot, and dancing around a bonfire. Staged against the bleak landscape and the cocoon of the derelict house, which the kids progressively tear down to feed the fire through the night, the scene is a Dionysian homage to the myths and icons of 1970s youth culture. It stands out as one of the most primal and personal moments in all of Assayas's work. The extensive soundtrack of songs from the period adds to the scene's hypnotic atmosphere. In this night-time sequence, the characters become pure figures of light, movement, and music.

Assayas considers *L'Eau froide* the film that fully comprises his conceptual and practical ideas about cinema through a return to an innocent, almost idealistic perception of the world, one that is breezy and even adolescent in nature:

> *L'Eau froide* all of a sudden established a link with that adolescent. Then I understood that it was through that person that I could find the key to what I could do with cinema. It is the same in life, by the way. Starting from there, I was able to introduce a form of freedom, a sort of carefree attitude into my cinema. And through this lightness and carefree attitude, I could be at the centre of a more valuable artistic practice. (Assayas 2005a, my translation)[21]

During the past decade, Assayas has been striving to maintain the freedom, levity, and unfettered approach he discovered in making *L'Eau froide*. Most of his 1990s films (*Irma Vep*, *HHH. Un portrait de Hou Hsiao-Hsien*, and *Fin août, début septembre*) were shot in Super 16mm with this intention in mind and were completed with a small crew in only a few weeks (Assayas 2004; Assayas 2005a). Even *Les destinées sentimentales*, which was a big production involving a large crew, complicated sets, hundred of extras, and starring two prominent French actresses, Isabelle Huppert and Emmanuelle Béart, stays true to Assayas's dedication to a 'light' approach to film-making.

Indeed, Assayas's films movement conveys the very essence of Assayas's idea of cinema as an art that expresses life through a process of becoming. The use of the mobile camera accentuates the twisted relations among family members, friends, lovers, and work colleagues, visually capturing the characters' social and psychological restlessness. Film critics Kent Jones and Thierry Jousse have eloquently commented on this aspect in Assayas's work. In an insightful overview of Assayas's oeuvre up to *Irma Vep*, Jones notes:

> Vertiginous speed is a fact of modern existence, and in the films of Olivier Assayas [...] speed is palpable: Assayas may be the only filmmaker who gives us the poetics of the digital age in all its mean perfection. This former *Cahiers du Cinema* [sic] critic must have the most rapturously mobile eye in modern movies. He makes an event out of every shape and spatial configuration that crosses his camera's field of vision. But each move, each colour, each visual rush is firmly connected to his characters in particular and quotidian existence in general [...]. 'Reality is always magic,' Renoir once said, and Assayas embodies that dictum more fully than any other modern director. (1996: 50)

Bodily movement and psychological anxiety find their parallels in the characters' travels. The journeys take place to and from many different locations, including within various sections of Paris, from the city to the outskirts, around other areas within France, and to the U.K. or even across continents to the United States. In *Clean*, Emily is played by Maggie Cheung, a Hong Kong star who was born and raised in the U.K. until the age of eighteen and whose career has spanned Asia and Europe, partly through her professional and personal partnership with Assayas.[22] Both within and beyond her films, Cheung's multicultural identity participates in today's global reality. Jean-Michel Frodon, chief editor of *Cahiers du Cinéma* since 2003, emphasizes the cosmopolitan aspects of *Clean* in an editorial for the magazine. The issue features a still from the film on its cover. The shot is a close-up, pulled from the film's ending sequence, of Emily singing in a San Francisco recording studio. The city, emblematically, is where she gave birth to her son and where she has temporarily returned to record an album of songs she wrote with a woman she met while in jail and possibly start a new career, this time clean from drugs. The photo suggests the narrative's global reach, which Frodon underlines in his review:

> This world is immense and complex: the scenario goes through four countries (Canada, France, England, United States), two continents, and an ocean; it evidently convenes by way of the sole presence of Maggie Cheung, the Asian horizon, the agent by which people speak Chinese as well. This world is cosmopolitan without being concerned about being so; this endlessly reflecting world gives meaning to Emily's rectilinear trajectory (Frodon 2004: 23, my translation).[23]

The jet-setting aspect of many Assayas films demonstrates that for the film-maker, cinema is a medium capable of rendering the immediacy of the present, offering a way for people to synchronize with the syncopated, scattered structure of present-day life (Assayas 2004; Fornara and Signorelli 1995; Peranson 2003). Assayas aims to convey the loss of spatial and temporal linearity in our post-Euclidean culture and to render the vectorial nature of people's inter-relations and communications within a new technologies- and media-saturated environment. The elliptical narrative structures and dynamic *mise-en-scène* and cinematography of Assayas's films translate into a figural language that captures the rapid reconfigurations of spatial and temporal data characteristic of twenty-first-century western society. In this sense, his films point to a major issue in contemporary art, aesthetic theory, and philosophy: how to capture and synthesize the relation between sensory and conceptual elements that sustain the subject's relation to the world (Dufrenne-Formaggio 1981; Merleau-Ponty 1964; Ricoeur 1977).

Assayas's post-figurative approach to film-making exemplifies what Gilles Deleuze, in *Cinema-Two: The Time-Image* (Deleuze 1989), identifies as a type of cinema that conveys pure optical and sound situations and in which movement is subordinated to time (1989: 3). Deleuze contrasts the 'time-image' (which for him coincides with modern cinema) to the 'movement-image' (loosely coincident with classical cinema), a more action-oriented type of cinema in which causality and linearity are privileged. In the narrative mode of the time-image 'sensory-motor situations have given way to pure optical and sound situations' (ibid.: 128) 'movement can tend to zero [...] the fixed shot' or 'may also be exaggerated, be incessant, become a world-movement [because] what is important is that the anomalies of movement become the essential point instead of being accidental or contingent' (ibid.). In *Reading the Figural, or, Philosophy after the New Media* (2001) David N. Rodowick Deleuze's concept of the time-image is predicated upon the idea that modern cinema (which for Deleuze begins at the end of World War II with Italian neo-realism) is more than a cultural manifestation or an aesthetic reflection of a historical or ideological climate: it is a form of thinking that implies a new relation between time and thought (2001: 172–77). Rodowick perfectly summarizes the importance of Deleuze's notion of the time-image for the development of a post-dialectic philosophy in contemporary cinema (ibid.). According to him, the time-image proposes a genealogic rather than dialectic approach to history and stresses the importance of philosophy as an act of affirmation of difference and change (ibid.: 200–02). Likewise, Assayas's post-figurative cinema does not refer to a transcendental or immanent meaning: it conveys the tension between real and virtual and presents cinema as an experience 'in the making,' as well as a new way of addressing the representation of reality after the crisis of classical aesthetics. From this perspective, the figural functions in Assayas's films as a departure from previous or established strategies of cinematic address and meaning formation and as an instance of cinema's particular relation to present-day reality.

From this perspective, the film that best represents Assayas's effort to develop a film-making aesthetics in line with the post-ontological approach to the image typical of new media society is *Demonlover*. In this film, Assayas deals with the over-saturated media culture characteristic of contemporary society and offers a critical portrayal of present-day circumstances, one that is predicated upon his belief that cinema is both about reality and informed by the reality in which it is produced. *Demonlover* in fact highlights the relationship between digital culture and globalization and the central role that both play in the formation of the economic, ideological, and social. The film was inspired by the theories of French Marxist philosopher and Situationist activist Guy Debord. Since the 1960s, and until his self-inflicted death in 1994, Debord wrote books and made experimental films that denounced the effects of the media on social and interpersonal relations. On the conceptual level, *Demonlover* was informed by Debord's Marxist-informed analysis of the 'society of spectacle' – a phrase Debord uses to describe our social condition – as summarized in a book titled *La Société du spectacle* (Debord 1992, [originally published in 1967]), subsequently adapted into a film by the same title, which included audio excerpts of the text, accompanied by illustrative images and written comments in subtitles or intertitles. The introductory paragraph of Debord's book, also featured in the film, gives an idea of the parallel existing between Debord's political stance and Assayas's conceptual purpose in making *Demonlover*:

> Understood in its totality, the spectacle is both the outcome and the goal of the dominant mode of production. It is not something added to the real world; it is not a decorative element, so to speak. On the contrary, it is the very heart of society's real unreality. In all its specific manifestations – news or propaganda, advertising or the actual consumption of entertainment – the spectacle epitomizes the prevailing model of social life. (Debord 1992: 17–18, my translation)[24]

To be sure, *Demonlover* departs from Debord's dialectic and anti-aesthetic approach to film-making, which is strictly anti-narrative and iconoclastic and involves the frequent use of still shots, sub- and inter-titles, and black screen, with or without voice-over commentary. On the contrary, Assayas's films flaunt a glossy visual style and a jarring narrative structure. Some film critics have even suggested that *Demonlover* is rather compliant with the incoherent flow and flashy style associated with digital media. At the 2002 Cannes Film Festival, where *Demonlover* had its world premiere, critics raised questions, as Jonathan Romney puts it, 'about the film's apparent collapse into incoherence, about its seemingly compromised fascination with the digital-age glamour it seeks to dissect, and about its over-conscious effort to be hip' (Romney 2004).

Appropriately for a film about the digital age, *Demonlover* features a narrative, *mise-en-scène*, and editing style that folds back upon itself like a digital palimpsest through its use of multiple layerings and surfaces and overlapping graphics and sound. The film's complex and twisted narrative structure is a case in point, as evidenced by the film's difficult reception at its Cannes premiere. During the promotional campaign that followed, Assayas insisted that the film's convoluted structure was a purposeful representational strategy on his part. Commenting on *Demonlover*'s unsettling plot twists in an interview with film critic Mark Peranson, he maintained that he deliberately went against generic conventions and audience expectations. He also emphasized that his intention was to break with the classical dramaturgic mode of the thriller and 'dive into the subconscious of the characters,' aiming to let their secret motivations, as well as the invisible surface of things, unfold the plot (Peranson 2003: 32–33).[25] Finally, he claimed he was trying to establish a different relationship with the film spectator, an alternative to the conventions of 'safe storytelling [in which film spectators] are manipulated by their own subconscious, by their own inner logic, or absence of logic' (ibid.: 33).

The film's visual and sound editing also recalls the processes of digital media. The lack of establishing shots, the use of sudden cuts that re-locate the action from one continent to another, and the purposeful avoidance and subversion of diegetic markers combine to make the film spectator, much like the Internet surfer, uncertain about the location and context of certain scenes. Sound bridges and soundscapes cunningly incorporate diegetic and extra-diegetic audio. Digital media noises associated with information technologies such as computers, Internet servers, mini-DV cameras, cellular phones, and automatic teller machines are mixed into Assayas's remix of the mesmerizing musical score by Sonic Youth.[26] Such digital references and motifs seem to be the only organizing principle of the film's structure, resulting in a style consistent with Assayas's unconventional narrative and editing strategies. Conversely, the purpose of editing in what are considered to be the film's more 'classical' scenes, including two car-chase sequences and a driving sequence set on a rainy Paris night is, paradoxically, to suggest a non-Euclidean, multi-layered configuration of space and time, one that is typical of virtual reality.

Additionally, the film's allegorical nature is obvious in the *mise-en-scène*, which features a vectorial and videogame-inspired approach to figure blocking and movement. As with virtual reality, settings and lighting blur the boundaries between indexical and virtual imagery, between live-action and animated figures, and between perception and hallucination. This style resonates with the development of the narrative in which characters seem to respond to the commands of a game consul rather than to emotional or rational motivations. Ultimately, *Demonlover* does more than appropriate narrative and visual characteristics of digital forms or mimic the sensory and cognitive experiences of digital media. The film explores the relation of cinema to the digital on the material level by alternating between 35mm film, digital footage from pre-existing animation films and videogames, and original DV and website images created by Assayas and his director of photography Denis Lenoir (using DV and further elaborated in post-production). Furthermore, the film adopts visual and narrative strategies that recall particular digital forms, most notably videogames, and re-create sensory effects generally associated with digital media. The airport sequences and scenes in the Japanese nightclub are magisterial examples of this techno-bending. The film's narrative also tackles digital culture and its economic foundation by focusing on the economic and ideological power held by media corporations. In particular, the film explores ethical and social issues related to the production, circulation, and reception of violent and exploitative images through softly regulated digital and communications technologies. Finally, *Demonlover* proposes an up-to-date political view of the 'postmodern condition' by calling attention to the reification of digital culture in present-day global society.

Thierry Jousse made very similar remarks in his enthusiastic review of *Demonlover*, which he symbolically inserted as the 'Afterword' to a collection of his 1990s *Cahiers* articles (Jousse 2003). The film had just been released when the anthology was going to press. Jousse's epilogue resonates with the book's 'Preface,' in which Assayas espouses Jousse's talent for recognizing cinema that grasps the spirit of the time. Jousse's article champions this very quality in *Demonlover*. He identifies in *Demonlover* an allegory of the system of circulation that regulates the regime of the visible in global culture. He appreciates Assayas's ability to capture the temporal and spatial flux of contemporary society through panoply of settings and locations. In this respect, he argues that

> *Demonlover* is at the same time a film of the vertigo of sameness and of the most exact singularity. It is in this sense that the film is properly realistic, because being realistic today is no longer just reproducing the impression, more or less diffused, of physical reality or of life as it unfolds, but it is penetrating from the interior a no man's land of time changes, of diffused projections, of mental images, of tricky perspectives, of disconnected spaces, of ghostly gaps. (Jousse 2003: 244, my translation)[27]

Demonlover also serves as an instructive example of Assayas's effort not only to move beyond the point of no return marked by the *nouvelle vague* auteur's postmodern approach to film-making, but also to give a new place to cinema in the age of new audio-visual media and post-ontological relation to reality. Predicated upon the close relationship of film theory and practice, Olivier Assayas's approach to film brings a new dimension to the role of authorship in contemporary French cinema, that of a mediator between the conceptual, symbolic, and practical elements of film production and reception orientation linked to the ubiquitous cultural changes in the new media society.

The case studies included in the second part of this book propose a similar model of authorship, one that maintains a dialectic relation with previous authorial traditions and practices, yet is the product of new trends in the audio-visual industry. This typology of film author blurs the boundaries between art house and mainstream, national and international film production and reception, and partakes in a trans-national film culture produced by the convergence of local and global circuits of audio-visual distribution. The film author of the new generation indicates a different type of singularity vis-à-vis the anonymity of collective and standard systems and methods of film production and distribution than the one attributed to the New Wave film author. In the era of global media, the film author is no longer associated with notions of aesthetic originality and personal expression, but instead with reflexive tactics of re-appropriation and re-inscription of cinema's formulaic and commercial characteristics.

Notes

1. The development of organized film discourse and cinema institutions in post-World War II France is illustrated in the first chapter of this book.

2. 'Comunque a quel tempo la cinefilia non era per me qualcosa di essenziale, nel senso che ció che mi attirava nel cinema era la possibilitá di trovare una via per esprimere le cose che avevo dentro, ma non passava affatto attraverso l'indigestione di film e la fascinazione per il cinema del passato, che erano molto frequenti nelle persone della mia generazione che volevano fare dei film.' The quotation is taken from an interview that took place between Assayas and Italian film critics Bruno Fornara and Angelo Signorelli in Paris in January 1995. The interview was published in the catalogue accompanying a retrospective of the film-maker's work at the 1995 Bergamo Film Festival in Bergamo, Italy.

3. Assayas worked as an assistant editor on *Superman*.

4. The most important theorist of the Situationist movement was the philosopher and film-maker Guy Debord (Chollet 2004: 78–95). On the occasion of Debord's death in 1994, Assayas wrote a commemorative piece about him in *Cahiers du Cinéma* titled 'Dans des circonstances éternelles du fond d'un naufrage,' (*Cahiers du Cinéma*, 487, [janvier 1995]: 46–49). In 2005, he also wrote a book in which he describes his youth within the context of the Situationist movement, titled *Une Adolescence dans l'après-mai. Lettre à Alice Debord* (Assayas 2005b). The book is written in first person as a letter to Alice Debord, Guy Debord's widow, with whom Assayas collaborated to publish his film work on DVD.

5. For a complete bibliographical account of Assayas input in the *Cahiers du Cinéma*, please go to the Cinémathèque française website: http://195.115.141.14/catalogue/index.php?collection=P&Textfield=assayas.

6. Assayas also talked about Hong Kong film-makers and their relation to Hollywood at a round table with Christophe Gans and Charles Tesson at the 2000 Locarno film festival. The proceedings were published by the *Cahiers du Cinéma*'s press in 2001 (Tesson, Paquot and Garcia 2001).

7. All these these short films, except for *Copyright*, are available on the French DVD version of his first feature film, *Désordre*.

8. 'Mon lien privilégié avec les *Cahiers* s'explique par la tradition de la revue, qui a toujours été plus ou moins faite par des genes qui avaient envie de faire des films. C'est le seul endroit où écrire sur le cinéma n'est pas contradictoire avec le désir d'en faire. Et c'est vrai, toute cette période de réflexion m'a été indispensable pour préciser mes orientations.'

9. His commentaries are available on the DVD editions of *Les Destinées sentimentales* and *Demonlover*, as well as on the recent DVD versions of films that were previously released on VHS (*Désordre*), films that had never been released before for home viewing (*L'Eau froide*), and films whose previous DVD editions did not contain commentaries (*Irma Vep*). The above-mentioned DVD collection of Debord's films, edited by Assayas, came out in 2005.

10. 'Je crois pourtant que quelque chose d'une foi réelle dans le cinéma, dans le sens de l'expérience humaine que recouvre ce mot, se trouve précisément dans cette vérification. Elle est le lieu géométrique où passe une frontière, celle qui sépare pensée et pratique, vieille distinction dont on sait que tout ce qui aura compté dans la pensée du xxè siècle l'a remise en cause: on peut même dire qu'à toute époque, dans les arts, la modernité aura eu lieu dans la négation de cette frontière, dans la fluidité, dans la liberté de circulation de l'un et l'autre côté, dans l'un et l'autre sens, indifféremment.' Assayas extensively discusses the relation between film theory and practice in an interview with Peranson published on the occasion of the North American release of *Demonlover* (Peranson 2003: 35–37).
11. I discuss this politics in the introduction and in chapter 1.
12. 'tre cinéaste c'est cela, c'est être respectueux des contingences. Prendre en compte l'économie et prendre en compte le public, c'est encore la meilleure façon qu'on ait trouvée d'être de son époque. Car si chacun admit bien volontiers que l'auteur préexiste à l'oeuvre, on peut pareillemment affirmer que l'époque préexiste à l'auteur.' I am using the male gender to be consistent with the French text. On this article, see also Maule 2003.
13. 'Il ne s'agissait pas tant d'Aurenche ou de Bost, ni du *Journal d'un curé de campagne* ou de Bresson. Il s'agissait d'opposer un scénario de scénaristes à un film d'auteur.'
14. '[...] le bégaiement et le radotage qui triomphent, prônés par des vedettes auto-satisfaites et narcissiques, leur agents qui les encouragent, et leur distributeurs qui dans leur calculs à courte-vue y trouvent leur compte.'
15. 'Nulle surprise alors, qu'on baigne aujourd'hui dans un retour aux valeurs artisanales du travail bien fait, du propre, du fini. Qu'on ait une teller répugnance du signifié qu'on en soit – sans vergogne – à nous vanter les mérites des publicités et de leurs réalisateurs. Dès lors qu'on ne croit en rien, il n'y a plus que la forme qui demeure. Objet de tous les soins elle devient une fin en soi. On sent très bien aujourd'hui le scénario à nouveau se renfermer sur lui-même. On sent le retour des valeurs de technique, d'achèvement. Et du mépris de soi qui les accompagnent.'
16. On the situation of the European film industry and the debates about Europe's inability to counteract Hollywood's monopoly in the mainstream market, see the introduction and, among others, Ilott (1996), Jäckel (2003), and Puttnam (1997).
17. On this, see my comment about Assayas's compliance with Michel Marie's definition of the *nouvelle vague* film author's style and methods at the beginning of this chapter.
18. François Mauriac is one of France's most famous twentieth-century writers, a member of the Académie Française and winner of the 1952 Nobel Prize in literature. His novels, inspired by his idiosyncratic Catholicism, include *Thérèse Desqueyroux* (1927) and *Le noeud de vipères* (1932). Julien Green, a writer born in Paris to American parents, who lived most of his life in France, specialized in sober psychological novels dealing with death and violence, including *Léviathan-The Dark Journey* (1929) and *The Distant Lands* (1987). Jacques Chardonne, the author of some 50 novels focusing mainly on romantic relationships, wrote, besides the aforementioned *Les destinées sentimentales* (1934), *Claire* (1931), *L'Amour c'est beaucoup plus que l'amour* (1937), and *Romanesque* (1938). After World War II his fortunes declined, due to the scandal surrounding his support of Nazism and his right-wing political position. Assayas has talked about Chardonne and his work in several interviews, especially those made at the time of *Les destinées sentimentales'* theatrical release.
19. Several film critics remarked on the modern sensibility of the film, particularly *Cahiers du Cinéma*, which devoted a long dossier to the film upon its release. Among the articles published in this dossier,

see Bouquet (1999) and Assayas's interview with some of the magazine's film critics and editors (Assayas 1999a).

20. It is worth noting that *figure* in French means both the face and the contours of the body.

21. 'L'Eau froide a, tout d'un coup, établi un lien avec cet adolescent-là. J'ai alors compris que c'était à travers cette personne que se trouvait la clé de ce que je pouvais faire de mieux au cinéma. Comme dans la vie, d'ailleurs. A partir de là, j'ai réussi à introduire une forme de liberté, une sorte d'insouciance dans mon cinéma. Et à travers cette légèreté et cette insouciance, à être au coeur d'une pratique de l'art plus valable.'

22. Cheung, who had previously starred in Assayas's *Irma Vep*, was Assayas's companion and wife for some years. She won the Best Actress Award at the 2004 Cannes Film Festival for her role in *Clean*.

23. 'Ce monde est immense et complexe, le récit traverse quatre pays (Canada-France-Angleterre-États-Unis), deux continents et un océan, il convoque évidemment, de part de la seule présence de Maggie Cheung, l'horizon asiatique, fait en sorte qu'on parle aussi chinois. Ce monde-là est cosmopolite sans paraître y songer, c'est à la mesure de son miroitement infini que prend sens le caractère rectiligne de la trajectoire d'Emily.' The phrasing has been changed from the French version to preserve the meaning of the original text.

24. 'Le spectacle, compris dans sa totalité, est à la fois le résultat et le projet du monde de production existant. Il n'est pas un supplément au monde réel, sa décoration surajoutée. Il est le coeur de l'irréalisme de la société réelle. Sous toutes ses formes particulières, information ou propagande, publicité ou consommation directe de divertissements, le spectacle constitue le *modèle* présent de la vie socialement dominante.' [Italics in original.] The book was subsequently published in several different editions; the latest came from Gallimard in 1992 and featured a foreword by Debord, in which the author claims that he had not felt that it was opportune to revise the original text because his critical theory 'did not need any changes; so long as the general conditions of the long historical period that this theory has been the first to define with exactitude will not have been destroyed' (Debord 1992: 7, my translation).

25. In the same interview, Assayas condemns conventional dramaturgy as 'part of today's alienation, be it in independent cinema or Hollywood cinema' (Peranson 2003: 34). To be sure, he puts great importance on the writing phase of his work and considers making films a natural continuation of writing about them.

26. On the collaboration between Assayas and Sonic Youth in the making of *Demonlover*'s soundtrack, see, among others, Piégay, Baptiste. Sonic Youth dialogue avec Olivier Assayas. *Cahiers du Cinéma*, 564 (janvier 2002): 28–29; and Howard Hampton's commentary on *Demonlover*'s soundtrack, 'Demonlover,' which appeared in the 'Sound and Vision' section of *Film Comment*, 39/5 (Sept/Oct 2003): 16.

27. '*Demonlover* est à la fois le film du vertige du même et celui de la singularité la plus exacte. C'est en ce sens qu'il est proprement réaliste, car être réaliste aujourd'hui, ce n'est plus seulement reproduire l'impression plus ou moins diffuse de la réalité physique ou de la vie telle qu'elle va mais pénetrer de l'intérieur dans un no man's land de fuseaux horaires, de projections diffuses, d'images mentales, de perspectives truquées, d'espaces deconnectés, de trouées fantomatiques.'

References

Assayas, O. 1980a. SPFX news (1ère partie): ou situation du cinéma de science-fiction envisagé en tant que secteur de pointe. *Cahiers du Cinéma*, 315: 19–27, septembre.

—. 1980b. SPFX news (2ème partie): ou situation du cinéma de science-fiction envisagé en tant que secteur de pointe. *Cahiers du Cinéma*, 316: 36–40, octobre.

—. 1980c. SPFX news (3ème partie): ou situation du cinéma de science-fiction envisagé en tant que secteur de pointe. *Cahiers du Cinéma*, 317: 22–33, novembre.

—. 1980d. SPFX news (suite et fin): ou situation du cinéma de science-fiction envisagé en tant que secteur de pointe. *Cahiers du Cinéma*, 318: 34–40, décembre.

—. 1981a. Jean-Pierre Mocky: le malentendu. *Cahiers du Cinéma. Situation du cinéma français I*, 323–324: 95, mai.

—. 1981b. George Lucas: un cinéma conceptuel. *Cahiers du Cinéma*, 328: 24–26, octobre.

—. et al. 1982a. *Cahiers du Cinéma. Made in USA*, 334–335: avril.

—. 1982b. Un auteur-artisan. *Cahiers du Cinéma*, 336: 30;32, mai.

—. 1982c. Entretien avec Jean-Pierre Mocky. *Cahiers du Cinéma*, 336: 31;33, mai.

—. LE PÉRON, S. and TOUBIANA, S. 1982d. Entretien avec John Carpenter. *Cahiers du cinéma*, 339: 15–23, septembre.

—. 1983a. Sur une politique. *Cahiers du Cinéma. Cinéma d'auteur: la côte d'alerte*, 353: 22–25, novembre.

—. 1983b. Eastwood in the country. *Cahiers du Cinéma. Cinéma d'auteur: la côte d'alerte*, 353: 56–57, novembre.

—. and TESSON, C. 1984. Hong Kong Cinema. Paris: *Cahiers du Cinéma*, 360–361, septembre.

—. and Tesson, C. 1985. Le sourire "off": entretien avec Clint Eastwood. *Cahiers du Cinéma*, 368: 22–29, février.

—. 1985. Du scénario achevé au scénario ouvert. *Cahiers du Cinéma*, 371–2: 7–8, mai.

—. 1986. L'émotion pure: entretien avec Olivier Assayas. *Cahiers du Cinéma*, 389: 8–11, novembre.

—. and Björkman, S. 1990. *Conversations avec Bergman*. Paris: Cahiers du cinéma.

—. 1999a. Le passé devait trouver sa place au coeur de ma vision du cinéma. Entretien avec Olivier Assayas. *Cahiers du Cinéma*, 548: 35–41.

—. 1999b. *Fin août, début septembre*. Paris: Petite bibliothèque des Cahiers du cinéma.

—. 1999c. *Kenneth Anger: vraie et fausse magie au cinéma*. Paris: Cahiers du cinéma, Collection Auteurs.

—. and Fieschi, J. 2000. *Les destinées sentimentales*. Scénario d'après le roman de Jacques Chardonne. Paris: Petite bibliothèque des Cahiers du cinéma.

—. 2001. Cassavetes, Posthumously. (*In* Charity, T. (ed.). *John Cassavetes: Lifeworks*. London: Omnibus Press, pp. 199–203.)

—. 2003. Préface. (*In* Jousse, T. *Pendant les travaux, le cinéma reste ouvert*. Paris: Cahiers du cinéma.)

—. 2004. Personal interview. Paris: 20 and 29 December.

—. 2005a. 'Pour moi, la vérité est dans le geste.' Interview with Olivier Assayas by Thomas Sotinel. *Le Monde*. [Online]. Available: http://www.lemonde.fr/cgibin/achats/acheter.cgi?offre=archives&type_item=art_arch_30j&objet_id=911806.

—. 2005b. *Une adolescence dans l'après-mai. Lettre à Alice Debord*. Paris: Cahiers du cinéma.

Bordwell, D. and Thompson, K. 2006. Lessons from Babel. (*In David Bordwell's Website on Cinema*. [Online.] Available: http://www.davidbordwell.net/blog/?p=147).

Bouquet, S. 1999. Les Temps modernes. *Cahiers du Cinéma*, 548: 32–34.

Chollet, L. 2004. *Les situationnistes: l'utopie incarnée*. Paris: Gallimard.

Darke, C. 1993. Rupture, Continuity and Diversification: *Cahiers du Cinéma* in the 1980s. *Screen*, 34 (Winter): 362–79.

De Baecque, A. 1991. *Histoire d'une revue. Tome 1: Les Cahiers à l'assault du cinéma: 1951–1959*. Paris: Cahiers du cinéma.

—. 2003. *La Cinéphilie: Invention d'un regard, histoire d'une culture. 1944–1968*. Paris: Fayard.

Debord, G. 1992. *La Société du spectacle*. Paris: Gallimard.

Deleuze, G. 1981. *Francis Bacon: logique de la sensation* (2 vols.). Paris: Editions du Seuil.

—. 1989. *Cinema 2: The Time Image*. [1985]. Tomlinson, H. and Galeta, R. (trans). Minneapolis: University of Minnesota Press.

Dufrenne, M. and Formaggio, D. 1981. *Tratto di estetica. Volume 1*. Milano: Mondadori.

Fornara, B. and Signorelli, A. (eds). 1995. *Olivier Assayas*. Bergamo Film Meeting '95 (exhibition catalogue).

Frodon, J-M. 2004. Où vas-tu, Emily? *Cahiers du Cinéma*, 593 (septembre): 22–24.

Hayward, S. 1993a. *French National Cinema*. London: Routledge.

—. and Vincendeau, G. (eds). 1990. *French Film: Texts and Contexts*. London: Routledge.

Ilott, T. 1996. *Budgets and Markets: A Study of the Budgeting of European Film*. London and New York: Routledge.

Jäckel, A. 2003. *European Film Industries*. London: BFI.

Jones, K. 1996. Tangled Up in Blue: The Cinema of Olivier Assayas-French Film Director. *Film Comment*, 32.1 (January): 50–58.

Jousse, T. 2003. *Pendant les travaux, le cinéma reste ouvert*. Paris: Cahiers du cinéma.

Lyotard, J-F. 1971. *Discours, figure*. Paris: Klincksieck.

Marie, M. 1998. *La Nouvelle Vague: une école artistique*. Paris: Nathan Université.

Maule, R. 2003. The Multiple Commitments of the Film Author. (*In* ANTONINI, A. (ed.) *Il film e i suoi multipli/Film and its Multiples*. Udine: Forum, pp. 241–50.)

Mazdon, L. (ed.) 2001. *France on Film: Reflections on Popular French Cinema*. London: Wallflower.

McCabe, C. 1985. *Theoretical Essays: Film, Linguistics, Literature*. Manchester: Manchester University Press.

Merleau-Ponty, M. 1964. *L'oeil et l'esprit*. Paris: Gallimard.

Peranson, M. 2003. Reattaching the Broken Thread: Olivier Assayas on Film-making and Film Theory. *Cinema Scope*, 14 (Spring): 30–39.

Powrie, P. (ed.). 1997. *French Cinema in the 1980s: Nostalgia and the Crisis of Masculinity*. Oxford: Clarendon Press.

—. 1999. *French Cinema in the 1990s: Continuity and Difference*. Oxford: Oxford University Press.

Puttnam, D. 1997. *The Undeclared War: The Struggle of the World's Film Industry*. London: Harper Collins.

Ricoeur, P. 1977. *The Rule of Metaphor: Multi-disciplinary Studies of the Creation of Meaning in Language*. [1975]. Czerny, R., McLaughlin, K. and Costello, J. (trans). Toronto and Buffalo: University of Toronto Press.

Rodowick, D. N. 1997. *Gilles Deleuze's Time Machine*. Durham and London: Duke University Press.

—. 2001. *Reading the Figural, or, Philosophy after the New Media*. Durham & London: Duke University Press.

Romney, J. 2004. Stop Making Sense. *Sight & Sound*. [Online.] Available: http://www.bfi.org.uk/sightandsound/feature/238/.

Tarr, C. and Rollet, B. 2001. *Cinema and the Second Sex: Women's Film-making in France in the 1980s and 1990s*. New York and London: Continuum.

Tesson, C., Paquot, C. and Roger Garcia, R. (eds). 2001. *L'Asie à Hollywood*. Paris: Cahiers du cinema/ Festival International du Film de Locarno.

Truffaut, F. 1954. Une certaine tendance du cinéma français. Cahiers du Cinéma, 31: 15–28, janvier.

Vincendeau, G. (ed.). 1995. *Encyclopedia of European Cinema*. New York: Facts on Life.

—. 1996. *The Companion to French Cinema*. London: Cassell.

—. 1998. Issues in European Cinema. (*In* Hill, J. and Church Gibson P. (eds). *The Oxford Guide to Film Studies*. Oxford: Oxford University Press, pp. 440–48.)

PART TWO: THE FILM AUTHOR IN THE NEW AUDIO-VISUAL SYSTEM

4

FOR AN IMPURE CINEMA: GABRIELE SALVATORES AND THE HYBRID NATURE OF FILM AUTHORSHIP IN CONTEMPORARY ITALIAN CINEMA

Italian film critics and theorists usually situate Gabriele Salvatores within the framework of Italy's 'nuovo cinema' (new cinema), an expression that refers to Italy's post-New Wave generation of film-makers who made their débuts during the 1980s and the 1990s. The expression denotes less a coherent movement than a constellation of cinematic practices spread across independent and state-funded modes of production, whose only common trait is a minimalist approach to film-making (Brunetta 1998; Marrone 1999a; Micciché 1998; Montini 1988b; Sesti 1994 and 1996; Zagarrio 1998a).[1] Typical aspects of the films produced within the nuovo cinema are small budgets, low-key aesthetics, and simple narratives featuring contemporary contexts and characters, yet devoid of any socio-political critique. In her introduction to a 1999 special issue of the Italian literary journal Annali d'Italianistica devoted to this film trend, Gaetana Marrone notes that the absence of stylistic affiliations with previous cinematic traditions and the political disengagement of the nuovo cinema disoriented Italian film critics and by and large provoked their dismissal of this new generation of film-makers (Marrone 1999b: 7–8).[2] This reaction, she notes, was 'a direct consequence, and a further manifestation, of the hiatus between author and critic that will definitively change the dynamic of their relationship in contemporary Italian cinema (ibid.: 8, my translation).[3]

Undeniably, Salvatores's profile as a film director is quite extraneous to a national model of authorship over-determined by the prestigious tradition of Italy's great neorealist and post-war film directors and internationally identified with the intellectual and aesthetic sophistication of New Wave film-makers such as, among others, Marco Bellocchio, Bernardo Bertolucci, Liliana Cavani, Pier Paolo Pasolini, and the Taviani brothers. His preference in fact goes to popular film genres and hybrid film forms and techniques, also reproducing other audio-visual media's aesthetics. On his side, Salvatores deliberately rejects Italy's authorial tradition (which he considers heavily influenced by the French model of the *nouvelle vague* auteur) because anchored in the idea of the film director as an individual creator, responsible for both writing and directing a film (Salvatores 2005). Quite the opposite, Salvatores likes to work in team and has a particularly carefree attitude vis-à-vis screenwriting credits. While during the past decade he has been partaking more and more in the writing process of his films and even single-authored a script, he mainly relies on professional screenwriters and throughout his career has directed several adaptations from theatrical and literary works.[4]

Salvatores's predilection for hybrid and popular forms is not just a pointer to the *nuovo cinema*'s refusal of the aesthetic and technical criteria set by Italy's illustrious film tradition or departure from the cultural and political engagement of the New Wave film authors: it advocates a necessary amendment of the authorial discourse typically found in the critical reception and the scholarly discussion of European cinema. From this perspective, Salvatores's position vis-à-vis film authorship helps reconsider a fundamental principle of the *politique des auteurs* and in auteur theory, which however was never been fully applied to European cinema: the intention to abolish pre-established hierarchies between arts, genres, and cinematic modes. Undeniably, this purpose informed the *politique des auteurs*'s take on French cinema and contributed to emancipate the national film production from its cultural subordination to literary and theatrical texts and canons, especially through the figure of the *nouvelle vague* auteur. Yet auteur-oriented film criticism and scholars theorized the film author mainly within the framework of Hollywood as the mainstream cinema *par excellence*, while they rarely discussed the auteur within the framework of Europe's mainstream film production.

As Salvatores and the entire generation of Italian and Western European film directors considered in this book demonstrate, the necessity of addressing European film authorship within a large framework of film modes and aesthetic parameters became all the more pressing with the advent of the new audio-visual system. In the case of Italy, the authorial individuality of the *nuovo cinema* film directors is the result of a dialectic rapport established between experimentalism and production strategies within an audio-visual system characterized by the decline of the national film industry and the monopoly of Hollywood films in the domestic film market. Italian film-maker and renown film author Liliana Cavani makes this point in an interview with Gaetana Marrone published in the aforementioned issue of *Annali d'Italianistica* on Italy's *nuovo cinema* (Cavani 1999: 247–51). Marrone further comments on Cavani's analysis as follows:

> [...] the new authors found themselves having to eliminate all the mediations that the fact of belonging to Cinecittà [the production studios based in Rome, headquarters of the Italian film industry] historically involved. In acknowledgement of their own alterity vis-à-vis a school derivation, they declared their specificity in being an orphan generation, 'lost in the dark' (Marrone 1999b: 9, my translation).[5]

The overall purpose here is not to refashion the romantic model of the auteur as a film director who establishes her/his personality against the anonymity of industrial strategies of film production and reception. Instead, the intention is to demonstrate that the new generation of film directors emerged in Italy since the 1980s allows for a reconsideration of one of the most important propositions of the *politique des auteurs*: to assess cinema's aesthetic values regardless of preconceived ideas about high art and to break the ancillary rapport of films with canonic texts and forms derived from literature and theatre.

Originally a stage director in one of the most prolific and innovative companies specialized in experimental theatre, Gabriele Salvatores brought many of the aesthetic and technical features (markedly trans-disciplinary) adopted in this early phase of his professional career to cinema, to which he exclusively devoted himself starting from the late 1980s. Furthermore, some of his films are theatrical or literary adaptations or else use audio-visual media (including the Super 8 millimeter camera and projector, the videogame, the videotape, and television) as narrative elements, mimicking their aesthetics though cinematographic processes, digital techniques, or editing solutions.[6] In an article published in an anthology on 1980s Italian cinema, Francesco Casetti describes Salvatores's poetics as an example of 'impure cinema' (Casetti 1998). The Italian film scholar uses a term coined by André Bazin in his article 'Pour un cinéma impur: défense de l'adaptation,' originally written in 1951, in which Bazin argues that adaptation enables cinema and the other arts (especially literature and theatre) to reciprocally enhance one another (1971).[7] Impure does not have a negative or diminishing connotation, quite the opposite: as Bazin specifies in the closing paragraph of his essay, cinema, now matured into an autonomous form of expression, is rather 'adding a new dimension that the arts had

Gabriele Salvatores (on the left) and his crew

gradually lost from the time of the Reformation on: namely a public' (1971: 75). Bazin's concept of impure cinema perfectly applies to Salvatores's approach to film-making, open to inter-textual and trans-medial exchanges and experimentations, as well as cross-fertilizations among different forms and genres within literature, theatre, and film, and conceived for a larger audience than the one generally connected with author cinema.

Salvatores's penchant for an unconventional aesthetic drawing on other art disciplines and audio-visual media also resonates with another definition of cinema, rarely used in relation to authorship: that of 'imperfect cinema.' This expression appears in Cuban film-maker and theorist Julio García Espinosa's foundational essay titled 'Por un cine imperfecto,' originally published in 1969 (Espinosa 2000). In his essay, Espinosa rejects stylistic perfection and elitist forms and argues that imperfect cinema is the goal of Latin American revolutionary cinema (ibid.: 287–88: 291–92).[8] As with Espinosa, Salvatores views cinema as an artistic activity with a social purpose, for which inspiration is to be found in real life, and of which the product is derived from a popular conception of art (Espinosa 2000). Also like Espinosa, Salvatores dismisses the authorial role of film directors and endorses a film-making method founded on a collaborative, inter-disciplinary work (ibid.). This affinity partly stems from Salvatores's ideological perspective: that of a left-wing film-maker committed to resisting cultural hegemony and intellectual elitism. Additionally, Salvatores transposed to his film-making practice the idea of popular and collective art that he had cultivated during the years spent as a stage director at the independent theatre collective based in Milan 'Il Teatro dell'Elfo' ('The Elf Theatre') during the 1970s and 1980s. Salvatores comments on this transition as follows:

> I grew up in an epoch in which people's contributions were not only accepted but even requested and in which we did not believe that a work was owned by a single person. And I still strongly believe this with respect to cinema: how can you not consider the editor as an author? And the screenwriter? And the actors? I offer this premise to say that I don't feel a film for which I have not written the screenplay is any less mine (Malavasi 2005: 12–13, my translation).[9]

From this perspective, his impure cinema is also, and foremost, a model of imperfect cinema.

To be sure, Salvatores still claims authorial signature regarding his role as a film-maker, a position that differentiates his work in theatre from his work in film: the former is a facilitator of dialogue between actors and audiences, the latter organizes the work of the actors through aesthetic choices (Salvatores 2005). Similarly, when discussing his films in interviews, he often embraces quite a traditional auteur-oriented discourse, in the sense that he describes not just aesthetic and technical solutions, but also recurring motifs in his work as the products of personal and intentional decisions. Nevertheless, he makes no claims about individual creativity since he recognizes that film-making is always a collaborative effort (Salvatores 2005). Conversely, Salvatores's statements about collaborative authorship should not be mistaken for a demagogic or opportunistic declaration from one of the most financially successful among the Italian film-makers of the *nuovo cinema* generation, whose films are mainly promoted in relation to his name, in Italy and abroad [where he gained some notoriety since he won an

Academy Award for his film *Mediterraneo* in 1992]. Salvatores is fully aware that cinema is also an industry and that realizing one's artistic goals is always contingent upon financial support and commercial viability (ibid.). Rather, the insistence on the popular and communal spirit of his film-making approach is consistent with the cultural politics that informed his career in the theatre (ibid.). For this reason, the following examination of his career and filmic corpus will refer to Salvatores's authorship less in terms of an individual than of a collaborative contribution to an impure and imperfect cinematic practice.

Praise of the liminal: Salvatores's impure cinema

Dudley Andrew establishes a direct link between André Bazin's essay on impure cinema, as well as other articles on adaptation that the French critic wrote in the early 1950s and were mainly published in the early issues of *Cahiers du Cinéma*, and the *politique des auteurs*, launched in those years in the same film magazine (Andrew 1990: 190). Appropriately so, Andrew notes that the young film critics who launched this policy applied Bazin's ideas in their own ways, pointing out how Bazin notoriously had 'major reservations about this highly romanticized view of film creation as issuing from a single and privileged consciousness' (Andrew 1990: 190). Yet Andrew also underlines that Bazin's thoughts on mixed cinema and adaptation were quite in line with the *Jeunes Turcs*' attack on the institutional cinema represented by France's 'Tradition of Quality,' vehemently expressed by François Truffaut in his 1954 article 'Une certaine tendance du cinéma français' (Andrew 1990: 201–05). The *politique des auteurs* gave authorial credential to the film director with the purpose to isolate a distinctive expertise and an individual imprint in the collective and industrial practices involved in film-making. At the same time, the figure of the film director as auteur allowed these film critics to emancipate cinema (French cinema in particular) from authorial models derived from other arts (literature and theatre above all). In this respect, the *politique des auteurs* and auteur-theory put in terms of individual signature what Bazin in his essay on impure cinema appreciated as a new direction in the evolution of film aesthetic.

According to Bazin, cinema had then just entered a phase of maturity, of which the idea of impure cinema foreshadowed the full accomplishment: in this new era of cinema's history, films were finally recognized for their intrinsic qualities, and filmic adaptations established a truly equal exchange with the other arts (Bazin 1971: 74–75).Andrew stresses this point, specifying that Bazin's evolutionary view of film history was grounded on the conviction that cinema originated and developed as a medium out of two sets of historically determined circumstances: on the one hand, the aesthetic and artistic impulse toward realism; on the other hand, the industrial and sociological framework of commerce and public entertainment (Andrew 1990: 174–75). [Andrew also remarks that Bazin inexplicably overlooks the role of technology in his account (1990: 175)]. As Andrew correctly underlines, the underlying thread that links Bazin and Alexandre Astruc's image of the '*caméra stylo*' to the notion of auteur is the idea and 'that the cinéaste can at least be considered the equivalent of the novelist, letting his style be dictated by the necessity of his material and his personal attitude toward that material' (Andrew 1990: 181). In the closing paragraph of Bazin's essay on impure cinema the *caméra stylo* lurkes beneath the suggestion that '[t]he time of resurgence of a cinema newly independent of novel and theatre will return. But it may be then because *novels will be written directly onto film*' (Bazin 1971: 75).[10]

As this chapter and the discussion of authorship in this book offer, the hybrid thread informing the notion of auteur cinema (across high and popular art, romantic, bourgeois aesthetics and industrial, mass consumer culture), liberally developed from Bazin's idea of impure cinema, should be reinvested in the consideration of the European film author as a sociology-of-production constituted outside of institutional systems and canonic forms of cultural production and reception.

Francesco Casetti makes reference to the three characteristics of impure cinema appraised by Bazin, which he finds in Salvatores's early cinematic works. The first is theatrical inspiration, with a particular emphasis on the adaptations of his first two films from plays, both of which Salvatores had previously directed on stage. The second is stylistic heterogeneity, drawing from different media. The third is a reliance on extra-cinematic elements informing the actors' performance styles, in line with Bazin's conception of the historical relativity of the work of art (Casetti 1998: 156–63). This framework is useful for thinking not only about Salvatores's early films, but also for illuminating his entire oeuvre. Casetti's first postulate regarding the theatrical origins of Salvatores's works in the 1980s, illustrates Bazin's polemic quite clearly (1998: 156–59). For most of the 1980s, Salvatores, in fact, primarily worked as a stage director and made his first foray into cinema when he was still involved full time in this capacity. Originally from Naples, he moved to Milan as a teenager. After high school, he attended the Accademia del Piccolo Teatro, one of Italy's most prestigious theatre schools. The school was affiliated with Il Piccolo Teatro ('The Piccolo Theatre'), Italy's foremost residential theatre company, which at the time was under the directorship of Giorgio Strehler, who had a worldwide reputation as one of the greatest stage directors of the post-war period. In 1973, Salvatores graduated from the Accademia del Piccolo Teatro and he, along with a group of friends, founded the aforementioned experimental theatre company Teatro dell'Elfo.

The influences of theatre, as well as of different artistic forms and genres on Salvatores's cinematic works are numerous. His first two films were based on two plays that he had already directed for the stage. Italian television networks commissioned both films. An executive of the state network channel Rai Due asked Salvatores to direct a film version of Sogno di una notte d'estate after having seen the play at the Teatro dell'Elfo. The deal took place during a time when Italy's state television was becoming increasingly involved in film production. The play, itself a liberal stage adaptation of William Shakespeare's A Midsummer Night's Dream, was Salvatores's most successful stage production, running for three consecutive years. Salvatores's cinematic début (1983) took the same title as the Italian play. He decided to devote himself to the cinema while making his second film, Kamikazen-Ultima notte a Milano/Kamikazen, Last Night in Milan (1987), co-produced by Reteitalia, a film and television production company owned by Italy's former prime minister, Silvio Berlusconi and Salvatores's newly founded production company Colorado Noir. The film was an adaptation of Comedians, a 1975 play by British playwright Trevor Griffith. Salvatores had previously directed two different stage versions of the work. He helmed the first production in 1985 for the Teatro della Versiliana in Marina di Petrasanta, Tuscany and directed the second version for his own company in 1987, the same year that he made his filmic adaptation. For the film adaptation, he worked with screenwriter Enzo Monteleone and two other collaborators.

During his sixteen-year tenure at Teatro dell'Elfo, Salvatores became an expert in what would later become a staple of his film-making practice: the blending of elements and techniques from various artistic traditions and media. As Salvatores himself stresses, his theatrical pieces were heavily indebted to cinema, especially US independent cinema, and occasionally included cinematic effects and filmic references.[11] Teatro dell'Elfo specialized in free adaptations of popular and classic texts, including, besides the aforementioned texts, One Thousand and One Nights, The Odyssey, Petronio's Satyricon, Ben Johnson's Volpone, Bram Stoker's Dracula, George Büchner's Woyzek, and Carlo Collodi's children's classic Pinocchio. The adaptations frequently involved transposing original stories onto contemporary situations and infusing them with political commentary via filmic and literary intertexts. In Kamikazen, for instance, Salvatores transformed the self-reflexive content of the original text into a bitter portrayal of the entertainment industry. He also re-located the play's setting from Manchester to Milan in order to highlight Italy's rich theatre culture. The featured setting, actors and comedians were representative of the familiar theatrical milieu in which Salvatores was involved.

Salvatores's preference for heterogeneous sources and techniques is evident in the screen adaptation of Sogno di una notte d'estate (1983), which blends not only cinema and theatre, but also integrates dance and rock music (one of the film's protagonists is the famous Italian rock star Gianna Nannini). The film borrows heavily from the rock musical genre and, particularly, the midnight cult movie The Rocky Horror Picture Show (Jim Sharman 1975). The hybrid aesthetic simultaneously recalls filmed theatre, music videos, and realist comedy. Music was Salvatores's first passion; in his early twenties, he played in several rock bands (Malavasi 2005: 5). In the second half of the 1980s, he directed three lyric operas: La gatta inglese/The English Cat (Edward Bond, 1982) in 1986; Cirano/Cyrano de Bergerac (Edmond Rostand, 1897) in 1987; and La figlia del reggimento/The Daughter of the Regiment (Gaetano Donizzetti, 1840) in 1989. Sogno di una notte d'estate, which premiered at the 1983 Venice Film Festival in a section dedicated to young Italian film-makers, had a mixed critical reception and a poor box office run. Its ambiguous style and technical 'mistakes' not only put off many film critics but also kept domestic audiences away from theatrical screenings. These technical imperfections – discontinuous framing and editing, inconsistent lighting – were partly voluntary and partly due to the fact that Salvatores was still mostly unfamiliar with the cinematic medium.

Luca Malavasi suggests that Sogno di una notte d'estate should be considered less Salvatores's cinematic début than a logical extension of his theatrical work. He states that the film is 'a contamination experiment conducted from within theatre, which explores the existential possibilities offered by the cinematic medium' (2005: 20, my translation).[12] As such, he classifies Kamikazen as Salvatores's first film, but with a similar prefatory comment. He claims that the motivation behind making Kamikazen was to broaden Salvatores's theatrical audience by reaching more people (ibid.: 20). Significantly, Salvatores's alleged intention to use cinema to open up his work to a larger audience finds an echo in Bazin's above quoted closing remarks on impure cinema, in which he claims that cinema helps to make theatre and literature more accessible, rather than being in competition with these artistic forms (1971: 75).

Many film critics consider the films released between *Marrakech Express* (1989) and *Puerto Escondido* (1992) as the most consistent in Salvatores's oeuvre because they are interconnected by similar themes, narrative structures, stylistic solutions, generic formulations, and production methods. From a thematic point of view, the most prevalent motif in these films is that of the 'fuga' ('escape'). The concept of escape, which is illustrated in the films by the protagonists' trips to exotic locations, functions as a metaphorical response to the general discontent that people experience in contemporary society. Film critics also identify the nuances of male friendship as a principal concern in Salvatores's work of this period. Based on Salvatores's own experiences, the films focus on the complacency, disillusionment, and social mal-adjustment of thirty-something men living in the wake of the ideological activism of the 1960s and the social protest movements of the 1970s.[13]

In *Marrakech Express*, four former best friends who had lived together during the 1977 Italian student protests – a movement prevalent in northern urban areas (Milan above all) and in many universities in northern and central Italy[14] – get together after ten years apart to rescue another ex-comrade, who is allegedly jailed in Morocco for the possession of hashish. The film's narrative concentrates on the adventurous road trip they take together, in which the four risk their lives and reconsolidate their friendship. The film is a coming-of-age story: the expedition, besides triggering nostalgic memories, forces the characters to come to terms with their differences. The men, now in their thirties, have either conformed to a comfortable, bourgeois lifestyle and mentality or confined themselves at the margins of a society which they refuse (Cedro), having lost the ideals that nourished their student lives. *Turnè* (1990) deals with the same issues, but from within a world well known to Salvatores, that of the theatre. The narrative features two male friends with very contradictory personalities: both actors, they have undertaken very different career paths, one starring in commercial television series, the struggling to pursue a difficult career on stage. Both are in love with the same woman who, in the end, cannot choose between them. The two men's differences come to a head when they perform together in a touring production of Anton Chekhov's *The Cherry Orchard*. It is during this road trip that the two men, and their common love interest, are forced to reconsider their relationships with one another.

Mediterraneo (1991), the third instalment in the 'escape' series, is a period film set during World War II, yet with an epilogue set in the early 1990s. The narrative follows the bizarre destiny of a small contingency of Italian soldiers who are mistakenly forgotten on a remote Greek island during Mussolini's Balkan campaign of 1940 and 1941. The soldiers end up spending some years there, in complete isolation and unaware of geo-political events. When the company is finally rescued at the end of the war, one of the soldiers decides to stay on the island and another returns there after a short time, disappointed by the direction of change back in Italy. *Puerto Escondido* concludes the series of social comedies and is the third of Salvatores's films set in exotic settings, after *Marrakech Express* and *Mediterraneo*. The film also has a strong connection to the thriller, a genre Salvatores will return to frequently in the subsequent years. The adventure-filled plot, adapted by Enzo Monteleone and Pino Cacucci from Cacucci's eponymous novel, is about a bank executive from Milan who witnesses a murder by a corrupt police inspector and tries to escape danger by moving to Mexico. Resettled in the small sea town of Puerto Escondido, the protagonist finds himself embroiled in a petty drug deal devised by an Italian couple living there. In the end, the man lands in jail, along with his accomplices and the murderous inspector, who had tracked him down in order to kill him and instead gave up this plan to start a new life with a local woman.

As Casetti noted in his article, if we consider these films as generic comedies, we should nevertheless think of them as 'open containers' of formulaic variants (1998: 160). Indeed, Salvatores's social comedies of the 1980s and early 1990s (and even earlier, in *Kamikazen*) mix the tones and narrative development typical of the Italian comedy with those of the stand-up act or stage monologue. These two forms of comedy performance were familiar to most of the actors featured in his early films since many of them had either worked with Salvatores in the Teatro dell'Elfo or had come from similar theatrical backgrounds. His films also depart from the conventions of Italian comedy and drama by adopting elements of the western (*Marrakech Express*), the road movie (all of them), the adventure film (*Marrakech Express, Mediterraneo*), the romantic comedy (all of them), and the thriller (*Puerto Escondido*). Malavasi also stresses Salvatores's propensity for generic fluctuation in his close textual analyses of Salvatores's later works, from the mid-1990s to 2005. In this respect, the notion of impure cinema best defines Salvatores's work during the past ten years; these films are characterized by a pronounced alternation and recombination of various genres, styles, and techniques.

Film critics attribute the thematic and stylistic heterogeneity of Salvatores's films to his 'restless' temperament as an artist. With only a few exceptions, they view his films as either technical failures or refer to them pejoratively as 'essays' whose innovative edge does not compensate for their lack of quality. On his end, Salvatores disagrees with the critics' classification of his early comedies within a coherent corpus. In a recent interview with Malavasi, he noted that the apparent continuity of these films is less a result of directorial intention than of specific production circumstances (Malavasi 2005: 7–8). Based on Salvatores's claim, it is important to keep in mind that these films are all produced collaboratively and, therefore, not simply the result of a unified, individual artistic vision. Furthermore, Salvatores makes no deliberate efforts to pursue aesthetic or thematic continuity. Instead, he views his theatrical and cinematic career as a 'work-in-progress' united by one very specific intention: to tell stories that call attention to the complexity of reality and the meaning of representation (Salvatores 2005). In this respect, his position parallels Bazin's assertions that not only is cinema a medium in which various arts may converge, but also that art *should* be open to other art forms rather than 'defend itself' against external influences (Bazin 1971: 75).

As Salvatores remarked in a recent interview, at the end of the 'escape' cycle, dissatisfied with the outcome of *Puerto Escondido* and eager to move away from his usual themes and formulas, he decided at this point to embark on a more diversified type of film-making (Salvatores 2005). Since the mid-1990s his films deal with more existential and philosophical themes, tackling the transformation of Italy's post-industrial and cosmopolitan society and the economic and cultural phenomenon of globalization. Concomitantly, they resort a more explicitly formulaic style, including heavily coded genres as science fiction (in *Nirvana*) and film noir (in *Quo vadis, baby?* (2005)), as well as to generic hybridization such as the fusing of social drama with the

Quo vadis, baby?: Giorgia

western in *Sud* (1994) or with the thriller in *Io non ho paura/I'm Not Scared* (2003). Salvatores's most recent production also features new film-making techniques, frequently pillaging from the aesthetics and the forms of other media.[15] Finally, another new trait prominent in the most recent part of Salvatores's filmic corpus is the less linear narrative and filmic style. On a personal level, Salvatores acknowledges a shift in his treatment of narrative and visual development and attributes this change to the influence that the reading of Amitav Ghosh's *The Calcutta Chromosome*, published in 1995, had on him (Malavasi 2005: 103–05). Salvatores tried to adapt this postmodern sci-fi story for the screen, but eventually abandoned the project. Yet the novel was a main source of inspiration for his subsequent film, *Nirvana* (1997), the only screenplay Salvatores wrote entirely by himself.

Sud deploys a number of different camera styles (including the frenetic tracking and dolly shots and fast zooms typical of the hyper-mobile camera), editing techniques (such as fast-motion and music video-style inter-cuts) to invoke the anxiety felt by the characters and the music video

Nirvana: Bombay City

culture in which they are immersed. Music is a very important factor in this film, as in most of Salvatores's work, starting from his early social comedies, where music scores comment on or abridge narrative sections or accompany montage sequences. Oftentimes, the music inserts in these films are well-known pieces from popular Italian songwriters (such as, for instance, Francesco de Gregori's songs in *Marrakesh Express*, which punctuate the salient moments of male bonding in the narrative). *Sud's* musical score, which is comprised of songs from the Italian rap-music genre called 'reggae muffa,' features political lyrics that denounce the marginalization and exploitation of extra-communitarians and workers in the southern regions and invoke an alternative society. *Amnèsia* (2002) weaves three parallel sub-plots about the generation gap between fathers and their children and uses a split-screen framing device to physically express the gap felt between the older and younger generations.[16] To be sure, the split-screen has been around since the very first decades of cinema. However, this technique, only sporadically used in films, has made a remarkable comeback in other audio-visual media, such as videogames and some recent television shows.

Salvatores's impure approach to cinema is best manifest in his most recent films in the use of different genres (particularly film noir) and digital technology, as well as in the film director's involvement, along with his production partner Maurizio Totti, in international co-productions and different artistic forms (literature) and media (television). In the mid-1990s, Salvatores began to experiment with audio-visual media other than film, starting with video (in some of his music videos), and then digital cinema.[17] His excursions into digital technology matured with *Nirvana*, a sci-fi film about virtual reality which employed digital editing and numerous digitally shot scenes, and culminated with the decision to shoot *Quo vadis, baby?*, Salvatores's latest released film, with a high-definition digital camera. The latter project was also the result of his investment in an editorial series of noir novels, Colorado Noir. In 2004, Salvatores and Totti, an independent film producer, sponsored the new series for the Italian press Mondadori, with the assistance of two noir experts, Sandrone Danzieri and Giorgio Gosetti. One of the main purposes for inaugurating the series was to monitor potential material for filmic development.

The first fruit of this initiative was *Quo vadis, baby?*. Adapted for the screen from Grazia Verasani's eponymous novel, the film stars, for the first time in Salvatores's career, a female protagonist, Giorgia, a forty-something, single, independent woman who works with her father as a private detective and carries heavy family baggage: her mother died when she was a young girl, a suicide according to the official record, though the woman was actually pushed from a balcony by her jealous husband. Ada, Giorgia's younger sister, who witnessed her mother's murder as a child, led a tumultuous life in perennial conflict with her father before hanging herself in early adulthood. These haunting family traumas resurface due to the arrival of a package containing a series of videotapes that Ada recorded in the weeks preceding her death, in which she addresses Giorgia and tells her about her new life in Rome as an aspiring actress. The film follows Giorgia's attempt to resolve the mystery surrounding her sister's death and which the arrival of the videotapes has prompted her to deal with. Salvatores's experience in making *Quo vadis, baby?* marked two significant changes in his career. First, the film is Salvatores's first foray into digital film-making and it enabled him to explore the aesthetic possibilities of digital technology by creating interesting 'noir' effects and atmospheres. The format also allowed him to re-create the appearances of the different audio-visual media featured in the film: the faded graininess of the 8mm colour home movies through which Giorgia's childhood memories are illustrated; the early 1980s black-and-white, fuzzy video images Ada recorded; and excerpts from VHS transfers of Lang's M. and Bernardo Bertolucci's *Ultimo tango a Parigi/Last Tango in Paris* (1972), the film from which Grazia Verasani took inspiration for the title of her book, using a line with which Paul (Marlon Brando), the protagonist, at one point addresses Jeanne (Maria Schneider), the co-protagonist, and is contained in one of the clips shown in Salvatores's film.

Quo vadis, baby? is also Salvatores's most daring example of impure film-making so far, mixing different media and genres both at the narrative and technical levels. The final sequence of the film is exemplary in this respect. The truth about Ada's death is contained in the last of the videotapes that the woman made, which had remained inside her video camera, which Giorgia recuperates from a friend of her sister. In the end of the film, Giorgia plays the tape which had remained inside the video camera, which contains a recorded version of Fritz Lang's M. (1931), Giorgia distractedly watches the film in her TV monitor while preparing supper, before going out on an impromptu date. The last part of the sequence scene takes place in Giorgia's empty apartment, as the video recording is still playing. The shot shows the TV set at a medium long distance on the right hand side of the shot. As the final credits of M. are running, the image is suddenly interrupted and replaced by Ada's final, tragic video recording, revealing her father's moral responsibility for her death.[18] Film, television, and video, and their respective aesthetics, are mixed in this long sequence, which proposes a *mise en abyme* of genres (the recording of a noir film within a film noir), of formal solutions (the use of the off-screen sound throughout the sequence, which echoes the same technique famously deployed in M.), as well as of representational levels (the video recording of a film and of a home movie played in a TV monitor diegetically inserted in the scene) and address (in the very end, when Giorgia leaves the home, the viewing situation reproduced in the scene draws attention to itself, so that the film spectator becomes interpellated as such, also as an inter-medial spectator).

Finally, filming *Quo vadis, baby?* with an HD video camera permitted Salvatores to produce a small-budget film that could circumvent the limitations of Italy's theatrical distribution system, which, as Salvatores stressed in a recent interview, is monopolized by the media corporation Medusa and Italy's state television network RAI (Malavasi 2005: 9).

Making films, politically: imperfect cinema as popular art

In 'Por un Cine Imperfecto,' considered the manifesto of Cuba's post-revolutionary cinema, Julio García Espinosa proposes an alternative kind of cinema that runs counter to mainstream, art house, and auteur-informed film practices. According to Espinosa, 'imperfect cinema' is a cinema of social struggle. It is a form that draws from reality and aims at intelligence, emotion, and intuition. Its aesthetic strategies do not offer an explanatory or contemplative view of contemporary issues; rather, imperfect cinema submits its hard-hitting and immediate representations of these issues to the audiences' judgments. Its mode of reception rejects film criticism – the traditional mediating apparatus between film and audience – and attempts to establish a direct connection between film and its spectators. As well, its production and distribution methods circumvent the conventional circuits by jettisoning film stars and authors as marketing strategies. For Espinosa, cinema is *not* about the celebration of individuality embodied in the star system or in the figure of the film author; it is about the celebration of plurality and community through the acknowledgment of film-making as a collaborative effort (Espinosa 2000).

Salvatores's conception of cinema and theatre is based on one of the main tenets of Espinosa's essay: the conviction that art is a popular activity, but an activity that must be differentiated from populist or mass art (Salvatores 2005). Salvatores's method also draws upon his own artistic principles developed during his time spent at the Teatro dell'Elfo; that is, to make popular art informed by contemporary society and to be open to new narrative and aesthetic strategies. With his transition from theatre to film in the mid-1980s – a period coincident with the waning of radical ideology stemming from the social unrest of the previous two decades – he transposed the spirit of Teatro dell'Elfo onto cinema by making films that, much like his theatrical productions, were at the same time entertaining and political. His approach to film-making is also wholly aligned with Espinosa's call for a partisan and committed type of cinematic poetics, a poetics that is anti-elitist and whose aim is to dispense with traditional film forms and aesthetics. To be sure, the collective model associated with the radical politics of the 1970s – the system in place at Teatro dell'Elfo – could not have been productively applied to an industrially based activity such as film-making. Yet at Colorado Film, as well as on the sets of Salvatores's films, the Teatro dell'Elfo's practice of co-authoring shows found a new manifestation in the collegial collaboration among film-makers, producers, screenwriters, actors, and technicians.[19] Some film critics in fact attribute the spontaneity and realistic touch of Salvatores's films to the professional and social relationships between the film director and the cast and crew members that work on his films, many of whom are friends in real life.

Salvatores insists that all his films are political, even those that some film critics have dismissed due to their affinities with mainstream genres and spectacular techniques. He believes that cinematic entertainment and aesthetics, if they convey one's beliefs and opinions, are in themselves political (Salvatores 2005). For instance, his social comedies of the 1980s and early 1990s exposed, with humorous bravado, the uncertainties, myths, illusions, and crises experienced by the members of his generation after suffering the loss and disappointment of abandoning the political activism and social ideals of their youth in order to adjust to a conservative and bourgeois society. These comedies proposed sharp ideological critiques of Italian society during the 1980s, an era referred to as *anni del riflusso* ('the reflux years'). The expression 'reflux' refers to the Italian people's ideological withdrawal from radical politics after the failed struggles of the 1960s and 1970s, leading Italians to seek refuge and gratification in the domestic and professional spheres.

The mid-1990s onward reveal, on a thematic and formal level, a more overtly political discourse in Salvatores's films, also conveyed through a self-reflexive technique of representation pointing at the tyrannical and constraining role of audio-visual media in everyday life. *Sud* (1994) tackles the century-old question of social exploitation and political corruption in Italy: the narrative, inspired by a real life event, follows the occupation of a social centre by a group of young people to protest against its foreclosure by local administrative authorities. In real life, this incident galvanized left-wing intellectuals including Salvatores, who wrote – along with Sandro Bernini and Angelo Pasquini – and directed *Sud* on the spur of the moment. *Sud* illustrates the attempt on the part of unemployed people living in a small town near Naples to expose the corruption of a powerful local politician. The young protesters forge a ballot and occupy a polling station. Together, they accidentally kidnap the politician's daughter who was anonymously casting her vote at the time. The film's core narrative follows the long siege and concludes with a special police squad storming into the place and opening fire on the occupants and ends with the protesters being arrested and treated like criminals by the police in full view of the media. The political climate in which *Sud* was released encouraged left-wing film critics to put aside their reservations about the film's narrative and stylistic inconsistencies and support it unconditionally. Positive reviews of the film appeared in most Italian film magazines, as well as in national newspapers.

Nirvana was completed only after a five-year hiatus brought on by the film's complex production circumstances, which included an elaborate set, hundreds of extras, and a very detailed storyboard. *Nirvana* was very expensive according to European standards and featured an international cast that included two French stars: Christopher Lambert (the star of Luc Besson's hit *Subway* (1985)) and Emmanuelle Seigner. Despite its big budget and formulaic format, *Nirvana* is considered one of Salvatores's most political films. The film is set in the near future (2005) in an unspecified megalopolis. Divided along class lines, the city's topography mirrors its social reality, with free and secure affluent areas contrasted against restricted and dangerous poor areas. The worst neighbourhoods, Marrakesh and Bombay City, are rigidly controlled by a violent police agency that uses computerized security and identification systems. This setting is an obvious metaphor for contemporary Italian cities which, at the time, were adjusting to a new global context of labour and the consequent migration from developing countries, changing class and ethnic configurations, and fragmentation of and fluctuation in economic and social networks. Additionally, through the film's futuristic setting and a sub-plot that takes place within the world of a videogame, *Nirvana* also offers a provocative critique of the new media society. The film's narrative pushes the domination of peoples' private and social lives by digital and audio-visual technologies to the extreme, speculating about a phenomenon that had only started to manifest itself in Italy in the mid-1990s.

The political discourse on contemporary Italian reality also runs through Salvatores's next films. *Amnèsia*, which on the surface seems to return to the themes of Salvatores's early comedies, takes a very different direction. The film tells the tale of two male friends going through a mid-life crisis who relocate to Ibiza and get involved in criminal activities. In spite of its familiar premise, instead of focusing on male friendships and middle-class malaise, *Amnèsia* explores the generation gap between fathers and their children through the use of unconventional narrative structures, such as multiple parallel plots, and aesthetic devices, such as the split-screen frame. In *Io non ho paura* Salvatores goes back to Italy's southern question by adapting on screen Nicola Ammaniti's best-selling novel about a diffused activity in organized criminality during the 1970s, the kidnapping of wealthy people from the north of Italy for ransom. Salvatores is presently filming an adaptation from Ammaniti's latest novel, Come Dio comanda (2006), another best-seller. Like the previous film adapted from this writer, Salvatores co-wrote the script with the author. The film is a co-production between Colorado Film and Rai Cinema, the film production branch of Italian television's state networks. Salvatores sets the social thriller in a fairy-tale atmosphere with Shakespearean tones, which recalls his theatrical play *Sogno di una notte d'estate* and filters the *fait divers* through the mythical structures of the western and the Elizabethan play.[20]

More recently, Salvatores's commitment to popular art can be seen in his exploration of the film noir genre. As mentioned above, Colorado Film sponsored a series of noir novels called Colorado Noir in 2004. Known as *gialli* – 'yellow' in Italian, referring to the colour of the paperback editions – the aim of the series was twofold: first, to discover new literary talents and second, to select from those texts published suitable material for filmic adaptations, keeping an option on the most promising novels. Currently, Colorado Film is developing a noir television series, provisionally titled *Black Book*, which will be co-produced with an Italian network through the television branch of Capri Films.[21] Needless to say, Salvatores is a fervent supporter of the noir genre. He feels that the genre's narrative conventions best reveal the uncanny contradictions of everyday life. On the main page of Colorado Noir's website, he states:

> I believe that the noir as a genre was born with a strongly realistic connotation, in those years when realism also had a fundamental importance in politics, while in our days it has transformed itself and is teaming up with deformation, abnormality. Today the noir is the most entitled among the literary genres to tell the reality in which we live, which is highly abnormal, obsessive, illegal: it is a deviant worldview, and for a film-maker the first thing to do is look for a worldview, the 'black worldview'. This is one of the reasons why we enthusiastically founded Colorado Noir. (My translation.)[22]

Salvatores's purpose with Colorado Noir is both to rehabilitate a genre generally dismissed as unrefined within Italian literature and cinema and to propose an alternative approach to realism separate from the dominant traditions of Italian neo-realism and social comedy. The foundation of Colorado Noir responds to Espinosa's exhortation to abolish elitism in artistic practices. Indeed, the mandate of Colorado Noir finds correspondence in folk art, a form depicting people's lived experiences and intended for popular consumption. Salvatores's 'imperfect cinema' has taken yet a new direction through the combination of noir genre conventions and high-definition digital formats in his latest film, *Quo vadis, baby?*. For this project, Salvatores opted to use a digital camera to make a low-budget film in which he explored the potential of the high-definition digital camera for reinventing the noir, a popular genre *par excellence*. Back in 1969, inspired by the new aesthetics necessitated by lightweight equipment and restrictive budgets, Espinosa claimed that 'cinema is no longer interested in quality or technique,' and that '[i]t can be created equally well with a Mitchell or with an 8mm camera, in a studio or in a guerrilla camp in the middle of the jungle' (2000: 296).

Popular cinema, collective practices: Salvatores and the redefinition of film authorship in the New Italian Cinema

To fully understand the political undertone of Salvatores's films and the discursive context in which the collaborative type of authorship that he represents emerges, one has to consider his position within Italy's film system and industry. Salvatores's films resist traditional distinctions between 'popular' cinema and 'author' cinema especially insofar as they alternate between independent and industrial systems of film production and distribution. Although Salvatores has always maintained Colorado Film, he has also co-produced many projects with the largest film production and distribution company in Italy, the Cecchi Gori Group. In addition, Italy's largest distribution companies: Penta Distribution and Medusa (the latter is a part of Silvio Berlusconi's media conglomerate) bought the rights to some of his films. Some of Salvatores's films – most notably *Mediterraneo*, which won the Academy Award for Best Foreign Film in 1992, and *Io non ho paura*, which received critical acclaim both in Italy and abroad – have been widely distributed through international film circuits, including North American venues. Early in his career, Salvatores received a state subsidy for developing *Marrakech Express* and *Turnè*, specifically, the government's special aid fund for cultural films called *articolo 28*.

However, Salvatores's mode of production remains first and foremost identified with the independent and median-ramge area of film production and distribution. Since the very beginning of his career, Salvatores founded his own production company, the Colorado Film, which he maintains up to these days, together with Maurizio Totti and stand-up comedian and actor Diego Abatantuono, whose crass comedies and television shows had already made him famous in Italy. The company represents the prototype of the collaborative method that Salvatores also assumed in his film-making practices. Since *Kamikazen* and during the first part of his career he established a long working partnership with Enzo Monteleone, a young and talented screenwriter who wrote three of Salvatores's subsequent films, *Marrakech Express*, *Mediterraneo*, and *Puerto Escondido*.[23] His consecration as a film-maker with *Marrakech Express* was a pre-packaged project commissioned to Salvatores by the independent producer Gianni Minervini and written by Monteleone in collaboration with Umberto Contarello and the future film-maker Carlo Mazzacurati. The film was made thanks to the fact that the script had won the 1987 edition of the Solinas Award, designed to bring original screenplays by emerging authors to the attention of film producers. In spite of the commissioned nature of the film, Salvatores succeeded in adding a very personal input to the project by gathering together a team of technicians and actors who had worked with him throughout the 1980s and constitute the core team which would collaborate with him through the early 1990s and even beyond. This crew of regulars includes director of photography Italo Petriccione (a friend who got his start in cinema alongside Salvatores and has been the DOP for all his films), editor Nino Baragli (who had worked on most of Pier Paolo Pasolini's films, and whom Salvatores considers his sole 'film teacher'), sound editor Tiziano Crotti, and costume designer Francesco Panni. Salvatores's inveterate group of actors in the 1980s and early 1990s were Diego Abatantuono, Gigio Alberti, Claudio Bisio, Fabrizio Bentivoglio, Giuseppe Cederna, and Ugo Conti. Indeed, what film critics consider being the most consistent phase in Salvatores's filmic corpus, his late 1980s and early 1990s social comedies, is rather the result of production circumstances and of a collaborative system of production. From *Marrakech Express* to *Mediterraneo*, Salvatores and his collaborators made three films back to back in less than three years by shifting the same crew and cast from one set to the other and overlapping the post-production of one film with the pre-production of the next.[24] The last instalment in the series (and the last film written in collaboration with Monteleone) was *Puerto Escondido*.[25] Furthermore, these films arguably set

Salvatores's reputation as the most successful film author within the generation of the *nuovo cinema* film directors working mainly in independent systems of production and being able to survive within the difficult context of Italian cinema's production also thanks to their own production companies. A decade before them, Nanni Moretti inaugurated this new production trend with his sensational 1976 début film, *Io sono un autarchico/I Am Self Sufficient*. The film was self-produced, shot in Super 8mm, and blown up to 16mm. It was so successful that it made Italian film critics anticipate a renaissance in Italian cinema. Along with *Io sono un autarchico*, Moretti's subsequent social comedies proved that independently produced films that subvert traditional narrative structures and propose personal, self-reflexive, and critical views of Italian society could achieve national film distribution and box office success. In many ways, Salvatores followed in Moretti's footsteps by founding his own production company through which he maintained his independence from the Italian film industry and its institutions. The studio also assured Salvatores's professional continuity by allowing him to work for long periods of time with the same faithful team of collaborators and actors. As Malavasi notes, Salvatores's production system 'is not simply a production structure but an original form of *industrial organization* and of *creative collaboration*' (2005: 57, my translation).[26]

Many Italian film critics have characterized Italian cinema during the 1980s and 1990s as some of the worst cinematic work in history. At best, Lino Micciché describes it as 'dull'; at worst, Morando Morandini refers to it as 'desolate.'[27] Micciché describes the effects of this dull period on Italian culture as a whole. He writes:

> And the "lesson" of what happened to us in the 1980s is also that a cinema poor in ideas, lacking inspiration, falling back on itself, incapable of dealing with reality, removed from the spectators' objective and subjective lives, negligent with respect to almost all of the country's issues, incapable of reformulating people's experiences on the screen, results in a structural and cultural crisis comparable to an epochal disaster. (1998: 14, my translation)[28]

On his part, Morandini blames the mediocrity of 1980s Italian cinema on a combination of industrial, institutional, and creative problems. The state's monopoly in producing culturally oriented films via government funds and national television networks resulted in the conformity and linguistic flattening of 1980s Italian films. According to Morandini, the 'anemic' condition of Italy's new cinema was the consequence of several factors, including the 'analphabetism' of the domestic film audience, which has been captivated and addled by television, advertising, and mass culture, and misinformed by a compliant press; the hegemony of the American films appearing on Italian screens; the crisis of theatrical film exhibition; and the lack of interest shown by Italian film producers in developing films within the domestic market.[29.]

By and large, Salvatores managed to avoid the mediocrity above described and, while not appreciated as a film author, he was immediately singled out as an original film director. In particular, what set Salvatores's films apart from the desolate horizon of 1980s new cinema is their ability to sense the pulse of Italy's new generation. This characteristic was apparent even in his first two film projects, *Sogno di una notte d'estate* and *Kamikazen*, and particularly in his early comedies.[30] Another element that contributed to Salvatores's success was his capacity to move beyond the boundaries of Italian society to reach international audiences. In this respect, the Italian film historian Gian Piero Brunetta considers Salvatores to be the key figure in 1990s Italian cinema. During this decade, observes Brunetta, Italy's new cinema expanded its geographical boundaries, moving outside the closed spaces in which most of the 1980s films were set (Brunetta 2004a: 390–91). From this perspective, Brunetta contends that Salvatores's films are among those 'which allow Italian cinema to regain a national and international "visibility" [through] storytelling that tries to widen its own narrative boundaries by joining together different worlds and realities which, until now, have remained separate' (ibid.: 391, my translation).[31] While not all of Salvatores's films have been box offices, they contributed to create a median niche within the domestic film market, sparking a particular interest amongst young adult, middle-class filmgoers who prefer entertaining yet cultivated and intellectually stimulating cinema over Hollywood exports and the commercial Italian comedies that crowd the domestic film market.

In this respect, it is fair to say that his position within the authorless context of *nuovo cinema* was that of a household name within a median range of film reception. Yet a more appropriate definition of his status would be that of a popular author. A comparative examination of Salvatores and Moretti's relation to the notion of authorship will help illuminate this point. If we assume the author as a sociology-of-production, then Salvatores is, together with Moretti, a representative of Italy's latest generation of film authors according to Italy's New Wave tradition.[32] Like Moretti, he explores new narrative and stylistic forms and depicts, with irony and critical distance, the personal and ideological crises of his generation. Yet Salvatores's cinematic culture and film references are quite different from those cherished by Moretti. Although Salvatores does not (as Moretti does) overtly reject Italy's cinematic tradition and has, in fact, been associated with the *commedia all'italiana* (Italian-style comedy, the national film subgenre notoriously abjured by Moretti), his films are indebted less to Italian films than to American independent films. Salvatores himself acknowledges that he watched more US independent films in his youth than Italian films in a recent interview with Malavasi published in Malavasi's monograph on the film-maker (2005: 6).

From the perspective of Italy's authorial tradition, Salvatores also differs from Moretti in his cinematic address. Salvatores adopts an objective, chorus-style narration while Moretti uses more self-referential and self-reflexive techniques, often mediated by his on-screen presence as a fictional character. As Manuela Gieri has aptly observed, Moretti's self-referential and ironic films provide 'a "cruel" self-portrait of their author and consequently of a segment of Italian society that is homogeneous from a social, generational, and political point of view' (ibid.: 226). In Salvatores's films, self-referentiality and self-reflexivity are expressed through characters, dialogues, and situations that best reflect his personal views and do engender, as in Moretti's films, distancing strategies of representation. Yet, by and large, Salvatores's films are more open to experimentation than those of Moretti. As noted earlier by Casetti, Salvatores's cinema is an impure one; it is an admixture of various forms and techniques. From this perspective, Salvatores's impure style redefined Italian cinema and established a new type of authorial practice, moving beyond the parameters set by Italy's filmic tradition. Malavasi foregrounds this aspect of Salvatores's cinema by dividing his oeuvre into two distinct periods: the early social comedy period and the later more experimental period. Concentrating on the latter period, Malavasi suggests that *Nirvana* – a film that uses and remarks on digital imaging technology – is the transitional marker for the second, more multimedia-oriented phase of Salvatores's career (ibid.: 103–05).

Following this periodization, if 1980s Italian cinema finds in Moretti the last representative of its authorial tradition, then Salvatores symbolizes the emergence of the *nuovo cinema* author as a popular author. From this point of view, Salvatores's authorship is also connected with the reconfiguration of certain generic conventions present in neo-realist film and *commedia all'italiana*, which have often over-determined the production and reception of Italian films. Gieri, among others, stresses Salvatores's affiliation with the Italian comedy as well as with neo-realism, pointing to his references to Vittorio De Sica's *Sciuscià/Shoeshine* (1946) and the *commedia all'italiana* masters in *Kamikazen*; and his allusions to Roberto Rossellini's *Paisà/Paisan* (1946), Ettore Scola's *C'eravamo tanto amati/We All Loved Each Other So Much* (1974), and Mario Monicelli's *La grande Guerra/The Great War* (1959) in his trilogy of 'road movies' (*Marrakech Express, Turnè, Puerto Escondido*), and his World War II film, *Mediterraneo* (Gieri 1995: 222–23).

Salvatores has been the subject of several studies in Italy, including three monographs and numerous chapters in anthologies or in magazine special issues on Italian new cinema.[33] Yet, over the years, he has received tepid reviews. Moreover, national and international film critics have yet to recognize Salvatores as an auteur. As mentioned in the introductory section of this chapter, the reasons for this oversight are mainly due to Salvatores's predilection for popular genres and stylistic heterogeneity. Only recently have some critics reconsidered their positions, although not without reservations. The release of *Io non ho paura* was met with unanimous critical praise, the first and only of Salvatores's films to receive such a positive reaction (Malavasi 2005: 29). Significantly, *Io non ho paura* is also Salvatores's most 'conventional' film according to auteur-oriented criteria. Its linear narrative construction and use of eye-pleasing imagery conforms to what critics expect from an auteur film, while its virtuoso camera movements are just experimental enough to appease their desire for aesthetic innovation. From another perspective, Malavasi finds Salvatores's status as an author in the way he combines reality and entertainment, a strategy Salvatores uses to reflect and comment on reality, rather than merely reproduce it. In this manner, Salvatores develops a distinctive authorial voice and a subversive political discourse about the realities of contemporary Italy (ibid.: 22–29).

Yet if critics were ready to accept Salvatores into the auteurist fold with *Io non ho paura*, his next film, *Quo vadis, baby?*, would put this acceptance at risk. The film's more fervent experimentation with digital technology coupled with its unrepentant alignment with popular genre fare (as seen in its unabashed use of film noir conventions) is a marked departure from Salvatore's previous works. In this respect, Salvatores has gone further than even Moretti in distancing himself from the tradition of Italian authorial cinema. Moretti's film practices in fact coincide with the French-based auteur model that holds that the auteur is the ultimate authority who integrates directing, screenwriting, and producing. As mentioned above, Salvatores rejects this model.

More than any other film-maker of the new generation, Salvatores has dispelled the cliché that author cinema is inaccessible to a wide audience, a preconception that Moretti has challenged before but from a more moderate perspective. Moretti still makes films with a select audience in mind and his status as a a film author has been established on the international scene, especially in France, where he is considered as the most important Italian film author of his generation. On the other hand, Salvatores stridently makes films for popular consumption and, for this reason, has been denied a widespread reputation as a film author in Italy and within international film culture.

Salvatores's most recent films and projects speak to his pragmatism regarding the commercial nature of film-making. *Quo vadis, baby?* was distributed in North America by Capri, a Toronto-based Canadian film and television distribution company that has been collaborating with Colorado Film Production since 2005 and whose president and CEO is the Italian producer Gabriella Martinelli. Capri presents itself as a 'vertically integrated and diverse multi-entertainment company' (http://www.caprifilms.com/capri_television.html). The company produces small-budget, independent films, as well as big-budget, all-star productions, and internationally co-produced TV movies and popular series. Rumours have it that Salvatores is currently developing a noir TV series with Capri, an Italian-Canadian venture featuring a female detective inspired by the protagonist of *Quo vadis, baby?* Capri is also set to co-produce Salvatores's announced next film project, provisionally titled *The Rules of Love*, based on the 1999 novel *The Loves of Judith* by Meir Shalev.[34] In 2008, Salvatores started filming his second adaptation from Niccoló Ammaniti, *Come Dio comanda*, the novelist's latest and very popular novel. Salvatores has also in view another film to be co-produced by Capri Film and Colorado Film, titled *Cargo*. The film's script is co-written by Salvatores and established Italian screenwriter Umberto Contarello, who collaborated with Carlo Mazzacurati and Enzo Monteleone on the script for Salvatores's first success, *Marrakech Express*.[35]

Finally, another of Salvatores's announced projects is the adaptation of a successful novel published by Colorado Noir in 2005, *La scala di Dioniso* by Luca di Fulvio. The story, set in London at the turn of the nineteenth century, is about a serial killer who murders the wives of rich stockholders. Salvatores and Maurizio Totti purchased the rights for the film adaptation even before the book was published and have been working on the screenplay since 2005.[36] The budget for the film is estimated at thirty million euros and involves an international co-production team, large, complicated sets, and a prestigious English-speaking cast, possibly led by Gary Oldman, Anthony Hopkins, or Edward Norton. Regarding the film's high cost and use of international stars, Salvatores makes no apologies. He does not view this excursion into international mainstream production as a defeat for authorial cinema. Rather, he sees it as a necessary step to counter Italy's lack of initiative in funding domestic productions. According to him, the government, under the leadership of Silvio Berlusconi during most of the past decade, 'declared war' on Italian cinema by cutting financial support and pulling distribution support from culturally oriented films (Salvatores 2005 and Malavasi 2005: 9). Instead of waiting for a radical institutional change, Salvatores has resorted to his own revolutionary action: making popular films, politically.

Notes

1. Italian film critics' position vis-à-vis the *nuovo cinema*'s style will be also discussed in chapter 9.
2. The poor critical reception of *nuovo cinema* is further discussed in this chapter and in chapter 9.
3. '[...] una diretta conseguenza, e un'ulteriore manifestazione, di quello iato tra autore e critico che cambierà definitivamente la dinamica del rapporto nel cinema italiano contemporaneo'.
4. Detailed information about screenwriting credits in Salvatores's films will be provided further on in this chapter.
5. [...] i nuovi autori si sono trovati a dover eliminare tutte le mediazioni che tradizionalmente l'appartenenza a Cinecittà comportava. In riconoscimento della propria alterità rispetto a una derivazione di scuola, hanno dichiarato la propria specificità nell'essere una generazione orfana, "sperduta nel buio".' The expression 'sperduta nel buio' refers to the title of a film directed by Nino Martoglio in 1914, *Sperduti nel buio*, of which no copy survives today. The film is considered a prototype of Italian cinema's realist tradition and had a strong influence on the development of neo-realist aesthetics (although the remake directed in 1947 during the neo-realist era, directed by Camillo Mastrocinque and featuring Vittorio De Sica was a conventional melodrama that betrayed the realist spirit of the original version).
6. Specific examples will be provided further on in this chapter.
7. Hugh Gray translated the title 'in Defense of Mixed Cinema' (1971). The term 'impure' is here preferred, and is also used by Casetti.
8. Since its original publication in 1969, the essay has been translated into English and published in several books and film journals. I here use the version that appeared in Stam, R. and T. Miller, (eds). *Film Theory: An Anthology*. (Malden Mass.: Blackwell Publishing, 2000).
9. 'Io sono cresciuto in un'epoca in cui il contributo delle persone veniva non solo accettato ma addirittura richiesto e in cui si credeva che la proprietá di un'opera non fosse di una singola persona. E lo penso ancora fortemente rispetto al cinema: come fai a non chiamare autore il montatore? E lo sceneggiatore? E gli attori? Faccio questa premessa per dire che non sento meno mio un film a cui magari non ho lavorato sulla sceneggiatura'.
10. The emphasis is mine.
11. Salvatores comments on the influence of film on his theatrical work and vice versa in an interview with Luca Malavasi that opens Malavasi's book (2005: 5).
12. '[...] un esperimento di contaminazione condotto dall'*interno* del teatro, che il cinema contribuisce semmai a dilatare nelle sue possibilitá "esistenziali"'.
13. On these themes see, among others, Casetti (1998: 156–63), Gieri (1995: 221–24), and Quaresima (1994: 40).
14. The most radical and violent fringe faction called its followers 'Metropolitan Indians' and advocated the re-appropriation of urban spaces and social opportunities for the youth. At universities, the protests targeted humanities departments, which they accused of being old-fashioned and self-propagating academic environments, and called upon to re-organize and modernize their structures and methods. Not ideologically linked to any political position or party, the protests were instead a manifestation of a generation's uneasiness in trying to find its own space in society. The 1977 movement also expressed a generalized disdain for the existing establishment and its institutions.
15. Specific examples will be provided further on in this chapter
16. Malavasi remarks on this technique in a review published in *Cineforum* (2002), and further develops his comments into a close analysis of *Amnèsia* that appears in his above-mentioned book on Salvatores (2005: 123–32).

17. A possible influence on the multi-medial character of his latest production is Salvatores's own involvement in other media, making music video and television commercial formats: in the early 1990s he directed several music videos and commercial spots that deployed advanced technical solutions and featured some of his regular actors (including Diego Abatantuono, Ugo Conti, Gigio Alberti, and Bebo Storti).

18. After Ada addresses the camera, the recording reveals a violent fight with her father, who has arrived at her apartment unexpectedly to bring her back home. During the clash, he reproaches her self-indulgent lifestyle and she accuses him of having killed her mother. He responds to her allegations by insulting and hitting her. Soon after the man leaves, Ada commits suicide.

19. Malavasi foregrounds the continuity of Salvatores's political commitments and suggests that the radical-left model of collective theatre finds its reincarnation in the collaborative spirit of Colorado Film and of Salvatores's working methods (2005: 56–57).

20. Malavasi offers an inspired reading of Io non ho paura (2005: 132–44). He was among the Italian film critics who noted the film's Shakespearean plot components, an aspect that international film reviewers, who were generally appreciative of the film, nonetheless missed. Phillip Kemp's review in Sight and Sound, for instance, considers the film only in regard to its obvious homage to Charles Laughton's Night of the Hunter (1955) (Kemp 2004).

21. For more about Colorado Film Production and Colorado Noir, please check their websites. Available: http://www.coloradofilm.it/ita/site.htm and http://www.coloradonoir.it/.

22. 'Credo che il noir come genere sia nato con una connotazione fortemente realistica, in quegli anni in cui il realismo aveva un'importanza fondamentale anche in politica, mentre in questi anni si sia trasformato approdando nella deformazione, nella non normalità. Oggi il noir è il genere letterario più titolato a raccontare la realtà in cui viviamo che è fortemente anormale, ossessiva, illegale: è uno sguardo deviato e per un regista la prima cosa da fare è cercare lo sguardo, "lo sguardo nero". Questo è uno dei motivi per cui abbiamo fondato con entusiasmo la Colorado Noir.' Quoted from the Colorado Noir website (http://www.coloradonoir.it/).

23. The only script to which Monteleone did not contribute was Turnè, written by Italian Francesca Marciano (who is also a film director and a film actress) and Fabrizio Bentivoglio. Bentivoglio, who is primarily an actor, was also one of the film's protagonists, together with Abatantuono. Bentivolgio and Abatantuono had previously starred together in Marrakech Express. Some years later, Marciano co-wrote (with the writer Nicola Ammaniti, the author of the source novel) Io non ho paura. Other important screenwriters who collaborated with Salvatores are Franco Bernini (Sud), Andrea Garello (Amnèsia), and Fabio Scamoni (Quo vadis, baby?).

24. Salvatores recalls these circumstances in his interview with Malavasi (2005: 7–8).

25. Salvatores and Abatantuono are also credited as collaborators on the screenplay. The actor, who plays the film's lead, improvised many of the dialogues on the set.

26. '[...] non è semplicemente una struttura produttiva ma una forma originale di organizzazione industriale e di collaborazione creativa.' The italics appear in the original text.

27. Micciché used the term 'dull' in the title of his anthology on 1980s Italian cinema in which Casetti's article is published; 'Schermi opachi' translates as 'opaque, dull screens'. The adjective also recurs in the editor's article, which opens the collection, whose title ('Il lungo decennio grigio,' 'The long grey decade') is as connotative as that of the book (Micciché 1998). The volume appeared on the occasion of a symposium held at the 1998 edition of the Pesaro Film Festival. Morandini characterized the 1980s as 'desolate' at a symposium on 1980s Italian cinema held in Milan on 18 March 1991.

The conference was titled 'Voci, volti, storie per gli anni '90. Quali personaggi e quali attori per il cinema italiano?' (Zagarrio 1998: 34).

28. 'E la "lezione" di quello che è accaduto a noi negli anni Ottanta è anche quella che un cinema povero di idee, carente d'ispirazione, ripiegato su se stesso, incapace di fare i conti con la realtá, lontano dalla vita oggettiva e soggettiva degli spettatori, assente rispetto a quasi tutta la problematica del paese, incapace di riaffabulare sugli schermi il vissuto delle persone finisce per sommare crisi strutturale e crisi culturale con risultati da disastro epocale.'

29. I am paraphrasing Zagarrio, who makes reference to a talk Morandini gave at a non-referenced colloquium in the opening section of his above-mentioned article, published in Micciché's anthology (1998: 34). Zagarrio summarizes Morandini's analysis into ten points, which I have condensed and grouped differently.

30. In his above-cited book on Salvatores, Malavasi introduces the film-maker within the context of 1980s cinema by referencing Micciché's essay on the 'dull 1980s' (Malavasi 2005: 17–19).

31. '[...] che consentono al cinema italiano di riguadagnare una "visibilitá" nazionale e internazionale [...] un racconto che cerca di allargare i propri confini narrativi, che vuol mettere a contatto mondi finora separati e realtá destinate sempre piú a incrociarsi nel prossimo futuro.'

32. The film magazine *Cinecritica* published a discouraging report on the new Italian cinema in a double issue appearing at the beginning of the 1990s (*Cinecritica* 1990/1991). The report contains, among others, an article by Morando Morandini developed from the same talk mentioned by Zagarrio in the above-cited chapter on 1980s cinema (Zagarrio 1998). On the new film-makers that appeared in the 1980s, see Montini (1988b). Montini dedicates a chapter to Salvatores in a previous anthology on new Italian film authors (1988a).

33. The monographic studies include Canova (1996), a study focusing on *Nirvana*; Facchinaro (1997); and Merkel (1992).

34. The film was recently announced on the website for the Italian Minister of Culture's promotional film company *FilmItalia*. Available: (http://filmitalia.org/film.asp?lang=ing&documentID=29019). However, the film does not appear on the official website of Capri Films.

35. Information about Capri Films is available on the company's official website, at http://www.caprifilms.com/index.html. The news regarding Salvatores's new film project appears on the Internet Movie Database at the following address: http://www.imdb.com/title/tt0437462/.

36. Salvatores and Maurizio Totti announced the project at the book launch of *La scala di Dioniso* in the summer of 2005 in Milan and discussed the project on several occasions, including a press conference held on 20 September 2005 in Montreal, on the occasion of the North American première of *Quo vadis, baby?* at the short-lived New Montreal Film Festival.

References

Inchiesta: il cinema italiano e gli anni '90. 1990/1991. *Cinecritica*, XIV(19–20): 56–74, ottobre / marzo.

Bazin, A. 1971. In Defense of Mixed Cinema. (*In* Gray H. (ed. and trans.) *What Is Cinema?* Berkeley, Los Angeles, and London: University of California Press, pp. 53–75.)

Brunetta, G. P. 2004a. *Cent'anni di cinema italiano*. Bari-Roma: Laterza.

——. 1998. *Storia del cinema italiano: dal miracolo economico agli anni novanta 1960–1993*. Roma: Editori Riuniti.

Canova, G. 1996. *Sulle tracce del cinema di Gabriele Salvatores*. Milano: Zelig.

Casetti, F. 1998. Gabriele Salvatores, o del cinema impuro. (*In* Micciché, L. (ed.). *Schermi opachi: il cinema italiano degli anni '80.* Venezia: Marsilo, pp. 156–63.)

Cavani, L. 1999. *Piccoli e grandi schermi: il cinema in televisione. Intervista a cura di Gaetana Marrone.* (*In:* MARRONE, G. (ed.). *New Landscapes in Contemporary Italian Cinema.* 17: 247–52.)

Espinosa, J. G. 2000. Por un cine imperfecto. (*In* Stam, R. and Miller, T. (eds). *Film Theory: An Anthology.* Malden Mass.: Blackwell Publishing, pp. 287–97.)

Facchinaro D. 1997. *Territori di fuga. Il cinema di Gabriele Salvatores.* Alessandria: Falsopiano.

Gieri, M. 1995. *Contemporary Italian Film-making: Strategies of Subversion. Pirandello, Fellini, Scola, and the Directors of the New Generation.* Toronto: University of Toronto Press.

Kemp, P. 2004. I'm Not Scared. *Sight and Sound,* 14 (3): 46–47.

MALAVASI, L. 2002. Amnésia. *Cineforum,* 414: 68–69.

—. (ed.) 2005. *Gabriele Salvatores.* Milano: Il Castoro.

Marrone, G. 1999a. Il nuovo cinema italiano: pregiudizi, realtá e promesse. (In

Marrone, G. (ed.). *New Landscapes in Contemporary Italian Cinema.* 17: 7–13.)

—. 1999b. *New Landscapes in Contemporary Italian Cinema.* 17.

Merkel, F. 1992. *Il cinema di Gabriele Salvatores.* Roma: Dino Audino.

Micciché, L. 1998. Il lungo decennio grigio. (*In* Micciché, L. (ed.). *Schermi opachi: il cinema italiano degli anni '80* . Venezia: Marsilo, pp. 3–16.)

Montini, F. (ed.). 1988a. *Una generazione in cinema. Esordi ed esordienti. 1975–1988.* Venezia: Marsilio.

—. 1988b. *I novissimi, gli esordienti nel cinema italiano degli anni '80.* Torino: Nuova Eri.

Quaresima, L. 1994. Gabriele Salvatores. (*In* Costa, A. (ed.). *Dossier: Cinema italiano anni novanta. Lettera dall'Italia,* 9 (36), pp. 27–43.)

Salvatores, G. 2005. Interview with the author on 20 September 2005. Montréal. [Cassette recording in possession of author.]

Sesti, M. 1994. *Nuovo cinema italiano: gli autori, i film, le idee,* Roma: Theoria.

—. (ed.). 1996. *La « scuola »italiana. Storia, strutture e immaginario di un altro cinema (1988–1996).* Venezia: Marsilio Editori.

Zagarrio, V. 1998a. Polveri e arcipelaghi. Movimenti, incontri, attraversamenti del decennio. (*In* Micciché, L. (ed.). *Schermi opachi: il cinema italiano degli anni '80.* Venezia: Marsilo, pp. 34–53.)

5

A DIFFERENT TYPE OF CINEPHILIA: ALEJANDRO AMENÁBAR AND THE NEW GENERATION OF SPANISH FILM AUTHORS

In the mid-1990s, Spanish cinema began to emerge from a long financial crisis. The upswing led to radical changes in government subsidy policy and investment on the part of financial corporations (notably Grupo PRISA's affiliated companies Sogetel/Sogepaq and Canal+ España) and television networks in the business of domestic film production. During this time, a vast contingency of aspiring film directors made their feature film-making débuts, including

The Others (Nicole Kidman)

Alejandro Amenábar, Juanma Bajo Ulloa, Icíar Bollaín, Daniel Calparsoro, Isabel Coixet, Augustín Díaz Yanes, Manuel Gómez Pereira, Chus Gutiérrez, Alex de la Iglesia, Fernando León de Aranoa, Julio Medem, Gracia Querejeta, Marc Recha, Santiago Segura, David Trueba, and Enrique Urbizu.[1] What distinguished these newcomers from their predecessors was their determination to attract domestic audiences within a theatrical exhibition circuit dominated by Hollywood films. Yet their responses to the crisis facing Spanish cinema were diverse. Some, such as de la Iglesia, Segura, and, in part, Bajo Ulloa and Calparsoro, openly embraced mainstream cinematic forms such as generic film-making and sequels.[2] Others, notably Recha and Medem, continued within the metaphorical style of Spain's authorial tradition. The majority of others, such as Amenábar, Bollaín, Coixet, Díaz Yanes, Gutiérrez, León de Aranoa, and Querejeta, made films within the framework of an audience-oriented cinema that was more in keeping with contemporary Spanish society and the new audio-visual system.

Alejandro Amenábar is arguably the most significant and successful representative of the latter group. Only twelve years into his career and with four feature films to his credit Amenábar is one of the most marketable Spanish film directors of the past decade, both at home and abroad. He partakes in contexts of film production and reception set across different contexts and circuits of film production and distribution, as well as their relative cultural and discursive formations and institutions. Amenábar's films are in many ways connected with Spanish author cinema. His working methods are in line with those generally associated with an authorial mode of production, involving responsibility for a film's conception and development. Although he does acknowledge the support of collaborators such as his friend and co-screenwriter, Mateo Gil, with whom he has written all his films except The Others/Los otros (2001) and his mentor/producer, film-maker José Luis Cuerda, he takes credit for writing and directing films according to original ideas and supervises every phase of film production and post-production, including the music score, which he personally composes.[3] Furthermore, the links with Spain's authorial tradition include intertextual references and thematic parallels with canonical films directed by nuevo cine film authors, such as Víctor Erice and Carlos Saura, as well as, like in most of the films produced within this movement, in stylistic solutions and formulas derived from classical Hollywood cinema.

In spite of these connections, Amenábar does not overtly recognize his connection with Spain's author cinema. When discussing aesthetic influences on his work, he tends to obliterate Spanish affiliations and instead considers the films of international film directors in classical or post-classical Hollywood such as, for instance, Alfred Hitckcock, Stanley Kubrick, and Steven Spielberg, to have a strong impact on his approach to film-making style.[4] Additionally, while on his part his production systems are still consistent with those of author cinema, he has also become a household name in the mainstream area of film production and distribution, occasionally associated with Hollywood co-productions and partnerships (as it was the case for The Others). Finally, he foregrounds a pragmatic and commerce-oriented attitude toward film promotion, which he monitors through publicity material (notably his personal website and the production information included in the DVDs of his films) that allows him to maintain at the same time a very low-key public persona and a maximum visibility within the international film market.

Amenábar's self-distancing attitude vis-à-vis Spanish author cinema is shared by most contemporary Spanish film-makers. This position responds in part to the disavowal of a sector of Spanish cinema that Spanish filmgoers historically snubbed, in part to the generalized effort in Spanish cinema to become more integrated into the global dimension of the film industry. This attitude is both constituted by, and responds to the economic and cultural conditions of an audio-visual system owned by trans-national media corporations, and one that not only controls the means of production and circulation, but also the cultural reception of films. From this perspective, Amenábar's authorship represents a sociology-of-production and a discourse about cinema established within the commercial conditioning of this audio-visual system and prompts, to use Timothy Corrrigan's words, a 'renewed attention to the layered pressures of auteurism as an agency that establishes different modes of identification with its audiences' (1991: 135–6).[5] In the case of Amenábar, authorial agency identifies postmodern tactics of professional orientation set at the global/local interface of a new generation of Spanish film directors whose films contain the overtone of a distinctively national author tradition and of its Hollywood-oriented cinephilia, even though they refuse to be confined within the production systems and the aesthetic parameters consolidated by this tradition and identified with the metaphorical style of the *nuevo cine*.

Spanish cinema's industrial renaissance and the post-authorial generation

Film discourse tends to identify European cinema with art- and auteur-oriented film production. The literature on Spanish cinema is no exception. Until very recently, most publications on this national cinema adopt film authorship as the primary interpretive framework, even when these publications concentrate on questions of national identity and cultural representation.[6] One obvious example of this scholarship is Peter William Evans's anthology *Spanish Cinema: The Auteurist Tradition* (1999), which includes a preface by José Louis Borau, one of the most highly regarded film authors of the *nuevo cine* movement. In his piece, Borau defines Spanish film authors as the backbone of Spain's film industry and underlines the specificity of Spain's authorial film practices in comparison to those developed in Western Europe and North America. He states:

> [T]he work of the auteurs is not the exceptional product of an industry characterized by commercial triumphs and local themes, as was the case of the American cinema in its heyday or of France (and its famous directors) in the 1930s. In Spain it was precisely the auteurs who, above all after the first screening of *¡Bienvenido, Mr. Marshall!* in the spring of 1953, accepted responsibility for guiding and redefining the film industry to which they belonged, trying to endow it gradually – perhaps without too much collective consciousness, but through personal effort and inspiration – with themes, forms, and styles that replaced old practices and created new guidelines, defining our film industry for audiences abroad and – with greater difficulty – for home audiences, or at least those sections that were most critical and demanding. (Borau 1999: xviii)[7]

Borau also admits that the 'success' of Spanish authorial films is measured less by their reception by 'mass audiences' than by the reactions of international film critics, scholars, and cultural institutions (ibid.: xx). He attributes the domestic audience's disaffection for authorial cinema to the Spanish film spectators' inability to decode the cryptic style to which oppositional film-makers had to resort to avoid censorship (ibid.: xix). What Borau does not acknowledge (and what contemporary specialists in Spanish cinema instead emphasize) is the connection between Spain's policies on film and authorial film practices. From the Francoist period until the mid-1990s, Spanish author cinema mainly relied on government subsidies and film modes committed to promoting and exporting the country's culture abroad. This system disregarded the lack of interest on the part of domestic film audiences in this type of cinema.

The Spanish population's disaffection for Spanish cinema was largely due to the ways in which this cinema portrayed the country. During the regime, formulaic and populist films that presented a retrograde and unrealistic image of Spain dominated the national circuit of film production and exhibition, which was strictly controlled by the censorship board. The few authorial films that were distributed in domestic film theatres were also unpopular, in spite of the fact that one of the major goals for Spanish film authors was to represent Spain's social reality. Several specialists on Spanish cinema attribute the poor commercial turnout for Spanish cinema in domestic film theatres to the formal and narrative complexity of 'oppositional' cinema during Franco's dictatorship. Complex narratives were used as a strategy to avoid state censorship, and they remained a characteristic feature of films produced even after Franco's death and the abolition of state censorship in 1975.[8] As Virginia Higginbotham puts it, 'One of the legacies of Franco to Spanish film is the aesthetic. This metaphorical convoluted style, which has become a national genre of postwar cinema, will never reach a large audience in a country in which developments in film remain known only to a small, select group of film students, intellectuals, and an educated minority' (1988: 135). During the 1980s, authorial cinema under the socialist government did not fare better with domestic audiences: the historical and literary origins of the films produced within this decade's institutional framework constituted an unlikely match for Hollywood blockbusters and Euro-pudding co-productions.

In 1999, the same year Evans's anthology was published, Luis García Berlanga made a provocative statement about Spain's authorial tradition at a special screening of his film *¡Bienvenido, Mr. Marshall!* in Coruña.[9] Together with Juan Antonio Bardem, Berlanga is considered the initiator of Spanish cinema's renaissance and one of the participants in the Salamanca Congress in 1955. The Congress gathered Spanish film-makers from different political positions to re-conceptualize Spanish national cinema in light of the constraints of censorship and to develop a model of cinema that was closer to Spain's social reality. One of the main influences driving the conception of the new model was Italian neo-realism. More than forty years later, at the aforementioned screening of *¡Bienvenido, Mr. Marshall!*, Berlanga contended that the Salamanca Congress had in actuality led the Ministry of Culture to develop an institutional mode of production that was out of touch with social reality and national audiences: '[W]ith the excuse of going into the street and providing testimony, some pedantic and boring films came out, influenced by neo-realism. The cinema then left the studios to lock itself into the offices of the Ministry of Culture' (as cited in Payān 2001: 9, my translation).[10]

In Borau's opinion, Spanish cinema began to reconnect with its audiences only after it shifted its thematic and stylistic focus from an aesthetic that was overly 'convoluted' to one that better reflected the country's social realities and shared fantasies of national identity. This shift was led by Pedro Almodóvar (Borau 1999: xx). The *movida*-informed style championed by Almodovár contributed to propelling the viability of Spanish cinema in the domestic and international film markets throughout the 1980s and early 1990s. The laudatory reception of Almodóvar's films, as well as the films of Vicente Aranda and Fernando Trueba, were not, however, representative of a general improvement in the situation of Spanish cinema in those years. Film producer Antonio Saura (son of Carlos Saura, Spain's most prestigious film-maker of the *nuevo cine*) observes that in 1994, despite the recent international success of Fernando Trueba's *Belle Epoque* (1992), which won an Academy Award for Best Foreign Picture, 'the Spanish film industry was going through one of its pandemic crises of confidence' (Saura 1997: 104, my translation).[11] John Hopewell agrees that in the first decade of the post-Franco period, the success of a few film-makers did not translate into an economic boom in the Spanish film industry, which, in terms of production, remained relatively slow until the mid-1990s (Hopewell 1982 and 1991). With only a few exceptions, the gap between Spanish author cinema and domestic film reception even widened during these years. In an article written in that period, Hopewell forecasted that this situation would change and predicted what would actually become a major trend in Spain's film industry: the increasing importance of television productions and of films targeting a wider audience. (Hopewell 1991: 120)

The film industry's ongoing difficulties prompted the socialist government to change its policy towards national film production. In 1994, the new minister of culture of the socialist government, Carmen Alborch, set aside the traditional system of advance credits meant to assure the production of culturally oriented films to privilege a system of automatic subsidies based on box office receipts. The purpose was not only to encourage a palatable domestic cinema for

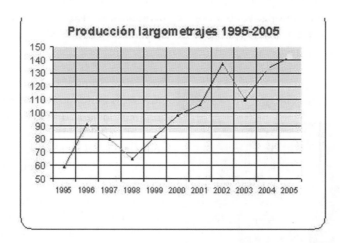

	1995	1996	1997	1998	1999	2000	2001	2002	2003	2004	2005
TOTAL	94	87	115	122	124	108	169	171	137	185	161

Table 11: 'Spanish Cinema in Figures and Data.' Ministry of Culture. http://www.mcu.es/cine/MC/CDC/Evolucion/GraficosEvolucion.html.

Spanish audiences but also to put an end to the polemics surrounding the Socialist government's approach to national subsidies. The criticisms surrounding subsidies had become particularly heated during the tenure of film-maker Pilar Miró, Alborch's predecessor. The accusations concerned Miró's excessive expenditure on films conceived within the framework of Spain's long-celebrated authorial tradition. Public opinion felt that these films were no longer as daring or original as the offerings from internationally acclaimed masters of the post-Salamanca realist renaissance and of the *nuevo cine* movement.

Alborch's 1994 reform provided a safety net for films produced through advanced aid, a sum no larger than the producer's investment and limited to a maximum of 50 million pesetas per film. According to the new decree, all Spanish movies released in movie theatres would receive 15 per cent of their gross box office revenue as a non-returnable subsidy in the first two years of their release, up to a maximum of 100 million pesetas. The films that were not made with advanced subsidies could receive either a sum equivalent to 25 per cent of their gross box office revenue or 33 per cent of their producer's investment, provided that the film earned gross box office revenue of 50 million pesetas in the first two years. These rewards were limited to a maximum of 150 million pesetas and no more than 75 per cent of the producer's investment or 50 per cent of the film's cost. Concomitant with the new decree, the national television network Radio Televisión Española (RTVE) announced important investments in film production. Additionally, Spain's media corporation Promotora de Informaciones, S.A. (PRISA) founded a film distribution company, Sogepaq, and a film production company, Sogetel (Heredero 1999: 49; Jordan and Morgan-Tamosunas 1998: 3–4; Benavent 2000: 17–18). The impact these new developments had on Spain's domestic film production and distribution was immediate. Only one year after Alborch's decree came into effect, 1995 appeared to be a miracle year for the country's film industry. Film production increased almost 30 per cent totalling 59 films compared to 44 in the previous year. Moreover, domestic theatrical film attendance increased by a considerable margin, with 9.3 million more spectators than in 1994 (Jordan and Morgan-Tamosunas 1998: 4).

Alejandro Amenábar and DOP Javier Aguirresarobe

Ever since, Spanish cinema has continued to improve its performance at the box office and has maintained a significant volume of production (table 11).[12] The prosperity has not gone unnoticed by national and international media. For instance, a website dedicated to international film festivals highlighted Spain's 'ebullient film market' on the occasion of the 2000 Cannes Film Festival and described the late 1990s as the 'golden age' of Spanish cinema (2000). This period is marked by the emergence of commercially successful film-makers such as Alejandro Amenábar, Juanma Bajo Ulloa, Mariano Barroso, Agustín Villaronga, Jaume Balaguero, Imano Ribe, and José Luis Cuerda (see 'A new golden age of Spanish cinema is in the works'). Since the late 1990s, Spain has also been increasing its Latin American co-productions through television networks and digital corporate ventures such as PRISA's digital channel Canal Satélite Digital, TVE, and Canal+ España.

The 1990s also saw a shift in the institutional position of the author in Spanish cinema. The new generation of film directors steered clear of the much criticized government-funded systems of film authorship and found new opportunities for developing author-informed, personal modes of production within the national film industry thanks to the backing of veteran film-makers. Pedro Almodóvar produced films by Alex de la Iglesia, Mónica Laguna, and Daniel Calparsoro; Fernando Trueba was a producer for Juanma Bajo Ulloa, Chus Gutiérrez, and Emilio Martinez Lázaro; Fernando Colomo worked with Icíar Bollair, Mariano Barroso, Azucena Rodriguez, and Daniel Calparsoro; and José Luis Cuerda acted as producer for Amenábar. The figure of the film director-producer created a system of mentorship that allowed for a new synergy between Spanish author cinema, the national film system, and the domestic film market. These producers were, in fact, film directors with an established reputation as film authors who were nonetheless relatively successful at the box office. They helped a number of young, talented film directors make their break into feature film-making while maintaining an autonomous position vis-à-vis the commercial constraints of the film market. The film director-producer became commonplace and took over the role of the independent film producer, which with only a few exceptions (as with Elías Querejeta, the producer to many film-makers of the *nuevo cine*) was never very popular within the Spanish film industry.[13]

1995, the miracle year that marked the economic revival of Spanish cinema, was also the year when Alejandro Amenábar made his first feature film, *Tesis/Thesis* (1996). This début was indeed the most spectacular result of the new production policies and of the director-producer system of authorial mentorship. The film received funding through government film subsidies amounting to about 64,000 pesetas (equivalent to $500,000 US). The film was produced by film-maker José Luis Cuerda's company, Las Producciones del Escorpión. *Tesis* became one of Spain's biggest box office hits of the decade and won seven Goya Awards for direction, screenplay, cinematography, and music. Amenábar's subsequent films have consistently reached top box office positions in Spain and have fared well on the international film market, including the notoriously inaccessible US theatrical film circuit. *Tesis'* success assured Amenábar a bigger budget of 370 million pesetas (about $2,850,000 US) for his next project, *Abre los ojos/Open Your Eyes* (1997). The film had the support of EUROIMAGE funds and involved an international co-production and distribution collaboration that included Cuerda's Las Producciones del Escorpión, the French production company Les Films Alan Sarde, the Italian distribution company Lucky Red, and the Spanish media companies Canal+ España and Sogetel. This second film was also well received abroad, notably in the United States, where it grossed $368,000, a quite respectable result for the work of a foreign and still unknown film-maker. The film also earned very positive reviews in the international press. *Abre los ojos* caught the attention of Hollywood star Tom Cruise, who bought the rights to the script for a Hollywood remake, *Vanilla Sky* (Cameron Crowe, 2001). The remake was produced by Cruise, who also starred.

Cruise then went on to co-produce, along with Miramax and Las Producciones del Escorpión, Amenábar's third film, *The Others*. The film starred Nicole Kidman and an international, all-English-speaking cast. The budget was 'only' $17,000,000 US, tiny by Hollywood standards but still above the average for European productions. *The Others* was the top-earning Spanish film in 2001, earning 26,560,672 euros in receipts (about $34,000,000 US). It won eight Goya Awards including those for Best Director, Best Cinematography, and Best Leading Actress. The movie also became a box office hit in the international film market, grossed almost $100 million in the United States alone, and received much critical attention globally. Despite its commercial appeal, even auteur-oriented film magazines such as *Cahiers du Cinéma*, *Positif*, *Sight and Sound*, and *Cineforum* took notice of the film (see Guerin 2001; Garbarz 2001; Mount 2001; Smith 2001; and Manzoli 2001). Remarkably, the Hollywood partners imposed no constraints on the film-maker's vision and working method during the shooting of *The Others*. Amenábar was granted director's cut and worked with an all-Spanish crew, including the pre-eminent director of photography Javier Aguirresarobe (Amenábar 2001: 171–74; 176–78; Marchante 2002: 147–49; 154–58).

By the same token, Amenábar's leap into big budget film-making, international co-production, and global marketing did not affect his decision-making on his next project, *El mar adentro/The Sea Inside* (2004). The film is Amenábar's most 'nationally' intimate work to date and primarily a Spanish venture. Support came from a number of national institutions: the Ministry of Culture; the audio-visual production company Filmanova; the media corporations Sogepaq and Sogecine; the national and regional television networks Televisión Española (ETV) and Televisión de Galicia (TVG); and Amenábar's own production company, Himenoptero. French television network Canal+ and Europe's subsidy fund EUROIMAGE provided additional funding. The film was well received in Europe and won several prestigious awards including six Goyas and the Special Jury Silver Lion Award at the Venice Film Festival. Although *El mar adentro* was not very popular with audiences in the United States, it was praised by American film critics and received the most prestigious accolades in North America: a Golden Globe Award and the Academy Award for Best Foreign Picture. The Oscar, in particular, consecrated Amenábar's international reputation as one of Spain's most prominent film-makers. Undeniably, *El mar adentro* changed Amenábar's authorial profile within the international film community: even the most orthodox film magazines, which until then had considered Amenábar just a talented film director specializing in thrillers, praised this film as the work of an inspired and mature auteur.[14]

The delayed acknowledgment of Amenábar's authorial status on the part of the specialized press and the film festival circuit is understandable. On the surface, his films are well-manufactured products meant for the larger circuit of theatrical distribution in domestic as well as international film markets. They pay direct tribute to classical Hollywood style, use aesthetics and cinematic techniques drawing from top popular film genres such as the thriller or the horror film, and (much like Hollywood films) tackle universal themes and issues without forwarding any political point of view or social cause. Amenábar's association with the concept of authorship has less to do with specific contexts of film production and reception or with the engaged and oppositional agenda of the Spanish authorial tradition than with self-conditioned responses to a postmodern context where, as Lawrence Grossberg argues, 'different cultural practices, as well as different popular sensibilities, are constantly opposing, undercutting and reinflecting each other within the unstable formation of everyday life' (1988: 179).

Spanishness and Spain's authorial tradition

Spanish authorial cinema has complex links with the concept of Spanishness. By and large, Spain's auteurist tradition emerged in reaction to the representation of Spanishness in Francoist cinema. In this filmic context, Spanishness was an ideological construct that offered an unrealistic image of the country, mainly derived from regionalist strands and folkloristic versions of Romantic and post-Romantic works from the Spanish literary tradition, as well as from Spain's popular arts and entertainment. Since the inception of the new *nuevo cine* in the early 1950s, many film authors of the pre- and post-Franco period have either parodied or subverted the cultural icons and stereotypes of Spanishness proposed by the regime, or else reformulated Spanishness on the basis of different aesthetic criteria and ideological systems, most importantly Italian neo-realism and Hollywood cinema. The literature on Spanish cinema frequently concentrates on the political and anti-hegemonic agenda of the *nuevo cine* film authors. Marvin D'Lugo views the critique of the Francoist iconology of Spanishness as a recurring motif in the films of Carlos Saura, as well as in those of some post-Francoist film authors, including Pedro Almodóvar and José Luis Bigas Luna (1991a and 1991b). Kathleen M. Vernon highlights the 'strategic uses of American film in constructing an alternative "imaginary" in opposition to dominant cultural practices in Spain' (1997: 36). She notes that the subversive function of the Hollywood intertext in Spanish postmodern cinema, particularly in the films of Pedro Almodóvar, is used 'to articulate a position on the margins of Spanish social and cultural institutions, one that challenges the validity of master narratives, of whatever ideological stripe, in the representation of past and present realities and the relation between them' (ibid.: 43). Like D'Lugo and Vernon, Marsha Kinder considers Almodóvar the most significant example of a post-Franco film-maker who trans-culturally re-inscribes Spanishness through the interplay of neo-realist and Hollywood film aesthetics (ibid.: 247–62).

Spanish film authors' take on Spanishness is complicated by the institutional nature of the Spanish film industry under Franco and the particular function of authorial film practices in the national cinema, both during and after the dictatorship. Since the end of WWII and at least until the mid-1990s, auteur-oriented films in Spain depended on a system of public support committed to promoting Spanish culture through national themes and artistic canons. The institutional foundation and the emphasis on the country's cultural identity and heritage in Spanish authorial cinema are legacies of Franco's regime. The fascist state's investment in this type of cinema had a double and contradictory purpose: to intensify protection against a growing cultural opposition and, at the same time, to promote a more "liberal" image of Spain abroad. At the end of Franco's dictatorship the state remained the main source of financing for Spanish film authors, especially when the national film industry underwent a long period of economic crisis. The institutional hold on authorial film practices then took another direction: once the state had dismissed its controlling and propagandistic function, it enhanced its role as a promoter of Spain's national culture both at home and abroad. The task proved particularly difficult within a domestic film market dominated by Hollywood films. The failure was most evident with respect to films developed from canonical literary works or depicting historical or cultural aspects of the country. The government's ineffectiveness in promoting Spanishness via authorial cinema culminated with the aforementioned Miró Law in 1983.

The Hollywood subtext is also prominent in the new generation of Spanish film directors, including Alejandro Amenábar (Marchante 2002; Payán 2001: 42–44), and a major contribution to the consolidation of their authorship as a culturally specific discourse within the context of a global audio-visual industry dominated by Hollywood products.

Intertextuality, Spanish style: death, authorship, and cultural re-inscription

Alejandro Amenábar grew up during the audio-visual revolution of the 1980s watching films on television and video (Marchante 2002: 31–33). His cinematic style reflects this audio-visual culture, which Antonio Saura describes in these terms:

> It's a generation with an aesthetic sense generated from America's violence and the linear narrative, from skepticism, a generation defined by protagonists without values and with doubts and shadows about their future. It's a generation of people disillusioned about the present and with great faith in their own talent. By and large, they are linked to a considerable general culture, although they make sure to dissimulate this in their public appearances; they are very conscious of the power of mass communication and have developed very sophisticated personal strategies to relate to the media, and they

El espíritu de la colmena: Ana meets Frankenstein

under no circumstances brush with provocation. They come from the middle class and they have grown up watching American cinema. Some of them have studied outside of Spain, but most of them are autodidacts and practitioners of the healthy art of short film-making. (1997: 109, my translation)[15]

Amenábar perfectly matches Saura's profile since both his cinephilia and his professional expertise are less the product of his university education than of personal training. For instance, Amenábar developed his own style by watching films and learned the techniques of film-making, along with all the practical aspect of his profession, on the sets of his own films. He has a vast knowledge of classical and contemporary Hollywood cinema and particularly privileges the adventure film, western, horror, and film noir genres (Sempere 2000: 105–07). His favourite film-makers are Alfred Hitchcock, Stanley Kubrick, and Steven Spielberg, to whom he pays homage in his own work (Amenábar 1996: 7; Marchante 2002: 81–90; Sempere 107–113; Payán 2001: 42; and Garbarz 2001: 19). In his interviews, he makes pointed references to films that are related to his work and often comments on the stylistic and technical strategies associated with specific film-makers (Amenábar 1996: 6–7; Marchante 2002: 58–59; 81–90; 100–06; 139–58). He also quotes other directors extensively (Amenábar 1996; Garbarz 2001; Rouyer and Peck 2002; Marchante 2002: 81–90, 107–13; Amenábar 2001: 163–205; Payán 2001: 38–50). His cinéphilia, combined with his multifarious and quasi-maniacal interest for film techniques, assured Amenábar professional credibility very early in his career, an authority reinforced in interviews through punctual relations made between the formal aspects of his films and specific strategies and solutions used in films directed by film-makers that he likes.

Amenábar cultivated his passion for cinema at a young age and at the margins of official institutions, although he did study film production at the Facultad de Ciencias de la Informacíon

('Department of Informational Sciences') at the Universidad Complutense in Madrid. Amánábar was, in fact, very dissatisfied with the theoretical content of the courses offered and the limited availability of equipment and production facilities offered there (Marchante 2002: 42–45; Sempere 2000: 20–24). For this reason, he often avoided classes and instead hung out with his friend and classmate Mateo Gil, watching films and talking about cinema (ibid.). Together, they also spent hours discussing and preparing film projects. During this period, Amenábar collaborated with Gil and other film students and friends in writing and directing shorts (ibid.). He completed three short videos with cameras purchased with his savings: La cabeza (1991), Himenóptero (1992), and Luna (1994). As Amenábar himself remarks, these early essay films contain the germ of his future work. In 1995, Amenábar remade Luna on

El espíritu de la colmena: Ana meets Frankenstein

35mm with Eduardo Noriega, the future male lead in *Tesis* and *Abre los ojos*, in the role Amenábar had originally played. *La cabeza* and *Luna* anticipated the themes of *Abre los ojos* and *Himenóptero* was the blueprint for *Tesis* (Marchante 2002: 46–47).

Amenábar's short films won several awards at a number of Spanish short film festivals, including top prizes at the Festival de Elche and the Festival de Cine de Carabanchel. His immediate success on the short film festival circuit made him the youngest and most promising director of Spain's new cinema. His second short, *Himenóptero*, caught the attention of José Luis Cuerda, who offered to produce his first feature film on the condition that Amenábar came up with a good script (Amenábar 1996: 5; Sempere 2000: 24–27). As a result, Amenábar took a hiatus from his studies in 1995 and co-wrote a script with Gil. With this first feature film project, Amenábar established his trademark production system, a process that involves a methodical pre-production stage. For example, he often uses detailed storyboards, paying close attention to character and narrative development. Being a self-taught musician, he composes the soundtracks for all of his films and oversees their orchestration. Along with directing a regular cast and crew, he is also heavily involved in the editing process and oversees the final edit (Payán 2001: 46–47; Garbarz 2001: 16).

Even if Amenábar maintains an approach to film-making which complies to Spain's authorial tradition and, much like within the lineage of this tradition, works within independent and national systems production he does not depend on Spain's institutional systems of production generally connected with author cinema and does not use formal strategies associated with the authors of the *Cine Nuevo* movement, notably allegorical narratives and political sub-texts. Yet his affiliation to the same film culture that has informed Spain's *nuevo cine* film authors is manifest in the intertextual relations that some of his films present with canonical works of that movement, as well as with the Hollywood genre and stylistic solutions that informed those films. Most film scholars have stressed the connection in *Tesis* and Víctor Erice's *El espíritu de la colmena/The Spirit of the Beehive* (1973) and Carlos Saura's *Cría cuervos/Raise Ravens* (1976) (Berthier 2002; Buckley 2002; Maule 2000). In a less obvious way, his least Spanish film, the English-language, Hollywood-produced *The Others*, also shares a thematic link with *El espíritu de la colmena* and *Cría cuervos*. Amenábar admits a voluntary reference to the Erice film in *Tesis*, whereas he has never made any reference between *Tesis* to the Saura film or between *The Others* and either of these masterpieces of the *nuevo cine*.

In the Erice and Saura films, Ana Torrent plays a sensitive and imaginative girl named Ana who is obsessed with death. In *Tesis*, the same actress stars as Ángela, a university student examining media representations of violence and death. Surprisingly, at the time *Tesis* was released, Amenábar did not acknowledge the obvious links between his film and the films in which Torrent had made her screen début as a child actress two decades earlier, claiming that he was oblivious to the intertextual coincidences. In a 1996 interview with the Spanish film magazine *Plano Corto*, he declared that his first choice for the role of Ángela was Penelope Cruz, one of Spain's rising stars at the time. However, due to Cruz's unavailability, Cuerda convinced him to opt for Torrent instead. Indeed, Amenábar did cast

Cruz as the protagonist in his next film, *Abre los ojos* (Amenábar 1996: 6). It was only much later that Amenábar acknowledged the influence of Eríce's film on *Tesis*; that is, when his reputation as a film-maker was already firmly established at home and abroad. Amenábar's published conversation with film critic Oti Rodríguez Marchante at the time of *The Others'* release is an interesting case that indicates that Amenábar might have voluntarily understated *Tesis'* connection to Spanish author cinema at the time of the film's release, given the low prestige that this typology of Spanish cinema had at the time. Even in the interview made in 2001, he only partially acknowledges a direct association between his work and Spanish authorial cinema, admitting the influence that *El espíritu de la colmena* had on him as a child (Marchante 2002: 94). Yet the only explicit reference to that film that Amenábar admits, according to him, did not make the final cut (Amenábar 2001: 201; Marchante 2002: 94).

In *Tesis*, Ángela, a sociology student, is writing her thesis on the representation of violence in contemporary society. While trying to find audio-visual materials for her research, she discovers a sordid plot involving snuff videos, which she suspects are the product of a perverse alliance among some students and professors.[16] Her private investigation of this criminal activity develops a plot within the plot in which the pursuer becomes the pursued. Ángela's overtly scientific and academic interest in violent images conceals a secret compulsion: to experience death vicariously through its visual representation. This unsettling desire aligns Ángela with viewers of snuff films for whom the ultimate goal is to witness an actual death.

The parallels between the characters played by the young Torrent in the two earlier films and the character of Ángela played by the adult Torrent in *Tesis* are especially evident in two scenes. During the opening credit sequence of *Tesis*, which takes place in a crowded subway station, Ángela unsuccessfully tries to get a glimpse of a dead body lying on the subway tracks. The first shot of the film is pitch black, and nothing is discernable except for a voice on a loud speaker instructing people to remain calm. The darkness finally lifts revealing the image of a train coming to a dead stop during a power outage. Security personnel direct a line of passengers towards the exit. The camera focuses on Ángela and follows her as she leaves the subway platform, which has been cordoned off by police to prevent people from looking over the railing at the tracks where the suicide has taken place. From this point, the sequence proceeds partially in slow motion, alternating between long shots of Ángela walking and point-of-view shots of her partial view of the tracks and of the gathered police officers that frustrate her attempts to get a peek. The narrative tension and viewer's expectations mount to a crescendo mirrored by the suspenseful musical score. The scene climaxes when Ángela finally breaks away and runs towards the platform, past the security guards, and glances over the edge of the railing. Her desire to see is once again denied when she is hastily pushed away by a police officer.

The second significant scene, in which Ángela's morbid curiosity is sated, follows shortly after the credit sequence. The sequence is filmed using a similar technique of partial slow motion and long takes. The camera follows Ángela as she enters a university library and makes her way to a projection room where she discovers the body of her thesis advisor next to a video projector. The man died while watching videos that Ángela had asked him to retrieve from a section on pornography and violence in the university video archives. The videos are restricted to students and allegedly contain very graphic material. When Ángela finds her professor dead, she does not run away in fear. Instead, she approaches the corpse in a sort of trance and cautiously touches its forehead.

Ángela's reaction to her brush with death is reminiscent of Ana's behaviour in *El espíritu de la colmena*, the film that launched Erice's reputation as an important storyteller and film-maker. In the film, a five-year-old girl living in a secluded house with her parents and older sister in post-civil war Spain is haunted by images of the monster in James Whale's 1931 classic horror film, *Frankenstein*. She finds a wounded man (who was probably shot by a villager for being a republican) in a shed and befriends him. Ana first discovers him when she follows a trail of blood through the open door of the shed. Interestingly, as in *Tesis*, this sequence is filmed in slow motion using a point-of-view long take to progressively reveal the trail of blood shining in the doorway and leading into the dark interior. Ana's discovery is immediately interrupted by the arrival of her father, who has been looking for her in the fields. His appearance makes the girl suspicious and she runs away. Oblivious to his calls, she takes refuge in the woods where she spends the night. While the villagers search for her, she daydreams about meeting the monster. The sequence explicitly invokes scenes from Whale's film, specifically the scene in which Frankenstein accidentally drowns a little girl who has befriended him, and the scene in which people from the girl's village gather to look for the missing child.

Tesis also 'quotes' the style and narrative content of *Cría cuervos*. In the latter film, the young Ana finds her father's dead body in his bedroom. Mesmerized by the sight, the child climbs onto the bed to get a better look at the corpse. She slowly reaches out her hand to caress its head, a gesture repeated by Ángela in *Tesis* upon her discovery of her professor's corpse. Furthermore, Ana's encounter with death is filmed in a slow-motion long take, the same strategy used in *Tesis* for the subway sequence and the scene in the library. Even if we allow that *Tesis*' connections to *El espíritu de la colmena* and *Cría cuervos* may be unintentional, the intertextual coincidences are still significant insofar as they signal the persistence of death as an important trope in Amenábar's cinema. However, in the case of Amenábar's films, the theme of death is no longer associated with Spain's turbulent history, but rather with contemporary global image culture.

Catherine Russell comments that New Wave 'film-makers began to articulate various forms of sexual and political desires within self-conscious forms of cinematic representation [in which] death [...] is the vehicle of an antiauthoritarian challenge to the discourses of control' (1995: 25). In this respect, she opines that death in New Wave cinema functions as both a rhetorical and a narrative device, constituting the spectator 'as the constructed subject of narrative desire and the mortal, historical body outside the text' (ibid.). As was the case with other New Wave movements, the *nuevo cine* had an anti-regime agenda. This preoccupation is apparent in the New Wave films *El espíritu de la colmena* and *Cría cuervos*. Both films draw upon a national cultural heritage of representational motifs in which death is an allegory for pressing social and political issues.

Marsha Kinder argues that *El espíritu de la colmena* and Saura's *La prima Angélica/Cousin Angelica* (also released in 1973) express 'the memories and fantasies of individuals who were emotionally stunned as children and interpellated as permanently infantilized subjects by the traumatic events of the Spanish Civil War' (Kinder 1993: 132). Kinder's comment indeed applies to Ana's situation in Saura's *Cría cuervos*. Set at the end of Franco's dictatorship, the girl is convinced that she is responsible for the death of her father, a stern military man who was involved in Franco's regime. Ana believes that she killed her father through her intense secret wish to punish him for being cruel and unfaithful to her mother, who recently succumbed to cancer. Flash-forward monologues interspersed throughout the film and narrated by the adult, Ana, reveal the child's motivation. In these segments, actress Geraldine Chaplin, who also appears as Ana's mother in the girl's daydreams and recollections, speaks to the camera from an empty room about the misery of her childhood and her plan to take revenge against her father for his cruelty towards her mother. Ana's residual anger towards her severe, self-serving militarist father echoes larger societal sentiments about Franco's regime.

At the beginning of *El espíritu de la colmena*, Ana attends a local screening of *Frankenstein* and Erice inserts the sequence from the film in which the little girl encounters the monster. This scene makes a strong impression on Ana who, as Kinder notes, absorbs 'both monster and victim as her own doubles' (Kinder 1993: 128). The *Frankenstein* excerpt chosen depicts the moment of the girl's drowning. The scene was originally cut to meet the Hays Code so that the death takes place off-screen. Spanish censors further cut the scene to remove the off-screen death all together (ibid.), Kinder explains:

> [...] Ana reinscribes the Gothic myth to suit her own Spanish melodrama, just as it had earlier been reinscribed by Whale to suit the Hollywood horror genre. Only she as a child and Erice as a film-maker (working under repressive censorship practices rather than commercial pressures) foreground nonverbal images and concrete sounds and their impact on the personal plane while the narrative resolutions and political implications regarding Francoist Spain remain implicit and oblique. Yet the film implies that the children of Franco would turn out to be the children of Frankenstein. Thus, in *El espíritu de la colmena*, it is the *process* of cultural reinscription that is emphasized more than the conventions being reinscribed. [...]Ana's relation to the monster points not only to the internalised trauma that marks the post-Franco generation, but also to Erice's reinscription of the Civil War through Hollywood cinema. (Ibid.: 128–29)

The young protagonists of *El espíritu de la colmena* and *Cría cuervos* eventually confront their pasts and move on with their lives. At the end of Erice's film, Ana finally gets out of bed, where she has been lying in a cataleptic state for days following the event in the woods, and walks to the open window. She calls out to the monster, which she believes to be the resurrected creature from Whale's film, thanks to her sister's teasing. Ana's gesture points less to a regression into her childhood fantasy than to her readiness to overcome her fears. Similarly, in the last sequence of *Cría cuervos*, Ana and her sisters go to school in the morning, finally leaving the house in which the entire film has taken place and which symbolizes Ana's sadness and confined childhood. As Ana goes outdoors, her demeanour changes completely, becoming happy and carefree. She soon loses herself in the crowd of children at school. According to Marvin D'Lugo, this closing sequence suggests that Ana is 'moving toward the ideal of lucidity that her future self in 1995 has already achieved' (1991: 137). For the film's final shot, Saura strategically positions the camera so that dozens of children pass in front of it, most of them out of focus. The scene ends with a freeze-frame in which Ana has been enveloped by the other children and becomes indistinct from them, signifying her successful entry into society and her adaptation to its conventions.

In some ways, Tesis begins where El espíritu de la colmena and Cría cuervos left off. The flash-forwards in Cría cuervos are set twenty years after Ana encounters her dead father. In Tesis, Ana Torrent not only plays a character with similar obsessions; it is as if her role is a continuation of the one that marked her cinematic début. Lika Ana, Ángela is haunted by death. Her experiences with death perhaps help her resolve her fixation, but as the film's final sequence hints, she cannot escape the pervasiveness of visual images that reproduce death and are themselves a metaphor for death. The last scene of Tesis takes place in a hospital where Ángela is recovering from the shock of having almost been a victim of the serial-killer/snuff film-maker, Bosco (played by Eduardo Noriega); she was supposed to 'star' in his next film. Just as her friend Chema enters Ángela's room, one of Bosco's movies is about to air on television and the two wait eagerly with their eyes fixed on the television monitor. When the film is about to begin, Ángela gets out of bed and the two flee the hospital. The camera pans across the room and stops on the television screen. An announcer explains that it is not easy for the network to show the violent images, yet their documentary value is invaluable because they are unquestionably real. Afterwards, the television screen fades to black and a warning about the affecting nature of the broadcast appears. At the moment when the snuff film is about to start, Tesis' closing credits begin to roll. This ending, wherein the viewer's vision is cut short, aims to frustrate the viewer's scopophilic desire, a technique used throughout the film. This strategy underlines Tesis' central theme and demonstrates that the scopophilic drive is not only formed by ubiquitous audio-visual culture, but that audio-visual culture is also a response to, and in many ways created by, our desires.

Although The Others is not usually discussed in relation to El espíritu de la colmena or Cría cuervos, the film contains many thematic connections to the nuevo cine classics. The Others is a gothic thriller set in the secluded countryside of Jersey Island in the British Channel at the end of World War II. In the film, Grace, played by Nicole Kidman, is a strict Catholic woman mourning the death of her husband who was presumably killed in the war. Grace lives in an isolated mansion that is apparently haunted by ghosts with her two children, Anne and Nicholas, who both suffer from a rare form of photosensitivity and cannot be exposed to sunlight. Like the protagonists of the Erice and Saura films, Grace's daughter, Anne, is both fascinated and repelled by death. Her narrative destiny also parallels those of Ángela and the young protagonists of El espíritu de la colmena and Cría cuervos. All these characters share a contradictory attraction-fear relationship with death, and all manage to free themselves of their morbid desires by experiencing death close up. Anne is the only one who can see the ghosts in the house and is not afraid of them. Indeed, Anne communicates with the ghosts, draws their pictures, and even befriends one of them, a ghost child her own age named Victor. Like Ana's older sister in *El espíritu de la colmena*, Anne takes perverse pleasure in scaring Nicholas by telling him stories about Victor. In so doing, she provokes panic attacks in the boy and angers her mother, who punishes her for telling lies. Anne and her mother reconcile only when the latter also begins to sense the spectres around the house and, eventually, discovers that their servants are indeed phantoms. Yet Anne is resentful of Grace throughout the film, even before their disagreement over the presence of ghosts in the house. She seems suspicious of her mother, although the cause of her suspicion is not explained. Anne vaguely hints to Nicholas and their nanny, Mrs Mills, that a dreadful incident occurred in the house many years ago involving the family, one that was caused by Grace's temper. It is revealed only in the end that her insinuations are true; in a moment of anger, Grace accidentally killed Anne and Nicholas and, in her grief, committed suicide. She and her children had continued living as ghosts in the same house, unaware of the fact that they are dead. Hence, the actual ghosts in the house are Anne and her family and the servants who once lived there. The people Grace thought were ghosts, that is, the people who bought the house following the tragic death of Grace and her children, are, in fact, the only living inhabitants of the mansion and have been trying to perform an exorcism with the help of a medium. Anne's acceptance of her situation is summed up by her nanny's sentiment: the dead and the living must learn to live together. As such, Anne's trajectory is similar to those of the two young protagonists in *El espíritu de la colmena* and *Cría cuervos*, who both learn to live with their ghosts.

In *The Others* (as well as in *Tesis*), no political allegory subsumes the protagonist's encounter with death, as it was the case in the films of the *nuevo cine*: the reference is rather to the postmodern condition as one in which the subject's relation to reality is problematized by the dominance of mass media and visual technologies.

In *The Others*, Amenábar's intertextual references to traditional Spanish cinema and his adoption of Hollywood genre conventions is again at the centre of Amenábar's meta-cinematic discourse and authorial negotiation of competing cultural and cinematic interests. As Nancy Berthier proposes:

> It's precisely this double movement of assimilation of the codes of the best American cinema and of the creation of an absolutely personal universe within the framework of European-style authorial cinema that allows us to explain the paradox of [Amenábar's] third film, *The Others/Los otros*, produced in the United States but in which the film-maker has at no moment renounced his authorial exigencies. Going well beyond the simple pretension of competing with the North American industry in Spain, Amenábar, with this film, has gone as far as to challenge it on its own terrain, utilising its own capital to – maybe... – propagate another way of making cinema. (2002: 130, my translation)[17]

With *The Others*, the process of cultural re-inscription of Hollywood into Spanish cinema that Vernon describes in terms of 'strategic uses of American film in constructing an alternative "imaginary" in opposition to dominant cultural practices in Spain' (1997: 36) moves to another level. While Hollywood is no longer an oppositional practice for contemporary Spanish cinema, it is not a hegemonic ideology that has co-opted its national cinema either.

The Others demonstrates that Hollywood and Spanish authorial cinema may live together, and that contemporary Spanish cinema may revive cinema's future by appropriating Hollywood's past filmic styles and classical film genres.

Life is a (virtual) nightmare: authorship in the new media society

Alejandro Amnábar's authorial discourse based on a *cin phile*-informed approach to cinema is apparent through the self-reflexivity and intertextuality of his films. His films flaunt their artifice by overtly placing themselves within the cinematic tradition, whether this is conveyed through borrowings from a variety of films or through themes, characters, and situations that refer to the pervasiveness of audio-visual media in contemporary society. In cinema, reflexivity has primarily been associated with experimental and political films that embrace modernist aesthetics or Brechtian techniques to develop abstract and non-representational forms of meaning. Reflexivity has also been used ironically to question the illusionist codes of classical and dominant cinema.

In defining modern cinema's self-reflexivity, Linda Hutcheon refers to William Siska's argument that the modernist impetus to contest narrative and representational transparency 'takes the form of an insistence on formal intransitivity by such techniques as the rupturing of the chain of causation upon which character and plot motivation depend, spatial or temporal fragmentation, or the introduction of "alien" forms and information' (Siska 1979: 889). Picking up Siska's assertion, Hutcheon remarks that reflexivity serves a different purpose in the postmodern context of signification where it becomes a de-naturalizing and self-referential tactic of representation (Hutcheon 1989: 109). Using the films of Woody Allen as an example, Hutcheon declares that their use of parody and meta-cinematic references both exploit and recontextualize the notion of 'humanist-modernist wholeness' (ibid.) typically associated with the modernist mode of self-reflexivity. She concludes, 'Showing the formation process not just of subjectivity but also of narrativity and visual representation has become a staple of metacinema today. The postmodern variant of this kind calls attention to the very acts of production and reception of the film itself' (ibid.: 110).

Hutcheon's emphasis on reflexivity as a postmodern technique that reveals and questions the constructedness of subjectivity and of representation from within an aesthetic and industrial framework of film discourse is pertinent to the examination of Amenábar's postmodern authorial approach to film-making. Yet Amenábar's films do not adopt a postmodern aesthetic of representation; quite the opposite, they use narrative and formal techniques to reinforce diegetic and discursive coherence. The intertextual and meta-cinematic references in his films invoke postmodern modes of filmic signification and reception in which subjectivity and representation are undermined at the outset. From this perspective, Amenábar is a postmodern author insofar as he partakes in commercial tactics of enunciation and reception that, while undermining personal authority as a principle of coherence behind the film text, engage with a self-reflexive, *cinéphile*-oriented discourse on cinema where authorship informs intertextual and extra-textual strategies of meaning formation.

Amenábar's use of reflexivity is particularly relevant in his treatment of death, the most distinctive and frequently recurring motif in his films. Amenábar has projected his discourse on death onto a meta-cinematic level since his début film, Tesis. Tesis explores the snuff film, the death film *par excellence*, to point to a theme at the basis of all Amenábar's films: the doomed fate of cinema in the present audio-visual society. As Nancy Berthier observes, Tesis is a meta-film that takes a position vis-à-vis an urgent question in mid-1990s Spain: the crisis of its national cinema. The film explicitly refers to this crisis in an early scene in which a film professor (who is involved in producing snuff films) advises his students to challenge Hollywood and save Spanish cinema from its imminent death by making films that give audiences what they want (Berthier 2002: 119–20). Furthermore, Berthier suggests, Tesis is itself a response to the crisis in Spanish cinema in that it intelligently negotiates both formulaic Hollywood codes and Spanish authorial cinema styles (ibid.: 129–30).

The representation of death in Amenábar's films also comments on the functions and consequences of cinematic violence. By revealing the artifice of cinema and quoting from film history, reflexivity reduces everything, including violence, to clichés, thereby desensitizing the viewer. The challenge of orientating the self within an audio-visual environment saturated with representations of death is a difficult one, especially as the boundaries between reality and representation become more and more tenuous. Amenábar's films regularly show the limits of our ability to experience reality by drawing attention to the pervasiveness and invasiveness of electronic media and their impact on our perception of reality. In Tesis, reflexivity resolves a fundamental question: How does one account for the complicity of the viewing subject in today's audio-visual systems? In Tesis, the snuff film functions as the endpoint of cinema; it is not only an image of death in the Barthesian sense shared by all photographic representations, it is actually the image of a death event (see Barthes 1981). Ángela's ambivalent stance vis-à-vis violent images interpellates the viewer's position in relation to such images. The unexpected change in Ángela's position from a passive viewer to an active participant in the creation of violent images foreshadows the film's central question: To what extent is the viewer complicit in the fetishism and sadism of what he/she watches? In raising this issue, Tesis proves, in extremis, Carol Clover's classic argument about the reflexive nature of horror films: 'there is in some sense no original, no real or right text, but only variants, so that 'the "art" of the horror film, like the "art" of pornography, is to a very large extent the art of rendition or performance, and it is understood as such by the competent audience' (Clover 1992: 11).

Reflexivity is at the very core of Amenábar's second film, Abre los ojos (1997). The protagonist, César (Eduardo Noriega), a wealthy, handsome, selfish, twenty-five-year-old playboy is confronted with his own narcissism and mortality when he is the victim of a violent car accident that leaves him heavily disfigured. His carefree life as a philanderer dramatically comes to a full stop. Unable to regain his good looks, even after reconstructive surgery, he plunges into a psychotic delirium in which reality and fantasy become intertwined. In the end, he realizes that his only hope out of this nightmare is to commit suicide. The narrative suggests that César might, in fact, already be dead, having committed suicide in a desperate moment after signing a contract with a cryonics company called 'Life Extension'. Apparently, César was so unhappy with his new fate that he resorted to preserving his body so that it could be resurrected years later when medical science had developed the means to restore his face. In the meantime,

César lives on in a dream life generated by a computer program. Following this narrative, as it is carefully constructed in the film, what César experiences as his life is nothing more than an artificial simulation from which he can only escape by committing virtual suicide. This would allow him to be resurrected back into a 'real,' albeit new and unknown, life. The film ends the same way it begins, in a darkened room with a voice speaking to César, instructing him to open his eyes. The mystery is left unresolved: the scene depicts either the protagonist's rebirth into the future or the beginning of the next phase in his dream life.

Apropos to Pascale Thibadeau's writing on *Abre los ojos* and Mateo Gil's *Nadie conoce a nadie* (1999), these films inscribe themselves into Spain's literary tradition insofar as they propose contemporary versions of Pedro Calderón de la Barca's play *La vida es sueño/Life Is a Dream* (1636–1637) and *El gran teatro del mundo/The Great Theatre of the World* (1635), respectively (Thibaudeau 2002: 143). Thibaudeau suggests that in recalling de la Barca's questioning of the nature of reality (informed, I suggest, by baroque philosophy's inquiries into the essence of mind and body and the unverifiable status of truth), these films offer a culturally specific approach to two central issues in contemporary film: the blurring between reality and virtuality and the crisis of subjectivity. (Ibid.)[18] According to Thibaudeau, *Abre los ojos* and *Nadie conoce a nadie* reinstate the primacy of reality over the virtual. In so doing, they point to the demons of contemporary reality:

> In this transitional epoch, in which a number of parameters that have been in place for centuries are re-opened, where the human species is in the process of mechanisation and mutation, where robots are given artificial intelligence and life is commercialised, cinema articulates the concerns of contemporary society and puts them into images. What these paradoxically iconoclastic films ultimately reveal is that images themselves are demonic; they abolish the boundaries between dreams and reality, between games and reality, and between fiction and reality. In redefining the limits of the real, by privileging the virtual over the actual, man loses his soul. Science and technology, those instruments of power based on optimisation and performance, negate reality by refuting the mortal body and condemn man to live...in hell. (Thibaudeau 2002: 160, my translation)[19]

Thibaudeau notes that *Abre los ojos'* ambivalent view of reality is reflected in its narrative structure. This structure challenges the 'regimen of belief' according to which cinematic enunciation creates a doubling effect wherein the spectator identifies with the protagonist's 'reality', opening up the filmic text to the discursive possibility of difference (in interpretation), as in an interactive game (ibid.: 144–47). By complicating the perceptions of the protagonist, the film calls into question the notion of subjectivity and the process of identification associated with classical cinema and the narrative system (ibid.: 147–53).

While far from developing anti-narratives or meta-narratives, Amenábar's films propose narrative structures and formal solutions that point to a reflexive use of the medium. Nancy Berthier links the relationship between on-screen and off-screen representation in *Tesis* to André Bazin's theory that cinema, unlike painting, is the centrifugal art *par excellence*. Bazin postulated that while painting confines the image within a frame, cinema uses images metonymically to represent a complete diegetic world beyond the frame; cinema, in effect, propels the image outwards (1971: 188). Berthier argues that in *Tesis*, Amenábar plays with the centrifugal tendency of cinema to produce an 'aesthetic of frustration, which creates desire and scopic pulsion to better deceive [the viewer]' (2002: 129, my translation).[20]

On his part, Jacques Terrasa focuses on the use of the black screen in *Abre los ojos*, a technique, he reminds us, that is equally prominent in the opening shots of *Tesis* and *The Others*, and which, I would add, returns in *El mar adentro*. This technique draws attention to the spectator's perceptual and cognitive processes and registers the expectations brought about by the act of viewing. He concludes:

> At this stage – that of a degree zero of the icon – the film, be it veiled or non-exposed (be the screen white or black), situates itself at the extreme points of iconicity, when the exacerbated desire of the film-maker and of the film spectator converge to regulate the flux and give birth to forms. Is it because this torrent of light that presses behind the black film is so intense, so violent, that Alejandro Amenábar's first three films open diegetically on such extreme situations? (Terrasa 2002: 171, my translation.)[21]

The self-reflexive framework of Amenábar's films is related to their extra-textual discourses, including promotional material, reception in film magazines and at film festivals, and the director's interviews and personal statements. The opening page of Amenábar's official website states that 'my movies are not movies of answers but of questions',[22] which points to the films' relationships with their sociocultural milieu. Additionally, the website cites Amenábar's comments on each of his films following their synopses, consistently reinforcing the self-reflexive nature of his work. For example, Amenábar writes of *Tesis*:

> The public, that is mainly interested in the images, is 'punished' this way but, this punishment is compensated by a script full of tricks and designed for the public's entertainment. However, the script, in several moments, proposed a reflection – while avoiding a teaching style-about the future of the audio-visual market: The pressure of the American Movie Industry, main example of movies dominated y economic interests, the growing diffusion of the 'snuff movies' (in which human beings are murdered in front of the camera) in the video circuits; the legitimisation of violence in TV news; the dominance of images over words, the individualisation of the public by means of TV and video, their insensibilization and loses of contact with reality.[23]

The promotional website for *Abre los ojos* (http:// www.sogetel.es/abrelosojos.htm, no longer operative) offered another example of marketing that focused on the self-reflexive character of Amenábar's work.[24] As Jean-Paul Aubert explains in his detailed analysis of *Abre los ojos*, the website echoed the film's atmosphere and themes without making direct reference to them (2002: 138). In this way, 'the website of *Abre los ojos* addresses itself to an informed spectator/ Internet user and allows him to continue an exploration to which the film already invited him' (2002: 140, my translation).[25] Aubert concludes that *Abre los ojos* contains a meta-cinematic reference to a different medium and that this reference is central to its narrative:

The film solicits the virtual universe of the Internet and the Internet site refers back to the film. However, this back-and-forth does not advocate any subordination of one support to the other. In privileging a spectator who is both a *cinuphile* and an Internet user, it may simply suggest a widening of the boundaries of the two media (ibid., my translation).[26]

Genre and transnational politics of authorial representation

Alejandro Amenábar's films are most readily associated with the thriller genre. In their discussion of film genres in contemporary Spanish cinema as instances of cultural re-inscription from a national and transnational point of view, Barry Jordan and Rikki Morgan-Tamosunas categorize *Tesis* within the subgenre of the psychological thriller because it aims at understanding the nature of psychopathology. Jordan and Morgan-Tamosunas claim that *Tesis* is 'an example of a film in which male violence, torture, mutilation and murder are dealt with in a more serious though no less commercial manner' (1998: 103–04). For this reason, they observe, there is 'an obvious contradiction between the film's rejection of male violence and aggression and the clear commercial potential arising from showing (simulated) examples of such behaviour' (ibid.: 104).

Violence features prominently in Spanish genre films of the last generation. The aim of these films is to create sensational effects by borrowing the conventions of Hollywood cinema. The commercial function of violence in contemporary Spanish cinema is markedly different from the way authors of the *nuevo cine* deployed violence as a form of political dissidence and social critique. As Marsha Kinder remarks, 'the graphic depiction of violence is primarily associated with an anti-Francoist perspective' (1993: 138) in the works of *nuevo cine* film-makers such as Erice, Saura, José Luis Borau, Ricardo Franco, Manuel Gutiérrez Aragon, Pilar Miró, and Augustín Villaronga. However, even for the *nuevo cine*, cinematic violence had another function: to attract domestic audiences. Kinder states:

> Moreover, this graphic violence had commercial appeal, especially in the post-Franco era when foreign pornography began to flood Spanish screens and Spanish spectators were drawn to the violent excesses of foreign cinemas. Thus, this oppositional system of representation developed against a double hegemony: domestically, it had to be distinguished from the conventions of the Counter-Reformation (particularly remolded by the Fascist aesthetic), where violence was eroticized as ritual sacrifice; globally and commercially, it had to be distinguished from Hollywood's valorization of violence as a dramatic agent of moral change (Kinder 1993: 138).[27]

According to Kinder, the films of the *nuevo cine*, proposed a 'radical cinema of cruelty' that 'eradicates the distinction between impure and purifying violence on which all social order is allegedly based' (1993: 154). She borrows her interpretation of violent sacrifice in Spain's Counter-Reformation culture from French anthropologist René Girard and, particularly, his book *Violence and the Sacred* (1977). For Girard, she explains, sacrifice is a ritualized form of expression that serves to maintain social order (Kinder 1993: 176–96). Kinder examines the ritualized representation of historical violence in Spanish films made after the Franco era, among which she singles out Ricardo Franco's *Pascal Duarte* (1976) and Augustín Villaronga's

Tras el cristal (1985). She remarks, '[...] the contemporary historical massacre (the Civil War or the Holocaust) is a structuring absence that helps to generate the escalating acts of primitive sacrificial murder that control the narrative, for, as Girard claims, "in order to retain its structuring influence, the generative violence must reimain hidden"' (Girard (1977: 309), quoted *in* Kinder 1993: 185). Kinder also observes that in the two aforementioned films, the murderous protagonists 'are presented not as deviant individuals but as violent subjects who have been constructed by a perverted culture' (1993: 196).

On-screen violence and its extreme manifestation, murder, are still prominent in Spanish films but without the attending social critique. The representation of violence in recent postmodern Spanish cinema is apolitical and ahistorical, conforming to what Catherine Russell observes as the dominant discursive trend in films coming out of the 1980s and 1990s. She states that 'violence is more systematically stylized and believability no longer an issue of morality, politics, or representation' (1995: 27). If one assumes that *Tesis*, (or, by the same token *Abre los ojos* and *The Others*) is primarily a genre film, then one can easily position it within the niche market of what some video distributors categorize as 'Euro-trash' cinema, indiscriminately lumping art house films by Jean-Luc Godard and Michelangelo Antonioni together with low-budget horror films. According to Joan Hawkins (1999: 15), this distribution category supports Carol Clover's point that horror films overturn the traditional distinction between 'high' and 'low' culture (Clover 1992: 11). This loss of distinction is particularly strong in European film production, distribution, and exhibition, where the 'operative criteria [...] is affect: the ability of a film to thrill, frighten, gross out, arouse, or otherwise directly engage the spectator's body' (Hawkins 1999: 16). Mainly relying on the categories prescribed within the video rental market, Clover believes that this type of categorization best captures 'what the public senses to be the 'horror' of the 'Euro-trash' film. This category indiscriminately groups big-budget dramas or horror thrillers with a large selection of 'lowbrow' and 'exploitation' films (Clover 1992: 5).

Regardless, Amenábar's films hardly belong in the exploitation category as he refuses to adopt the technique of sensationalism to create suspense or elicit fear. He states that his approach to thriller and horror films is different from that of most Hollywood and mainstream products insofar as he privileges subtlety over shock value. In an interview with Amenábar published in the auteur-oriented film magazine *Positif* upon the release of *The Others* in France, film critic Franck Garbarz acknowledged, with reference to the film-maker's tendency to let the horror take place off-screen, 'it's what one doesn't see that is the most terrorizing' (Garbarz 2001: 16, my translation).[28] Amenábar further developed on this point saying:

> It's an old theory that some Hollywood producers would not repudiate. Yet, in fact, horror cinema most of the time is happy with accumulating special effects – which I do not find frightening. Repulsive, maybe, impressive for a moment, but this [device] does not mark you. As for me, I prefer to play with the spectator's mental projections, to make fear emerge from him by suggesting what is behind the door, what's hiding back there. I find this much more interesting. The ghosts that float in the air and pass through walls – I don't find this frightening at all. My films – notably *The Others* – are inscribed within an approach opposite to that of *The Haunting* [Jan de Bont, 1999] – the remake of the

original [Robert Wise, 1963] – whose special effects are extraordinary, but which has nothing frightening about it. (Garbarz 2001: 16–17, my translation)[29]

Commenting on this characteristic of Amenábar's cinema in her aforementioned essay, Berthier argues that in using a technique of 'scopic frustration,' *Tesis* negotiates an alternative position for Spanish cinema, one that fuses Hollywood genre with Spanish cinema's styles and approaches. She contends that Amenábar

> [...] does not condemn American cinema; after all, it is one of his major points of reference and his cinematic education took place at a time when [Hollywood] inundated the screens. He even enjoys citing and borrowing certain elements of American cinema's aesthetics, and, occasionally, of the thriller, a formulaic and overexploited genre even by North American industry standards. But he stops his gathering here. From there, he adapts his subject to Spain in the 1990s. He sets his characters in a specifically Spanish cultural context that is notably represented by the Faculty of Sciences of Information – profoundly Spanish characters, young people his age who look like him, and an actress, Ana Torrent, that establishes a strong link with the Spanish cinema of his predecessors. In fact it is no coincidence that he makes an actress whose gaze, one could say, was represented in Víctor Erice's *El espíritu de la colmena* (1973) and Carlos Saura's *Cría cuervos* (1975) the heroine of his own film about the gaze. (Berthier 2002: 129, my translation)[30]

With *El mar adentro* (2004), Amenábar explores the social drama for the first time, using his own cultural frame of reference. The film is set in Galicia, one of Spain's autonomous communities situated on the Northwest of Spain's Atlantic coast. The narrative is inspired by the true story of Ramón Sampedro, a quadriplegic man who made national headlines in the 1990s for his struggle against the Spanish government to win the right to medical euthanasia. Sampedro, who became paralysed in his early twenties due to a diving accident, was bedridden for almost 30 years. During this time, he fought for legal permission to commit assisted suicide and lost. However, he did eventually commit suicide with the help of a friend in 1998. He wrote a book about his experience, which became a best-seller in Spain. The event caused quite a commotion, galvanizing public opinion and engendering a strong critical backlash from the Catholic Church.

Robert Sklar observes that Amenábar's ascent within the international film community, which was already apparent with *The Others*, is further reinforced by this film:

> At this point his genre-based work appeared to place him on a familiar transatlantic, if not Hollywood-bound, trajectory, and some who followed his career applauded his breaking free from what they regarded as Spanish cinema's self-absorption with the nation's past and present dilemmas. *The Sea Inside* may mark a new turn, or return, for Amenábar, but it also maintains the authorial tropes of his thrillers, a predominant concern with questions of consciousness and personal perception. (2005: 53)

Rather than a new turn or a return, *El mar adentro* marks a step forward in Amenábar's career as a postmodern author, commercially minded within a transnational framework of reception, yet, nonetheless, maintaining a very distinct and culturally over-determined position.

Jay Beck's apropos remark about Pedro Almodóvar and Julio Medem's works and their relation to Spanish culture and identity also applies to Amenábar. According to Beck, Almodóvar and Medem 'take pains to avoid issues of rethinking the Francoist legacy and turn instead to using cinema as a tool to write the future of Spanish identity in the era of transnational commerce and culture' and 'unlike the generic reinscription proposed by Kinder and others, the genre-based tropes used in the films function as synechdotal markers of deeper issues, almost always related to questions of identity, national, and personal' (Beck 2000: 141–42). In the case of Amenábar, his preference for the genre film is at the same time a symptom of cultural conditioning and a way to reposition Spanish films within the contemporary film market.

Notes

1. On these and other film-makers who débuted in the 1990s, see Heredero 1999.
2. I am thinking specifically of the three instalments of Segura's police action-thriller *Torrente*, featuring the director in the role of the protagonist (*Torrente, el brazo tonto de la ley*, 1998; *Misión en Marbella*, 2001; and *Torrente 3: El protector*, 2005). For his part, de la Iglesia has specialized in gothic and surrealist comedies, a film cycle he inaugurated with the top-grossing films *Acción mutante* (1993) and *El dia de la bestia* (1995), and recently revamped with *Crimen ferpecto* (2004). Segura and de la Iglesia, who are friends, have occasionally made public declarations about which one of them earned more box office receipts.
3. About Amenábar's professional relationship with Gil, see Marchante 2002: 33–39; 49–50; 65–69; 84–85; 91; 101–02; 157; and Payán 2001: 43. On his work with Cuerda, see Marchante 2002: 46–49; 54–55; 68–73; 97–99; 106; 136; 158–59; 165–66; 171–72; and Payán 2001: 43.
4. Amenábar's references to these film directors will be further discussed in another section of this chapter.
5. Italics are in original text.
6. Some recent approaches to Spanish cinema move away from the auteur paradigm. Included in this set, among others, are Jordan and Morgan-Tamosunas 1998; Talens and Zunzunegui 1998; and Benavent 2000.
7. *¡Bienvenido, Mr. Marshall!/Welcome, Mr. Marshall!* (Luis García Berlanga, 1952) was a landmark film for Spanish cinema. The film's director, Luis García Berlanga, borrowed generic conventions from the American western film. As with Berlanga's other comedies and farces throughout the 1950s and 1960s, *¡Bienvenido, Mr. Marshall!* is a social allegory that presents a metaphorical yet sharp critique of Spanish society and politics under Franco's regime.
8. See Kinder's book on Spanish national cinema (Kinder 1993), as well as the anthology she edited some years later (Kinder 1997), in which she wrote a chapter on the topic of formal and narrative complexity in post-Francoist Spanish cinema, 'Documenting the National and Its Subversion in a Democratic Spain' (Kinder 1997: 65–98).
9. Berlanga was active as a film director and producer up until 2002. He is the Honorary President of the Academia de las Artes y las Ciencias Cinematográficas de España (A.A.C.C.E.), founded in 1985 by film producer Alfredo Matas to support and implement the strategies of the Spanish film industry.

10. 'Que con la excusa de salir a la calle y dar testimonio salieron unas películas pedants y aburridas, influidas por el neorrealismo [sic]. El cine abandonó entonces los platós para recluirse en los despachos del Ministerio de Cultura.' The quotation appears in José Louis Payán's short introduction to the book, titled 'Introducción. Los Gozos y las sombras del cine español'. Berlanga's linguistic pun involving the repetition of the verb 'salir' (literally 'to go out' or 'to come out') is untranslatable into English. On the Salamanca Congress, see Payán's introduction and, among others, Kinder (1993: 26–28). Note that Payán dates the Congress 1956, while Kinder and other scholars set the event in 1955.

11. '[...] la industria atravesaba una de sus pandémicas crisis de confianza.' Saura's comments appear in a double issue of Viridiana (Saura 1997: 104). Viridiana publishes film scripts of emerging film-makers. In the aforementioned issue, the screenplays are Icíar Bollaín's Hola, estas sola? (1996) and Augustín Díaz Yanes's Nadie Hablará de nosotras cuando hayamos muerto (1995).

12. Data pertaining to annual film production and attendance is available on the online portal of the Spanish Ministery of Culture, Department of Cinema and Audio-visual Arts, available at: http://www.mcu.es/cine/MC/CDC/index.html.

13. On this subject, see Jordan and Morgan-Tamosunas (1998: 5).

14. See, among others, the following articles and reviews: Goodridge and Wilson 2005; Martinez 2005; Sklar 2005. On the other hand, Cahiers du Cinéma wrote quite a negative review ('Mar adentro.' Cahiers du Cinéma, 36: 35–38, février 2005).

15. 'Es una generación con un sentido estético hijo de la violencia, de la narración lineal americana, del esceptismo, una generación definida por unos protagonistas sin valores y con dudas sobre su futuro. Es una generación de desencantados del presente con una gran fe en el propio talento. En general, atesoran una considerable cultura general, aunque procuran disimularlo en su comparencias públicas: son muy conscientes del poder de la comunicación y han desarrollado estrategias personales muy sofisticadas de relación con los medios, que en algunos casos rozan la provocación. Vienen de la clase media y han crecido viendo cine americano. Algunos han estudiado fuera de España, pero los más son autodidactas y praticantes del sano arte del cortometraje.'

16. Tesis was distributed under the title Snuff in some countries.

17. 'C'est précisement ce double mouvement d'assimilation des codes du meilleur cinéma hollywoodien et de création d'un univers absolument personnel dans le cadre du cinéma d'auteur à l'européenne qui permet d'expliquer le paradoxe de son troisième film, The Others/Los otros, produit aux États-Unis, mais dans lequel le réalisateur n'a à aucun moment renoncé à ses exigences de créateur. Allant bien au-delà de la simple prétention de concurrencer l'industrie nord-américaine en Espagne, Amenábar, avec ce film, est allé jusqu'à la défier sur son propre terrain, utilisant ses propres capitaux pour – peut-être... – y propager une autre façon de faire du cinéma.'

18. Among the films that address these issues, Thibaudeau (2002: 143) mentions David Cronenberg's Videodrome (1982), Paul Verhoeven's Total Recall (1990), Wim Wender's Until the End of the World (1991), David Lynch's Lost Highway (1996), David Fincher's The Game (1997), and Peter Weir's The Truman Show (1998).

19. 'À cette époque chernière où nombre de paramètres en vigueur depuis des siècles sont remis en cause, où l'espèce humaine est en voie de mécanisation et de mutation, où l'on dote des robots d'intelligence artificielle et l'on commercialise le vivant, le cinéma cristallise nos angoisses contemporaines en les mettant en images. Or, ce que nous disent en dernière instance ces films paradoxalement iconoclastes, c'est que c'est l'image elle-même qui est démoniaque car c'est elle

qui abolit les limites entre le rêve et la réalité, entre le jeu et la réalité, entre la fiction et la réalité. En perdant la référence au réel, en privilégiant le virtuel face à l'actuel, l'homme perd son âme, en refusant la réalité du corps mortel par le recours aux nouvelles performances scientifiques et technologiques, ou par le truchement d'un jeu et de médias niant la réalité, il se condamne à vivre ... un enfer.'

20. [...] esthétique de la frustration, qui créée [sic] le désir et la pulsion scopique pour mieux les décevoir.'

21. 'À ce stade – celui d'un degré zéro de l'icône –, la pellicule, qu'elle soit voilée ou non exposée (que l'écran soit blanc ou noir), se situe aux points extrêmes de l'iconicité, lorsque le désir exacerbé du cinéaste et du spectateur convergent pour réguler le flux et donner naissance aux formes. Est-ce donc parce que le torrent de lumière qui se presse derrière la pellicule est si intense, si violent, que les trois premiers films d'Alejandro Amenábar s'ouvrent diégétiquement sur des situations extrêmes?'

22. Available: http://www.clubcultura.com/clubcine/clubcineastas/amenabar/intro.htm.

23. Available: http://www.clubcultura.com/clubcine/clubcineastas/amenabar/tesis.htm. Original syntax, spelling, and punctuation have been retained.

24. *Abre los ojos* appears in the filmography of Sogetel's website. [Online.] Available: http://www.sogecinesogepaq.com/ficha.asp?id=3&pelicula=ABREpercent20LOSper cent20OJOS.

25. '[L]a page web de *Abre los ojos* s'adresse à un spectateur-internaute averti et lui permet de prolonger une exploration à laquelle le film l'invitait déjà.'

26. 'Le film solicite donc l'univers virtuel d'internet: le site internet renvoie au film. Cependant, ce va-et-vient ne prône pas une quelconque soumission d'un support à l'autre. En privilégiant un récepteur à la fois *cinéphile* et internaute, peut-être suggère-t-il simplement l'elargissement des frontières de ces deux médias.'

27. According to Kinder, Francisco Goya's counter-hegemonic model of representation using mainly strategies of parody and allegory influenced a number of Spanish film-makers, including Carlos Saura. In her book, she finds direct allusions to Goya in Saura's *Llanto por un bandido* (1963), as well as in the second episode of the three-part anthology film produced by Elías Querejeta *Los desafíos/The Challenges* (1969), directed by José Luis Egea (Kinder 1993: 156–160; 176).

28. 'C'est ce que l'on ne voit pas qui est le plus terrorisant.'

29. 'Il s'agit d'une vieille théorie que ne renieraient pas certains producteurs hollywoodiens. Mais, dans les faits, le cinéma d'horreur se contente la plupart du temps d'accumuler les effets spéciaux – ce que je ne trouve pas effrayant. Répugnant peut-être, impressionnant pendant un moment, mais cela ne vous marque pas. Je préfère quant à moi jouer avec les projections mentales du spectateur, faire naître la peur en suggérant ce qu'il y a derrière la porte, ce qui s'y cache. Je trouve ça beaucoup plus intéressant. Les fantômes qui flottent dans les airs ou qui passent à travers les murs, je ne trouve pas ça effrayant du tout. Mes films – et notamment *Les Autres* – s'inscrivent dans une demarche inverse à celle de *Hantise*, le remake de *La Maison du diable*, don't les effets spéciaux sont extraordinaire mais qui n'a rien d'effrayant.'

30. '[...] ne condamne pas le cinéma américain, qui reste un de ses référents majeurs, ne serait-ce que parce que son éducation cinématographique s'est faite à une période où ce dernier inondait les écrans. Il va même jusqu'à s'amuser à le citer et à lui emprunter certains éléments de son esthétique, ici, en l'occurrence, un cadre générique surexploité par l'industrie nord-américaine, le thriller. Mais ici s'arrête la ressemblance. À partir de là, il adapte son propos à l'Espagne des années quatre-

vingt-dix. Il fait vivre ses personnages dans un contexte spécifiquement espagnol, représenté notamment par la Faculté de Sciences de l'Information, avec des personnages profondément espagnols, des jeunes de son âge, qui lui rassemblent, une actrice Ana Torrent, qui établit un fort lien de filiation avec le cinéma espagnol de ses aînés. Faire en effet de cette actrice dont le regard fut précisément, pourrait-on-dire, mis en scène par Víctor Erice dans *El Espíritu de la colmena* (1973), puis par Carlos Saura dans *Cría cuervos* (1975), l'héroïne d'un film sur le regard, n'est pas un hasard.'

References

A new golden age of Spanish cinema is in the works. [Online.] Available: http://www.filmfestivals.com/cannes_2000/market/europe_worldwide.htm.

Amenábar, A. 1996. Entrevista. *Plano Corto*, 11: 3–7.

—. 2001. *The Others: Guióon cinematográfico original*. Madrid: Punto de lectura.

Amitrano, A. 1998. *El cortometraje en España: Una larga historia de ficciones breves*. Valencia: Filmoteca Generalitat Valenciana.

Aubert, J-P. 2002. Quand le cinéma espagnol assume sa promotion. Étude de la page web d'Abre los ojos. (*In* Berthier, N., (ed.). *Penser le cinéma espagnol (1975–2000)*. Lyon: Grimh/Grimia, Université Lumière-Lyon 2, pp. 131–42).

Barthes, R. 1981. *Camera Lucida*. [1980]. Howard, R. (trans.). New York, N.Y.: Hill and Wang.

Bazin, A. 1971. *What is Cinema?* Gray, H. (trans. and ed.). Berkeley, Los Angeles and London: University of California Press.

Beck, J. 2000. Mediating the Transnational in Contemporary Spaish Cinema: Pedro Almodóvar and Julio Medem. *Lugares Sin Limites: Cinema of the 80s and 90s in Latin America, Spain, and Portugal*. (*In* Guízar Álvarez, E. and Brígido Corachán, A. (eds). *Torre de Papel*, Spec. Issue 10.1: 134–69, Spring.)

Benavent, F. M. 2000. *Cine español de los noventa*. Bilbao: Ediciones Mensajero.

Benveniste, É. 1980. *Le vocabulaire des institutions indo-éuropéennes: Pouvoir, droit, religion*. Paris: Édition de Minuit.

Berthier, N. 2002. Voir ou ne pas voir: la fonction du hors-champ dans Tesis (Alejandro Amenábar). (*In* Berthier, N. (ed.). *Penser le cinéma espagnol (1975–2000)*. Lyon: Grimh/Grimia, Université Lumière-Lyon 2: 119–30).

Borau, J. L. 1999. Prologue: The Long March of the Spanish Cinema towards Itself. (*In* Evans, P. W. (ed.). *Spanish Cinema: The Auteurist Tradition*. Oxford and New York: Oxford University Press, pp. xvii-xxii.)

Bordwell, D. 1985. *Narration in the Fiction Film*. Madison, WI: University of Wisconsin Press.

Buckley, C. 2002. Alejandro Amenábar's Tesis: Art, Commerce and Renewal in Spanish Cinema. *Post Script*, 21(2): 12–25, Winter-Spring.

Clover, C. J. 1992. *Men, Women, and Chain Saw*. Princeton, N.J.: Princeton University Press.

Corrigan, T. 1991. *A Cinema without Walls: Movies and Culture after Vietnam*. New Brunswick, N.J.: Rutgers University Press.

D'lugo, M. 1991a. Catalan Cinema: Historical Experience and Cinematic Practice. *Quarterly Review of Film and Video*, 13 (1–3): 131–46.

—. 1991b. Almodóvar's City of Desire. *Quarterly Review of Film and Video* 13.4: 47–66.

Evans, P. W. (ed.). 1999. *Spanish Cinema: The Auteurist Tradition*. Oxford: Oxford University Press.

Fiddian, R. W. and Evans, P. W. (eds). 1988. *Challenges to Authority: Fiction and Film in Contemporary Spain*. London: Tamesis Books Limited.

Garbarz, F. 2001. Alejandro Amenábar: jouer avec les projections mentales du spectateur. *Positif*, 491: 15-20, janvier.

Girard, R. 1977. *Violence and the Sacred*. [1972] Trans. P. Gregory, Baltimore, MD and London, Johns Hopkins University Press.

Goodridge, M. and Wilson, V. 2005. In a White Room. *Sight and Sound*, 15(3): 6, March.

Grossberg, L. 1988. Putting the Pop Back into Postmodernism. (In Ross, A. (ed.). *Universal Abandon?: The Politics of Postmodernism*. Minneapolis: University of Minnesota Press: 167-190).

Guerin, M-A. 2001. Catho hanté: *Les Autres* d'Alejandro Amenábar. *Cahiers du Cinéma*, 563: 81-82, décembre.

Hawkins, J. 1999. Sleaze Mania, Euro-trash, and High Art: The Place of European Art Films in American Low Culture. *Film Quarterly*, 53(2): 14-29, Winter 1999-2000.

Heredero, C. F. 1999. Cine español: nueva generación. *Dirigido*: 49-67, abril.

Higginbotham, V. 1988. *Spanish Film Under Franco*. Austin: University of Texas Press.

Hopewell, J. 1982. *Out of the Past: Spanish Cinema after Franco*. London: BFI.

—. 1991. Art and a lack of money: the crises of the Spanish film industry: 1977-1990. *Quarterly Review of Film and Video*, 14(4): 113-22.

Hutcheon, L. 1989. *The Politics of Postmodernism*. London and New York: Routledge.

Jordan, B. and Morgan-Tamosunas, R. (eds). 1998. *Contemporary Spanish Cinema*. Manchester and New York: Manchester University Press.

Kinder, M. 1993. *Blood Cinema: The Reconstruction of National Identity in Spain*. Berkeley: University of California Press.

—, (ed.). 1997. *Refiguring Spain: Cinema/Media/Representation*. Durham and London: Duke University Press.

Kovács, K. 1991. The Plain in Spain. *Quarterly Review of Film and Video*, 14(3): 17-46.

Leydon, Joe. 1998. Rev. of *Abre los ojos*, dir. Alejandro Amenábar. *Variety*, CCCLXIXX/9: 64, January 12.

—. Rev. of *Thesis (Tesis)*, dir. Alejandro Amenábar. *Variety*, CCCLXII/4: 73-74.

Malraux, A. 1978. *The Voices of Silence*. Princeton: Princeton University Press.

Manzoli, G. 2001. Riportando a casa I cari estinti. *Cineforum*, XLI(409): 19-21, October.

Marchante, O. R. 2002. *Amenábar, vocación de intriga*. Madrid: Paginas de Espuma.

Martinez, D. 2005. Mar adentro: l'évasion du poète. *Positif*, 528: 43-44, février.

Maule, R. 2000. Death and Cinematic Reflexivity in Alejandro Amenábar's *Tesis*. (In Guízar Álvarez, E. and Brígido Corachán, A. (eds). *Lugares Sin Limites: Cinema of the 80s and 90s in Latin America, Spain, and Portugal*. Torre de Papel Spec. Issue 10: 65-76, Spring.)

Mount, J. 2001. Dread Again. *Sight and Sound*, 53: 18-19, 53, November.

Payán, M. J. 2001. *Cine español actual*. Madrid: Ediciones JC.

Rabinow, P. (ed.). 1984. *The Foucault Reader*. New York: Pantheon Books.

Rodriguez-Ortega, V. 2005. 'Snuffing' Hollywood: Transmedia Horror in *Tesis*. *Senses of Cinema*, 36. [Online.] Available: http://www.sensesofcinema.com/contents/05/36/tesis.html.

Russell, C. 1995. *Narrative Mortality: Death, Closure, and New Wave Cinemas.* Minneapolis: University of Minnesota Press.

Saura, A. 1997. El nuevo cine español. *Viridiana*, 15: 103–17, March.

Sempere, A. 2000. *Alejandro Amenábar: Cine en las venas.* Madrid: Nuer Ediciones.

Siska, W. 1979. Metacinema: A Modern Necessity. *Film Quarterly*, 7(1): 285–89.

Sklar, R. 2005. The Sea Inside. *Cineaste*, XXX(2): 52–53, Spring.

Smith, P. J. 2001. The Others. *Sight and Sound*, 53: 53–54, November.

Talens, J. and Zunzunegui, S. (eds). 1998. *Modes of Representation in Spanish Cinema. Hispanic Issues*, 16. Minneapolis-London: University of Minnesota Press.

Terrasa, J. 2002. Les écrans noirs d'Alejandro Amenábar: des voix en quête d'images. (*In* Berthier, N. (ed.). *Penser le cinéma espagnol (1975–2000).* Lyon: GRIMH/GRIMIA, Université Lumière-Lyon 2, pp. 161–71.)

Thibaudeau, P. 2002. Réalités virtuelles et destines manipulés à travers Abre los ojos de Alejandro Amenábar et Nadie conoce a nadie de Mateo Gil. *In* Berthier, N. (ed.). *Penser le cinéma espagnol (1975–2000).* Lyon: GRIMH/GRIMIA, Université Lumière-Lyon 2, pp. 143–60.)

Vernon, K. 1997. Reading Hollywood in/and Spanish Cinema: From Trade Wars to Transculturation. (*In* Kinder, M. (ed.). *Refiguring Spain: Cinema/Media/Representation.* Durham and London: Duke University Press, pp. 35–64.)

6

Made in *Europa*: Luc Besson and the Question of Cultural Exception in Post-auteur France

In film discourse and criticism, the discussion of authorial practices in relation to specific roles and expertise varies depending on ideological and cultural frameworks. As mentioned in previous chapters of this book, authorial approaches to film traditionally concentrate on the figure of the film director, particularly since the emergence of auteurism. With respect to other professional figures, author-oriented studies tend to give priority to roles related to the aesthetic and visual component of film-making, such as the art director or director of photography. Another professional figure associated with the notion of authorship in film is that of the producer, especially in discussions of Hollywood classical cinema. Yet this typology of authorship is generally subordinated to that of the film director.[1]

Luc Besson's investment in film direction, production, and distribution within the French and international film systems reconfigures not only the importance of the producer as author, but also a central tenet in auteur-informed approach to cinema: the establishment of authorship outside of pre-established distinctions between 'art' and 'commercial' cinemas. As stressed elsewhere in this book, the discussion of the auteur in mainstream or industrial film modes mainly regarded Hollywood film directors and seldom applied to European film directors. The point here is not to present Besson as an instance of a European auteur involved in mainstream film practices and systems, but instead to demonstrate that the redefinition of auteurism is a central issue in current debates in France and other European countries about the repositioning of author cinema in the global audio-visual system. In this respect, Besson's role in French cinema and film discourse exemplifies the strident contradictions and ambiguities implicit in auteur-oriented views of French and European cinema still prevalent in France, not only among film critics and theorists, but also major players in the film industry. As such, the approach to authorship informing this chapter is also distinct from those sustained in recent studies of neo-

Hollywood director-producers such as, for instance, Francis Ford Coppola and Steven Spielberg as auteurs.[2] Before delving deeper into this question, an overview of Besson's role in domestic and international film arenas is in order.

An American in Paris? The transnational reputation of Luc Besson

Of the French film-makers who made their débuts during the 1980s, Luc Besson is one of the few working on a relatively high production scale within commercial circuits of national and international film distribution and exhibition. Since the beginning of his career, he has adopted mainstream film genres and formulas conceived for vast film audiences, in step with Hollywood's marketing strategies around the world. As a result, many film critics, in France and abroad, share the conviction that he is one of the most 'Americanized' European film-makers of his generation, a typical by-product of Hollywood's pervasive influence over national cinemas. In 1991, Andrew Sarris, the American film critic who imported the *politique des auteurs* to the United States and developed a North American version of auteurism, wrote:

> Luc Besson has been praised and disparaged as one of the new breed of high-tech, high-gloss, Americanoid, anti-auteur filmmakers who do not wish to provide an alternative to Hollywood's blockbuster confections, but merely to embellish them with some Gallic sauce. Mr. Besson has even been described as the French Steven Spielberg. (Sarris 1991)

This reputation has accompanied Besson for most of his career and, indeed, for his detractors, it constitutes a major point of critique. During the 1980s, Besson's American aura was associated with the director's penchant for action films and generic formulas and complemented his categorization within the *cinéma du look*, a film style allegedly aimed at younger generations accustomed to Hollywood blockbusters. Since the 1990s, this American image was substantiated by Besson's increasing collaboration with Hollywood, which involved the distribution of his films in the US mainstream circuit and production and distribution contracts with Hollywood studios.

To complete the picture, Besson has occasionally worked with multi-million-dollar budgets on English-speaking productions replete with Hollywood stars and actors. Ten years after *Le cinquième élément/The Fifth Element* (Besson, 1997), an action film starring Bruce Willis produced by Gaumont and distributed by Columbia Pictures, Besson is likely to further consolidate his American reputation with his latest directorial effort and first foray into animation, *Arthur et les Minimoys/Arthur and the Invisibles* (2006). The film, which mixes live action and 3-D animation sequences, cost more than $80 million US and was five years in the making. The live action portions are set on a farm in the USA (shot in France's Normandy) during the 1950s, and they feature a primarily American cast including Mia Farrow and emerging child actor Freddie Highmore in the lead roles. For the English version, Besson cast several American stars to voice the animated characters, including Robert De Niro, Madonna, Snoop Dog, and Harvey Keitel. These celebrities were prominently featured in the film's international promotional campaign.

Yet Besson has always maintained a certain professional distance from Hollywood. Although he has contracts with three American studios (a two-year contract with Warner Brothers, a three-year contract with Sony, and a three-year contract with Twentieth Century Fox), he has rarely worked on an American film set. The only film he has co-produced with an American film company is *Léon/The Professional* (Besson, 1994). Upon the film's US release, *Variety* represented Besson as an independent player, 'a dedicated auteur' yet 'unabashedly commercial,' a film-maker who 'does not feel like a "French" director' and is happy to work in Hollywood yet is 'not sure he wants to put the sunglasses on "full-time"' (Alexander 1994). Some years later, coinciding with the release of *Jeanne d'Arc/The Messenger: The Story of Joan of Arc* (Besson, 1999), the entirely French funded mega-production about France's famous martyr, *Variety* saluted Besson as an 'action auteur...largely unloved by his fellow French film-makers' (Williams 1999: 105). Somewhat ironically, his first official accolade from film critics in his own country was the 1997 César Award for Best Director for *The Fifth Element*, arguably his most characteristically American film.

Besson defends himself against French critics' accusations that he is 'trying to emulate American "commercial" cinema' and 'selling out for the American-style movies' by claiming that his narrative structures would be unacceptable in Hollywood and that he has yet to make sequels of his most successful films (Williams 1999). The latter point is less pertinent given that Besson has produced three more *Taxi* films since 1999. Furthermore, he intends to direct two sequels to *Arthur et les Minimoys* in the near future (Besson 2006). Then again, Besson wrote and produced but did not direct *Taxi* (1998), and he considers the three proposed *Arthur* instalments part of a single, unified project; that of adapting the four children's books Besson co-wrote with Céline Garcia between 2002 and 2004.[3] More generally, Besson has emphasized his cottage industry, author/producer approach to film-making, which he contrasts with Hollywood-based studio methods. Film critics have occasionally endorsed Besson by paradoxically invoking auteurist arguments about his unique style. The mainstream film magazine *Première*, the only French magazine that has consistently supported Besson's work, openly embraces this perspective. Chief Editor Alain Kruger (1994) saluted *Léon*, a film set in New York with an all-American cast, as the most '*bessonien*' film since *Le dernier combat/The Last Battle* (Besson, 1984). A few years later, in a review of *The Fifth Element*, Jacques-André Bondy noted, 'In Hollywood, when people work with such considerable budgets, they run the risk of trapping the film in ironclad moral – and

Jeanne d'Arc (Milla Jovovich)

Besson shooting *Léon* in New York (on the left, Gary Oldman)

commercial – rules, systematically transformed into script recipes. Besson, however, managed to stay himself' (Bondy 1997, my translation).[4]

An outsider to the French film system and culture, Luc Besson has, from the beginning of his career, carved out his own space and retained a margin of autonomy within the French and international film industries by combining independent and corporate systems of production and personal and conventional methods of film-making.[5] He has always chosen his own collaborators and maintained director's cut rights and general supervision even for the most costly and complex of his projects and at every stage of his films' pre-production and production. He can undertake this endeavour owing to his technical competence and indefatigable, meticulous working style. He has managed to maintain personal control over his films, even those with budgets to the order of 60, 80, and 90 million francs (*The Messenger*, *Léon*, and *The Fifth Element*, respectively), involving hundreds of technicians and a complex production organization. For the first two films, the crews were divided between two continents across various sets and laboratories. Although Besson entered the mainstream circuit at a very young age and has forged tight connections with sizable studios – mainly Gaumont, France's largest film company, with which he was associated from 1984 to 1999 – he remains a defender of the independent mode of production at the core of his film-making philosophy. His comments on his long collaboration with Gaumont indicate this sensibility:

During fifteen years, my relations with Gaumont have always been both good and difficult. Gaumont is an old lady, a big, heavy firm, and I have always been small and alone. Now, the interests of a big company are not always those of a person. [...] The people in charge at Gaumont have always been kind people, agreeable and attentive, but, this notwithstanding, each film has been a battle. They are open-minded businessmen, but they are not artists. Each time, I have had the impression of making a film against them. Never have I arrived with a project to hear them say to me: 'Yes, super, brilliant!' (Besson 2001: 80, my translation)[6]

Another distinctive aspect of Besson's self-determination is his detachment from France's 'high' film culture and national film institutions, including film festivals, cine-clubs, film journals, and academic film programmes and professional film schools. In a 2003 interview with the French magazine *Télérama*, Besson said:

A long time ago, I tried to enter the IDHEC (Institut des Hautes Etudes Cinématographiques, now called Fondation Européenne pour les Métiers de l'Image et du Son [FEMIS]). I was rejected ten minutes into the interview. They asked me to name my favourite directors. I said Spielberg, Scorsese, and Forman. They told me: 'Goodbye, young man.' A few years later, when they asked me to teach some classes, I refused. I had talked with Jean-Jacques Beineix, who had previously accepted the offer. Six months later, he was still disturbed by the pretensions of the students, who looked down on him... (Besson 2003: 35, my translation)[7]

Overlooked by film journals and scorned or ignored by film festivals due to his commercial status, Besson is notoriously secretive about his projects and gives very few interviews and limits these primarily to film magazines that have proven supportive of his work, such as *Première* and *Studio Magazine*. The coverage provided by *Première*, especially, has been almost an extension of the promotional campaigns for Besson's films. The popular magazine has published several articles and positive reviews of Besson's work and has displayed film stills and photos of Besson on its cover. The magazine's support for Besson has not flagged even when its reception of a particular film has been tepid; for example, with Besson's ninth feature, *Angel-A* (2006) (see Loustalot 2006a). Generally, Besson has regained credibility in the international film scene, particularly since the foundation of *Europa*. Indeed, Europa-produced films have had a strong presence at international festivals. In 2000, Besson was appointed Jury Director at the Cannes Festival. In 2004, he received the *Prix des Amériques* at the *Festival de Films du Monde* in Montréal.

The unresolved tension between Besson and France's art house and auteur-informed milieus of film criticism foregrounds some of the contradictions implicit in the demarcation of cultural and commercial film modes and reinstates traditional views of European and Hollywood cinemas as monolithic and antithetical film systems. In 'Issues in European Cinema,' Ginette Vincendeau regards the upsurge of new approaches in European cinema as an amendment to the traditional, misleading identification of European cinema with 'art cinema', which erases any distinction between films and film-makers, provides an incomplete account of actual film practices, and reinforces essentialist conceptions of Hollywood as the oppositional norm against which Europe delineates its difference (Vincendeau 1998: 447).

The increasing attention Besson has received at the Cannes Festival is a significant pointer to the ambivalent politics lurking beneath Europe's art and author cinema. Over the years, the film festival has ceded its reputation as the main showroom of Europe's art house cinema to become a meeting point for international sales agents and film distributors. Furthermore, Cannes has become an important occasion for Hollywood studios to culturally validate some of their films and personalities. Duncan Petrie remarks on the Cannes Festival's capacity to 'cross the perceived divide between the cultural and commercial sides of the industry: i.e. minority-audience "art house" films and mass market commercial productions' (1991:118). He further notes that 'particular films are targeted at particular markets depending on their form and content' (ibid.).[8] With regard to Besson's gradual acceptance into France's cinema elite, the Cannes Festival's graciousness points less to a significant shift in standards of taste and culture than to the fact that Europa Corp. has, since 2003, established a working relationship with Canal+/Vivendi, a company integral to the festival. Besson is now affiliated with one of the most powerful media corporations and largest art house film distributors in France. Moreover, Canal+/Vivendi's double investment in marketing and culture production parallels Besson's multiple commitments with Europa.

In her book *Luc Besson*, Susan Hayward (1998) suggests that the French film-maker's attitude toward production systems and film-making methods situates him within the French tradition of collective film modes, particularly the 1930s Poetic Realist movement of the Popular Front cinema (1998: 10). Undoubtedly, Besson proposes a unique blend of individualistic and collaborative working styles. If his political and aesthetic purposes differ considerably from those of the Popular Front film-makers, they certainly offer a similarly uncompromising and autonomous stance with respect to France's state cinema and cultural establishment, inspired by national popular ideas concerning cinema's function in modern society.

Ideologically, Besson's idea of cinema as a narrative form of expression and entertainment may appear as simply a minor variation – no matter how personalized and culturally specific – of Hollywood and mainstream cinema's enviable situation: that of a 'flexible managerial culture and an open and innovative financial system that has adapted to changing economic and social conditions' (Miller 1998: 371). However, a crucial difference exists between Besson's approach and that of Hollywood: whereas for the latter creative purpose is subordinated to industrial and commercial considerations, Besson privileges creativity and individual style. He affirms the primacy of his vision to his practice in a 2002 interview with *Première*: 'The machine scares you in the beginning.... But today, I detach myself, I take pleasure in the gesture, in the writing. The camera, like style, must be light as a feather. A creator must have a suppleness that allows him to be more inventive. One does not have to become ossified or let oneself be grabbed by the apparatus' weight' (Besson 2002: 94, my translation).[9] Without falling into essentialist dichotomies of industry and art, it is valid to say that Besson's markedly individualistic and anti-institutional practices are incompatible with studio modes of production. Though he avoids obvious markers of intellectual value and remains loyal to the film industry, Besson's films demonstrate that while he believes in the significance of box office revenues, they are not an essential aspect of his work. Besson has stated, 'Once a film is a success, people always talk about a marketing "coup." At the beginning, however, there is a sincere wish to simply see a story' (2003: 34, my translation).[10]

Since October 2000, Besson's independent attitude regarding both French and American film contexts has concretized in his film production and distribution company Europa Corp.[11] A studio based entirely in France, located on the director's estate properties in Paris and Normandy and financed through the reinvestment of box office revenue from the films Besson directs and produces. The enterprise is a logical development within the film-maker's cohesive trajectory of self-determination and reinstates his assertive stance regarding the importance and centrality of French and European cinema in the international film market. Besson's initiatives at Europa have been enmeshed in French and American debates about 'cultural exception' (France's stance against the United States for the treatment of films as cultural products) and have punctuated some of the most salient stages in French cinema's attempt to maintain a double standard regarding its economic and cultural interests vis-à-vis Hollywood. In the summer of 2001, less than a year after the foundation of his new studio, Besson gave a strongly negative assessment of his relationship with Hollywood. Although his comments rely on contrasting clichés about Hollywood's assembly plant methods with his self-enterprising, individually coordinated mode of production, they also capture the daily reality of a production system that Besson has personally lived through and walked away from. In the interview, he affirms:

> In the studio system, when you make a film, you take the risk of getting fired, so... everyone tries not to make films! This is the spirit of the studios. You don't make a film until you cannot do otherwise. Except for the unavoidable projects, like Spielberg or Tom Cruise, the studios practically never give the green light. I've spent three years at Warner: they have never 'greenlighted' any of my projects. At Sony, it was the same. They say: 'Super, super!' until the studio head has himself fired and a new team arrives. Everybody is paid, the weather is beautiful, the guys beat it at 4:00 pm. It's their life, but it is not mine. They have a mentality all their own. They don't want to take any risks. They want some product. And if you are not there to make their product, it doesn't work. Sure, they say they love the European artists, they only ask them to give a little tone to their films. Like, we make the cake and you put the cherry on top. (Besson 2001: 79, my translation)[12]

Besson has a more flexible view of French cinema, one that acknowledges the interface of commercial and artistic constituents of a national film context largely backed by state subsidies and predicated upon cultural priorities, yet also accountable to a large mainstream audience and market. Commenting in *Première* on the present situation of the French film industry, he opines:

> In France, about twenty people control the cinema in its entirety. They are producers, directors, managers, people who have an economic responsibility but who must also

love cinema. If they don't have this love, it's the cinema as a whole that is in deep shit. What is important is that they recognize a good equilibrium. If they are twenty people that think of nothing else but making money, it's going to be a catastrophe. If they love cinema, they are going to divide things into parts: producing certain films because, economically, the whole of the business needs it; then, producing other more demanding films because we also need those. [...] I don't know these people well enough to know if they are all aware of this. I am aware of this and it's one hell of a responsibility. (Besson 2002: 94–95, my translation)[13]

Undoubtedly, Besson's defence of a national popular model of cinema reveals the cinematic imagination of a long-time mainstream filmgoer. Besson himself often insists on his status as a popular movie fan. He goes as far as to affirm that cinema is an art mostly useful for people from 10 to 25 years old, as it is preparation for appreciating other arts (Besson 2003: 36). His cinema lineage is based in a film market dominated by Hollywood blockbusters and French mainstream films. His professional competence is the result of a long and humble apprenticeship on film sets, progressively moving his way up to the position of assistant director.[14] Not long ago, Besson's tense relationship with French critics came to a head when Besson was ordered to pay the legal fees for two court cases he initiated against French magazines that had criticized his films (Guichard 2004). In 2006, in an exclusive interview with *Première* prior to the release of *Angel-A*, his first film in seven years, Besson explicitly put the blame on critics for his long absence: 'I had lost the pleasure, the will to make films. You need to have a lot of energy to be able to work for two years, be trashed by the press, be fashionable for fifteen days, and then go home' (Besson 2006, my translation).[15]

If Besson's cinematic preferences stem from an aesthetically and historically naïve perspective, they also suggest an open-minded consideration of cinema and a rejection of the categorizations that have for years biased the discussion of French cinema in the direction of its construction and commendation as the ceremonial banner of Europe's art and author cinema. Ginette Vincendeau reminds us that 'French cinema is *also* – and for its home audience, primarily – a "popular cinema"' (1996: x). For Vincendeau, the most idiosyncratic characteristic of French cinema is its cultural vitality, supported not only by discriminatory institutions such as film festivals, cine-clubs, and specialized film journals, but also by a wide-ranging typology of audiences and media. Lucy Mazdon adds to this point by stressing the difference between the domestic perceptions of French cinema and perceptions from abroad. In her introduction to an anthology on popular 1990s French films, she explains why the distinction between art and popular cinema is problematic and concludes:

It would seem that what we perceive to be an 'art' or a 'popular' film depends as much upon the particular context of reception as upon the identity of the film itself. This is not to suggest that such definitions are entirely redundant. Evidently some films are more aesthetically or thematically challenging than others and will demand quite different modes of reception to those invited by the mainstream product. However, such definitions are a highly complex matter, subject to change and influenced, as we have seen, by production, exhibition, and reception. (Mazdon 2001: 5)

The pre-eminent labelling of French films as art films, as films developed for a non-mainstream circuit, is one of the reasons for the limited distribution of France's popular films abroad. This restriction is only occasionally broken by box office phenomena such as, to pick three recent examples, two films adapted from the *Astérix* comic strip and the universal hit *Le fabuleux destin d'Amélie Poulain/Amelie* (Jean-Pierre Jeunet, 2001). As Mazdon notes, the box office success *Taxi* (Gérard Pirès, 1998), produced by Besson's company Leeloo, was promoted in the United Kingdom with the slogan: 'Hollywood doesn't make them like this any more' (Mazdon 2001: 5). This particular (anti-) Americanization strategy is the antithesis of the tactic Columbia adopted in 1994 to promote *The Professional (Léon)* in the United States, which described the work as an 'American film by the director of *La Femme Nikita*' (the North American title for *Nikita*) (Alexander 1994: 10). Whereas *Léon* is an action film set in New York and co-produced by Columbia, *Taxi* is set in Marseille, displays typical French comedy conventions and was entirely produced and distributed by a French company. It includes the classic ingredients of the Hollywood action film, adopting the speed-on-wheels plot inaugurated by *Speed* (Jan de Bont, 1994). *Taxi* foregrounds car chases and stunts, yet, as with all of Besson's films, it weaves in French cultural motifs. The British promotion hits the right note by revealing Besson's ambition: to make films with the same production values as Hollywood but with a distinctive tone and setting.

The configuration of Besson's work: auteur, art, and national discourse

Susan Hayward (1998) analyses Besson's films 'in context,' stressing the film-maker's alterity with respect to the French lineage of state- and television-supported author cinema. She reminds us that Besson resists the label 'auteur,' and she prefers to use the director's definition of himself as a *metteur en scène*, which in French means film director but is also a figure that the 1950s French auteur-oriented critics contrasted to the auteur to delineate a stylistically talented though not conceptually unique film-maker (Hayward 1998: 2–10). Besson distances himself from the French auteurist tradition: 'Since the *nouvelle vague*, the *"milieu"* keeps using narrow minded and fixed ideas: only an elite should be able to make films; the auteur is sacred, and all he does is good since he is an artist. For me, cinema is a creative triangle: writer, director, actor. It is a compromise that should bring humility' (Besson 2003: 34, my translation).[16]

To be sure, Hayward's approach suggests that whereas Besson positions his personal style and world-view within mainstream film-making practices, he could also be categorized within the tradition of the auteurist directors.[17] Indeed, in spite of the derision that auteur-oriented critics have outwardly expressed towards Besson, he heralds authorial film practices that trespass the surreptitious boundaries of 'art' and 'popular' cinema. Ultimately, though, deciding to which auteurist typology Besson belongs and even debating whether Besson is an auteur at all is not the point. The issue at stake is identifying what pre-established assumptions and classifications of film practices and modes are subsumed under the notion of auteur, in France and internationally. This task is performed with the awareness that, as Timothy Corrigan (1991: 101–37) observes, the film author is a historically and contextually variable manifestation of an aesthetic category and promotional strategy.

Besson's position as a 'popular' film-maker and film author should be considered within a national and international context, particularly with respect to the role of European cinema in

LUC BESSON

arthur
et les minimoys

INTERVISTA

Cover of the first of the three tomes on the *Arthur* saga written by Luc Besson

the global audio-visual market. As Stephen Crofts suggests, the 'European-model of art cinema,' promoted after World War II to counteract Hollywood, has been modified by 'the suppression of existentialism by later 1960s political radicalism and subsequent apoliticism,' as well as by 'Hollywood's development of its own art cinema' (1993: 51). Crofts also underlines the exchanges that many European art cinemas and film authors have established with Hollywood styles and genres, a claim that is at the centre of many critical approaches to European national cinemas, including Thomas Elsaesser's study of New German Cinema and Marsha Kinder's examination of Spanish *nuevo cine*. Many scholars (see Crofts 1998; Durovicová 1994; Moran 1996; and Petrie 1992) and film industry players (see Finney 1996; Ilott 1996; and Puttnam 1997) have stressed that the idea of European cultural unity is both purely theoretical and hardly applicable to either past or present European conditions. As mentioned in the Introduction, according to Victoria de Grazia, during the post-World War II period the logic of each European nation state was that of integrating 'Europe on a societal level around a common material culture' while maintaining its economic distinction through protectionist laws against the competition of the US cinema (1998: 27).

France's policy regarding Hollywood cinema is an example of the flagrant contradiction existing between Europe's claim for cultural specificity and unity and the actuality of the nation state's economic and political orientations. In the endorsed homeland of European art house and auteur cinema's mystique, two popular film types contributed to saving France's film industry in the 1980s: the heritage film and the *cinéma du look*. France reinforced its protectionist policies against foreign films, not found in other European countries such as the United Kingdom, at the same time that French film corporations were merging their distribution circuits with US majors, including, to mention two of the earliest such mergers, Gaumont with Buena Vista in 1993 and U.G.C. with Fox in 1995. As much as these commercial strategies were profitable for the development of French cinema abroad through international co-productions, they obviously clashed with the country's resolute stance on retaining its cultural distinction from Hollywood.

For the French film industry, Besson has perennially represented a major source of box office receipts and secured access to the US market. Indeed, Besson solidified efforts by the French Minister of Culture Jack Lang and Producer Daniel Toscan du Plantier – the head of Gaumont in the early 1980s and then of Unifrance, the state's promotional agency for French films in foreign markets – to reinstate France's prominence in domestic and international film distribution. Moreover, he is the only film-maker identified with the *cinéma du look* to overcome the crisis that this type of cinema faced in the early 1990s.[18]

Although firmly rejecting any affiliation with Europe's high-art or intellectual film tradition, Besson has often acknowledged his position within the French and European film contexts with respect to an alleged cultural heritage. Decidedly, Besson does not align himself with the French (and European) claim for the 'cultural exception of cinema' through which France argued its position against the United States at the 1993 Uruguay Round of the General Agreement on Tariffs and Trade (G.A.T.T.). To this day, the issue remains a hotly contested topic for the United States and its Hollywood representative, the Motion Picture Association of America, as well as with different factions of the French film industry. On this issue, Besson's statements are resolute while still consistent with his conception of cinema:

> There is no cultural exception. We have to keep the word 'culture'. That's all. Culture is the identity card of a country. Period. We don't say 'the passport exception'. We say 'passport'. With culture it's the same, we don't even have to fight over this. They can't take out an organ from us. The culture is in us, is our heart. It won't be possible to take it out of us. Or it will be necessary to kill us all. (Besson 2001: 95, my translation)[19]

Besson mitigates his view of the cultural exception by defending cultural diversity. Yet within the context of a French film culture shared by film critics and author-oriented film-making practices, a negative position on cultural exception is equivalent to an anti-nationalist declaration about French cinema. Some months after Besson had proclaimed his opinion on the matter, Jean-Marie Messier abruptly declared that 'cultural exception is dead.'[20] He made this announcement at the time of his acquisition of Canal+ and provoked a vast polemic that echoed among French film critics and film-makers. The discussion of cultural exception has reinforced strong partisanship within the French film system. But France's claim for cinema's cultural exception is predominantly a symptom of unresolved contradictions within the French and international film industries. The widely publicized confrontation between France and the US at the 1993 G.A.T.T. illustrated less the struggle between the guardian of cinema's cultural values (France) and the commercial usurper (the United States) than a battle between two contestants representing opposite interests in the same important sector of the culture industry.

Quoting Michael Chanan, Angus Finney concludes that the real issue behind the G.A.T.T. crisis was 'the result of a move during the 1980s by the US to change the arena for international regulation of intellectual property [...] the move corresponds to the growing importance of the culture industry in the global market-place, now including not only entertainments but also information' (1996: 7). Finney argues that the temporary resolution of the 1993 G.A.T.T. wrangling between France and the US was an 'exception' to the inclusion of films in the trade agreement (see also Jäckel 1996; and Puttnam 1997). According to Finney, the agreement brought no substantial modifications to the pre-existing situation, insofar as it 'only sanctioned those protectionist measures that were already in place' (1996: 8). Toby Miller argues that the international meeting that followed and replaced the G.A.T.T. in 1995, the World Trade Organization (WTO), turned the attention of the audio-visual sector toward other controversial issues, namely the TV-film nexus and satellite programming. Miller gives a Marxist-oriented interpretation of the G.A.T.T. and European Union (EU) cultural politics, noting that

> The abiding logic of the Community's audio-visual policy is commercial: it clearly favors large concerns that can be built upon further [...] the seeming discontinuity with earlier concerns, when the E.C. had a primarily economic personality, is misleading: a notion of cultural sovereignty underpins concerns vis-à-vis the U.S., but so too does support for monopoly capital and the larger states inside its own walls. (Moran 1996: 80)

With Europa, the 'post-Hollywood' Besson is proving that (successful) movies can be made and distributed outside of the constraints and limitations of Hollywood's global control and France's stance in favour of the cultural exception. Conceived from within a national popular perspective, the film production and distribution company targets the international film market and thrives on the ideological inconsistencies of France's pretensions about its 'cultural' specificity. From this perspective, the studio's foray into the Asian market – established in April 2002 through the creation of Europa Corp. Japan, which linked Europa with the Japanese film distribution company Asmik Ace – offers a way out of the conflicting interests that bind European cinema, and particularly French cinema, to Hollywood, by creating new forms of partnership within the international film arena as well as France.

Europa Corp. and the politics of France's (inter)national film marketing

Besson likes to present Europa as the result of a fortuitous encounter among people with various connections to the film business. About the creation of Europa he stated:

> – [Q] What was your ideal in creating Europa? – [A] Quite honestly? To have fun! It's the only thing that we thought of. The excitement of saying to ourselves: 'We are going to be able to make the films that we dream about.' After that, we had to get organized and do things seriously so as to be able to master the entire production line, from the conception of the project to its diffusion in film theatres and on video. But the first impulse was that: to have fun! (2001: 81, my translation).[21]

Nevertheless, a calculated professionalism may be read behind the rationale in Besson's bringing together the expertise of a previous manager of Gaumont, an emerging producer, and an art house actor turned agent. Besson's senior partner, Pierre-Ange Le Pogam, is a former Gaumont executive with eighteen years of experience in the studio's highest ranks (when he left, he was general assistant director). Among other things, Le Pogam heads Gaumont Buena Vista International (GBVI), the company that sealed the contract between Gaumont and Disney. Through Le Pogam, Disney distributed Europa's first film, *Kiss of the Dragon* (Chris Nahon, 2001), in the international film market. The other two Europa associates have slightly less clout. The young Virginie Silla, Besson's wife since August 2004, had worked for a few years at Gaumont in the international relations department, the distribution department, and as an assistant producer, before joining Besson's team, three years before the foundation of Europa. The third partner, Michel Feller, is a former art house actor – he played the protagonist of Olivier Assayas's *L'Enfant de l'hiver/Winter's Child* (1989) – who became a talent scout at Artmedia. Such managerial variety supports Europa's diversification of films, genres, marketing sectors, and financial investments, alternating nationally and internationally distributed action films with small domestic comedies.

An important asset to Europa is its sophisticated recording studio, Digital Factory, located in one of Besson's properties, a seventeenth-century castle in Normandy where the director had also filmed some sequences of *The Messenger*. Besson also fitted the property for the live-action shooting of the film, and built an animation studio at Pantin, in the Paris suburbs, in which *Arthur et les Minimoys*'s animated sections were made. At the beginning of his Europa venture, a proud

Besson said to *Studio Magazine*, 'Up to $25 million [US], Europa is at present able to produce a film without the help of Americans' (Besson 2001: 79, my translation).[22] In the same interview, he claimed to have turned down many offers from Hollywood studios to assist in the production of *Kiss of the Dragon* (Chris Nahon), which was eventually bought by Fox for international distribution. Franck Priot discusses these counter-Hollywood production methods in an article about Europa in *Télérama*: 'At least 150 companies dream about making a film with Jet Li. Besson convinced him thanks to his *pedigree* and his fast reaction: the comedian had only six months off between two shoots. Six months were enough to finance and shoot *Kiss of the Dragon*' (Ferenczi 2003: 38, my translation).[23]

Late in 2001, Europa made a dramatic turn toward higher production volume by signing a three-year deal with Vivendi-Universal, France's former multinational corporation, run by the French financial scout and manager Jean-Marie Messier. At the time, Messier was in the midst of a spectacular financial rampage that would eventually cost the corporation 13.6 billion euros ($11.8 billion US) and force his resignation as CEO in July 2002, although he was well remunerated with a $20 million compensation package. Messier had created his financial empire through the privatization of the French state-owned water company, Compagnie Générale des Eaux. Messier progressively transformed the company, renamed Vivendi, into a media corporation that absorbed the French pay-TV channel Canal+, which had been a crucial player in French cultural film production and exhibition since 1984.[24] Vivendi was consolidated as a worldwide media corporation with the purchase of Seagram, previously controlled by the

Jet Li, star of *Kiss of the Dragon* (Europa Corp.'s first production)

powerful Montreal and New York–based Bronfman family and its subsidiaries Universal Studio and Universal Music. The conglomerate also swallowed the US satellite television company EchoStar Communications and Barry Diller's USA Networks.

In exchange for exhibition rights to some of Europa's films, the deal with Vivendi aimed at financing Digital Factory and building new studios for post-production, music recording, and animation. Besson's negotiations were upset by Messier's acquisition of Canal+ and, soon after, the firing of the company's director, Pierre Lescure, one of Besson's long-standing professional partners. Lescure's culturally oriented agenda was incompatible with Messier's mainstream production interests and partnership with the Hollywood studio Universal. Messier's move caused enormous controversy in France and rekindled criticism against the executive, his lavish lifestyle, and his public displays of corporate power. Besson never took an official position on the Lescure affair and did not renew the loyal affiliations he had often demonstrated in his career, most recently with Bill Mechanic at Fox.

Six months before the incident, when *Studio Magazine* asked Besson if Lescure's rumoured departure from Canal+ would affect his agreement with Vivendi, he diplomatically answered that, although his collaboration with Canal+ was primarily the result of his long-term friendship and partnership with Lescure and Nathalie Bloch-Laîné, his contract with Vivendi had already been signed and would remain valid regardless (Besson 2001: 95). An ambiguous comment about Vivendi's acquisition of Canal+ appeared on Besson's website in which Princess L (a *nom de plume* which Besson was using at that time) makes sarcastic remarks about Messier and the regal party that was held at the Louvre Palace to celebrate the takeover. The remarks compare Messier (referred to by his nickname 'J6M'),[25] a member of the corporate royal class, with King Louis XIV, who at the time was featured in the French historical drama *Le Roi danse/The King Is Dancing* (Gérard Corbiau, 2000), the latest Canal+ film. Princess L censures Canal+ as a 'dead' network that lacks creativity and inspiration and, with somewhat less venom, accuses Messier of 'killing' it. She also lampoons Messier for being less committed to promoting art than Louis XIV.

Despite its links with big corporations such as Disney and Vivendi-Universal, Europa started as a relatively small enterprise. In the beginning, the studio employed approximately fifty people, although the employees doubled within a few years. The firm rapidly increased its pool of projects, varied in both type and budget. To a certain extent, Europa is Besson's response to his problematic relationship with the Hollywood studios and his unwillingness and inability to create within their industrial and managerial structures (Ferenczi 2003: 38). The deal with Vivendi-Universal was indeed a considerable test of Besson's position vis-à-vis corporate financing and the studio's production philosophy, especially when Messier was attacked by the French media for firing Lescure. Besson's response was to keep a low public profile, reinforcing his introverted behaviour toward the media. He gave fewer interviews and discontinued his contributions to his website. However, Besson recently talked more openly about Vivendi, criticizing the lack of creativity he sees at the heart of the enterprise and comparing it to his own Europa, whose structure he claims is entirely dedicated to nurturing artistic creation (see Besson 2003: 34).

Certainly, Europa has pursued a growing and successful production line that expands beyond the precedents set by Besson's earlier films. Besson describes his film producer role as one of facilitation. Europa produces and distributes films ranging across a variety of genres, involving both international and French casts and crews. One area of Europa's expertise, at least until 2005, has been big-budget action flicks with martial arts stars. In two years the film company produced and distributed Chinese star Jet Li's vehicle *Kiss of the Dragon* and Hong Kong actor and director Corey Yuen's *The Transporter* (2003). Yuen co-directed *The Transporter* with French first-time director Louis Leterrier, whose second film for Europa, *Danny the Dog/ Unleashed* (2005), features Li in an unusual Scottish setting, surrounded by a prestigious international cast that includes Morgan Freeman and Bob Hoskins. Other Europa films that play with generic and transcultural hybridism, albeit often resulting in stereotyping, are *Wasabi* (Gérard Krawczyk, 2001) – set in Japan and starring one of Besson's cherished actors, Jean Reno, and Japanese teenage pop idol Ryoko Hirosue – and *Yamakasi* (Ariel Zeitoun, 2001), an action movie starring a group of young people who jump from buildings, which the film's promotional tag describes as: 'The samurais of the modern times.' There are also comic strip adaptations – which, over the past few years, have become almost a subgenre in French cinema – such as *Michel Vaillant* (Bernard Bonvoisin, 2003) and thrillers, such as *Banlieue 13* (2005) and the sequel to Mathieu Kassovitz's successful *Les rivières pourpres/The Crimson Rivers* (2000) titled *Les rivières pourpres 2: Les anges de l'Apocalypse/Crimson Rivers 2: Angels of the Apocalypse* (Olivier Dahan, 2004). As previously mentioned, sequels are just beginning to represent an important investment initiative for Europa, from the *Taxi* franchise to *The Transporter* sequel directed by Louis Leterrier in 2006.

The studio caters to audiences across Europe, North America, and Asia and also addresses a range of domestic audiences. The vast variety of Europa productions includes veteran French director Bertrand Blier's *Les Côtelettes* (2003), French comedies such as Patrick Alessandrin's *15 Août/August 15th* (2001), *Moi César, 10 ans 1/2, 1m39/I Cesar* (Richard Berry, 2003), and *Quand j'étais chanteur* (Xavier Gianolli, 2006), starring French star Gérard Depardieu. Many Europa films have international art cinema clout, such as Italian film-maker Mimmo Calopresti's *La felicità non costa niente/Happiness Costs Nothing* (2002), Québécoise film-maker Manon Briand's *La Turbulence des fluides/Chaos and Desire* (2002), and the directorial débuts of three big-name actors, *Peau d'ange/Once Upon an Angel* (2002), by French star Vincent Perez; *Cheeky* (2003), by British actor David Thewlis; and *The Three Burials of Melquiades Estrada*, by Hollywood star Tommy Lee Jones (2005). Besson has always shown an interest in producing actors' first directorial projects. Indeed, one of his first major productions was Gary Oldman's *Nil by Mouth* (1997), which was an official selection at the Cannes Film Festival.

Since *The Messenger*, Besson has emphasized themes and projects that champion new French film-makers and actors-turned-film-makers, many of whom come from his own professional team. This is the case with Aruna Villiers, a veteran script supervisor who worked with him on *The Messenger* and completed her first film, *À ton image*, in 2004. Perez finished directing his first film immediately before appearing in two Europa productions, the intimate drama *La felicità non costa niente* and the spectacular remake of *Fanfan la tulipe* (2003), directed by Gérard

La turbulence des fluides (2002), by Québécois film-maker Manon Briand, co-produced by Europa Corp.

Krawczyk. Krawczyk is one of the most prolific film-makers on the Europa team and his film starred Perez in the lead role opposite Penélope Cruz. Other projects from French actors include Bernie Bonvoisin's all-star costume adventure *Blanche* (2002), Richard Berry's above-mentioned *Moi César, 10 ans 1/2, 1m39*, and Isabelle Doval's *Rire et châtiment/Laughter and Punishment* (2003), featuring Doval's husband, José Garcia (who also appears in *Blanche*), and the director herself in the main roles. Doval's next film, *Un château en Espagne*, is also being produced by Europa.

At the same time, Besson has co-produced films outside France, some of which are by critically acclaimed but not commercially viable directors, such as Briand and Calopresti. Other international Europa productions include those by genre directors intended for the mainstream circuit; for example, the films of Hong Kong action directors such as Corey Yuen and the Pang brothers, whose *Jian gui/ The Eye* (2002) was released in France by Europa. In 2005, Europa hit the jackpot with the release of the internationally acclaimed *The Three Burials of Melquiades Estrada* (Tommy Lee Jones, 2005). Although it was a box office failure, the film won two awards at the 2005 Cannes Film Festival (for Best Actor and Best Screenplay) and represents the first real critical success the company has had on the international art house market.

Europa is not simply the fulfilment of Besson's individual and professional conception of cinema; it realizes an aspiration that many film production companies have pursued in Europe, generally with poor results: that of achieving an industrial and commercial alternative to mainstream cinema that is competitive with Hollywood. With Europa, Besson challenges Hollywood on his own terms, playing the big studios' game with fewer and more diverse means, which allow him more flexibility and freedom. In a sense, it is not surprising to hear Besson often compare himself to Steven Spielberg (Besson 2003). Besides being an influence on Besson, Spielberg's creation of his own studio, Dreamworks, is a precursor to Besson's Europa. Recently, Besson has also compared his Digital Factory studio to George Lucas's Skywalker Ranch studio, stressing, with an undertone of European cultural pride, that his studio is located in eighteenth-century buildings (Besson 2007). The studio responds to the needs of a reconfigured Europe, involving new strategies of development and promotion, management-oriented decision-making, diversified marketing, transnational co-operation, and investment in infrastructure, human resources, technologies, and cultural organizations. In many European countries, these strategies are supported by state and European Union aid programmes for audio-visual production and distribution, new independent and corporate film structures, and international television and film co-productions. In this regard, Europa is an exceptional and unique entity.

Europa reflects the tensions of Besson's position: maintaining his autonomy from American as well as French studios and avoiding the old Continent's aversion to combining cultural and economic interests, while remaining part of the economic systems at play in the international market. Besson's studio is moving into the intersection of local and global production and distribution from a position outside of corporate structures, although not completely free from their sphere of influence. In this respect, Europa's most original trait is its diversification of production and marketing niches, a difficult proposition for the Hollywood majors and large European studios.

Besson's Americanized image is based on the premise that European cinema is national and Hollywood is global; an assumption that overlooks the way that global film practices and industries debunk flimsy categories of national specificity and promote a distinctly transnational and cross-cultural agenda. While a Besson film may be promoted as an American or Americanized product, Hollywood studios also tailor their films and marketing to specific markets. As Toby Miller puts it:

> Part of the talent of international cultural commodities is their adaptability to new circumstances: the successes and meanings of Hollywood films need to be charted through numerous spatial, generic, and formatting transformations as they move through US release to Europe and Asia then domestic and international video, cable, and network television [...]. The Ford Motor Company has long worked with the adage 'To be a multinational group, it is necessary to be national everywhere.' (Miller 1998: 376–77)

Europa seems to be working with the Ford maxim particularly as far as the Asian market is concerned. The studio's most international productions, such as *Kiss of the Dragon*, *Wasabi*, and *Bandidas*, apply the laws of globalization to the letter. *Kiss of the Dragon* (2001), directed by Chris Nahon, is an action film that transposes the Chinese martial arts star Jet Li into a US context and narrative.[26] Li, who was discovered by American audiences playing the villain in *Lethal Weapon 4* (Richard Donner, 1998), and subsequently played the lead in the Hollywood blockbuster *Romeo Must Die* (Andrzej Bartkowiak, 2000), decided to co-produce *Kiss of the Dragon* with Besson based on their very similar conception of production. Like Besson, Li wants a project to come together quickly and special effects to be realistic.

Krawczyk's *Wasabi* (2001), an action thriller with comic undertones, is clearly indebted to the classic buddy film. The film centres on two French cops, the hero and his goofy pal, but adds an adolescent Japanese girl to the mix and sets the action against the cluttered urban environment of contemporary Tokyo. The script was 'commissioned' by Besson's long-time friend and collaborator Jean Reno, who wanted to make a film in Japan, where he has had immense popularity since *Nikita* (1990) and *Léon* (1994). Reno's co-star, Ryoko Hirosue, a young actress and singer, is a rising Japanese star. *Wasabi* deploys all the clichés of the cultural clash between France and Japan and exploits the two stars' screen personas, thus playing to a variety of audience expectations from different cultural backgrounds.

Europa recently produced *Bandidas* (Joachim Roenning and Espen Sandberg, 2006), a western written by Besson and starring Penélope Cruz and Salma Hayek as two women who become bank robbers in order to avenge their fathers and stop a renegade American land baron who is terrorizing their town. Capitalizing on the popularity of the most famous Latina actresses working in Hollywood, the film was nonetheless a huge commercial failure. The poor box office take of this and other globally oriented Europa films (such as Guy Ritchie's *Revolver* (2005)) may explain why the company has recently refocused attention on its domestic market through a series of *polars* (French-style thrillers). One of the most successful films within this genre is *Ne le dis à personne* (Guillaume Canet, 2006), starring François Cluzet and French-Canadian actress Marie-Josée Croze, which was well received in France and earned four awards at the 2007 edition of the Césars (the French equivalent of the Oscars), including one for Best Film Director and one for Best Male Lead.

Europa is also concentrating on the French comedy genre with two releases in 2007. *L'invité* (Laurent Bouhnik) stars popular French actors Daniel Auteuil and Thierry Lhermitte. *Michou d'Auber* features prominent French actors Gérard Depardieu and Nathalie Baye and is directed by Thomas Gilou, who ten years earlier made one of the biggest comedy successes, *La vérité si je mens* (1997). Interestingly, Europa is also producing remakes of successful Japanese thrillers, following the example of Spielberg's studio Dreamworks:[27] in 2007 Europa produced an English-language remake of *Himitsu* (Yojiro Takita, 2001) titled *The Secret*, directed by French film star Vincent Perez. Also, in 2007, Europa produced *Hitman* (Xavier Gens) inspired by the popular Japanese videogame franchise by the same title. This film shows that the company is maintaining the connection with the Asian cinema market that it has pursued since its foundation through projects like the two Jet-Li vehicles *Kiss of the Dragon* and *Danny the Dog*, *Wasabi* and the European distribution of the Pang brothers' *The Eye* (2002) and *The Eye 2* (2004).

In 2006, Besson returned to film directing after a seven-year hiatus. His two new films were greeted with a mixed reception. *Angel-A*, starring popular French actor Jamel Debbouze, represents Besson's hugest flop to date.[28] *Arthur et les Minimoys*, released a couple of months after *Angel-A*, was a huge financial success in France but received bad reviews and did very poorly in North America, even though the United States was Besson's explicit target market for the film. More than five years in the making and made entirely in Europa's studios, the partly animated, partly live-action fantasy constitutes Besson's most ambitious project to date. The film is an adaptation of a children's book by the same title that Besson co-wrote with Céline Garcia and published in 2002 in two volumes. The publisher is Intervista, a press owned by Europa. *Arthur et les Minimoys* is the most expensive French film ever made with French capital, and it is Besson's most direct challenge to Hollywood. The film capitalizes on one of the most popular

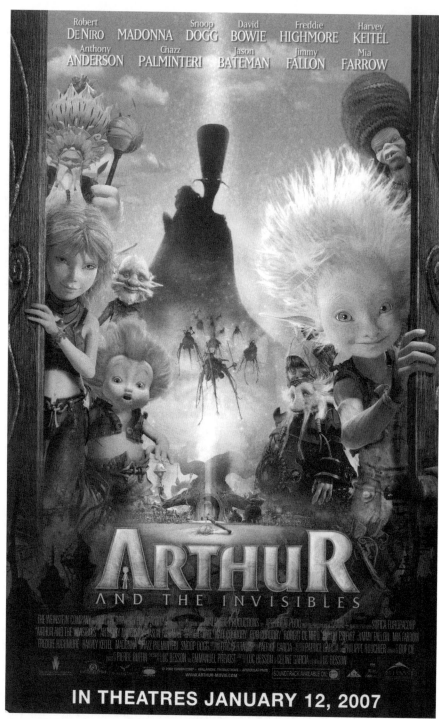

The North American poster of *Arthur et le Minimoys*

cinematic forms now circulating in the mainstream global film market, the computer-animated film. The promotional strategy employed follows the lead of the two most prominent animation studios: Pixar and Dreamworks. For example, both the domestic and international campaigns for *Arthur* highlighted the film and pop stars that lent their voices to the animated characters. The film's English version, designed for the international market, features global household names such as Madonna, David Bowie, Robert De Niro, and Harvey Keitel, among others. The French version credits the immensely popular French singer Mylène Farmer (known as the 'French Madonna') and Alain Bashung (who, like Bowie, is one of the most respected songwriters of his generation).

The film also borrows conventions from other films adapted from popular children's novels; for example, *Harry Potter* (2001–), *The Lord of the Rings* (Peter Jackson, 2001–2003), *Eragon* (Stefen Fangmeier, 2006), and *The Chronicles of Narnia* (Andrew Adamson, 2005). The formula backfired, especially in the United States and Canada. Film critics attacked both Besson's books and the script for their lack of originality, if not open plagiarism. Robert Koehler wrote in *Variety*:

> The sources and ideas that are borrowed, copied or stolen here include the tales of King Arthur to 'The Matrix Reloaded,' 'The African Queen,' 'Star Wars' and 'The Wizard of Oz.' Script, based on Besson's French tome 'Arthur et les Minimoys' (which spawned three sequels), apes the Joseph Campbell hero myth template that's become a bible for Hollywood's current generation – and offers proof the template is exhausted. (2006)

Neil Genzlinger of *The New York Times* similarly notes that *Arthur* 'resembles, at various times, *Honey, I Shrunk the Kids*, *The Sword in the Stone*, *Fraggle Rock* and assorted others' (2006). Despite its commercial failure in the United States, the film was nonetheless successful thanks to domestic support and strong box office scores in many European countries such as the United Kingdom, Spain, and Germany.[29] Above all, *Arthur* represents Europa's growing status as an international commercial studio employing the commercial and artistic strategies of Hollywood. The film's range and calibre of voice talent is itself a huge accomplishment.

Europa's ambition is to celebrate the impossible marriage between commerce and art upon which cinema is predicated. The company is self-sufficient and vertically integrated including everything from a post-production studio to international distribution capabilities. It employs a dependable professional entourage with connections in the French and international film industries. Every aspect of the studio reflects Besson's idiosyncratic view of cinema as a form of personal expression and of social consumption. However, the escalation of the Franco-American polemic over cinema's cultural exception and, more importantly, Europa's consolidation with Vivendi-Universal, may have a negative impact on Besson's vision. Intermittent revelations of professional exploitation and managerial unscrupulousness, some of which have had legal consequences, also cast shadows on Besson's intentions to keep Europa an independent pole of production and distribution. In March 2000, Besson faced charges of plagiarism for having allegedly stolen Kathryn Bigelow's script for *The Messenger*. Besson was accused of plagiarism again in February 2001 by Julien Séri and Philippe Lyon, co-writers of *Yamakasi*. The most serious accusation arrived on 4 June 2002, when Besson was charged with involuntary manslaughter for the death of cameraman Alain Dutartre, who had been the victim of a car accident while filming a stunt for *Taxi 2*. The charge concerned Besson denying a trial run to test the stunt that led to Dutartre's death and seriously injured his assistant Jean-Michel Bar and the car's driver. In August 2003, the French press listed Europa among the entertainment companies that made the most use of casual work contracts to avoid paying social benefits to employees.

Europa's willingness to bow to corporate interests raises questions over its claim to be an independent cottage industry with connections to the mainstream film circuit. Yet, the company brings attention to the necessity for European cinema, blending artistic and business attitudes in film production and distribution practices, while being equally attentive to the domestic and international markets from an economically autonomous standpoint.

Notes

1. Boschi and Manzoli note, 'However, if in these situations the producer imposes himself as an even more directive "double," an even more general (but at the same time more indirect) supervisor of the director, putting the latter in the role of a mere partial executor, at the same time he isolates and defines in a clearer way the director's specific function, that of directing the actors and the artistic and technical staff, freeing him from the burdens he is often unable or unwilling to take over' (ibid.).
2. About Coppola's authorial status, see Corrigan (1991: 108–15); on Spielberg, see a 2003 special issue of the British film magazine *Reverseshot*. [Online.] Available: http://www.reverseshot.com/legacy/aprilmay03/ghostly.html.
3. The titles of the four books are *Arthur et les Minimoys*, *Arthur et la cite interdite*, *Arthur et la guerre des deux mondes*, and *Arthur et la vengeance de Maltazar*. The first film depicts the events of the first two books, and Besson plans on two sequels, one expected in 2009 (*Arthur et la guerre des deux mondes*) and one in 2010 (*Arthur et la vengeance de Maltazar*).
4. 'À Hollywood, quand on atteint des budgets aussi considérables, le risque est d'enfermer le film dans un carcan de règles moralement – et commercialement – correctes qui se transforment en autant de recettes scénaristiques. Besson, lui, est resté lui-même.'
5. For a detailed description of those methods, see Hayward (1998: 13–21).
6. 'Pendant quinze ans, mes rapports avec Gaumont ont toujours été à la fois bons et difficiles. Gaumont est une vielle dame, une grosse société lourde, et moi, j'ai toujours été petit et seul. Or, les intérêts d'une grosse boîte ne sont pas toujours les mêmes que ceux d'une personne...Les responsables de la Gaumont ont toujours été des gens courtois, agréables et à l'écoute, mais, malgré tout, chaque film a été un combat. Ce sont des businessmen ouverts, mais pas des artistes. Chaque fois, j'ai eu l'impression de faire un film contre eux. Jamais je ne suis arrivé avec un projet pour m'entendre dire: "Oui, super, génial!".'
7. 'Moi, jadis, j'avais voulu faire l'Idhec [l'ancêtre de la Femis]. J'ai été recalé au bout de dix minutes d'entretien. On m'avait demandé mes cinéastes préférés. J'ai répondu Spielberg, Scorsese, Forman. On m'a dit: "Au revoir, jeune homme." Plus tard, quand on m'a proposé d'y donner des cours, j'ai refusé. J'avais parlé avec Jean-Jacques Beineix, qui, lui, avait accepté. Six mois plus tard, il ne s'était toujours pas remis de la pretension des étudiants, qui l'avaient regardé de haut ...'

8. Anne Jäckel (2003: 92) also quotes these passages from Petrie's book about cultural and commercial aspects of British film industry.

9. 'La machine fait peur au début...Mais, aujourd'hui, je me détache, je prends plaisir au geste, à l'écriture. La caméra, comme le style, doit peser le poids d'une plume. Un créateur doit avoir cette souplesse, cela lui permet d'être plus inventif. Il ne faut pas se scléroser ni se laisser happer par la lourdeur de la machine.'

10. 'Une fois qu'un film marche, on me parle toujours de "coup", de "promo". Pourtant, au départ, il y a l'envie sincère de voir simplement une histoire.'

11. Europa Corp. will be subsequently referred to as Europa.

12. 'Dans le système des studios, quand on fait un film, on prend le risque de se faire virer, donc chacun essaye de ne pas faire des films! C'est ça, l'esprit des studios. On ne fait un film lorsqu'on ne peut faire autrement. Mis à part les projets incontournables genre Spielberg or Tom Cruise, les studios ne donnent pratiquement jamais le "greenlight" [le feu vert]. J'ai passé trois ans chez Warner: ils n'ont greenlighté aucun de mes projets. Chez Sony, pareil. Ils disent: "Super, super!" jusqu'à que le responsable du studio se fasse virer et qu'une nouvelle équipe arrive. Tout le monde est payé, il fait beau, les mecs se barrent à 4 heures de l'après-midi. C'est leur vie, mais ce n'est pas la mienne. C'est une mentalité à part. Ils ne veulent prendre aucun risque. Ils veulent du produit. Et si vous n'êtes pas là pour faire leur produit, ça ne fonctionne pas. Bien sûr, ils disent adorer les artistes européens, ils ne leur demandent que de teinter très légèrement leur films. Genre, nous, on fait le cake et vous, vous mettez la cerise dessus.'

13. 'En France, une vingtaine de personnes gèrent le cinéma dans son ensemble. Ce sont des producteurs, des réalisateurs, des patrons, des gens qui ont une responsabilité économique mais qui doivent aimer le cinéma. Si elles n'ont pas cet amour, c'est le cinéma tout entier qui est dans la merde! Ce qui est important, c'est qu'elles sachent quel est le bon équilibre. Si ce sont vingt personnes qui ne pensent qu'à faire de l'argent, ça va être une catastrophe. Si elles aiment le cinéma, elles vont faire la part des choses: produire certains films parce que, économiquement, l'ensemble du métier en a besoin; ensuite, produire d'autres films, plus exigeants, parce que, créativement, on en a aussi besoin [...] Ces vingt personnes, je ne les connais pas suffisamment pour savoir si elles en sont toutes conscientes. Moi, j'en suis conscient et c'est une sacrée responsabilité.'

14. Besson was assistant director to Claude Faraldo for *Deux lions au soleil/Two Lions in the Sun* (1980), Raphaël Delpard for *Les Bidasses aux grandes manœuvres* (1981), and second assistant to Alexandre Arcady for *Le Grand Carnaval/The Big Carnival* (1983).

15. 'J'avais un peu perdu le plaisir, le goût de la réalisation. Il faut une sacrée énergie pour bosser pendant deux ans, se faire déglinguer par la presse, être à la mode pendant quinze jours, et puis rentrer chez soi.'

16. 'Le milieu traîne quand même des idées étriquées et figées depuis la *Nouvelle vague*: seule une élite pourrait faire du cinéma; l'auteur est sacré, et tout ce qu'il fait est bon puisque c'est un artiste. Pour moi, le cinéma est un triangle créatif: auteur, réalisateur, acteur. C'est un compromis qui doit pousser à l'humilité.'

17. According to Dana Polan, Hayward's reading of Besson is implicitly auteur-oriented, albeit informed by an intention to contextualize the director as: 'One highly significant element in a complex process of film production and reception which includes socioeconomic and political determinants, the work of a large and highly skilled team of artists and technicians, the mechanisms of production and distribution, and the complex and multiply determined responses of spectators' (Polan 2001: 76–7).

18. The momentum of the *cinéma du look* seems to have waned immediately after the international success of Besson's *Nikita* and the failure of Jean-Jacques Beineix's *IP5* (1992). The latter film, despite showcasing Yves Montand's last film performance, passed through the 1992 Cannes Film Festival without comment and was a commercial failure in France and abroad. After *IP5*, Beineix made *Otaku* (1994), a short film about Japanese men's hobbies, which was barely noticed at Cannes, and *Mortel transfer* (2001), which was very poorly received in France (Powrie 2001). Carax's next film after an almost ten-year absence, *Pola X* (1999), was equally ill-received at Cannes and at the box office.

19. 'Il n'y a pas d'exception culturelle. Il faut garder le mot "culture", c'est tout. La culture, c'est la carte d'identité d'un pays. Point. On ne dit pas l'"exception du passeport". On dit "passeport". La culture, c'est pareil, il n'y a même pas à lutter. On ne peut pas nous arracher un organe. La culture, c'est en nous, c'est notre coeur. On ne pourra pas nous l'arracher. Ou il faudra tous nous tuer.'

20. Quoted in 'Le scenario noir de J2M.' (*Le nouvel observateur*. [Online.] Available: http://www.nouvelobs.com/articles/p1938/a8398.html).

21. 'Quel étais votre idéal en créant Europa? - Très honnêtement? S'éclater! C'est le seul truc auquel on ait pensé. L'excitation de se dire: "On va pouvoir faire les films dont on rêve." Après, il a fallu s'organiser et faire les choses sérieusement afin de pouvoir maîtriser toute la chaîne, de la conception du projet à sa diffusion en salle et en vidéo. Mais la première impulsion a été celle-là: s'éclater!' (Bold in the original.)

22. 'Jusqu'à 25 M$, Europa est actuellement capable de produire sans l'aide des Américains.'

23. 'Il y a au moins cent cinquante sociétés qui rêvent de faire un film avec Jet Li. Besson a réussi à le convaincre grâce à son pedigree et à sa vitesse de réaction: le comédien avait six mois entre deux projets. Six mois qui ont suffi à financer et tourner Le Baiser mortel du dragon.'

24. On the consequences of the Vivendi-Canal+ merger on French film production, see Lequeret 2002.

25. www.besson.com, accessed 20/11/00. The nickname 'J6M' had been coined by Canal+'s satirical puppet show *Les Guignols*, which humorously made an acronym of the six 'M's in the phrase that the Messier puppet used to refer to itself: 'Jean-Marie Messier, Moi-Même, Maître du Monde' (Jean-Marie Messier, Myself, Master of the World).

26. The film also stars Bridget Fonda and Tchéky Karyo, who played, respectively, the female lead and Uncle Bob in the American remake of *Nikita*.

27. For instance, Dreamworks produced *The Ring* (Gore Verbinsky, 2001), a remake of *Ringu* (Hideo Nakata, 1998).

28. See the reviews of the film by Aubron (2006) and Nesselson (2006). For a detailed account of *Angel-A*'s home box office results, go to: http://www.allocine.fr/film/boxoffice_gen_cfilm=61511.html.

29. For a detailed account of *Arthur*'s box office results, go to: http://www.boxofficemojo.com/movies/?page=intl&id=arthurandtheinvisibles.htm.

References

Alexander, M. 1994. A Gaul in Hollywood. *Variety*, 356.10: 10, October.

Aubron, H. 2006. Angel-A. *Cahiers du Cinéma*, 608: 42, January.

Besson, L. 2001. Le plus grand défi de Luc Besson: entretien avec Jean-Pierre Lavoignant et Christophe d'Yvoire. *Studio Magazine*, 169: 72–83.

——. 2002. Je n'ai plus peur: entretien avec Lionel Cartégini et Olivier de Bruyin. *Première*, 300: 92–7.

——. 2003. Le système B: entretien avec Aurélien Ferenczi. *Télérama*, 2781: 32–6, 30 April.

——. 2006. Interview Luc Besson. *Première*. [Online.] Available: http://www.premiere.fr/premiere/magazine-et-exclus/interviews/interview-lucbesson/(affichage)/interviewPage/(interview_id)/410269/(interviewPage_question)/9.

——. 2007. Press Conference. Montreal: Hotel Sofitel, 5 January.

Bondy, J-A. 1997. Le cinquième élément. *Première*, 244: 35, juin.

Boschi, A. and Manzoli, G. (eds). 1995. *Oltre l'autore I. Fotogenia*, 2.

Corrigan, T. 1991. *A Cinema without Walls: Movies and Culture after Vietnam*. New Brunswick, N.J.: Rutgers University Press.

Crofts, S. 1993. Reconceptualizing national cinemas. *Quarterly Review of Film and Video*, 14(3): 49–68.

——. 1998a. Authorship and Hollywood. (*In* Hill, J. and Church Gibson P. (eds). *The Oxford Guide to Film Studies*. Oxford: Oxford University Press, pp. 310–24.)

De Grazia, V. 1998. European cinema and the idea of Europe, 1925–95. (*In* Nowell-Smith G. and Ricci, S. (eds). *Hollywood and Europe: Economics, Culture, National Identity: 1945–95*. London: BFI, pp. 19–33.)

Durovicová, N. 1994. Some thoughts at an intersection. *Velvet Light Trap*, 34: 3–9.

Ferenczi, A. 2003. Sa petite entreprise ne connaît pas la crise. *Télérama*, 2781: 36–9, 30 April.

Finney, A. 1996. *The State of European Cinema: A New Dose of Reality*. London: Cassel.

Genzlinger, N. 2007. The Human and the Animated, Shrunk to Size. *The New York Times*. (12 January). [Online.] Available: http://movies2.nytimes.com/2007/01/12/movies/12art.html.

Guichard, L. 2004. Besson un peu débouté. *Télérama*, 2857: 26 October.

Hayward, S. 1998. *Luc Besson*. Manchester: Manchester University Press.

Hillier, J. (ed.). 1985. *Cahiers du Cinéma. Volume 1: The 1950s, Neorealism, Hollywood, the New Wave*. London: RKP/BFI.

Ilott, T. 1996. *Budgets and Markets: A Study of the Budgeting of European Film*. London and New York: Routledge.

Jäckel, A. 1996. European co-production strategies: the case of France and Britain. (*In* Moran A. (ed.). *Film Policy: International, National, and Regional Perspectives*. London and New York: Routledge, pp. 85–100.)

Koehler, R. 2006. Arthur and the Invisibles. Arthur et les minimoys. *Variety*. (21 December.) [Online.] Available: http://www.variety.com/review/VE1117932356.html?categoryid=31&cs=1&p=.

Kruger, A. 1994. Léon. *Première*, 211: 40, novembre.

Lequeret, É. 2002. Les inconnues de l'après-Canal+ (dossier). *Cahiers du Cinéma*, 570: 68–71, juillet-août.

Loustalot, G. 2006. Angel-A. *Première*, 348: 44, février.

Margolick, D. 2002. Vivendi's Mr. Universe. *Vanity Fair*, 500: 240–77.

Mazdon, L. (ed.). 2001. *France on Film: Reflections on Popular French Cinema*. London: Wallflower Press.

Miller, T. 1998. Hollywood and the World. (*In* Hill, J. & Church Gibson P. (eds). *The Oxford Guide to Film Studies*. Oxford: Oxford University Press, pp. 371–381.

Moran, A. (ed.). 1996. *Film Policy: International, National, and Regional Perspectives*. London and New York: Routledge.

Nesselson, L. 2006. Angel-A. *Variety*. 23, 28. 26 December.

Petrie, D. 1991. *Creativity and Constraint in the British Film Industry*. London: MacMillan.

——. (ed.). 1992. *Screening Europe: Image and Identity in Contemporary European Cinema*. London: BFI.

Polan, D. 2001. Auteur desire. *Screening the Past*. [Online.] Available: http://www.latrobe.edu.au/screeningthepast/firstrelease/fr0301/dpfr12a.htm.

Powrie, P. 2001. *Jean-Jacques Beineix*. Manchester: Manchester University Press.

Puttnam, D. 1997. *The Undeclared War: The Struggle of the World's Film Industry*. London: Harper Collins.

Sarris, A. 1991. Sarris' film column. *New York Observer*, 1 April.

Schatz, T. 2003. The Whole equation of Pictures. (*In* Wright Wexman, V. (ed.). *Film and Authorship*. New Brunswick: Rutgers University Press, pp. 89–95.)

Staiger, J. 2003b. Authorship Approaches. (*In* Staiger, J. and Gerstner, D. A. (eds). *Authorship and Film*. New York: Routledge, pp. 27–57.)

Vincendeau, G. 1996. *The Companion to French Cinema*. London: Cassel.

——. 1998. Issues in European Cinema. (*In* Hill, J. and Church Gibson P. (eds). *The Oxford Guide to Film Studies*. Oxford: Oxford University Press, pp. 440–48.)

Williams, M. 1999. French Filmmaker of the Year. *Variety*, 373: 105, 11–17 January.

PART THREE: THE FEMALE AUTHOR IN THE ERA OF POST-FEMINISM

7

AUTEURISM AND WOMEN'S CINEMA IN FRANCE, ITALY AND SPAIN

At the ninth edition of the Festival International de Films de Femmes (FIFF, 'International Women's Film Festival') held in Créteil, France, in 1987, Chantal Akerman declared women's cinema to be 'outdated.'[1] The Belgian-born film director was not only voicing a widespread opinion at the time, but one that still holds true today among women film-makers who have 'made it' in the male-dominant tradition of film direction in Western Europe over the past twenty years, both in mainstream and author-informed contexts of film production and reception. These film-makers tend to demarcate themselves from gender-specific feminist categories, even when their films privilege female characters and focus on women's issues. As much as this position implies if not an acceptance then certainly an oversight of the patriarchal ideology still prominent in many contexts of film production and reception, it also reveals a pragmatic strategy of disengagement from the ideological constraints that have traditionally confined women's subject positions and professional roles in Western European cinema and society.

In a *Screen* article, 'Women's Cinema, Film Theory and Feminism in France' (1987), Ginette Vincendeau inquires into the origins of post-feminist politics in France during the 1980s. The article opens with a direct reference to Akerman's statement at FIFF and follows with a damning indictment about 'the connection between theoretical debates about gender and feminism and women's film-making in France' wherein Vincendeau describes the situation as 'oblique and at worst conflictual' (Vincendeau 1987: 5).[2] She attributes this gap between feminism and female film directors in France to three factors: the lack of feminist approaches in film criticism and academia; the 'general decline of political militancy both as an activity and a theoretical approach' since the early 1980s; and, finally, the small output of feminist publications and films which tend to be polarized between ultra-chic presses such as Editions des Femmes and Librairie des Femmes and colour feature films on the one hand and on minimalist bulletins of the Mouvement de Libération des Femmes (MLF, 'Women's Liberation Movement') and black-and-white informational videos produced and distributed by feminist collectives on the other (Vincendeau 1987: 5–8).

Regarding the link between feminism and women's authorial film practices, Vincendeau opines, 'Given that the model for the auteur is still the individual genius, or at least the artist driven by "internal necessity" towards self-expression, this has had the paradoxical result of pushing French women directors into heightened individualism on the one hand and alignment with male "colleagues" on the other' (ibid.: 9). According to Vincendeau, only a few female film-makers 'seem to be aware of the crippling effect of this individualism' (ibid.). Among them she mentions Jeanne Labrune, who puts the blame on the lack of institutional programmes (comparable to those existing in Germany) aimed at promoting women's films in France. Vincendeau concludes, 'The French inability to think collectively means that French women cannot experience their practice in any other way than as auteurs, thinking that they are doing very well out of this individualistic game, whereas very often they are at the same time being 'had', in terms of their contracts, of distribution, etc.' (Ibid.)

Carrie Tarr and Brigitte Rollet share Vincendeau and Labrune's take on French women film-makers, including those involved in authorial film practices. In the introduction to *Cinema and the Second Sex: Women's Film-making in France in the 1980s and 1990s* (2001), Tarr and Rollett emphasize that the French concept of auteur did not help women, with the exception of Agnès Varda, gain access to France's 'overwhelmingly male' cinematic milieus and institutions when authorship became a critical and professional category associated with the *nouvelle vague* (Tarr and Rollet 2001: 9–11). They add that the French figure of the auteur has contributed to undermining, rather than highlighting, gender-specific elements and perspectives in the films of French female film-makers:

> The figure of the auteur/artist as it has been constructed and valued in French universalist discourses, is understood to transcend the particularities of gender, sexual orientation and ethnicity, thus obviating debates on the lack of representation on the part of women, gays and lesbians, and ethnic minorities. In this context, it is not surprising that French women directors routinely reject the label of 'women director' [...], since claiming a supposedly gender-neutral auteur status is often the best way to gain legitimacy and recognition within the film industry. (Ibid.: 10)

Although Tarr and Rollet acknowledge that 'an acceptance of auteurism has enabled women to impose themselves as directors to an extent that is unique to France,' they also stress that this acceptance implies a gender-neutral context of production and reception (ibid.: 10–11), particularly 'during a period dominated by "postfeminist" assumptions [and] a strong backlash against feminism in politics, culture and the media' (ibid.: 4).

These circumstances leading French female film directors (especially those recognized as 'auteurs') to part from the concept of women's cinema and to distance themselves from feminism apply to most Western European women film-makers working in different modes of cinematic practices. This is the case even though feminism motivated women's efforts to break through the male-dominant national cinemas of this geo-political area during the late 1960s and the 1970s. Female authorial practices developed in this context since the 1980s prompt a re-thinking of the notion of women's cinema as a type of agency premised on pragmatic and localized tactics of personal and professional affirmation that purposefully ignore sexual difference and gendered identity as binding and limiting concepts. This position resonates with recent feminist approaches to the notion of female authorship, focusing less on textual marks of feminine expression than on pragmatic strategies of consumption and appropriation of artworks and discourses (Bean and Negra 2002; Gerstner and Staiger 2003; Maule 2005a, 2006; Rabinovitz 2005; Wright Wexman 2003). Lauren Rabinovitz describes these new views as follows:

> Authorship in this regard then is not merely a unity across the text but is established in relationship to human agency within industrial or artisanal networks and practices. Authorship as a practice is therefore contingent on securing a position and power within institutional frameworks and reception. (2005: 27)

Seen from this perspective, the gender-oblivious stance in Western European female authorship signals less the abandonment than the continuation of women film-makers' political discourse within patriarchal society in the heyday of the Women's Movement through different strategies and means. Indeed, the most recent theoretical discussions of female authorship assume post-feminism less as a superseding paradigm than a different take on women's identity politics.

Gender politics in the age of post-feminism

Sarah Projansky provides a comprehensive illustration of post-feminism in her book *Watching Rape: Film and Television in Postfeminist Culture* (2001: 66–89). She identifies five categories of post-feminist discourse: 1.) linear post-feminism (which follows feminism as a historical phenomenon); 2.) backlash post-feminism (which involves antifeminist and revisionist positions); 3.) equality and choice post-feminism (which illustrates feminism's achievements and suggests that liberated women no longer need feminism); 4.) (hetero)sex-positive post-feminism (which rejects feminism as anti-sex and endorsement of women's individuality and independence from men); and 5.) men-as-feminists post-feminism (which claims that men can also be feminists, as women are now equal to men) (Projansky 2001: 66–89). Women film directors' reluctance to address gender in contemporary Western European cinema finds justification in all the post-feminist positions described by Projansky. According to Projansky, post-feminism is 'a cultural discourse – an attitude, a reaction formation, an always available hegemonic response to feminism – not entirely linked to any particular historical moment' (2001: 88).

Post-feminism constitutes a standpoint from which Western European female film-makers disentangle their agency from unresolved issues in feminist praxis and theory: how to identify and develop feminine identity and expression within a society and a film system founded on male-dominant models of subjectivity and aesthetics. In this respect, their post-feminist approach to film-making involves: 1) a reconsideration of gender as one of the elements constituting women's subject position, to be constantly renegotiated and adapted to specific contexts and situations; and 2) a disengagement of female authorship from notions of gendered subjectivity imbricated in oppositional or binary mechanisms of identity formation.

Another definition of post-feminism particularly suitable for the discussion of women's authorial film practices in Western Europe over the past twenty years comes from a post-theoretical framework that supersedes post-structuralist redefinitions of subjectivity and proposes a pragmatic and materialistic approach to film aesthetics. In *Deleuze and Cinema: The Aesthetics of Sensation* (2002), a book inspired by the writings of the French philosopher Gilles Deleuze, Barbara M. Kennedy associates post-feminism with a theoretical framework that rejects the psychoanalytic and occularcentric paradigms of 1970s and 1980s feminist film theory and, instead, develops a post-theoretical, post-Cartesian and non-transcendental approach to subjectivity: 'In contrast with the contentious deliberations across feminisms of "difference" a *post-feminist* agenda is concerned with the micrology of the lived experiences, across and between the spaces of any fixed, sentient, or even fluid gendered subjectivity' (2002: 21).

These and other discussions of post-feminism in relation to cinema (Projansky 2001; Modleski 1991) offer a position from which to address the general disregard for gender-specific issues and the dismissal of feminist politics in women's authorial film practices since the 1980s, especially in Europe. Post-feminism also represents a counter-hegemonic discourse whose manifestations vary depending on the cultural and geographic context and the specific feminist traditions from which it develops and has, for instance, different connotations within the three national contexts examined in this book. For this reason, an overview of the impact of the Women's Movement in French, Italian, and Spanish cinema is necessary to situate the post-feminist agenda assumed by female film-makers in these national cinemas during the past twenty years.

Feminism and the discourse on difference in France, Italy and Spain

The discussion of sexual difference was especially prominent in France and Italy and typified by the concept of *écriture feminine* (feminine writing) and the *pensiero della differenza* (difference thought), respectively. *Écriture féminine* refers to female authorial identity conceived outside of the western Logos and its linguistic and logical processes. Italian feminists were influenced by the French theories of difference, especially the ones proposed by the group Psychanalyse et Politique ('Psych & Po') and by theorists Luce Irigaray and Adrienne Rich. Italian feminists also assumed an idiosyncratic approach to difference; unlike the French feminists, they did not emphasize the symbolic dimension of difference. Italian feminists have gone even further than their French counterparts in pursuing a politics of difference in that they do not only refuse equality as an implicit re-instatement of male subjectivity as the norm but hypothesize female difference as being-woman, within a dual conceptualization of being (Bono and Kemp 1991: 16). As Luisa Passerini underlines in the article 'The Women's Movement in Italy,' Italian feminism, 'despite its awareness of possible alliances against the patriarchal system, [...] broke away from the student and youth movements' (1993: 175). In this respect, Bono and Kemp stress that, 'By comparison with French, British, and American feminism, the most surprising feature of Italian feminism is its non-institutional basis' (1991: 2). Rather than an essentialist position, the 'subjectivism' of Italian feminism entails an empirical and political gesture, linked to women's experience and thought (ibid.: 18–19).

The dissociation of Spanish women film-makers from feminist discourse developed differently than in France and Italy. Indeed, because of the dictatorship (whose patriarchal traits were further reinforced by strong links with the Catholic Church), feminism became an issue only after Franco's death in 1975, which marked the celebration of the United Nations' International Women's Year (IWY). In this country, even more than in Italy, the question of 'double militancy' (in socio-political parties and in the Women's Movement) contributed to creating divisions among the militants and undermining the influence of feminism in Spanish society. Ana Pereira Prata compares the development of feminism during the democratization processes of Italy and Spain, 'two Southern European countries that experienced authoritarian rule and were predominantly catholic' (Pereira Prata 2003: 143). She argues that, in Spain, 'the democracy movement lived in constant fear of a reactionary coup, which led women's organizations to work closer with political parties that were democratic, but not explicitly feminist' (ibid.: 144). Hence, the subordination of women's issues in the first years of the post-Franco era was a consequence of 'consensus politics,' a moderate platform that Spanish parties and unions encouraged in order to avoid socio-political instability (ibid.: 145).

Since the 1980s, feminism has produced different strands of thought and action in these three national contexts. The editors of the aforementioned anthology on 1980s French feminism note that by the mid-1980s, 'most of the writings about sexual *différence* had fallen out of fashion in France, much sooner, in fact, than they did in the United States' (Célestin, DalMolin, and de Courtivron 2003: 1). The theory of difference has been replaced by a theory of differences, located at the interface of local and global, specific and universal politics (ibid.: 6–11). According to Kelly Oliver and Lisa Walsh, the authors of a more recent book on the same subject, in trying to overcome the epistemological deadlock of difference, French feminism 'continue[s] to be a necessary moment in the struggle towards a sense of subjectivity incorporative of both same and other – whether that other be figured as belonging to another sex, race, nation ...' (2004: 9).

This new generation of feminists tackled the issue of difference by stressing the national/global interface related to women's political and legal rights in France. In this regard, French feminists have also rejected the French notion of universalism, firmly criticized during the 1980s as a concept that erases women's identity in the name of 'human' equality and progress. The Tunisian-born feminist theorist Gisèle Halimi, for instance, opposes this 'deceptive' universalism to a framework that foregrounds the role of place and specificity in women's identities (Halimi 2004). In the final paragraph of her essay, she remarks:

> To regain a shred of energy and a voice with which to speak, women need to oppose this deceptive universalism with another universalism, still republican, but truly universal. A universalism in which women refuse the erasure of their identity as women and build our humanity together with men. A universalism which recognizes its own diversity. (Ibid.: 39)

Yet, although the universalistic stance of the so-called 'Third Wave' of French feminism has been the object of national debates and foreign critiques (especially on the part of North American feminists), it has also provided a political standpoint for gaining civic rights such as the introduction in 2000 of France's 'parity law,' which guarantees women equal representation in political parties.

Like in France, in Italy the feminist movement prompted the approval of a series of laws for women's social and legal advancement, including the general reform of the Family Law, the law for equal gender treatment in the workplace in 1977, the law on abortion in 1978, and the institution of the 'consultori familiari' ('family centres') all over the country beginning in 1975. At the level of social activism, Italian feminism underwent two phases: the first began with the 1968 movement and ended in the early 1970s; the second started in the mid-1970s with women's creation of new, informal groups and organizations (Passerini 1993: 176–77). Giuliana Bruno and Maria Nadotti underline the difficulty and ambivalence involved in the feminists' move from an initial 'dual militancy' (Marxist and feminist) to the creation of 'small, uncentralized groups, both consciousness-raising groups and *gruppi dell'inconscio*' (unconsciousness groups) (1988: 10). These groups, they add, 'followed a path which began with, traversed, Marxism, and naturally led to reaching and traversing psychoanalysis' (ibid.).

Since the 1980s, women's centres and associations in Italy have remained in place and diversified their objectives and orientations. Conversely, gender issues are still largely disregarded within institutional and academic circles. In part, the absence of gender discourse in Italy's public sphere and culture reflects a specific choice on the part of Italian feminists, as Bono and Kemp maintain in 1991:

> Italian feminism bridges the gap between institutional, theoretical feminism and active/ political feminism. Until now, there have been no 'women studies' (in the sense of degree courses, departments, chairs or lectureships) in Italian universities. There are, of course, women in academia, many of whom have an interest in studying or teaching other women's work, or in bringing their lives as women to bear upon their subject disciplines and their modes of research. Instead of trying to institutionalize these issues, however, they manage to carve out a space in the curriculum *as it is*. In this respect they infiltrate and exploit the grey areas of academic organization. (1991: 3)

In the past decade, women have reached more visibility in Italian academy and Gender Studies has been integrated in some universities' curricula. Yet, Italian feminist discourse is still primarily confined to community-based organizations and networks.

The fact that Spanish women's political equality was not accompanied by a strong feminist discourse made the emergence of post-feminism even easier than in France and Italy. In Italy, starting in the early 1980s, the feminist movement became dispersed in small groups and organizations. Similarly, in France, once women gained recognition on the levels of legislation and politics (abortion was legalized in 1985 and a growing number of women were publicly appointed under the socialist government's two mandates), feminism was soon relegated to a historical phenomenon. As the feminist organization 'Murejeres progresistas' ('Progressive women') argues on its website, in spite of the evident fragmentation of the country's feminist movement since the 1980s,

> The most important phenomenon produced during these years is the existence of a current of opinion among women, one which is oriented towards rupturing old behavioural

patterns and rejecting the patriarchal attitudes of male systems of power. This attitude of rupture is reflected in women of different ages, social classes, and professions and is concretized in a growing desire to gain independence within the economic sphere as well as personal and professional spheres (http://www.fmujeresprogresistas.org/feminismo4.htm, my translation).[3]

Feminism and women's cinema: a contested relationship

In most of Western Europe, feminism was an important component of the cultural activism organized within the 1968 movement, except in countries that were under dictatorship during the late 1960s and early 1970s such as Spain and Greece. Because of its connection with the revolutionary and counter-institutional activities of the 1968 movement, feminist cinema was mainly located in independent networks of film production and distribution. In each national context, feminist collectives and groups supported film and video projects on gender-specific topics and used cinema as a means to sensitize and educate women about their condition. However, these initiatives had no impact on national film systems and institutions. In fact, quite the opposite happened: the sociocultural divisions between the sexes remained in place within most national film industries, as well as academic programmes and cultural circles, both during and after the waning of the Women's Movement.

The only exception to this situation is a particular strand of feminist film practice developed in Germany and the United Kingdom within the framework of counter-cinema. Feminists reacted against the patriarchal ideology implicit in mainstream and classical cinemas by making films that both criticized and avoided formal and narrative conventions such as naturalistic representation, character identification, narrative continuity, aestheticism, and closure. The purpose was to create a new cinematic language and to address gender-relevant topics. In West Germany and the United Kingdom, feminist counter-cinema involved public institutions.[4] Feminist discourse was integrated into pre-existing government programmes or institutions such as, for instance, the British Film Institute (BFI) and the National Film Theatre (NFT) in the United Kingdom or the subsidy for auteur films in Western Germany. Furthermore, the government and public institutions subsidized and promoted academic courses, cultural events, and publications on women's cinema. For example, in 1973, the NFT launched a retrospective on Dorothy Arzner curated by feminist film critic Claire Johnston. Johnston put together a pamphlet for the occasion called *Notes on Women's Cinema* (1973), featuring articles written by feminist scholars including herself. The feminist film journal *Frauen und Film* (*Women and Film*) was founded by the German film-maker Helke Sanders in 1974. In the United Kingdom, the film journal *Screen* reserved special attention for feminist film theory, with contributions by Johnston, Christine Gledhill and Laura Mulvey.

In the rest of Western Europe, feminist initiatives remained limited to independent and local activist groups and collectives, and had only sporadic or peripheral connections with institutional structures and regular circuits of film distribution. In France, feminism was largely ignored by the film industry and the government. Françoise Audé, who has long been the only feminist film critic in France, suggests that feminism was not a serious consideration for the many women who began making feature films in the 1970s, both in mainstream and auteurist contexts of film production (1981: 105).[5] With regard to the films made by female directors in this decade, she comments:

> Characterized by different political, aesthetic, and ethical options, these films are heterogeneous. They are not all feminist; far from it. Not all female film-makers proclaim their commitment as women in their work and at the service of the feminist cause. Some, who did not disdain the interest that was given to them as samples of feminine creativity, are the authors of films impregnated with ordinary stereotypes of French misogyny. Not every woman's film is the champion or the privileged representative of the women's liberation movement. As any man's film, a woman's film typifies – at the outset – nothing more than itself (1981: 134, my translation).[6]

To be sure, several female film-makers, film critics, scholars, and actresses publicly manifested their feminist militancy during the 1960s and 1970s. Some of them developed film projects based on women's social struggle and activism in community groups, documentation centres, collectives, and associations. Audé devoted a chapter of her book to the influence of the Women's Movement on French cinema titled '1968, Le cinéma au service de la libération des femmes' ('1968: Cinema at the service of women's liberation') (1981: 105–16). In this chapter, she refers to pro-abortion initiatives such as the text published in the *Nouvel Observateur* in 1971 in which 343 female film directors and actresses admitted to having illegal abortions (ibid.: 105). She also lists a series of militant films including *Histoires d'A*, directed by Charles Belmont and Marielle Issartel in 1973 but blocked by the Ministry of Culture and released only the following year. These educational films were shot on Super 8mm and made within academic and research contexts (Paris VIII and the Centre National de Recherche Scientifique (C.N.R.S.)). Audé's list also includes a number of documentary films about the women's liberation movement produced and distributed through independent circuits (ibid.: 105–116).[7]

In the 1970s, the most important feminist association dealing with cinema in France was Musidora, named after the French silent film actress, director, and producer, best known for her role as Irma Vep in Louis Feuillade's serial *Les Vampyres/The Vampires* (1915). Musidora was founded in 1973 by a group of women interested in film: their purpose was to produce and distribute videos made by female directors and to promote research on women's cinema. Musidora was also behind the establishment of the first international women's film festival, which took place in Paris in 1974 and anticipated the creation of a regular women's film festival in the country, the Festival International de Films de Femmes. Finally, in 1976, the association founded a publishing company, *Paroles ... elles tournent* (a pun that translates literally as 'Words... they go around' but also 'Words... women shoot films').

In spite of these initiatives, feminism did not change women's position in French cinema. Although the French government approved important laws assuring women's civic rights and health services (notably legalized abortion, consensual divorce, and stricter sanctions on rape), it did not promote any programmes to guarantee women's professional status within the arts, including cinema. By the time the socialist government took power and implemented new policies to promote French cinema, especially during Jack Lang's two mandates as minister of culture (1981–1986 and 1988–1992), the Women's Movement had already lost momentum at the level of French legislation. As Roger Célestin, Eliane DalMolin, and Isabelle De Courtivron remark in the introduction to the anthology *Beyond French Feminisms: Debates on Women, Politics and Culture in France, 1981–2001*:

> As had been the case in 1945 when the first wave of feminism in France slowed down after gaining the vote for women, the second wave of the seventies lost steam once the Left came to power and institutionalized part of this second wave's agenda. The French media in the eighties were therefore quick to relegate feminism to a sort of 'historical epiphenomenon.' (Célestin, DalMolin, and De Courtivron 2003: 2)

Tarr and Rollet associate some of the women's films from the second half of the 1990s with the 'retour du politique' (return of politics), that is, a revival of the socio-political engagement which had marked the 1960s and 1970s in relation to issues of immigration, social exclusion, economic disparity among classes, and cultural specificity (1998: 6–7).

Since the 1990s, French female authors have also explored new forms of female identity through subversive representations of sex and the body, particularly in the cinema. In this respect, Célestin, DalMolin, and De Courtivron suggest:

> Perhaps more than women writers, women film-makers have inherited the burden of operating in the borrowed world of male myths and images. They also acquired from their predecessors the desire to react to the normalized voyeuristic impulse that characterizes the representation of women and has been implicitly accepted by them, ultimately defining the way women perceived themselves. (2003: 9)

In Italy, the confinement of feminist cinema to independent and educational circuits of film production and distribution (except for sporadic projects funded by national television) reflects the oscillation between oppositional and accommodating attitudes typical of the Women's Movement in this country. This tenuous position was evident vis-à-vis both the dominant system and political parties and groups identified with the counterculture. Throughout the 1970s, film-makers and screenwriters (among others, Armenia Balducci, Giovanna Gagliardo, Annabella Miscuglio, and Gabriella Rosaleva), as well as writers and intellectuals (Dacia Maraini, Adriana Monti) involved in the feminist movement, made feature films that portrayed women's stories and conditions. Miscuglio and other female film directors also made educational and information films to distribute through militant collectives or directed educational programmes about women's experiences. Some of the latter were produced by Italian state television (RAI), the most famous examples being the series *Si dice donna/They Say Woman* (1977) and *Processo per stupor/Rape Trial* (1979), a film made by a collective of six women that documented a real-life rape trial.

In the aforementioned book *Offscreen: Women and Film in Italy* (1988), Giuliana Bruno and Maria Nadotti sample testimonies, documents, and essays about these examples of Italian feminist cinema. They also illustrate the Italian feminists' use of cinema as an educational tool, such as the collaboration of the film scholar Giovanna Grignaffini with the Women's Research and Documentation Centre in Bologna and the film-related seminars of the '150 Hours Courses' offered by feminist intellectuals and activists co-ordinated by Adriana Monti and Giulia Alberti in Milan (Bruno and Nadotti 1988: 11). The '150 Hours Courses' featured free classes on literacy, social history, sociology, photography, and graphic design. The programme, which ran from 1974 until 1982, was initially conceived for female factory workers but was later opened to housewives and pensioners. The curriculum included a seminar on film titled 'The cinema as representation: the place of the female in Hollywood cinema' (1979/1980) (ibid.: 101–03). Within the framework of the courses, Monti directed a 40-minute documentary film shot on black-and-white 16mm film using free equipment. *Scuola senza fine/School without end* (1979) recorded the workshops over a period of two years.

Italian feminists also maintained an ambivalent position vis-à-vis the national film industry and film community. As in France, feminist film-makers had very little access to regular channels of film production and distribution and worked either within independent structures or through national television networks devoted to cultural and educational programmes. Indeed, most Italian female directors in those years were able to make movies exclusively within these frameworks. On the other hand, feminist activists kept their distance from the national film industry, which they considered inescapably compromised because of its place within the patriarchal system. Significantly, Lina Wertmüller and Liliana Cavani, the only Italian female directors with professional power and prestige within the national and international 1970s art house film circuit, declared themselves feminists. Yet, the thematic and stylistic qualities of the films these women made in this period set them apart from those produced by militant feminists. Wertmüller and Cavani were criticized by several feminist scholars, especially in North America, for re-instating feminine clichés and even furthering misogynistic representations of women.[8]

Since the 1980s, several women have begun making feature films in Italy. Although only a few have managed to distribute their films on the national film circuit (besides Archibugi, Cristina and Francesca Comencini, Roberta Torre, Fiorella Infascelli, Cinzia Th. Torrini), female film directors have been active within different areas and modes of film-making. In 1999, at the twentieth edition of the Women's International Film Festival in Florence, film critic Gabriella Imperatori gave an encouraging overview of the role of women in Italian film practices, while stressing the fact that contemporary film-makers adopt a less critical perspective than the feminist film-makers of the past. She describes the new generation as follows:

> [They] are now far from the historical models of denunciation that characterized the 1970s (in the *Io sono mia* collective, for instance); instead they are more inclined to develop stories in which the ultimate judgment emerges spontaneously from the plot. By and large, [women film-makers are] more mature and professional, more capable of providing answers to questions about both women's world and the world at large. They are ready to accept comparisons or to continue on their own, to experiment and to recuperate, pursuing new technology on a passionate and fascinating quest (Imperatore, quoted in Massara 2006, my translation).[9]

The lack of concern with gender issues has been a constant in Spanish cinema. In *Feminist Discourse and Spanish Cinema: Sight Unseen* (1999), the first book dedicated to the representation of women and women's cinema in Spain, Susan Martin-Márquez denounces the lack of visibility of the very few women film directors in Spain, within both the film industry and national film discourse:

> Gender-specific blind spots and analytical oversights are evident here; women directors especially have been subject to patronizing dismissals, received only cursory attention, or been omitted completely. The case of Rosario Pi, Spain's first woman film-maker of the sound era [...] is instructive [...]. It appears that over the years women working in the Spanish film industry have not simply been denigrated and dismissed, they have also been erased. (1999: 5–6)

Martin-Márquez reminds us that few women who had important roles in Spain's national film industry before the 1990s assumed feminist positions, even when they seemed to advocate its cause. This was the case of the actress/film director Ana Mariscal, the only prominent woman in 1950s and 1960s Spanish cinema. Regarding Mariscal's feminist status, Martin-Márquez states that 'despite the apparently feminist nature of some of her pronouncements [...] [they] would have hesitated to use that term [feminism]' (1999: 9). She also provides the example of Pilar Miró, who started her career within the context of Spain's resistant *nuevo cine* movement toward the end of Franco's regime and continued to make films in the post-Franco era. During the 1980s, she served two terms as Minister of Culture for the socialist government (ibid.). Miró, notes Martin-Márquez, 'has for several decades engaged in public diatribes against those who would seek to categorize her or her work as feminist' (ibid.).

The contradictions implicit in Miró's rejection of gender as a subject position emerged particularly during the 1980s when she became the most powerful woman in the Spanish audio-visual system. She was general director of the national film industry from 1983 to 1985 and head of the national television network from 1986 to 1989. During both mandates, she was heavily criticized for her conservative support of 'high culture' in film production and her excessive expenditures on costumes and settings. Her political career also had consequences for her work and its critical reception. In particular, the films she made between her first and second appointments were stigmatized (also outside of Spain) for being too stylized, the products of a 'woman of power' with the means to produce artistic films with high production values.[10] The debates raised during Miró's appointment as head of Spanish state television are symptomatic of the ambivalence underlying discourses on gender within Spanish society. The main accusation against Miró concerned the fact that she included personal items in her budget under the pretext that she considered them 'professional expenses.' On this occasion, she resorted to her femininity as a justification, claiming that a woman attending official events needs more apparel than a man, who can always wear the same tuxedo.

This controversy brings new insight to the stern rejection of gender-specificity as discriminatory among Spanish female film directors of the latest generation. A perfect example of this position appears in a short article by Icíar Bollaín in 2003 in a special issue of the feminist journal *Duoda*, titled 'Cine con tetas' ('Cinema with tits'). In her piece, the acclaimed film-maker defines sexual difference as a biological detail with no bearing on cinematic practices. In her frank words, 'The difference between men and women is that they are men and we are women, basically. They have a penis, we don't. We have tits, they don't' (Bollaín 2003: 51–52, my translation).[11] Bollaín's declaration is all the more surprising if one considers that the three feature films she has completed to date are centred on women's personal and social problems in contemporary Spain. *¿Hola esta sola?* (1995) deals with two young women who suffer affective troubles within their respective families and find refuge in their mutual friendship. *Flores de otro mundo/Flowers from Another World* (1999) depicts the integration of female immigrants in a small community in rural Spain. *Te doy mis ojos/Take my Eyes* (2003) touches upon the widespread phenomenon of domestic violence against women in the country; a theme that Bollaín first explored in the short film *Amores que matan* (2000). As is the case with the French and Italian female film-makers discussed earlier, in distancing herself from gender-specific definitions of personal expression or cinema aesthetics, Bollaín does not overlook the conditions and problems specific to women. Rather, she refuses to assume essentialist views of feminine creativity and identity.

From *différence* to differences: gender politics in the age of post-feminism

During the 1970s and 1980s the European cultural mode of film production underwent a paradigm shift due to the increased participation of independent film producers and television networks. A large number of women film-makers went into feature film-making at this time. The new production system was mainly conceived for television broadcasting; hence, these women's works were exposed to only a very small, niche theatrical audience. The female film-makers of the new generation did not benefit from any special subsidy or opportunity programme; they had the same opportunities as their male colleagues and went through the same type of formation.

For this reason, neither the personal development nor the professional experiences of female film-makers have been significantly marked by gender-specific circumstances. Most of the women who have started their careers as film-makers since the 1970s have received a formal education in film production and had long apprenticeships in the film industry, in various roles (i.e. as independent directors of short films, screenwriters, directors of films or programmes for national television networks, or directors of commercials). These experiences consolidated their professional status and built important connections within the national and international film context. As such, these film-makers can be considered auteurs according to the French *nouvelle vague*'s usage of the term; that is, film-makers who maintain complete control over their films (Marie 1998: 63). Indeed, many women film-makers based in Western Europe have succeeded in staying autonomous vis-à-vis public film systems, national film industries, and independent film companies throughout their careers (Claire Denis and Francesca Archibugi are cases in point). The authorial discourse associated with Western European female film-makers points to a post-feminist disavowal of gender difference which either subsumes the notion of gendered subjectivity into a larger discussion of sociocultural identity and politics or adopts a post-subjective perspective on issues of cinematic aesthetic and address. For this reason, the treatment of female authorship in Western European cinema requires a consideration of feminist and post-feminist discussions of gender.

Feminist approaches to film informed by Freudian and Lacanian psychoanalysis have concentrated on the semantically absent and culturally fluctuating role of the female subject in western representation, especially through the lens of classical Hollywood cinema. As Mary Ann Doane has pointed out, Sigmund Freud's definition of female identity in his lecture 'Femininity' is conveyed through a section from Romantic poet Heinrich Heine's *The North Sea*. As Freud presented the passage, metonymic figures hint to the ultimate mystery, 'the riddle of the nature of femininity' (Doane 1990: 41). Yet, as Doane reveals, the poetic devices ultimately do not ask the question 'What is Woman?' but rather 'what signifies Man?' (Ibid.) Hence, Doane concludes, 'The question in Freud's text is thus a disguise and a displacement of that other question, which in the pre-test is both humanistic and theological. The claim to investigate an otherness is a pretense, haunted by the mirror-effect by means of which the question of the woman reflects only the man's own ontological doubts' (ibid.: 42). According to Freud, femininity has no specific connotation; it simply conveys male identity as opposite or 'other.' Likewise, Doane argues that in the patriarchal structure of the cinematic apparatus and its mechanisms of meaning production and reception, the female subject can only be detected through mechanisms of metonymic displacement (1990: 42–43).

Some feminist film-makers have appropriated the notion of femininity and associated it with a counter-aesthetic of radical alterity. In her essay 'Textual Politics' (1990), Annette Kuhn credits the British feminist theorists Claire Johnston and Laura Mulvey for having addressed, more or less directly, the relation of femininity to cinema as a resistant feminist practice. For Johnston and Kuhn, constructing a feminist counter-cinema involves '"an analysis of the functioning of signs within the discourse" and then a subversion of this discourse by means of antirealist or anti-illusionist textual strategies' (Kuhn 1990: 252).[12] Kuhn opines that Mulvey, in her 1975 article 'Visual Pleasure and Narrative Cinema,' 'rais[es] the questions of specularity and gendered subjectivity' and implicitly addresses a crucial issue: that of 'a specifically feminine film language and its potential for feminist counter cinema' (ibid.). Kuhn envisages two categories in which feminist film practices have developed counter-strategies of representation: 1) through the deconstruction of dominant cinema; and 2) through the development of a 'feminine writing' (ibid.: 253). In relation to the latter, she argues that the purpose is to 'privilege relations of subjectivity which are radically "other" to the fixity of the subject relations set up by dominant forms of signification' and specifies that 'the "otherness" of such texts is related to, or emerges from, their articulation of feminine relations of subjectivity' (ibid.: 259). According to Kuhn, strategies of representation that highlight 'alternative' feminine subjectivity, seek new forms of filmic pleasure. These include 'relations of looking, narrativity, and narrative discourse, subjectivity and autobiography, fiction as against non-fiction, and openness as against closure (ibid.: 260).

Most Western European female film-makers, including those generally identified as authors, do not claim any relation to feminist counter-aesthetics or strategies of representation. However, these film-makers make use of some of the formal strategies that Kuhn associates with feminist cinema; furthermore, their attention to women's complex relations to the private and public spheres still recalls the purpose of early feminist film-making. In this respect, their films may be considered as a particular manifestation of 'women's cinema,' one that Tarr and Rollet have associated with French female film authors in the 1980s and 1990s (2001: 12). Tarr and Rollet underline that the feminist notion of 'women's cinema' does not apply to French contemporary female film-makers (2001: 11-12). They clarify that this term in France (and, I add, in other Western European film contexts without a tradition of feminist film discourse and counter-cinema) simply denotes films directed by women and not necessarily those that address gender issues or a female audience. Yet, they concede that the critical feminist elements of women's cinema can indeed be found in the auteur-oriented films made by French female directors:

> Many, if not most, of the psychological auteur films discussed here center their narratives on female protagonists, displacing the hegemonic male gaze and foregrounding female desires and subjectivities in ways that justify the term 'women's films'. At the same time, they rarely address their spectators as the autonomous or women-centered women of feminist films (and their second films are often less female-oriented than their first films). (2001: 12)

The point here is not to define women's cinema from an essentialist perspective that would assume all films made by women as instances of women's cinema. Likewise, in discussing female authorship and women's cinema within a post-feminist discourse the idea is certainly not to provide a practical definition of post-feminist authorship or to suggest what is a post-feminist type of female author. Finally, the issue at stake is not to tell 'feminist' and 'post-feminist' practices in women's film authorship. Instead, the purpose is to propose that women's authorship in film is a strategy to assert agency within contexts of film production and reception, as well as within a cultural framework that does not recognize gender or feminist discourse as specific standpoints and/or even consider these perspective historically and conceptually outdated or professionally counter-productive. Female authorship in a post-feminist era is therefore a praxis that allows women to take position within a gender-blind or biased context.

Notes

1. Reported in Vincendeau (1987: 4). The FIFF is one of the oldest and most important among the film festivals dedicated to women. The festival was inaugurated in Sceaux in 1979 and moved to Créteil in 1985 (Tarr and Rollet 2001: 17). On the FIFF, see also Rollet (1998: 30-32).

2. The previous year, Vincendeau wrote another article on the Créteil film festival, focusing on the issue of female auteurism (Vincendeau 1986).

3. 'El fenómeno más importante que se ha producido, no obstante, durante estos años es la existencia de una corriente de opinión entre las mujeres que se orienta hacia la ruptura de viejas pautas de comportamiento, y rechaza las actitudes patriarcales de los sistemas de poder y de los hombres. Esta actitud de ruptura se refleja en las mujeres de diferentes edades, clases sociales y profesiones, y se plasma en un creciente deseo de alcanzar una independencia en lo económico y en lo afectivo, en lo personal y en lo profesional.'

4. The literature on 1970s feminist counter-cinema is vast and cannot be comprehensively listed here. Some writings from that epoch include: 'Feminism and Film: Critical Approaches,' (Editorial. *Camera Obscura*, 1: 3-10, Fall 1976.); Armatage, K., 'Feminist Film-making: Theory and Practice.' (*Canadian Women's Studies*, 1(3): 49-50, 1979.); Gledhill, C., 'Recent Developments in Feminist Criticism.' (*Quarterly Review of Film Studies*, 3: 457-474, 1978.); Johnston, C., 'Women's Cinema as Counter-Cinema.' (In Johnston, C. (ed.). *Notes on Women's Cinema*. London: SEFT, 1974); Johnston, C., 'Feminist Politics and Film History.' (*Screen*, 16(3): 115-24, Autumn 1975); Johnston, C., 'The Subject of Feminist Film Theory/Practice.' (*Screen*, 21(2): 27-34.); Kaplan, E. A., 'Avant-garde Feminist

Cinema: Mulvey and Wollen's *Riddles of the Sphynx*,' (*Quarterly Review of Film Studies*, 4: 135–144, 1979.); Kuhn, A., *Women's Pictures: Feminism and Cinema* (London: Routledge & Kegan Paul, 1982); Lesage, J., 'The Political Aesthetics of the Feminist Documentary Film.' (*Quarterly Review of Film Studies*, 3(4): 507–23, 1978.); Mayne, J. *The Woman at the Keyhole: Feminism and Women's Film* (Bloomington: Indiana University Press, 1990) (especially her discussion of European feminist film-makers Helke Sander, Ulrike Ottinger, and Chantal Akerman); Mulvey, L., 'Visual Pleasure and Narrative Cinema.' (*Screen*, 16(3): 1975.); and Penley, C., 'The Avant-Garde and Its Imaginary' (*Camera Obscura*, 2: 3–33, 1978).

5. *Ciné-modèle. Cinéma d'elles. Situations de femmes dans le cinéma français 1956–1979* was the first book on women's cinema published in France, and it is still amongst a select few.

6. 'Traversés d'options politiques, esthétiques et éthiques différentes, ces films sont héthérogènes. Ils ne sont pas tous féministes, loin de là. Toutes les réalisatrices ne se revendiquent pas engagées dans leur oeuvre en tant que femmes et au service de la cause féministe. Certaines n'ont pas dédaigné l'intérêt qui leur était porté en tant qu'échantillon voyant de la créativité féminine, sont les auteurs de films imprégnés des stéréotypes ordinaires de la misogynie française. Le film de femme n'est pas inéluctablement féministe. Chaque film de femme n'est pas le champion ou le représentant privilégié du mouvement de libération des femmes'.

7. See also Brigitte Rollet's discussion of Coline Serreau's career within the context of French cinema since the 1960s (Rollet 1998: 25–34).

8. There is vast material about the critical reception of these two film-makers within North American feminist scholarship. See, among others, Diaconescu-Blumenfeld, R., 'Regista di Clausura: Lina Wertmüller and Her Feminism of Despair,' (*Italica*, 76(3): 389–403, Autumn 1999.); and de Lauretis, T., 'Cavani's *Night Porter*: A Woman's Film?' (*Film Quarterly*, 30: 35–38, Winter 1977).

9. The article was quoted by the feminist philosopher Donatella Massara in a paper presented at the twelfth Symposium of the Associazione Internazionale delle Filosofe (International Association of Women Philosophers), held in Rome from 30 August to 4 September 2006 and published in the latest issue of the online historical magazine *Donne e conoscenza storica* (*Women and Historical Knowledge*), (January-February 2006), http://www.url.it/donnestoria/film/storia/immstorsimposio06.htm.

10. Françoise Audé talks about the critical bias against Miró in a review of *Werther* (1986), where she defends this 'elegant' and original work against its many detractors in the French film scene (1987: 78).

11. 'La diferencia entre los hombres y las mujeres es que ellos son hombres y nosotras mujeres, básicamente. Ellos tienen cola, y nosotras no. Nosotras tenemos tetas, y ellos no.'

12. Kuhn quotes Johnston's 1973 pamphlet 'Notes on Women's Cinema.'

References

Historia del feminismo en España. [Online.] Available: http://www.fmujeresprogresistas.org/feminismo4.htm.

Audé, F. 1981. *Ciné-modèles cinéma d'elles: situations de femmes dans le cinéma francais 1965–1979*. Paris: L'Âge d'Homme.

—. 1987. 'Werther.' Rev. of *Werther*, dir. Pilar Miró. *Positif*, 322: 78, décembre.

Bean, J., and Negra, D. (eds). 2002. *A Feminist Reader in Early Cinema*. Durham: Duke University Press: 14–16; 27–138.

Bollaín, I. 2003. Cine con tetas. *Duoda*, 24: 83–88.

Bono, P. and Kemp, S. (eds). 1991. *Italian Feminist Thought: A Reader*. Cambridge, Mass.: Basil Blackwell.

Bruno, G. and Nadotti, M. (eds). 1988. *Women and Film in Italy*. New York and London: Routledge.

Célestin, R., Dalmolin, E. and De Courtivron, I. 2003. *Beyond French Feminisms: Debates on Women, Politics, and Culture in France, 1981–2001*. New York, NY: Palgrave Macmillan.

Doane, M. A. 1990. Film and the Masquerade: Theorizing the Female Spectator. (In Erens, P. (ed.). *Issues in Feminist Film Criticism*. Bloomington and Indianapolis: University of Indiana Press, pp. 41–57.)

Gerstner, D. A. and Staiger, J. (eds). 2003. *Authorship and Film*. New York:Routledge.

Halimi, G. 2004. A Deceptive Universalism. (In Oliver, K. and Walsh, L. (eds). *Contemporary French Feminism.* Oxford and New York: Oxford University Press, pp. 31–39.)

Johnston, C. 1973. *Notes on Women's Cinema*. London: BFI.

Kennedy, B. 2002. *Deleuze and Cinema: The Aesthetics of Sensation*. Edinburgh, UK: Edinburgh University Press.

Kuhn, A. 1990. Textual Politics. (In Erens, P. (ed.). *Issues in Feminist Film Criticism*. Bloomington and Indianapolis: University of Indiana Press, pp. 250–67.)

Marie, M. 1998. *La Nouvelle Vague: une école artistique*. Paris: Nathan Université.

Martin-Márquez, S. 1999. *Feminist Discourse and Spanish Cinema: Sight Unseen*. Oxford: Oxford University Press.

Massara, D. 2006. Storia delle donne nella storia del cinema delle registe. *Donne e conoscenza storica*. [Online.] Available: http://www.url.it/donnestoria/film/storia/immstorsimposio06.htm.

Maule, R. 2005a. Une histoire sans noms: les femmes et le concept d'auteur au cinéma des premiers temps. (In Maule, R. (ed.). *Femmes et cinéma muet: nouvelles problématiques, nouvelles methodologies*. Cinémas, Spec. issue 16(1): 35–58, Fall.)

—. 2006. The Dialectics of Trans-national Identity and Female Desire in the Films of Claire Denis. (In Dennison, S. & Lim, S. H. (eds). *Remapping World Cinema: Identity, Culture and Politics in Film*. London and New York: Wallflower Press, pp. 73–85.)

Oliver, K. and Walsh, L. 2004. *Contemporary French Feminism*. Oxford; New York: Oxford University Press.

Passerini, L. 1993. The Women's Movement in Italy and the Events of 1968. (In Cicioni, M. and Prunster, N. (eds). *Visions and Revisions: Women in Italian Culture*. Oxford: Berg, pp. 167–82.)

Pereira Prata, A. 2003. Women's Political Organizations in the Transition to Democracy: An assessment of the Spanish and Italian Cases. *Journal of Women's History*, 15(3): 143–47, Autumn.

Projansky, S. 2001. *Watching Rape: Film and Television in Postfeminist Culture*. New York and London: New York University Press.

Rabinovitz, L. 2005. Past Imperfect: Feminism and Social Histories of Silent Film. (In Maule, R. (ed.). *Femmes et cinéma muet: nouvelles problématiques, nouvelles methodologies. Cinémas*, Spec. issue 16(1): 21–34, Fall.)

Rollet, B. 1998. *Coline Serreau*. Manchester, UK: Manchester University Press.

Staiger, J. 2003. Synthesizing Feminism, Theory, and History. Symposium Review. 2003–2004 Oberman Humanities Symposium. 101 Becker Communication Building, University of Iowa, Iowa City, IA, USA, 7 November 2003.

Tarr, C. and Rollet, B. 2000. *Cinema and the Second Sex: Women's Film-making in France in the 1980s and 1990s*. New York and London: Continuum.

Vincendeau, G. 1987. Women's Cinema, Film Theory, and Feminism in France. *Screen*, 28(4): 4–18.

—. 1986. Women as Auteur-e-s: Notes from Créteil. *Screen*, 27(3–4): 156–62, May-August.

Wright Wexman, V. (ed.). 2003. *Film and Authorship*. New Brunswick: Rutgers University Press.

8

FEMALE AUTHORS AND GENDERED IDENTITY IN FILM: CLAIRE DENIS'S POST-SUBJECTIVE REPRESENTATION

Although Claire Denis gives prominence to women's points of view in her films, she does not acknowledge femininity as an enunciative standpoint. For a film-maker concerned with issues of sociocultural marginality, such a blind spot might seem odd, albeit common in France among women film directors who consider gender-focused perspectives of their work limiting and even counter-productive.[1] Yet Denis's dismissal of gender resonates with important tenets in France's third-wave feminism: on the one hand, the articulation of identity within contexts of racial and social discrimination; on the other hand, the radical reconceptualization of feminine subjectivity involving a different approach to the female body.

In the first case, Denis's films offer a gambit which brackets subjectivity as a provisional term, continuously reframed and negotiated within an inextricable map of inter-personal relations and divides that are experienced in terms of social alienation and racism in colonial and post-colonial contexts, as well as problems of cultural estrangement in global society. This complex set of inter-relations is rendered through strategies of representation that, in eschewing causal and psychological development of characters and events and place, avoid an unresolved issue in feminist discussions of women's authorship: how to account for gendered identity and without falling into binary or essentialist definitions of femininity, connected to a western, white model of subjectivity. From this perspective, Denis's authorial position offers a viable solution to this epistemological impasse and addresses at the same time pressing concerns in French feminist discourse of the past two decades, as well as recent approaches in feminist approaches to women's cinema that propose post-colonial and post-subjective re-conceptualizations of feminine identity. Denis's films, in fact, transcend the author-informed idea of subjective expression in the sense that they do not foreground the point of view of a white French woman raised in colonial Africa and relocated in post-colonial France: instead, they develop a choral type of narrative which deflects fixed notions of subjectivity and cultural identity. In so doing, they avoid a paradox in post-colonial discourse: that although many western-based representations of non-western cultures attempt to disengage from totalizing subject positions, the theoretical basis of such projects remains essentially western- and Euro-centric.

Ella Shohat and Robert Stam, in *Unthinking Eurocentrism: Multiculturalism and the Media* (1994), describe Eurocentrism as 'the procrustean forcing of cultural heterogeneity into a single paradigm in which Europe is seen as the unique source of meaning, as the world's center of gravity, as ontological "reality" to the rest of the world's shadow' (Shohat and Stam 1994: 3). Shohat and Stam argue that cinema has contributed greatly to the construction of the Eurocentric imperial imaginary, due to its consolidation as the apparatus of bourgeois society, predicated upon the production of master narratives (ibid.: 101–03). In their opinion, cinema's imperialist mandate has continued even after the end of colonialism, hidden in elements of the narrative and manifested in the 1980s and 1990s European cinema's revival of imperialist epics and dramas (ibid.:123). Denis avoids the Eurocentric positions by proposing an unapologetic view of colonialism and by stressing the unresolved conflicts existing in post-colonial society.

Denis also evades authorial definitions connected with the concept of subjective expression through her particular treatment of the *mise-en-scène* and character development. For her, the act of film-making involves a relational process with the cast in which desire and erotic tension yet are not bound by restrictive patterns of sexual identity and difference. When Judith Mayne asked her in 2004 whether she sees herself as a 'woman film-maker,' she replied:

> I never think about the question. I think about it when I film a woman I always have the impression that the film is 'female' from the outset, but I share with men and with women [...] Even if I'm at the origin of the film, and the film is therefore 'feminine,' the work of filmmaking is a relationship. It's a relationship with the actors, and it is a very erotic relationship (Mayne 2005: 144).

By distancing herself from the notion of feminine expression, or from the category of 'woman film-maker,' Denis points to a type of authorship set outside of the usual mechanisms of signification attributed to subjective expression and enunciation which pose epistemological problems to feminist theorists. Several film scholars and critics (Beugnet 2004; Del Rio 2003; Smith 2005) have examined this aspect of Denis's work with regard to Gilles Deleuze's concept of the time-image, a metaphor for modern cinema's blurring of the rapport between physical and mental, subjective and objective, real and fictional aspects of representation (Deleuze 1989).

The importance of being marginal

As Martine Beugnet appropriately states in her monograph *Claire Denis* (2004), 'Denis's stories are stories of foreignness – a foreignness that is simultaneously physical and mental, geographical and existential' (2004: 2). In part, Denis's investment in this subject is explained through her own life story. Born in Paris in 1948, her parents brought her to Cameroon when she was only two months old. She lived in several West African countries, including Somalia, Djibouti, and

Burkina Faso, where her father worked for the French colonial administration. She returned to France at the age of fourteen when she and her sister contracted polio and needed hospital treatment. When her sister became paralysed as a consequence of her illness, her mother refused to join her husband back in Africa and the family eventually relocated to France. Denis missed her life in Africa; at 17 years old, she went to Senegal to attend high school and lived there for some time with friends of her parents (Reid 1996: 68). Upon her return to France, she had the impression of being a foreigner in her own country, a feeling that never left her (Denis 2000).

Indeed, Denis considers herself 'un être séparé' ('a separated being') and describes this state as 'an active principle. Complicated, sometimes painful,' typical of film-makers marked by inherent loneliness, even though they are constantly surrounded by people (Truong 2003: 74–75, my translation).[2] Because of the distinctive focus and style of her work, this mode of being is also applicable to a sense of professional alienation she frequently experienced as a film-maker. Throughout her career, she avoided the traditional institutions of film production and collaborated with independent film producers and small film companies or culturally oriented television networks (La Sept-Arté, BBC), and art foundations (Fondation Cartier). As a result, her films gained relatively sparse attention within both national and international contexts of film reception. In a 1996 interview, Chris Darke asked Denis whether her 'marginality has to do with the fact that [she's] a woman making films in France' (Darke 2000: 18). She replied in a manner that belies her conception of otherness as a political strategy:

> No. I don't think I make the sort of films which have the characteristic traits of French cinema, which is to say a lot of dialogue and a very social focus. Some suggest my marginality has to do with the fact that my films have a lot of marginal characters in them. But I don't think so. I think it's more that I don't express myself like mainstream French directors. But being marginalized is a way of being slightly protected – I'm doing my own thing with no one interfering and that suits me. (Ibid.: 18)

To be sure, Denis's conviction that marginality assures her freedom and mobility in her work is coherent with the auteur-informed idea of film-making that emerged in France in the late 1950s with the *nouvelle vague* movement. At the time, film directors maintained control over their projects and ensured their artistic freedom by working with small budgets and crews and obscure actors (Marie 1998: 63). In her book on Denis, Beugnet notes that Denis's film-making method and body of works is in keeping with auteur-informed cinema:

> In their superimposition of the personal (the distinctive style, the recurrent themes and the presence of autobiographical elements) and the historical (in the sense of the wider cultural, political, and socio-economical framework in which the films are elaborated) Denis' films may usefully be described as auteur cinema. (2004: 14–15)

From this point of view, Denis also partakes in a nationally specific type of auteur-oriented discourse and practice that constituted both reference points and problematic legacies for the French film-makers of her generation. Chapter 3 illustrated the ambivalent attitude of film-makers emerging in France since the 1980s vis-à-vis the *nouvelle vague* auteurs using Olivier Assayas as a case study. It is worth noting that Assayas and Denis, who started making feature films at the same time, are friends and have crossed paths on a number of film projects, share similar opinions on this subject.[3] In 1998, they participated, together with two other French film directors of their generation, Cédric Khan and Noémie Lvovsky, in a round-table discussion about the heritage of the *nouvelle vague*. Charles Tesson and Serge Toubiana, the editors-in-chief of *Cahiers du Cinéma* at the time, moderated the round table and the proceedings were subsequently published in the magazine (Tesson and Toubiana 1998). On that occasion, Denis and Assayas both acknowledged the legacy of the film movement in terms of a new freedom which, for instance, legitimized the possibility of making a film out of a personal desire to work with one's partner (ibid.: 72). Denis especially associated *nouvelle vague* cinema with an epoch marked by certain political, social, and cultural changes, among which she singled out post-colonialism, sexual freedom, and jazz, which, she believes, directly or indirectly informed the film-makers of this movement (ibid.: 70–71).

While the lesson of the *nouvelle vague* auteur was essential for Denis's approach to cinema, her film practice also significantly departs from the methods established by this model and does not follow the methods generally identified with the nouvelle vague auteur as a sociology of production in which the film director is given sole responsibility for a film (Marie 1998). She gives considerable credit to the small group of regular collaborators which has been with her since the beginning of her career: cinematographer Agnès Godard, screenwriter Jean-Pol Fargeau, sound technician Jean Louis Ughetto, and editor Nelly Quettier.[4] In discussing her films, she also highlights the input of the musicians who contributed to the soundtracks for her films, most notably the British band Tindersticks, which scored three of her films, and the band's leader Stuart Staples, who composed two scores for her. Furthermore, she often casts a number of actors, who appear in several of her films, including Grégoire Colin, Béatrice Dalle, Alex Descas, Vincent Gallo, Isaach de Bankolé, Katerina Golubeva, and Michel Subor. Given the importance that Denis assigns to professional collaboration, Beugnet is right in suggesting that the idea of auteur cinema she associates with Denis is not intended 'merely as the individual expression of a singular expression and personal concerns [but is also] avowedly inscribed in a wider historical context, including a background of cultural and artistic references and a framework of cinematic traditions' (2004: 15).[5]

Denis's authorship was internationally sanctioned only at the release of her fifth film, *Beau travail* (1999), more than ten years after her début as a film director. Jonathan Rosenbaum, a Chicago-based, worldwide reputed film critic who had not been until then a fan of Denis's cinema, not only enthusiastically reviewed *Beau travail*, but he listed it among the best films of 2000 (2001). Rosenbaum's review of this film synthesizes the elements that film critics recognize as Denis's aesthetic signature as auteur: plastic *mise-en-scène*; numerous subtle references to literary and filmic intertexts and loose literary adaptations; empathetic direction of very physical actors; anti-conventional representation of eroticism and sexuality; synesthetic *mise-en-scène* and editing, often compared to a musical composition. (Rosenbaum 2001) Yet these elements constitute less an auteur-informed veer in Denis's approach to film-making than a new emphasis

Beau travail (Denis Lavant as Galoup)

Beau travail The training routines (in close-up, Grégoire Colin, who plays Sentain)

put on the sensorial dimension of cinema set outside the visual prominence and narrative conventions of classical film representation.

The western woman, the native, and Otherness: representing the post-colonial body

Denis's first two feature films, *Chocolat* and *S'en fout la mort*, represent critiques of the master-servant dialectics underlying cultural and gender relations in contemporary western society. *Chocolat* investigates class and interracial relations in colonial and post-colonial Cameroon. Denis's two subsequent films, *S'en fout la mort* and *J'ai pas sommeil*, move this inquiry to post-colonial France and address the problems of multicultural and interracial integration in Paris during the 1980s. *Beau travail*, Denis's fifth feature, marks Denis's return to an African setting and explores the negotiation of power relations and masculinity in the French Foreign Legion via a narrative loosely inspired by Herman Melville's unfinished novella *Billy Budd, Sailor*, posthumously published in 1924. *J'ai pas sommeil* and *Beau travail*, which develop choral, multi-focal narratives centred on the portrayal of the male body, deflect binary configurations of sexual difference, identity, and identification often connected with cinematic representation.

Chocolat marks Denis's effort to depict Africa while avoiding nostalgic or western-centred biases. This endeavour is parlayed via a French woman, emblematically named France, who returns to Cameroon where she had lived with her parents as a child. Commenting on her preparation for the film, Denis said she used Frantz Fanon's book *Peau noire, masques blancs* (*Black Skin, White Masks*, [1952] 1967) as a filter to supplement those provided by the fictional framework and her collaboration with playwright Jean-Pol Fargeau (Reid 1996: 68). These filters allowed her to 'clear away a giant prejudice that is called Africa' (Gili 1988: 15, my translation).[6] France's return to Africa brings her memories to life in a long flashback that constitutes the core of the film's narrative. The flashback depicts the protagonist's childhood in 1950s Cameroon and the characteristic power relations of her colonial environment. The narrative is centred on the dialectic of desire between Aimée, France's mother, and her servant or 'boy,' Protée. The unspoken tension and perverse power games find their parallel in young France's close relationship with Protée, although without the sexual undertones. The situation is further complicated by the arrival of unexpected guests at the farm who bring their own troubled power dynamics. The tension is finally broken by two interrelated incidents that terminate the flashback and disrupt France's childhood memories. First, Aimée makes a sexual advance towards Protée, who proudly turns it down but is then confined to work outside the house. Shortly afterwards, Protée betrays his loyalty to France by letting her burn her hand on the hot pipe of a power generator after touching the surface to give her the false impression that it was not hot.

In *S'en fout la mort*, a film that further develops *Chocolat*'s quandary over 'the impossible desire for reconciliation between colonizer and colonized' (Butler 2002: 95), Denis focuses on non-western identities in post-colonial France. The film's protagonists are Dah (a character portrayed by Isaach de Bankolé, the actor who plays Protée in *Chocolat*), an immigrant to Paris from Beni who makes a living dealing fighting cocks for illegal gambling, and his associate Jocelyn (the first of Alex Descas's many roles in Denis's films), a cock trainer from the Caribbean. Hired to

Claire Denis on the set of *Chocolat*

Chocolat: from the left, Aimée, Protée, and France

organize an illegal gambling parlour, the two men are forced to live in a squalid basement beneath one of their employer's properties. Their boss is Ardenne (*nouvelle vague* star Jean-Claude Brialy), a restaurant and club owner who had lived for years in the Antilles and had been the lover of Jocelyn's mother.

Dah and Jocelyn react to the post-colonial racism and capitalist exploitation they face quite differently. Jocelyn, a quiet, withdrawn man, attached to his traditions and principles, is shattered by the circumstances in which he is trapped. Suffering under Ardenne's increasingly patronizing attitude (it is insinuated that Ardenne may be Jocelyn's father) and his secret infatuation with Ardenne's lover, he begins drinking heavily. Towards the end of the film, Ardenne's son stabs him to death. This dramatic scene takes place at the cockpit after Jocelyn arrives at a fight completely drunk and delirious and begins abusing the patrons in Creole. Jocelyn's aggression and descent into madness are consistent with Fanon's lucid description of the phenomenon of re-enacting colonizer-colonized relationships. Jocelyn's self-abasement recalls Fanon's discussion in *Les damnés de la terre* of cases of mental disturbance linked to the 'colonial war' (1961: 187–235). In contrast, Dah is proud and uncompromising. He resists Ardenne's attempts to take financial advantage of him and remains untouched by his harsh treatment. Denis gives Dah subjective perspective throughout the film, his voice-over functioning as narrative commentary and a resistant viewpoint. In the opening scene, Dah is filmed from behind while sitting in a van at night. His first words repeat the film's opening written text, a quotation from American novelist Chester Himes, one of Denis's favourite authors and a frequent contributor to the 'Noir Series' she read in her adolescence: 'Every human being, whatever his race, nationality, religion, or politics, is capable of anything and everything.'[7] In the film's final scene, after Dah attends a funerary ceremony for his friend and tells him about his upcoming reconciliation with his dead mother in the Antilles, Dah leaves Paris behind, taking with him the profits from the last fight.

According to Denis, *Chocolat*, *S'en fout la mort*, and *J'ai pas sommeil* form a trilogy on post-colonial issues inspired by Frantz Fanon's most renowned books, the above-mentioned *Peau noire, masques blancs* and *Les damnés de la terre,* published in 1961 (Reid 1996, 69). Indeed, these films seem to illustrate Fanon's warnings about the complexity involved in the de-colonizing process, the deep-rooted violence in colonial social relationships, and the colonizing perspective of modern western culture. Even the titles of the two films, *Chocolat* and *S'en fout la mort*, contain a double meaning that represents the unresolved tension between colonizer and colonized as a state of being. As Kathleen Murphy notes, both films deal with the notion of betrayal (1992: 63). *Chocolat* refers to colonial jargon for black people and also signifies 'to be cheated.' The film in fact depicts a double betrayal: that of the master towards the servant (Aimée has Protée ejected from the house for refusing her sexual pass) and that of the servant towards the master (Protée, in turn, transgresses his bond with France by purposely letting her burn her hand). *S'en fout la mort* is the name of Jocelyn's champion cock, whose death anticipates that of its trainer; Jocelyn's suicidal trajectory symbolically ends in the cockpit. The expression 's'en fout la mort' refers to a phrase that in Africa or the Antilles means a 'fetish against coming apart, death,' a reference to the survival challenge in post-colonial France that Dah, but not Jocelyn, will overcome (Murphy 1992: 63).

Denis's conscious rejection of any conciliatory representation of the problems and contradictions of colonial and post-colonial society has earned her a unique place within a group of film-makers who have dealt with France's colonial past. Dina Sherzner's introduction to the anthology *Cinema, Colonialism, Postcolonialism: Perspectives from the French and Francophone World* (1996: 6–7) includes Denis, Bertrand Tavernier (*Coup de torchon/Clean Up*, 1981) and Alain Corneau (*Fort Saganne*, 1984) among the film-makers who, in the 1980s and 1990s, shattered the long silence on France's colonial past (ibid.: 7). Shohat and Stam cite *Chocolat* as one of the 'few critical "nostalgia" films' about the colonial period that 'shift their focus from male aggressivity to female domesticity, and to the glimmerings of anticolonial consciousness provoked by transgression of the taboo on interracial desire' (1994: 123).[8] Yet their reading is reductive. As Butler demonstrates in *Women's Cinema: The Contested Screen* (2002), *Chocolat's* portrayal of colonial Africa does more than offer interracial desire as an easy way to reconcile western and colonial identities (2002: 107). In this regard, *Chocolat* arguably rejects essentialist views of 'European' versus 'non-European' subjectivities and presents a view of social relations that addresses 'historically configured relations of power' in which 'Eurocentrism is an implicit positioning rather than a conscious political stance' (Shohat and Stam 1994: 4).

French critics readily categorized *Chocolat* as an example of 'féminin colonial' ('colonial feminine') cinema. The expression refers to films made by French female directors who tackled France's colonial history (Strauss 1988: 29). These film-makers include, besides Denis, Marie-France Pisier, director of *Le bal du Gouverneur/The Governor's Party* (1990), and Brigitte Rouän, whose film, *Outremer/Overseas* (1988), came out the same year as *Chocolat*. Like Denis, Pisier was raised in Africa (Algeria) by a Catholic family that, like Denis's family, held a highly critical view of colonialism (Strauss 1988: 29–31). In the article 'Le Colonial Féminin: Women Directors Interrogate French Cinema' (1996), Catherine Portuges specifies that 'féminin colonial' refers to 'a cinema of memory, 'in which border crossings translate into a *mise-en-scène* that destabilizes hegemonic ideas of nationality, sexuality, and the family' (1996: 81). She adds that the 'féminin colonial' films offer 'more than merely self-promoting exercises in melancholic nostalgia or innocent complicity, for they reinscribe French colonial history within a visual space that – implicitly, if not explicitly – critiques prior erasures of women's subjectivity from the horizon of colonial stories' (ibid.). For Portuges, *Chocolat* represents Denis's coming to terms with history through the reconstruction of a childhood trauma, and an index of the film-maker's 'hybridized positionality' (ibid.: 83).

Denis's uncompromising post-colonial discourse in *Chocolat* and *S'en fout la mort* refuses both essentialist revisionism and politically correct solutions. Denis frequently addresses in interviews the problems and controversies that her particular outlook on racial representation poses, both for conservative and progressive viewpoints. When she presented *S'en fout la mort* in New York, Denis recalls being criticized by a group of young African Americans for her negative and tragic portrayal of Jocelyn. Her attempt to explain to the young men, via Fanon, the political meaning of having a black man die at the end of her film was unsuccessful. Denis says, 'Maybe I have gotten old and my thoughts [are] out of touch with the new generation. But I still don't think that serious social inequities can be solved by nonviolent means. I really believe this' (Reid

1996: 73). For Denis, re-acquainting oneself with one's colonial past and facing the reality of today's racial biases involves cultural shock and emotional disillusionment.

Many theoretical discussions developed in the context of post-colonial discourse acknowledge that since western epistemology is wedded to modernist categories and agendas, it will remain decidedly Eurocentric, even when formulated from a post-colonial standpoint. Post-colonial theorist Gayatri Chakravorty Spivak means to avoid this risk by adopting continuously shifting strategies, and by re-inflecting discursive subject positions, including her own, particularly when discussing Third World women from a feminist perspective. Robert Young, in his book *White Mythologies: Writing History and the West* (1990), cites Spivak as an example of scholarly awareness regarding unconscious reproductions of imperialist assumptions in radical criticism (1990: 162). However, he notes that Spivak's position is still problematic when she tries to combine deconstruction with Marxist theory and maintain heterogeneous discontinuity and differences within a 'syncretic frame' (ibid.: 173).[9]

Cultural quandaries occur most often in the objectification of so-called Third World women as privileged signifiers of difference. Peter Jackson and Jan Perose, in their introduction to the anthology *Construction of Race, Place, and Nation* (1993), underscore the necessity of going beyond essentialist assumptions of race and gender. In particular, they propose a diachronic and dynamic scrutiny of how these terms form a trans-national and class-specific position, from which place and nation are constructed and multifaceted entities, variously manifested in different geo-cultural contexts (1993: 19). The quandary surrounding the intersection of gender, race, and cultural identity is particularly difficult when considered in terms of cinematic representation, especially in cases like Denis's, a white female director whose work focuses on issues of colonial and post-colonial discourse. As Alison Butler reminds us in her aforementioned book (2002):

> [T]he question of white women directors' relationship with post-colonialism impinges on a number of difficult questions, concerning the extent and the nature of women's complicity and culpability in colonialism, the ways that white femininity signifies in racist ideology, and the meanings which white women have projected onto the colonized landscape and indigenous people. (2002: 105)

Commenting on Denis's position on gender and race issues, Judith Mayne opines:

> [T]he ways in which gender and race are addressed in her films can never be defined in terms of any one particular concept of what the cinema is, what 'should' be, or what it might be in terms of ways of seeing through the lenses of gender, race and nation. (2005: 29)

Denis is actually very conscious of the questions and debates she inspires with her unapologetic representation of colonial and post-colonial situations, especially in regard to her predilection for featuring black male characters.[10] About the difficulties she encounters casting black actors in leading roles in French cinema, she says:

Film producers react negatively to how I dramatize a topic in my films. They don't understand how I want to cast blacks; producers regularly suggest that if I cast black actors, they should be erotic 'objects.' In my films, black people are never objects. They are subjects who actively choose what they want. Producers usually have a very exotic idea about what black actors should do and where they should be seen. Producers' scripts would liken black characters to lions and elephants. In contrast, I think Blacks featured in my films are 'noir' ('black'). (Reid 1996: 69).

Radhika Mohanram situates subjectivity and political agency at the conjunction of body and place, examining pre-modernist, modernist, and postmodernist notions of subjectivity in relation to race. From this perspective, she offers a 'cartography of bodies' in which 'a postmodern understanding of identity is based on a comprehension of nation and race as arbitrary or as a political construct' (Mohanram 1999: xii). Integral to her discussion is the argument that western-centred theories of subjectivity have kept the body and the 'submerged concept of place/landscape' in a subaltern relation to notions of spirit, rationality, and civilization, identifying whiteness with spirituality and blackness with corporeality. Denis's approach to the male black body, from Chocolat to J'ai pas sommeil, disavows the western-centred association of blackness with corporeality that Mohanram delineates. Denis's mise-en-scène of bodies (particularly black male bodies) as sites of contention and metaphors for power relations in colonial and post-colonial social contexts is a progressive point of convergence in her work, particularly in her first three films. The representation of the body has become more and more important in Denis's work during the past ten years.

Bodies that matter: the re-contextualization of the post-colonial body
In J'ai pas sommeil and Beau travail Denis propounds a politically viable critique of western subject positions less by trying to resolve the contradictions that these films highlight, than by further problematizing them via the representation of physical and social bodies that transgress predetermined definitions of cultural identity. J'ai pas sommeil is based on a true criminal case that polarized public opinion in France in the 1980s. Thierry Paulin, a second-generation immigrant from Martinique was charged with killing and robbing dozens of old women in Paris, with the complicity of his lover. Denis was well aware that she was playing with a hotly controversial subject when she started working on the film (Denis 1994: 25). Throughout pre-production and production, she worked carefully to bypass the social and cultural clichés of both the Caribbean and gay communities, to the extent of making changes to actual people and places, which she researched heavily.

In commenting on the film's controversial material, Denis specified that she could not possibly have assumed a politically correct position in depicting a character who is '[t]he absolute inverse of what black characters should be in the cinema according to the schemas of the "politically correct"' (1994: 27–28, my translation). Indeed, she considers the expression 'politically correct' to be 'le corollaire du racisme' ('the corollary of racism') (ibid.: 28, my translation). Instead, she was careful to change the name of the real serial killer (who is called Camille in the film) and omit the sensational aspects of the criminal case. She also embedded Camille's narrative within other characters' stories, thus providing a more holistic picture of his circumstances in an effort to understand his actions, although not explain or justify them (ibid.: 26–27). To this end, the film does not engage in social commentary, and the representation of Camille's social and familial environment never becomes mere reportage on multi-cultural communities or ethnic minorities.

In *J'ai pas sommeil*, Denis's preoccupation with the marginal worlds of immigrants and ethnic minorities is relayed through a distinctly female gaze. This gaze has an on-screen equivalent in Daïga, the young Russian woman who arrives in Paris by car to try her fortune as an actress. She ends up staying and working in a small hotel where Camille and his partner live. Throughout the film, Daïga observes Camille from a distance and in the end she leaves Paris with the money she found in his room soon after the police caught him. An immigrant and victim of western and capitalist exploitation herself, Daïga reflects Denis's position vis-à-vis 'the troubled nature of masculinity' (Denis 2000: 42). Denis's nuanced treatment of gender and ethnicity constantly keeps racial stereotyping in check. Denis also avoided portraying Camille as a monster by contextualizing his story within a multiple narrative set in a Paris community where people's destinies accidentally intersect and, as Denis puts it, people live a condition of social otherness. In particular, the setting is the multicultural district of the eighteenth arrondissement (Denis 1994: 25–26). She developed the script and conceived the film's structure using the figure of the concentric circle, a sort of '*jeu de l'oie*' (literally 'goose game,' a French spiral board game) (ibid.: 25). This metaphor perfectly renders the image of Paris's concentric map divided into *arrondissements* ('districts'), with the eighteenth *arrondissement*, where this *fait divers* took place and where the film is set, at the centre. The film's structure is foreshadowed by an opening sequence showing two policemen flying over Paris in a helicopter and suddenly bursting into laughter. This apparently unrelated scene for Denis has a very specific purpose:

> For me, it was almost a theatrical image of the function of laughing, which fit with the way I see the characters of the policemen in this film. Because I wanted to maintain the form of a game, a progressive approach to the murders, it seemed to me that the police apparatus didn't have to create suspense, tension. All the characters move along with destiny casting the dice and, in this trajectory the policemen have a concrete function, they control the traffic, they look from the helicopter to see if there are any traffic jams, and they are there to eventually arrest the murderers, but mostly in a good-natured way. (Denis 1994: 26, my translation)[11]

The opening scene functions as a frame for the film's narrative puzzle and foreshadows the non-linear development of the plot. The scene is comedic and features two groups of immigrants, one from Martinique and the other from the former Soviet Union, crossing paths in parallel montage. The shots interweave characters and events from each group but without the two groups ever coming into contact. Furthermore, consistent with Denis's aim to follow a random, albeit advancing, narrative structure, *J'ai pas sommeil* does not seek narrative closure. Instead, the story progresses impressionistically, lingering on Parisian streets and in interiors, capturing moods and atmospheres, and portraying each character as indefinite and ambiguous. Finally, the film's style is comprised of cinematographic and editing strategies that multiply the points of view and suggest collective enunciation. In this respect, *J'ai pas sommeil* inaugurates a new

L'Intrus: the South Pacific Islands

narrative technique in Denis's career with which she experimented further in her subsequent films, most daringly in the recently released *L'Intrus*, and which not only deflects subject positions but blurs the boundaries between the real and the virtual.

Although not as overtly political as these other films, *Beau travail* is undoubtedly linked to colonial and post-colonial motifs. Denis returns to her exploration of the body as a site of contested power. Set in a former colony of West Africa, *Beau travail* centres on the neo-colonial situation established between the Foreign Legion and the local population and foregrounds a self-reflexive use of literary and cinematic references to imperial France. The ironic title translates as 'job well done,' the praise given to a soldier's correct execution of his duty, and is also a reference (as Denis has acknowledged in some interviews) to the Hollywood classic *Beau Geste*, particularly the 1939 version directed by William Wellman and starring Gary Cooper.

L'Intrus: dragging Trebor's body

The film is a very loose adaptation of Herman Melville's novella *Billy Budd, Sailor*, an unfinished work that was rediscovered and published in 1924, thirty-three years after Melville's death. In Denis's adaptation, besides having shifted the time and setting from eighteenth-century Great Britain to contemporary Africa, she also changes plot development and characters' names and fates. In *Billy Budd, Sailor*, Billy Budd, the handsome and good-natured sailor, accidentally kills Claggart, the master-at-arms, while they are gathered in the captain's cabin. Hearing that the evil and envious master-at-arms is unjustly accusing him of insubordination in front of the captain, Billy Budd punches Claggart in an outburst of rage, causing him to fatally hit his head. Although he sides with Billy Budd and considers the episode a tragic accident, the captain is obliged to sentence Billy to death to avoid the possibility of mutiny. After a private conversation with the captain, Billy dies heroically, blessing the captain with his last words.

In the film, Billy becomes a brave young soldier, named Sentain (Grégoire Colin), who has developed a harmonious relationship of mutual respect with his captain by way of his modest and cooperative attitude. The figure of Claggart is replaced by Galoup, a warrant officer ('*adjudant*') played by Denis Lavant. Jealous of the attention Sentain receives, Claggart tries to kill him by sending him on an expedition in the desert with a defective compass. Sentain is finally rescued by a caravan of merchants and Claggart dismissed from the Foreign Legion for his action. What does remain intact in *Beau travail* is the palpably homoerotic tone of the novella, especially manifest in the captain and the entire crew's infatuation with the handsome sailor, as well as Claggart's (Galoup in the film) twisted psychology.[12]

The soldiers' training takes place in isolation in a beautiful natural landscape. This setting is juxtaposed with the nearby small city where the men have their only exposure to women. Their encounters with the women they meet at the local disco extend the film's examination of power relations beyond the homosocial context of the military to heterosexual post-colonial African society. For the first time in this film, Denis works with an almost exclusively male cast (women play only extras), allowing her to explore class, race, and sexual relations within the purview of a homosocial environment. To prepare the actors for the training scenes, Denis did not hire a military expert but a dance choreographer, Bernardo Montet, who created eight dances and appeared in the film as a legionnaire. The soldiers' training routines consisted of Montet's artistic *mise-en-scène* accompanied by excerpts of Benjamin Britten's opera *Billy Budd*. At one point, Galoup and Sentain perform a short '*pas-de-deux*,' a concentric dance in which the warrant officer and the soldier end up face-to-face as unspoken rivals. The physicality of these scenes foregrounds the body's function as a site of power.

In the article 'Claire Denis: Films and the Post-colonial Body – with special reference to *Beau travail* (1999),' Susan Hayward opines that Denis's films propose a multiple model of post-colonial subjectivity that challenges the objectification of the colonized body as 'single unity and subjectivity whose multiplicities were deliberately dissimulated under [the] Western [Law of the Father] rule' (2001: 160). Such multiplicity, she notes, encounters many problems in expressing itself, as many post-colonial characters in Denis's films demonstrate (ibid.). In Hayward's analysis of *Beau travail*, she points to the relation between identity and place as a colonizer-colonized relationship that is key to the film and is complicated by notions of dislocation, displacement, context, and specificity. Hayward asserts that post-colonial bodies in Denis's work cannot be encompassed or contained within a western-oriented context of discourse. Rather, she infers, 'Denis shows in different ways the struggle, if not the impossibility, of reinscribing the self into the dislocated space and the impossibility of reinventing a narrative and myth (or reclaiming a memory)' (Hayward 2001: 161).

In a review of *Beau travail*, Scott Heller points out that the film is perhaps the culmination of Denis's interest in the body as a motif evident in the gallery of 'troubled' male characters in her earlier films, which included Protée, Dah and Jocelyn, and Camille and his brother, Théo (Heller 2000). About her 'fascination with watching men fighting or working' in *Beau travail*, Denis comments:

> I like writing stories about men not because I want to dominate them but because I like to observe and imagine them. A man is a different world and this masculinity interests me. French cinema is so full of talk – I couldn't care less about these people talking about their lives. Godard said that in cinema there are women and guns and I agree completely. That's to say, there's sex and violence. Cinema functions through these even if one is highly intellectual. (Darke 2000: 17)

The above quotation comes from an interview appropriately titled 'Desire Is Violence,' in which Denis formulates her work in terms of the dialectic of desire and violence: 'There must be violence for there to be desire, I think – and that's what's so beautiful about Oshima's films. I expect if I went into analysis I'd be found abnormal – I think sexuality isn't gentle. Desire is violence' (Darke 2000: 17).

Denis's approach to cultural identity and representing the body also resonates with theories and discourses of contemporary cinema that open new directions in the consideration of film and of the cinematic experience. As mentioned in a previous section, Denis's 'plastic' approach to film-making echoes Gilles Deleuze's description of the new relation between body and thought established by the time-image. In Denis's films, paraphrasing Deleuze, the body is 'no longer the obstacle that separates thought from itself, that which it has to overcome to reach thinking. It is on the contrary that which it plunges into or must plunge into, in order to reach the unthought, that is life' (1989: 189). Denis's concentration on the body is both stimulated by and stimulating a type of desire which supersedes the mechanisms of identification traditionally associated with the filmic experience, as well as those related to the hypostasis of subjective expression and reception at the basis of authorial approaches to film.

Body, soul, and thought: towards a corporeal cinema
Film critics have noted Denis's talent for working with bodies and her obsession with bodily expression as a metaphor for power relations. Denis herself acknowledges the importance of this aspect in her films. When two *Cahiers du Cinéma* critics noted in an interview that, with *J'ai pas sommeil*, she had succeeded in achieving the '*mise-en scène des corps*' that she had only hinted at in *S'en fout la mort*, she replied: 'Maybe this has taken shape... At any rate, there are first of all bodies in this film. This is not humour, filming bodies is really the only thing that interests

me. It's quite intimidating, especially when they are men's bodies' (Denis 1994: 25, my translation).[13] Her play on the French word for body (corps) in 'peut-être que ça a pris corps advantage' (untranslatable in English) cleverly connects her cinematic practice with her new filmic interests and motifs.

As mentioned in the previous section, although the film contains extensive training sequences, Denis hired a dance choreographer instead of a military expert to prepare the actors. As Scott Heller observes in his film review, the legionnaires' exercises 'begin as calisthenics, morph into martial arts, and become a vigorous form of modern dance' (2000: 42). Similarly, Stéphane Bouquet, in his article 'La hiérarchie des anges,' notes:

> For Claire Denis, putting dance and the army in contact is a way of interrogating the notion of a collective body. Dancer and soldier try to reach an ideal body, even if it is not exactly the same body. And to what point can one disappear into a super-body? To the point of becoming fused within the rhythm [the law] of another; and what pleasure is there in abolishing oneself as a subject in order to participate in the beauty of the group, of the norm? ("You are no longer an African, we hear, you are a legionnaire"). (2000: 49, my translation)[14]

For Bouquet, the ideal of beauty associated with the army has homosexual connotations (ibid.). Denis reckons that the film indeed presents an explicitly homosexual subtext, which she also finds present in Melville's novella. This theme caused problems during production, as Denis reveals in an interview with Jean-Marc Lalanne and Jérôme Larcher for Cahiers du Cinéma: 'We were forbidden to stay in Djibouti at night. The Legion's great phobia is homosexuality and people thought that my film was about that. We were threatened; I was told they would beat up the actors' (Denis 2000a: 52, my translation). Denis also describes her commitment to avoiding fetishizing or eroticizing the figure of the legionnaire. Throughout the film, she tried not to objectify the male actors' bodies (ibid.: 52–53).

Beau travail does not just mark Denis's most accomplished effort to use the body as a vector of thematic issues, but also as the catalyst of Denis's characteristic approach to cinema as a combination of the sensorial and conceptual elements underlying film-making. Film critics and scholars have variously discussed her approach in terms of sensation (Beugnet 2005: 152–98), sensuality (Garbarz 1997: 38), and desire (Beugnet 2005: 132–52; Mayne 2005: 59–80). Martine Beugnet discusses this topic in the final chapter of her monograph on Claire Denis, titled 'The mise en scène of desire: towards a cinema of the sense' (2004: 132–96). Beugnet argues that Denis's film-making style 'relies, first and foremost, on the sensuous apprehension of sounds and images that expands cinema's primarily visual powers of evocation' (ibid.: 132). She observes:

> In its mise en scène of desire, Denis' film-making not only creates correspondences between the senses, but [...] also confuses the traditional processes of identification and point of view. Desire thus emerges in its ambivalence and diversity, as inherently linked to transgression. It affects individuals regardless of their gender, race or nationality, and

as such, challenges the taboos and hierarchies erected by social orders that attempt to tame desire by designating its legitimate objects. It threatens the integrity of the body and of the self, and reveals the fragility of the human mind and flesh, beset by a sense of loss and lack and always at risk of dissolving into desire, to be 'consumed' by it. Ultimately, transgression takes place at the level of representation itself, when the boundaries between fantasy (where everything is still possible) and actualization (the reality of the consummation) are erased. (Ibid.: 132)

For Beugnet, *Nénette et boni* marks a turning point in Denis's move towards a 'cinema of the senses' in feature film, foreshadowed by a series of shorter films she directed in 1994 and 1995, the medium-length film *US Go Home* (1994) and the shorts *Duo* (1995) and *À propos d'une déclaration* (1995). *US Go Home* was part of a TV series produced by the cultural television network La Sept Art titled 'Tous les garçons et les filles de leur âge ...' (1994), in which six French film-makers of different ages and backgrounds were asked to depict stories of French adolescents interspersed with pop songs from a specific epoch. Denis's film follows the trajectories of three adolescents (Martine, her older brother Alain, and her friend Marlène) in the Parisian *banlieue* in the course of a twenty-four-hour period as they pursue their first sexual experiences. *Duo* was commissioned by the BBC within the framework of a series in which film directors were asked to provide their reflections on painting. *À propos d'une déclaration*, commissioned by the Foundation Cartier, gathered film-makers' contributions for an exhibition on the theme of love.

In these projects, Denis further explores the thematic and formal concerns of her earlier work. For example, in *Duo* she examines the representation of interracial relations. The film proposes a *mise en abyme* of the male gaze/female object-of-the-gaze binary across racial divides through a clever composition of visual fragments and editing. The soundtrack consists of the classic jazz tune *Tin Tin Deo*. The short film features a downward tilt over a painting by contemporary French artist Jacques de Loustal portraying the figure of a black man. The silhouette of a black man (Alex Descas) observes the painting and returns the camera's gaze. The camera moves to reveal the object of the two male figures' look: a nude white woman within the painting, her head cut off by the edges of the picture. *À propos d'une déclaration* further examines the representation of desire in relation to gender and race through strategies of framing and editing. The two-minute film features still images of a black man's hands placed against the window of an airplane, followed by a sequence in which a woman undresses and takes a bath, framed from the neck down as she shaves her pubic hair. The accompanying soundtrack includes wolf howls.

Nénette et Boni is set in a working-class section of Marseille and features two adolescent siblings, Boni and Nénette (played by Grégoire Colin and Alice Houri, who appeared as siblings in *US Go Home*, and with whom Denis wanted to work again). Estranged since their mother's suicide, the two are reunited when the girl finds herself pregnant and escapes from her boarding school. She goes to live with Boni, who shares their mother's old house with a group of other young men. Boni makes pizza for a living and daydreams about a voluptuous married woman in his neighbourhood (her husband is played by Vincent Gallo, who also appeared in *US Go Home* as a US G.I.). Boni initially turns his back on his sister, whom he resents for having lived under the tutelage of their father, a small-time crook. Both siblings, in fact, hate their father: Boni holds him responsible for his mother's suicide; Nénette strong rejection of his affection makes think that the man may have impregnated his own daughter. Boni becomes accustomed to his sister's presence and tries to dissuade her from giving up her baby for adoption. In the final scene, after Nénette has given birth, Boni kidnaps her baby from the hospital nursery and takes it home. In the last scene of the film, Boni cuddles the newborn while Nénette, just back from the hospital, stands in the backyard smoking a cigarette butt she found in an ashtray.

Several film critics and scholars have stressed *Nénette et Boni*'s tactile rendition of reality. In his review published in the film magazine *Télérama*, Jacques Morice describes the film in terms of sensorial apprehension:

> Fluid and solid, abstract and concrete, a strange filmic experiment – as one would speak of an experiment in chemistry or in physics – is this *Nénette et Boni*. A universe wherein one does not follow an action but rather one discovers the reactions, the combinations, and the transformations to come; a young woman cleaves the water in a swimming pool; a coffee machine gurgles the morning beverage; a man kneads pizza dough. We're positively situated in a cinema of substances and sensations. (1997, my translation)[15]

Morice concludes that, with *Nénette et Boni*, Denis 'confirms that she has a true talent for making places and characters come alive in a physical and carnal manner. She moulds her shots like a sculptor. In the end, she gives us a full-bodied film (Morice 1997, my translation).[16]

Positif's film critic Franck Garbarz also views chemical processes as core metaphors in the film. In an article titled '*Nénette et Boni*: Mère, pourquoi nous as-tu abandonnés?' (1997) Garbarz draws a parallel between the plastic representation of chemical processes and the narrative's trajectory, from the trauma of abandonment provoked by the death of the two adolescents' mother to the reconstitution of a new family outside of the Law of the Father:

> Making bread and kneading pizza dough physically illustrate this transformation of matter that is at the centre of the film: much like flour and water produce bread, so the reunion of Nénette and Boni re-establishes blood ties that constitute a suturing of the original abandonment. (Garbarz 1997: 39, my translation)[17]

The tactility, or sensuality, of Denis's films is closely tied to her aesthetic and intellectual interest in the politics of desire. In a 1995 documentary film titled *Claire Denis, la vagabonde*, made by Josef Lifshitz, Denis comments on the important role of desire in her work, both as a textual motif and as a metaphor for her personal approach to film-making. She insightfully explains that what interests her most about desire is its ability to maintain relations, situations, stories, and suspense. Beugnet reports the following passage from Denis's testimony:

> I am interested in primary things. For instance, I'm interested in desire. The growth of desire. And then something makes me stay there... Something makes desire self-sufficient, and that is often followed by frustration. Because it is so strong, that what follows, to respond to desire, is not strong enough to fulfil it. (2004: 136, my translation)[18]

Denis's exploration of desire finds its climax in *Trouble Every Day* and *Vendredi soir*, two distinctly different films which share a thematic focus: the representation of desire as a vehicle of transgression and danger. *Trouble Every Day* takes to the extreme Denis's belief that 'desire is violence' (Darke 2000). The film quite literally intertwines sex with physical violence, murder, and cannibalism. The film provoked a scandal at its première at the 2001 Cannes Film Festival and subsequently became a 'cult movie,' appreciated by some film critics and scholars for its unconventional treatment of the horror genre and its compelling atmosphere.

As with many of Denis's films of the past decade, *Trouble Every Day* presents parallel and intersecting plots set in the streets of Paris. The narrative follows the lives of two couples, Shane and Tricia, young Americans honeymooning in the city, and Dr Léo Semeneau and his wife, Coré, two Parisians living in the suburbs. Coré is afflicted with a mysterious illness that makes her dangerously cannibalistic whenever she has sex with men. In spite of her husband's efforts to keep her locked up in the house and sedated, she succeeds in escaping and finding the occasional victim. As the film proceeds, we learn that Shane is an ambitious young scientist who had once studied in Paris and conducted research with Léo in Africa. He has contracted the disease that affects Coré. Shane desperately tries to reach Léo with little success until a laboratory assistant clandestinely reveals Léo's home address. When Shane arrives at the house, he finds the door wide open and Coré wandering in a state of confusion, drenched in blood. She has just killed her neighbour, a young man who had been spying on her for days and had broken into the house. Partly in self-defence and partly out of pity, Shane kills Coré and leaves her in the house, now in flames, moments before Léo arrives. Shane soon succumbs to his murderous impulses, seducing and killing a young chambermaid at his hotel. In the final scene, Tricia enters the hotel room bathroom just as Shane finishes cleaning himself of blood. He tells her he wants to go home and embraces her. The film concludes ominously with Tricia spotting a stray trickle of blood on the shower curtain.

For her following film, *Vendredi soir*, an adaptation of the eponymous 1999 novel by Emmanuèle Bernheim, Denis took a 180-degree turn, both in tone and cinematic approach. She adapted a love story, writing the script with the book's female author instead of her usual partner, Jean-Pol Fargeau.[19] Furthermore, Denis abandoned her usual unrestrained approach to literary adaptations and stayed quite close to the source novel. Finally, she eschewed the multiple-narrative structure characteristic of her films and concentrated on a single plot line with only two characters (also unusual is that both of them are white). For the first time since *Chocolat*, the female character's point of view provides the film's focal narrative perspective. As the title suggests, *Vendredi soir* unfolds within the space of one night, portraying a brief, casual encounter between Laure, a shy, introverted woman (played against type by comedian Valérie Lemercier) who is about to move in with her fiancé, and Jean (Vincent Lindon), a quiet, melancholic stranger she meets and offers a lift in the middle of a transportation strike which causes a massive traffic jam in Paris's downtown. In the liminal intimacy created by the emergency situation, the two become increasingly attracted to each other and end up spending the night in an empty hotel. At dawn, she leaves the hotel room, running to meet her fiancé at their new home.

The story is based on a real event; during the 1995 transportation strike, people were encouraged on the radio to offer lifts to people stranded on their way home from work. The situation provides the premise and the context for a recurring motif in Denis's films: the transgression of interpersonal boundaries and social relations through sexual desire. To shoot the film, Denis spent several weeks on location in a couple of intersections near Place de la Concorde in Paris, which were closed to traffic for the occasion. She coordinated a complex mise-en-scène of outdoor scenes involving dozens of cars and extras. In spite of the choral backdrop, the film offers Denis's most intimate narrative based on close-ups, extreme close-ups, and details of the two protagonists' bodies as they interact in the car, a hotel room, and a restaurant. Denis's approach captures their impulses and hesitations with precision and sensitivity. Martine Beugnet considers Vendredi soir 'Denis' most "Deleuzian" of project' (2004: 186). According to Beugnet, 'the film is not constructed as plot development, but as an exploration of time as subjective and changing' (ibid.). Laure's story is deflected and multiplied by numerous potential plot developments and told through a hybrid technique that 'superimposes the banal and the dream-like, the physical reality of the context and the de-familiarising effect of the film-making process itself' (ibid.: 189). Beugnet recalls Deleuze's emphasis on banality in the cinema to 'superimpose the real and the imaginary' (ibid.). From this point of view, she adds, the spaces in Vendredi soir are both concrete and metaphorical. A significant choice on Denis's part was avoiding the use of voice-over to convey the protagonist's thoughts and feelings. As Beugnet observes, Denis 'abandons the kind of conventional sociological and psychological definition associated with the traditional characters of literature and film' (ibid.: 191). Instead, Beugnet concludes, Denis constructs a mise-en-scène of sensations and moves 'towards the invention of a cinema of the senses' (ibid.: 195).

In her analysis of Trouble Every Day, Beugnet discusses the overall climate of anxiety underlying the film's formal strategies and points out that DOP Agnès Godard also picks up on this when she describes Trouble Every Day as less a horror film than a 'terror film' ('un film d'effroi') (Beugnet 2004: 169). Beugnet demonstrates how 'the film [...] radically departs from the genres' main conventions' (ibid.). Among the formal elements that Beugnet connects with Trouble Every Day's mise-en-scène of terror are 'de-familiarising angles and framing' (ibid.), as well as the film's slow tempo, marked by obsessive repetitions of sounds in empty spaces (the trolley's clanking) or by interspersed shots of inanimate objects (ibid.: 170). Finally, she observes that the film provokes in its uncanny representation of indoor spaces and outdoor locations (ibid.: 170–71). In an article published in Kinoeye, Philippe Met takes the issue of the generic and aesthetic categorization of Trouble Every Day to a higher level. He views the film's various interpretations and controversial reception as a dialectic between lack and excess, contradictory film aesthetics and strategies associated with art house and horror films, respectively. He proposes that the very title, Trouble Every Day, hints at the 'lack-and-excess dialectic – titular litotes versus visual and notional hyperbole' (Met 2003). Yet Met also points out that this dichotomy undermines the coexistence of the two elements.

In this respect, Met quotes Denis's statement about the dangerous aspects of her characters in discussing the Thierry Paulin case depicted in her film *J'ai pas sommeil*: 'For me, the monster is invisible. If there is a thread running through all my films, it is that evil is never the other, everything is inside and never outside' (ibid.).

Met's assertion that *Trouble Every Day* represents 'the unthought of the body' (2003) resonates with Deleuze's description of an emerging bodily cinema marked by the rise of the time-image. With *Trouble Every Day*, Denis ventures into a cinema of bodily sensations in which 'desire as violence' addresses the post-subjective idea of 'becoming' illustrated in Deleuze's book (co-written with Félix Guattari), *A Thousand Plateaus: Capitalism and Schizophrenia* (1987: 272–79). Deleuze and Guattari refer to molecular becoming as an alternative way of conceptualizing relations and structures of identity outside of structuralist-psychoanalytic configurations (1987: 235–36). A figural, post-subjective idea of becoming is applicable to *Trouble Every Day*, which is an attempt at rendering the invisible, the unthought of the body. Met's remark about 'the philosophical care of *Trouble Every Day*' (2003) corresponds to Denis's exploration of a cinema of sensation in which what is at stake is no longer the sensorial depiction of a molecular body, but rather the sensation and the tension subsumed by the figural body as, paraphrasing Deleuze and Guattari, becoming-animal, becoming-intense.

Trouble Every Day and *Vendredi soir* are paradigmatic examples of Denis's approach to film-making based on the representation of the body as a vessel for thoughts, mental states, emotions, and feelings. Denis's representation of the body in these two films recalls a specific element of the time-image: the display of a *mise-en-scène* in which the body 'plunges into' thought (Deleuze 1989: 189) Deleuze views the time-image as a cinema of bodily attitudes and postures (which he derives from Bertolt Brecht's concept of 'gest,' that is, the development of attitudes in theatrical performance) referring back to the social and independent of the story or the role itself (Deleuze 1989: 192).

In her aforementioned book, *Deleuze and Cinema: The Aesthetics of Sensation* (2002), Barbara Kennedy depicts the shift from early feminist to post-feminist discussions of subjectivity in practices of film production and reception as a move from a 'cinepsychoanalysis [...] based within a radical feminist political arena and within a definition of film as apparatus' to 'theories of "material affect" and "sensation" and "becoming" and a neo-aesthetics as sexuality' (ibid.: 50–51). According to Kennedy, the former paradigm (exemplified by 1970s feminist film theory) designates 'the cinematic experience as a production of fantasy, identification, and, most importantly, a subjectivity, created through a series of primary (that is, actually experienced by us as individuals) psychical processes' (ibid.: 38). In between these poles, Kennedy places the post-structuralist determinations of a fractured, fluid, or multiple female subject (ibid.: 19).[20] Although she appreciates the 'materialist consideration of cinema' characteristic of post-structuralist feminism, which she describes as a 'refreshing return to aesthetics and a new consideration of the concept of the "body"' (ibid.: 51), she also estimates that its definition of subjectivity is still bound to traditional concepts of the mind/body relation and aesthetics.

For Kennedy, post-feminism colludes with a post-theoretical concentration on Deleuze's idea of becoming as a process that dissociates subjectivity from language and focuses on molecular assemblages and the materiality of experience. From this perspective,

> A definition of *post-feminism*, in an academic sense, may initially be described as a theoretical set of practices within which one may speak as a 'woman'. However, that very concept of woman becomes multiple, complex, and polysemic. I want to extend the term therefore to explain *post-feminism* as a desire to move outside a politics of difference or a politics of gendered subjectivities, to a micro-political pragmatics of *becoming* where subjectivity is subsumed to becoming-woman. Here the term 'becoming-woman' is, in my use of the term, synonymous with the affective forces of the material. (Kennedy 2002: 21)

Deleuze associates the time-image to film-makers affiliated with various typologies of modern cinema. Significantly, he connects the cinema of bodily postures to the work of French New Wave and post–New Wave film-makers who have a direct influence on Denis's work, Jacques Rivette above all, but also Jean-Luc Godard, Jean Eustache, Philippe Garrel, and Jacques Doillon (Deleuze 1989: 193–203). As well as the above, he discusses the cinema of 'body, brain and thought' to women film-makers such as Chantal Akerman and Agnès Varda who, during the 1970s, explored the relations between bodies and their environment as pointers to an individual and a social temporality (ibid.: 196–97). About women's relation to this instance of the time-image, he states, 'Female authors, female directors, do not owe their importance to militant feminism. What is more important is the way they have produced innovations in this cinema of bodies, as if women had to conquer the source of their own attitudes and the temporality which corresponds to them as individual or common gest' (1989: 196–97). To be sure, Deleuze's dismissal of feminism as the motor behind Varda or Akerman's cinema is problematic insofar as it completely obliterates the importance of feminist discourse in these film-makers' representations of the female body and feminine spaces (at least throughout the 1970s). Yet, his unapologetic oversight regarding feminist discourse should also be considered within the context of his view of cinema as a conceptual practice premised on a post-subjective approach to philosophy. From this perspective, his claim that female film directors' representation of the body as a vector of thought allows them to conquer 'a temporality which corresponds to them as individual or common gest' (Deleuze 1989: 197) also signals a move beyond models of cinematic expression and meaning formation premised on psychoanalytic and transcendental conceptions of the subject which sets women outside of western discourse and aesthetics. The same move characterizes Denis's approach to film-making.

'Je est un autre': sexual difference beyond subjectivity
In her films, Claire Denis deploys a very particular treatment of storytelling, replete of temporal ellipses, discontinuous narrative development, disjunctive editing, psychological character development, and multiple plot structures. Her particular treatment of the narrative produces

mixed reactions among film audiences and critics and often leaves spectators puzzled. When British film critic Chris Darke suggested to Denis that *J'ai pas sommeil* and *Beau travail* gave a sense of 'the development of an almost abstract film-poetry' (2000), Denis denied any intention to go in that direction. She referred to *Beau travail* as an example:

> You can't say to yourself 'I want to make an abstract film' – it's a bit dumb as a working method. But to try to capture someone's memories, Galoup's for example, to ask why he misses the Legion and Djibouti and to want to convey this cinematically inevitably becomes a little abstract. I think it's easier for me as someone who's marginal and isolated; I don't have a studio behind me telling me what not to do. But if I'd set out to make *Beau Travail* as a consciously anti-narrative film I would have failed – I don't think one consciously marginalises oneself, it just happens. European cinema is saturated by a form of storytelling that's almost televisual and American cinema remains, in plastic terms, very strong. Think of *Dead Man* and *Ghost Dog*. But there's also Hsiao-Hsien Hou and Ming-Liang Tsai in Taiwan, the young Kurosawa in Japan – these are people I feel very close to. I don't feel at all marginal in their company. (Denis 2000b)

Denis also denied wanting to do away with narrative, although she admitted her affinity for the 'plastic narration' that she finds mainly in Asian cinema. In another interview, significantly titled 'Je me reconnais dans un cinéma qui fait confiance à la narration plastique: Entretien avec Claire Denis' (Denis 2000a), Denis acknowledges that she is influenced by the 'plastic narration' of Asian film-makers such as Wong Kar-wai and Kiyoshi Kurosawa. All the same, she dismisses the suggestion that she would abandon classical narrative to 'express everything through questions of point of view, framing, bodies' positioning within a shot' (Denis 2000a: 52–53, my translation).[21] Martine Beugnet notes:

> Hence, another paradox of Denis' work lies with its ability to hold in tension the modernity of cinema with the lyricism of the romantic and novelistic traditions: no matter how stylized the approach, her story worlds and characters never take the form of disembodied entities. On the contrary, drawing their appeal precisely from that irreducible element of mystery that they evoke, her stories offer a deeply affecting and sensual viewing experience. (2004: 200)

Beugnet describes Denis's film-making style as a hybrid between the modernist film, which refuses closure and psychological development, and Deleuze's notion of the time-image wherein, in Beugnet's words, 'time and vision do not merely function as a codification allowing for the smooth unfolding of movements and actions towards a logical resolution, they become the actual texture of the film' (ibid.: 21). Beugnet also uses Deleuze's writings to argue that Denis's films ignore conventional narrative structures in favour of 'transitory, mutating spaces [... which] provide a wealth of connections and potential interpretations, and a multitude of lines of flights' (ibid.: 21–22).

When Jonathan Romney asked Denis at a London screening of *J'ai pas sommeil* if she was aware of the fact that her narrative style did not make things easy for the audience, she offered a justification of her unusual approach reminiscent of Deleuze's definition of the crystalline narrative:

> It's conscious and unconscious. Because again I am not trying to make it hard. I hate that. But I am trying to float on the impression of what a story could be. But for me, cinema is not made to give a psychological explanation, for me cinema is montage, is editing. To make blocks of impressions or emotion meet with another block of impression or emotion and put in between pieces of explanation, to me it's boring. Again, I am not trying to make it difficult but I think, as a spectator, when I see a movie one block leads me to another block of inner emotion, I think that's cinema. That's an encounter. I think cinema is linked to literature by a lot of social ways. Our brains are full of literature – my brain is. But I think we also have a dream world, the brain is also full of image and songs and I think that making films for me is to get rid of explanation. Because there is, I think, you get explanation by getting rid of explanation. I am sure of that. (Denis 2000b)

This new type of enunciation is related to a new regime of the direct time-image, which Deleuze identifies with narrative and editing structures in which 'images and sequences are no longer linked by rational cuts; which end the first or begin the second, but are relinked on top of irrational cuts, which no longer belong to either of the two and are valid for themselves (interstices)' (1989: 248). As David N. Rodowick notes in Gilles Deleuze's Time Machine (1997), these theories also redefine the links between movement, time, and thought from a post-ontological epistemology and culture, mainly influenced by Nietzsche's theories of time as eternal recurrence. At the narrative level, the time-image produces a falsifying narration where real and imaginary are indiscernible and the distinction between fiction and reality or between subject and object is blurred (ibid.: 155). Deleuze calls this type of narrative crystalline narration, where the crystal is a metaphor of an in-becoming image where spaces are 'direct representations of time [...] from which movement derives' (ibid.: 129). One of the ways in which Deleuze describes crystalline narration is in terms of a 'free, indirect discourse operating in reality,' a definition borrowed from Pier Paolo Pasolini and which, according to Deleuze, appears in Pasolini's, as well as in John Cassavetes, Shirley Clark, and Jean-Luc Godard's, films and best describes the ethnographic style of the Québecois documentary film-maker Pierre Perrault and of the main representative of the cinema vérité style, Jean Rouch (ibid.: 147–55). According to Deleuze, the free-indirect narrative creates an inter-subjective exchange of otherness between film-maker and character, the latter already belonging to a community and a minority 'whose expression they practice and set free' (ibid.: 153). This inter-subjective exchange is central in Denis's 'mise-en-scène' of post-colonial bodies and post-subjective identities in L'Intrus, her most recent film.

As freelance writer Damon Smith notes in the introduction to an interview with Denis upon the North American release of L'Intrus, 'With its triptych structure, each stage of which corresponds to a different geographical region and atemporal narrative, L'Intrus is an allusive memory-puzzle of sorts, dreamlike, beguiling and visually poetic' (Smith 2005). Smith connects L'Intrus's story with Deleuzean forms of narrative signification, epitomized by the metaphor of the 'bal(l) ade':

A tale of inner and outer travelling, *L'Intrus* is an exemplary illustration of what cinema theorist Gilles Deleuze, in his two-volume analysis of classical and postwar conceptual practices, termed the 'bal(l)ade' form, a pun on the French words for 'voyage' and 'ballad.' Under this rubric, a film introduces the theme of a wandering or journey that takes place through 'external or internal necessity, through the need for flight,' one in which pure seeing replaces action. (2005)

Elena Del Rio, in an article on *Beau travail* published in a *Kinoeye* special issue on Denis and Martine Beugnet, in her aforementioned book, both discuss Denis's approach to narrative in relation to Deleuze's time-image (Del Rio 2003). Beugnet (2003: 117–24) and Del Rio (2003) make this connection particularly in relation to *Beau travail*'s narrative structure and treatment of space and time. Beugnet also notes that 'although she always starts from the real, Denis's film-making has consistently eschewed the rules of strict logic and cause-effect in order to evoke a reality that is never entirely unified and knowable' (2003: 118). For her part, Del Rio observes, 'in its entirety, but particularly in its last scene, *Beau travail* presents an interesting, and slightly reconfigured, example of what Deleuze calls the "pure optical and sound situations" of modern cinema' (2003). Del Rio's references to Deleuze in her description of characters strolling in *Beau travail* are similar to those provided by Smith in regard to *L'Intrus*: 'characters [are] found less and less in sensory-motor motivating situations, but rather in a state of strolling, of sauntering or of rambling which define[s] pure optical and sound situations' (2003). Del Rio uses the final sequence of *Beau travail* to illustrate the connection between Denis's narrative approach and Deleuze's conception of spatial configurations in the time-image.

L'Intrus focuses on Louis Trebor (Michel Subor), a solitary and mysterious man in his late sixties who lives like a hermit in the Jura mountains in France, near the border of Switzerland. Trebor spends his time with his dogs and neglects his son (Grégoire Colin), who lives nearby. In need of a heart transplant, Trebor withdraws a conspicuous amount of money from his account in Geneva and looks for a donor heart on the black market. He finds one through a young Russian woman (Katerina Golubeva, who played Daïga in *J'ai pas sommeil*) who then pursues him through his trans-continental travels. Trebor first goes to Punan, Korea, where he convalesces after the transplant and buys a ship for his estranged son who lives in Tahiti. Subsequently, he goes to the South Pacific island of his childhood in search of his son. Soon health complications oblige Trebor to be hospitalized. While recovering, he is visited by a man who presents himself as his son. Upon leaving the hospital, Trebor visits the morgue, where he identifies the corpse of his French son, bearing a large scar on his chest, an indication that he may have been an unwilling heart donor for his father. Trebor leaves Tahiti, taking his dead son with him.

Throughout the film, the narrative remains ambiguous due to the lack of dialogue; a young woman is mysteriously slain near Trebor's house; the Russian woman and a young man drag Trebor's body in the snow; a bizarre meeting is held in Tahiti, presumably to select a man to impersonate Trebor's son. These events take place with little dialogue and no explication, leaving the viewer to mull over the impressionistic images. *L'Intrus* is also Denis's most complex film in terms of its intertextual layerings. Denis's inspiration for the script came from the short novel by the same title by Jean-Luc Nancy (2000), in which the French philosopher reflects upon his heart transplant in relation to philosophical and political reflections on the notion of strangeness. Keeping the heart transplant as an underlying narrative thread, Denis concocts a complex, multiple narrative structure based on muddled logic and spatial relations. Dreams, thought, and reality exist on the same plane. Spaces and characters' motions reverberate in what she describes as 'affective charges':

> Disparate sets...fit over each other, in an overlapping of perspectives [which] reverberate with each other in an affective realm that goes beyond subjectivity and character to involve the film body as a sensation-producing machine. It is as if the film were sending ripples of affect and thought across a diversity of its moments. Deleuze speaks of these affective charges as having the function of linking the film's parts. In other words, affective forces take over situations where space and time are no longer reliable or determinate: "Space is no longer determined, it has become the any-space-whatever which is identical to the power of the spirit, to the perpetually renewed spiritual decision: it is this decision which constitutes the affect, or the 'auto-affection', and which takes upon itself the linking of parts. (Ibid.)

Denis casts Michel Subor as the protagonist, the same actor she selected for *Beau travail* as an homage to one of her favourite films, Jean-Luc Godard's *Le petit soldat/The Little Soldier* (1963), in which Subor starred. In *Beau travail*, Subor provided a meta-filmic reference to issues of post-colonialism addressed in *Le petit soldat* and prominent in Denis's film. In *L'Intrus*, the actor brings the image he established when he was young in an adventure film by Paul Gégauff titled *Le reflux* (1965). Halfway into preparing *L'Intrus*, Denis inserted footage from a rare copy of *Le reflux* that took months to track down (Smith 2005). The clips function as flashbacks to Trebor's life in Tahiti as a young man. Other intertextual links include Robert Louis Stevenson's novel *The Reflux*, from which the Gégauff film was adapted, and Paul Gauguin's paintings and his memoir about his life in Tahiti. In the case of this film, the intertextual links have continued even beyond the film's release: Jean-Luc Nancy has written an essay about the links between the film and his book (Nancy 2005).

Smith notes about the film:

> If *L'Intrus* presents a field of vision that is at once boldly subjective and all-encompassing, it also comes alive with exhilarating images of bodily sensuousness and nature's own majestic vitality [...] As always, Denis's concern is to explore the literal and metaphorical borderlands where aliens and natives, intruders and guests go wandering, looking for signs of home within and beyond the barriers of nation, culture, sex and family. (2005)

Claire Denis's conception of film-making is a process she describes as follows: 'to plunge through an aesthetic construct, towards a more profound, more mysterious dimension' (Frodon 2001: 3).[22] This cinematic practice may offer an alternative to the subject-bound notion of authorship and, in return, free this category from the epistemological deadlock of sexual difference. From this perspective, Denis's description of herself as a separated being points to a definition of the author as an Other where otherness no longer primarily symbolizes the position of women in western culture.

Notes

1. According to Judith Mayne, '[a]ny reluctance on Denis' part to classify herself as a "woman director" is also a reflection of the particular status of women filmmakers in France' (2005: 27). She substantiates her statement by referencing a book discussed in chapter 6, Carrie Tarr and Brigitte Rollet's *Cinema and the Second Sex: Women's Film-making in France in the 1980s and 1990s* (2001) (2005: 27)

2. '[...] un principe actif. Compliqué, parfois douloureux.'

3. Assayas helped Denis make *J'ai pas sommeil*, for which she could not find financial backing, by introducing her to independent film producer Bruno Pesery, with whom Assayas had made *Une nouvelle vie* (1993). Assayas and Denis were among the seven film-makers who directed short films for a TV series produced by the cultural television network La Sept Art, titled *Tous les garcons et les filles de leur âge ...* (1994). For the series Denis directed *US Go Home* and Assayas *La Page blanche*. Finally, the two were to direct a collaborative horror film to be filmed in a hotel, an unrealized project for which the third contributor would have been Canadian film-maker Atom Egoyan. Assayas developed the original idea into a completely different project, his feature film *Irma Vep* (1996), in which Egoyan's wife and regular collaborator, actress Arsinée Khanjian, played a cameo role. Denis developed the idea years later for her project *Trouble Every Day* (Frodon 2001).

4. Fargeau co-wrote all of Denis's films with her except one, *Vendredi soir*, which Denis co-wrote with Emmanuèle Bernheim, the author of the 1999 source novel of the same name.

5. Beugnet's remark on Denis's authorship complies with the editorial line of the 'French Directors Series' by Manchester University Press, within which her study appeared. This editorial policy is discussed in chapter 6 of this book, in relation to another monography published within the Cambridge series, Susan Hayward's *Luc Besson* (1998).

6. '[...] se débarrasser d'une gigantesque idée reçue qui s'appelle Afrique.'

7. The quotation appears in Françoise Audé's review of the film in *Positif* (1990: 71) and in Tarr and Rollet's book *Cinema and the Second Sex: Women's Film-making in France in the 1980s and 1990s* (2001: 221).

8. Besides *Chocolat*, Shohat and Stam mention *Le bal du Gouverneur* and *Outremer*.

9. Vietnam-born and US-naturalized scholar and film-maker Trinh T. Minh-ha, whose subject position, like Spivak's, is at the juncture of Third World identity and western culture, explicates the conflicted position of Third World female theorists in her book *Woman, Native, Other: Writing Postcoloniality and Feminism* (1989).

10. Film journals also exhibit problematic attitudes regarding black actors, especially when it comes to identifying them. In the articles on *S'en fout la mort* here cited, the captions for photos of the two main actors swap the two men's identities. So in *Positif* Isaach De Bankolé becomes Alex Descas (Audé 1990: 71) and in *Film Comment* Descas is presented as 'Isaach de Bankholé' (Murphy 1992: 62).

11. 'Pour moi, c'était une image presque théâtrale de la fonction du rire, qui s'accordait avec la manière dont je voyais les personnages des policiers dans ce film. Comme je voulais que cela garde la forme d'un jeu, une approche progressive des meurtres, il me semblait que l'appareil policier ne devait pas procurer le suspense, la tension. Tous les personnages avancent selon des coups de dés de leur destin et, dans les cases successives de ce parcours, les policiers ont une fonction concrète, ils règlent la circulation, ils regardent de l'hélicoptère s'il n'y a pas de bouchon, et ils sont éventuellement là pour arrêter les tueurs, mais plutôt d'une façon bonhomme.'

12. On this subject, see Grant 2002.

13. 'Peut-être que ça a pris corps davantage ... En tout cas, il y a davantage de corps dans ce film. Ce n'est pas de l'humour, la prise de corps c'est vraiment la seule chose qui m'intéresse. Ç'est assez intimidant, surtout quand c'est le corps des hommes.'

14. 'Chez Claire Denis, mettre en contact danse et armée est un moyen d'interroger la notion de corps collectif. Danseur et soldat cherchent à rejoinder un corps idéal même si ce n'est pas exactement le même. Et jusqu'où disparaître dans un supra-corps? Jusqu'où se fondre dans le rythme (la loi) d'un autre et quel plaisir y a-t-il à s'abolir comme sujet pour participer à la beauté du groupe, de la norme? (« *Tu n'est plus Africain* entend-on, *tu es légionnaire* »).'

15. 'Fluide et solide. Abstraite et concrète. Etrange expérience de cinéma comme on parle d'expérience en chimie ou en physique – que celle de Nénette et Boni. Un univers où l'on suit moins une action que l'on ne découvre des réactions, des combinaisons, des transformations: une jeune fille fend l'eau d'une piscine; une cafetière crachote le breuvage matinal ; un homme pétrit de la pâte à pizza. On est bien ici dans un cinéma de substances et de sensations.'

16. '[...] confirme qu'elle a un véritable talent pour faire vivre les lieux et les personnages de manière physique et charnelle. Elle façonne ses plans comme un sculpteur. Au final, elle nous offre un film qui a du corps.'

17. 'La fabrication du pain et le travail de la pâte à pizza illustrent physiquement cette transformation de la matière qui est au cœur du film: tout comme la farine et l'eau produisent le pain, la réunion de Nénette et Boni a rétabli le lien du sang, constitutif de la réparation de l'abandon original.'

18. 'Je suis intéressée par les prémices des choses. Par exemple, je suis intéressée par le désir. La montée du désir. Et puis quelque chose fait que j'en reste là ... Il y a quelque chose qui fait que le désir se suffit à lui-même, et que souvent il est suivi d'une frustration. Parce qu'il est si fort, que ce qui vient, pour répondre au désir, n'est pas assez fort pour le combler.'

19. Denis and Bernheim were working together unproductively on another adaptation when the novelist suggested the short novel she had just completed in response to something Denis said about her wish to make a simple film with only two characters (Denis and Jones 2003).

20. Kennedy mentions Vivian Sobchack's *The Address of the Eye: A Phenomenology of the Viewing Experience* (Princeton, NJ, Princeton University Press, 1992) and 'Phenomenology and the Film Experience,' (*In* Williams, L. (ed.), *Viewing Positions*. New Brunswick, New Jersey, Rutgers University Press, 1994, pp. 36–59); and Miriam Hansen's 'Early Cinema, Late Cinema: Transformations of the Public Sphere' (*Screen*, 34(3): 197–210, Autumn 1993).

21. '[...] tout exprimer par des questions de point de vue, de cadrage, de positions de corps dans un plan.'

22. '[...] une plongée a travers une construction esthétique, vers un domaine plus profond, plus mystérieux.' I use Beugnet's translation of the original quote from the concluding paragraph of her book *Claire Denis* (2004: 200).

References

Ancian, A. 2002. Claire Denis:An Interview. Pruks, I. (trans.). *Senses of Cinema*. [Online.] Available: http://www.sensesofcinema.com/contents/02/23/denis_interview.html.

Audé, F. 1990. S'en fout la vie (S'en fout la mort). *Positif*, 356: 70–72, octobre.

Beugnet, M. 2004. *Claire Denis*. Manchester and New York: Manchester University Press.

Bouquet, S. 2000. La hiérarchie des anges. *Cahiers du Cinéma*, 545: 48–49, avril.

Butler, A. 1994. The Politics of Location as Transnational Feminist Practice. (*In* Grewal I. and Kaplan, C. (eds). *Scattered Hegemonies. Postmodernity and Transnational Feminist Practices.* Minneapolis, MN: University of Minnesota Press, pp. 137–52.)

—. 2000. *Women's Cinema: The Contested Screen.* London and New York: Wallflower Press.

Darke, C. 2000. Desire Is Violence. *Sight and Sound*, 10(7): 16–18, July.

Deleuze, G. 1981. *Francis Bacon: logique de la sensation* (2 vols.), Paris: Editions du Seuil.

—. 1986. *Cinema 1: The Movement-Image.* [1983] Tomlinson, H. and Galeta, R. (trans). Minneapolis: University of Minnesota Press.

—. and Guattari, F. 1987. *A Thousand Plateaus: Capitalism and Schizophrenia.* [1980] Massumi, B. (trans. and forewords). Minneapolis, MN and London: University of Minnesota Press.

—. 1989. *Cinema 2: The Time Image.* [1985] Tomlinson, H. and Galeta, R. (trans). Minneapolis: University of Minnesota Press.

— and Guattari, F. 1994. *What Is Philosophy?* [1991] Tomlinson, H. and Graham Burchell, G. (trans). New York: Columbia UP.

Denis, C. 1994. J'ai pas sommeil. Entretien aven Claire Denis. Jousse, T and Strauss, F. (interviewers). *Cahiers du Cinéma*, 479–80: 25–30, mai.

—. 2000a. Je me reconnais dans le cinéma qui fait confiance à la narration plastique: Entretien avec Claire Denis. Lalanne, J-M. and Larcher, J. (interviewers). *Cahiers du Cinéma*, 545: 50–53, avril.

—. 2000b. Claire Denis Interviewed by Jonathan Romney. *Guardian Unlimited*. [Online.] Available: http://film.guardian.co.uk/interview/interviewpages/0,,338784,00.html.

— and K. Jones. 2003. Audio commentary. *Friday Night*, DVD, Wellspring.

Del Rio, E. 2003. Performing the Narrative of Seduction: Claire Denis' *Beau travail* (*Good Work*, 1999). *Kinoeye: New Perspectives on European Film*, 3(7). [Online.] Available: http://www.kinoeye. org/03/07/delrio07.php.

Fanon, F. 1961. *Les damnés de la terre.* Paris: François Maspero.

Frodon, J.-M. 2001. Il s'agit de s'aventurer au-devant d'une forme. *Le Monde*: 3, 11 July.

Garbarz, F. 1997. *Nénette et Boni*: Mère, pouquoi nous as-tu abandonnés ? *Positif*, 432: 38–39, février.

Grewal, I. and Kaplan, C. (eds). 1994. *Scattered Hegemonies. Postmodernity and Transnational Feminist Practices.* Minneapolis, MN: University of Minnesota Press.

Gili, J. A. 1988. Entretien avec Claire Denis sur *Chocolat. Positif*, 328: 14–16, juin.

Grant, C. 2002. Recognizing Billy Budd in Beau Travail: Epistemology and Hermeneutics of an Auteurist 'Free' Adaptation. *Screen*, 43(1): 57–73.

Hayward, S. 2001. Claire Denis' Films and the Post-colonial Body – with special reference to *Beau travail* (1999). *Studies in French Cinema*, 1(3): 159–65.

Heller, S. 2000. Playing Soldier. *American Prospect*, 7(14): 42–43. June 5.

Jackson, P. and Penrose, J. (eds). 1993. *Construction of Race, Place, and Nation: Postmodernity and Transnational Feminist Practices.* Minneapolis: University of Minnesota Press.

—. 1994. *Construction of Race, Place, and Nation. Postmodernity and Transnational Feminist Practices.* Minneapolis, IN: University of Minnesota Press.

Kennedy, B. 2002. *Deleuze and Cinema: The Aesthetics of Sensation.* Edinburgh, UK: Edinburgh University Press.

Marker, C. 1999. Sleepless in Paris: *J'ai pas sommeil* (Denis, 1993). (*In* Powrie, P. (ed.). *French Cinema in the 1990s: Continuity and Difference.* Oxford, UK, Oxford University Press, pp. 137–47.)

Marie, M. 1998. *La Nouvelle vague: une école artistique*. Paris: Nathan Université.

Maule, R. 2006. The Dialectics of Trans-national Identity and Female Desire in the Films of Claire Denis. (*In* Dennison, S. and Lim, S. H. (eds). *Remapping World Cinema: Identity, Culture and Politics in Film*. London and New York: Wallflower Press, pp. 73–85.)

Mayne, J. 2005. *Claire Denis*. Urbana and Chicago, Ill.: University of Illinois Press.

Met, P. 2003. Looking for Trouble: The Dialectics of Lack and Excess. Claire Denis, Trouble Every Day (2001). *Kinoeye: New Perspectives on European Film*. [Online.] Available:http://www.kinoeye. org/03/07/delrio07.php.

Minh-Ha, T. T. 1989. *Woman, Native, Other: Writing Postcoloniality and Feminism*. Bloomington and Indianapolis: Indiana University Press.

Mohanram, R. 1999. *Black Body: Women, Colonialism, and Space*. Minneapolis, MN: University of Minnesota Press.

Morice, J. 1997. *Nénette et Boni. Télérama*. [Online.] Available: http://www.telerama.fr/cine/film. php?id=42008.

Murphy, K. 1992. The Color of Home. *Film Comment*, 28: 62–63. September-October.

Nancy, J-L. 2005. L'Intrus selon Claire Denis. [Online.] Available: http://remue.net/spip.php?article679.

Portuges, C. 1996. Le Colonial Féminin: Women Directors Interrogate French Cinema. (*In* Sherzner, D., (ed.). *Cinema, Colonialism, Postcolonialism: Perspectives from the French and Francophone World*. Austin, TX: University of Texas Press, pp. 30–102.)

Reid, M. 1996. Colonial Observation: Interview with Claire Denis. *Jump Cut*, 40: 67–73.

Rodowick, D. N. 1997. *Gilles Deleuze's Time Machine*. Durham and London: Duke University Press.

—. 2000. Unthinkable Sex: Conceptual Personae and the Time-Image. *Invisible Culture: An Electronic Journal for Visual Studies*. [Online.] Available: http://www.rochester.edu/in_visible_culture/issue3/ rodowick.htm.

—. 2001. *Reading the Figural, or, Philosophy after the New Media*. Durham and London: Duke University Press.

Romney, J. 2000. Claire Denis Interviewed by Jonathan Romney. *The Guardian Unlimited*. [Online.] Available: http://film.guardian.co.uk/interview/interviewpages/0,,338784,00.html.

Rosenbaum, J. 2001. The Hit Parade: Rosenbaum's Top 40 Films of 2000. *Chicago Reader*. [Online.] Available: http://www.chicagoreader.com/movies/archives/2001/0101/010105_3.html.

Sherzner, D. (ed.). 1996. *Cinema, Colonialism, Postcolonialism: Perspectives from the French and Francophone World*. Austin, TX: University of Texas Press.

Shohat, E. and Stam, R. 1994. *Unthinking Eurocrentrism: Multiculturalism and the Media*. London and New York: Routledge.

Smith, D. 2005. *L'Intrus*: an Interview with Claire Denis. [Online.] Available: www.sensesofcinema.com/ contents/ 05/35/claire_denis_interview.html.

Strauss, F. 1990. Mémoires d'exil. Féminin colonial. *Cahiers du Cinéma*, 434: 28–33.

Tarr, C. and Rollet, B. 2001. *Cinema and the Second Sex: Women's Film-making in France in the 1980s and 1990s*. New York and London: Continuum.

Tesson, C. and Toubiana, S. 1998. Quelques vagues plus tard: table ronde avec Olivier Assayas, Claire Denis, Cédric Kahn et Noémie Lvovsky. *Cahiers du Cinéma. Nouvelle Vague: une légende en question*, spec. issue: 70–75, décembre.

Toubiana, S. 1999. Beau travail!. *Cahiers du Cinéma*, 539: 28–31, octobre.

Truong, N. 2003. Claire Denis: 'je suis une être séparé'. *Le Monde de l'éducation*, 316: 72–77, juillet-août.

Young, R. 1990. *White Mythologies: Writing History and the West*. London and New York: Routledge.

9

FEMININE MATTERS: FRANCESCA ARCHIBUGI AND THE RECONFIGURATION OF WOMEN IN THE PRIVATE SPHERE

Francesca Archibugi is among the female film directors (including, among others, the sisters Cristina and Francesca Comencini, Fiorella Infascelli, and Cinzia Th. Torrini) who have made their débuts during the 1980s within the framework of Italy's 'new cinema.' In almost twenty years of feature film-making, she has developed a distinctive reputation in Italy and abroad as one of the most-appreciated female film directors of the new generation. Her films depict interpersonal relations and coming-of-age stories set within Italy's domestic and micro-social contexts, bringing attention to generational conflicts between children and parents. Although her films deal with contexts and narratives generally associated with women's issues, Archibugi dismisses gender as a significant standpoint in her work.

Archibugi's role within Italian cinema and culture exemplifies the complex relations that Italian female film directors entertain with the national discourse on film authorship. Archibugi embraces the realist aesthetic and the social focus typically associated with Italy's authorial tradition since neo-realism and connoted by male-focused perspectives and themes.

What is at stake here is certainly not to propose that the focus on female characters and gender issues in Archibugi's films are marks of a feminine discourse within a male-dominant society and gender-blind film context. Such an approach would propose an essentialist view of female authorship and of women's cinema altogether in terms of feminine tradition. Instead, the point is to underline the potential for a post-feminist approach to film-making to disentangle the concept of female authorship from binary or oppositional models of feminine subjectivity or expression.

It is not 'carino': Archibugi and the authorial articulation of realist cinema

In 1992, the Italian film scholar Leonardo Quaresima (1992) published an article titled 'Non è carino' in the Italian film journal *Cinema & Cinema* in which he commented on the work of film-makers who began their careers during the 1980s. The title, which translates as 'it is not cute' or 'it is not kind,' refers to one of the many labels Italian film critics used to characterize this decade's much-criticized 'new cinema.' Like Gabriele Salvatores and other Italian film-makers of that generation, Archibugi has been frequently associated with the *carino* genre. Yet her affiliation with the realist tradition of Italian cinema has assured her authorial status and salvaged her work from the anonymity of the *carino* cinema. Indeed, Archibugi maintains a double status in Italian film discourse and cinema. On the one hand, she is associated with the *carino* cinema's minimalist trend, also criticized for proposing degraded versions of the *commedia all'italiana* and television-informed narratives and formal solutions; on the other hand, she is seen as the inheritor of Italy's realist tradition, particularly as established through the post-war social comedy and drama. Archibugi's professional training and the varying reception of her films reflect this double standing.

Archibugi was born in Rome in 1960 to an upper-middle-class family of intellectuals. As an adolescent, she was selected among hundreds of high school students to play Ottilie in a television adaptation of J. W. Goethe's 1809 novel *The Elective Affinities*, directed by Gianni D'Amico (*Le affinità elettive*, 1979). Before making her own début as a feature film director, she acted in films by, or collaborated with, some of the most interesting film authors of the new generation, including Marco Tullio Giordana and Giuseppe Bertolucci (Bernardo's younger brother). She was trained as a film director at the Centro Sperimentale di Cinematografia, Italy's national film school, where she graduated at age 23 from the film directing programme. She also studied with some of the main proponents of Italian post-war cinema such as Ermanno Olmi, the prestigious film director of the post-neo-realist period, at his film school Ipotesi Cinema, based in Bassano, a small town in the north-east of Italy, as well as with the famous Italian screenwriter and in Rome with Furio Scarpelli, who was a member of the pre-eminent Age-Scarpelli team of screenwriters since the 1950s and, during his three decades in film-making, the screenwriter for dozens of successful comedies.[1]

Traditionally associated with Italy's post-war film directors, Archibugi's working methods are characteristic of authorial film practices. These include: cooperating with producers from national television networks and independent film companies on small-budget films; personally conceiving and developing the screenplays; supervising all phases of film production; collaborating with a trusted team of producers (including Leo Pescarolo, who produced Archibugi's first three feature films), screenwriters (such as Claudia Sbarigia and Gloria Malatesta, with whom Archibugi wrote three screenplays, including those for her first two feature films), and musicians (mainly Battista Lena, Archibugi's husband, who usually composes the scores for all her films); and privileging little-known and non-professional actors, especially children.[2] Furthermore, her films have received prestigious awards at international film festivals, are regularly discussed in auteur-informed film magazines, and have been given important tributes (in 2003, New York's Museum of Modern Art had a retrospective of her work).

Mignon è partita: Mignon says goodbye to Giorgio and his family

In spite of her links with Italy's author-informed film milieu and culture, Archibugi dodges authorial considerations of her work and is explicit about her intention to make films for a wide audience (Laviosa 2003a). Although not always successful at the box office, her films consistently reach the nation-wide circuit of theatrical exhibition. Some of her films have also achieved minor distribution overseas. Such local and foreign exposure is rather exceptional for Italian films, which are usually only distributed nationally, either through short-term engagements in selected theatres or, most often, via television networks and the home-viewing market. In this respect, like other Italian film-makers of her generation considered in this book (Gabriele Salvatores in particular), Archibugi partakes in modes of film production that encompass culturally and commercially oriented cinema. Also like Salvatores, Archibugi claims her affiliation with popular cinema, yet from a different perspective, her inspiration coming from post-war Italian realist comedy and drama.

Archibugi's approach to film-making draws from her formal training and professional apprenticeships, above mentioned, at the Centro Sperimentale, and under the mentorship of Olmi and Scarpelli, in Rome. During this period she made several short films, *Riflesso condizionato* (1982), *Lo stato delle cose* (1983), *La guerra è appena finita* (1983), *Il vestito più bello* (1984), *Un sogno truffato* (1984), and *La piccola avventura* (1985). She also wrote some screenplays with Gloria Malatesta and Claudia Sbarigia, including *La cintura/The Belt* (1989) and *L'estate sta finendo* (1987). With the same team of screenwriters she completed the script for *Mignon è partita*, which won First Prize at the Premio Solinas (Solinas Award), established in 1986 by the family of the famous Italian screenwriter Franco Solinas (who died in 1982) to promote unpublished scripts for feature film production. The film was made the following year and was a small co-production involving the Rome-based independent producer Leo Pescarolo and the French film company Chrysalide.

Mignon è partita foreshadows Archibugi's most typical themes and stylistic solutions, including the coming-of-age story, with an emphasis on generational tensions mostly between parents and children; an unobtrusive style; and combining well known and emerging actors with non-professionals, especially children, with no formal training or previous experience. The film centres on a Roman middle-class family and follows the trajectory of Giorgio, a sensitive, discrete, and studious adolescent who does not seem to fit in with his dysfunctional family. The family is made up of an unfaithful, absent father, an archetypical, self-sacrificing mother who pretends not to notice her husband's infidelity for the sake of her five children, and Giorgio's four siblings. The family's daily routine is disrupted by the arrival of the children's French cousin Mignon, who is the same age as Giorgio and was sent to live there because her wealthy father, Giorgio's paternal uncle, has been jailed for the accidental death of a worker at an unsafe construction site under his care. Giorgio is the only family member able to spend time and get along with the snobbish cousin. Indeed, Giorgio falls in love with Mignon but does not dare manifest his feelings for her. When she starts a fling with one of his brother's friends, he suffers in silence and makes an awkward attempt at suicide. In the end, Mignon pretends to be pregnant so that she can leave her cousin's house and return to Paris. *Mignon è partita* received five David di Donatello awards (Italy's equivalent to the Oscars), was embraced by critics, and did quite well at the box office. Italian film critics especially appreciated the film-maker's ability to capture everyday reality with sensibility and stylistic sobriety.

Archibugi wrote her second film, *Verso sera*, with the same co-writers, Sbarigia and Malatesta. The project was another Italian-French co-production involving the same companies that financed her first film. Two international stars were featured: the prominent Italian actor Marcello Mastroianni, and Sandrine Bonnaire, an emerging French actress who made her début as the wayward adolescent in Maurice Pialat's *À nos amours/To Our Loves* (1983). Again, the film takes place in Rome in 1977, a year marked by student protests at several Italian universities. The story depicts the short and troubled cohabitation of three cross-generational family members: Ludovico Bruschi, a wealthy and cultivated but disenchanted retired professor of Russian literature (Mastroianni); Stella, his anti-conformist, working-class daughter-in-law (Bonnaire) who recently separated from Bruschi's insecure and hopeless son, Oliviero; and Stella's daughter Papere, Bruschi's young granddaughter, of whom he is given temporary custody after her parents' divorce.[3] When Stella joins her daughter at Bruschi's house, many heated debates erupt between her and her father-in-law. Bruschi regards Stella as an opinionated yet ignorant young woman whose political activism lacks ideological foundation. In the end, the undisciplined and impetuous Stella and the well-mannered and cultivated professor succeed, in part, in resolving their differences. Yet Stella cannot stand being confined within Bruschi's house and the trappings of bourgeois life. Despite Bruschi's efforts to dissuade her, she takes off with her daughter for a student rally. Her decision marks the definitive break between Stella and her

Verso sera (Marcello Mastroianni and Sandrine Bonnaire)

Verso sera: 'collective consciousness' at home

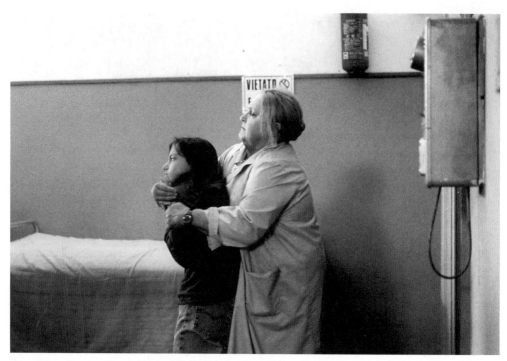

Il grande cocomero (Laura Betti and little Alessia Fugardi)

father-in-law, who decides to cut off contact with her and Papere, although he continues to provide for them financially. The film focuses on the generational and cultural gaps among the main characters, as well as the ideological contradictions each character represents. The dignified professor is a Communist who has always maintained his loyalty to the Party, yet he lives a bourgeois existence in Rome's most exclusive neighbourhood, the Parioli. Stella and Oliviero epitomize the generation (of which Archibugi is a part) that grew up in the aftermath of the 1968 revolution, without ideals and historical reference points. The film won two David di Donatello awards, including best film, yet it had a less favourable reception than Archibugi's first film. It was criticized by some film writers for its excessive use of dialogue, didactic treatment of characters, and uneven narrative structure.[4]

Archibugi's third film, *Il grande cocomero* (1993), released after a three-year hiatus, was produced through the same companies that backed her previous films, with the additional contribution of Canal+. Beginning with this film, and until *Renzo e Lucia*, Archibugi wrote her screenplays without collaborators. She also co-wrote her most recent film, *Lezioni di volo* (2006), with Doriana Leondeff, with whom she also co-signed the published script, *Lezioni di volo* (Venezia: Marsilio 2006).

As it has been the case with other films by Archibugi, *Lezioni di volo* had overall positive, yet never enthusiastic, reviews and did not do too well at the box office. *Il grande cocomero* widens the scope of her favourite subject matter (family relations) to the social sphere. The film in fact investigates one of Italy's most delicate and debated domains in public health research: child psychiatry. The film tells the story of Pippi, a twelve-year-old girl who suffers major epileptic seizures that seem to have a psychological origin. Arturo (Sergio Castellitto), a young neuro-psychiatrist who works at the hospital where Pippi was sent during one of her frequent crises, takes up her case out of sympathy. Suspecting that her condition has a psychosomatic origin, he uses psychotherapy to unearth the cause and eventually free Pippi from her self-induced epilepsy. *Il grande cocomero* signalled Archibugi's move towards more socially conscious issues. Film critics, both in Italy and abroad, praised her approach to the topic and her realistic depiction of the deficiencies and problems inherent in Italy's public health system. The film was also a box office success, both at home and in some foreign countries, and won several honours, including three David di Donatello awards.

However, Archibugi's next film, *Con gli occhi chiusi* (1994), an Italy-Spain-France co-production, had a rather negative response. Some film critics found the work too hermetic, preventing identification with the characters.[5] The narrative, a fairly faithful adaptation of the eponymous novel by Federigo Tozzi (1919), is set in the countryside around Siena, Tuscany, between the end of the nineteenth century and the beginning of the twentieth century. In the story, Pietro, the son of a rustic and despotic landowner, falls in love as a child with Ghìsola (played as a child by Alessia Fugardi, who was Pippi in *Il grande cocomero*), the daughter of one of the tenant farmers. As he grows up, he pursues his plan to marry her against his father's will, even when she relocates to the city to escape from him. Unaware that she is, at first, the mistress of a middle class man and then, after the man has gone bankrupt, a prostitute, Pietro keeps pursuing her. Blind to the evidence of her disparate condition, he remains committed to marrying her and goes to fetch her from the brothel where she lives. When he finds out that she is pregnant, he faints from the initial shock and then realizes that he no longer loves her and decides to leave. The film was a box office failure and left many critics perplexed. The film's poor performance deeply disappointed Archibugi, who did not return to feature film-making for four years.

In 1994, the same year she made *Con gli occhi chiusi*, Archibugi participated in an anthology film featuring Italian film-makers titled *L'unico paese al mondo*. In the next four years, she completed two documentary films. The first is an instalment of *Ritratti d'autore, seconda serie* (1996), an anthology film of interviews by young Italian film-makers with established Italian directors. Archibugi contributed with a segment on Marco Bellocchio. The second documentary, titled *La strana storia di Banda Sonora* (1997), is a road movie about a jazz band's tour around Italy organized by Archibugi's husband, jazz musician Battista Lena.

Archibugi's fifth feature film, *L'albero delle pere*, was co-produced by the film branch of the national television network RAI (RAI Cinemafiction), the national film institute Istituto Luce, and some independent film companies. This film marked Archibugi's return to her most typical themes and settings. The film is set in Rome during the Christmas holidays of 1997 and features, once again, an Italian family. This time Archibugi focuses on an atypical family structure, with children raised by parents from different marriages and common-law relationships. The story is told through the point of view of an adolescent fourteen-year-old boy named Siddhartha, who lives with his heroin-addicted mother, Silvia. The boy has a half-sister, five-year-old Domitilla, who lives with her father. Both of the children's fathers are separated from Silvia but are still attached to her, although they disapprove of her addiction. The two men are quite different: Siddhartha's father is an unsuccessful, rebellious, independent film director; Domitilla's father is a conservative, bourgeois lawyer, in keeping with his family's legacy of prominent legal figures. While Domitilla is spending the holidays at her mother's house, she accidentally pricks herself with one of Silvia's used syringes. Siddhartha witnesses the incident and, without telling his parents, gets his sister tested for viral infections, finding out that she has contracted hepatitis C. When the parents accidentally find out, a family crisis erupts. In the end, everyone tries to piece their lives together and help Silvia overcome her problems. But the woman falls back into her habit, snorting heroin at a friend's house. On her way home, she falls asleep at the wheel under the effect of the drugs and dies in a car accident. The film confirmed Archibugi's ability to work with children and elicit authentic performances from actors. Archibugi used many more outdoor scenes than in her previous films, following, with fluid camera movements, the restless protagonist on his hectic journey through the city. She also adopted a fast-paced editing style to render the young protagonist's frenzied schedule, punctuating the action with animated inserts displayed on Siddhartha's home computer in which a cartoon Siddhartha pops up to remind the boy of his daily appointments and duties. *L'alberto delle pere* was fairly successful with Italian audiences but received mixed reviews from critics. The popular success of the film shows Archibugi's talent for addressing sensitive issues in a straightforward manner and for directing children (the protagonist, Niccoló Senni, received the award for best emerging actor at the 1998 Venice Film Festival). Despite all this, the critics reprimanded Archibugi's use of repetitive motifs and patterns.

Archibugi's next two feature films were produced for television. *Domani* was the first Italian film made about the earthquake that shook Umbria in 1997. The film was co-produced by RAI but was meant for theatrical distribution: while it did not have popular success, it travelled the international film festival circuit and received laudatory reviews in Italy and overseas. The film recounts the daily problems related to the relocation of earthquake survivors after their houses have been condemned. The people are moved first to a trailer camp and then to a village composed of prefabricated housing units. Archibugi tries a different direction, developing a choral narrative and concentrating on the social sphere. The film was not successful in Italy, in spite of the strong critical reception from film magazines and newspapers. Film critics praised Archibugi for avoiding the clichés and typical visual techniques associated with television coverage of social events.

Next, Archibugi directed a segment for an anthology film about 9/11, *Un altro mondo è possible/Another World is Possible* (2001), to which several Italian film-makers contributed. She then returned to television production with the two-part TV movie *Renzo e Lucia* (2004), adapted from Alessandro Manzoni's canonical novel *I promessi sposi* (1842). The mini-series aired on Canale 5, one of the private television networks owned by the Italian media magnate and politician Silvio Berlusconi. Although following the nineteenth-century novel's main plot, Archibugi and her two co-writers, veteran screenwriter Francesco Scardamaglia and TV specialist Nicola Lusuardi, glossed over Manzoni's religious and ethical perspective. Instead, they adopted a psychological approach to the characters and offered original portrayals of the three main characters: Renzo and Lucia, the betrothed, and Don Rodrigo, the powerful Spanish aristocrat who falls in love with Lucia and tries, by any means necessary, to prevent the marriage. Archibugi's loose, modernist adaptation of the novel, which is set in the seventeenth century, received mixed reviews. Still, this TV movie proved Archibugi's ability to develop intimate views of inter-personal relationships, and her allegiance to the realist tradition of Italian cinema, as manifested in the film's faithful reconstruction of medieval life in the Lake Como countryside, including the epoch's settings and costumes.

Archibugi's latest film, *Lezioni di volo*, released in Italy in March 2007, was produced by Guido de Laurentiis for the emerging Italian production company Cattleya. The film is set in India and features an international cast, mixing, as Archibugi usually does, well-known actors (including Giovanna Mezzogiorno, one of the most respected actresses of her generation, art house cinema and television veteran Flavio Bucci, and established art house actress Anna Galiena, who played Pippi's mother in *Il grande cocomero*) and lesser known actors and people with no acting experience (the two young male protagonists). The film features two eighteen-year-old boys from a privileged socioeconomic background who travel to India on vacation and encounter an experience that will change their perspectives on life.

Flavia Laviosa, in her article 'Themes and Motifs in the Cinema of Francesca Archibugi' (2003b) appropriately identifies the cinematic trend with which Italian film critics have associated Archibugi's films as the 'carino' (cute) cinema:

> The carino genre has produced nice and sentimental films, criticized for revealing the contemporary directors' inability to narrate ambivalent, mysterious images or enigmatic ideas. This kind of cinema, denigrated with euphemisms such as "dignified, evasive, and promising" (Vitti 235), shows a disinterest in the exploration of the world of the soul and the mind, and insists on the complete removal of serious topics like history, politics or memory. (2003b)[6]

Laviosa suggests that Archibugi's 'carinismo speaks for her generation of parents in crisis and their children's new problematic contexts' (ibid.). In an address titled 'La macchina cinema' (The Cinematic Apparatus), Enrico Magrelli referred to the term *carino* at a round table on 'Italian Authors and Actors' organized by the Venice Biennale on 14 June 1998.[7] On that occasion, he described Italian 1980s cinema in terms of 'umbilical aesthetics,' a degraded form 'similar-to-television existentialism, an uncertain set (instead of a text), made of clumsiness' (Zagarrio 1998b: 13, my translation).[8] He also offered that 'the "cuteness" of the 1980s hides the aphasia; more than just stories, we see many Polaroid pictures, family videos, school snapshots in which a generation is posing' (ibid.: 13, my translation).[9] As for the few film-makers generally praised by film critics of the time, he concedes that '[o]ne can grasp metabolized fragments of *commedia all'italiana* in Moretti, Archibugi, Mazzacurati, Piccioni, Luchetti, etc,' (ibid.: 13, my translation).[10] Paradoxically, the same thematic and stylistic elements that prompt some film critics to categorize Archibugi's work in the minimalist vein of the *carino* cinema – due to her penchant for intimate stories focused on domestic settings and her inconspicuous style – also contribute to consolidating her authorial status in Italy and abroad.

A vehement defender of Archibugi's work in Italy is Alessandra Levantesi, a film critic who has published several articles and edited an anthology on the film-maker.[11] In the chapter devoted to Archibugi in the anthology on 1980s Italian cinema titled *Schermi opachi: Il cinema italiano degli anni '80* (1998: 107–115), Levantesi distinguishes Archibugi's work from the *carino* genre. At the beginning of her essay, Levantesi recounts having been bothered by some comments upon the release of *Mignon è partita* dismissing the film as 'a cute comedy, minimalist, full of good feelings' (Levantesi 1998: 107). On the contrary, Levantesi praises the film for its precise rendition of the social context, lifestyle, and psychology of contemporary adolescence, as well as its frank portrayal of the disillusioned 1968 generation twenty years later:

> In a new Italian cinema oscillating between narcissism and confusion, intellectualist abstractions and nonrealism, such a concrete and timely declaration of intents seemed unusual [...] the unknown film-maker allowed herself the transgressive gesture of representing two former 1968 activists, belonging to the generation of 'eternal children,' in the unprecedented role of parents migrating from the ideological left to an existential, petit-bourgeois twilight zone. He is a bookseller, a failed writer, and a third-rate Don Juan; she is a wife and mother resigned to matrimonial unhappiness, like a grandmother. (Levantesi 1998: 108, my translation)[12]

Likewise, Italian film historian Gian Piero Brunetta expresses a rather positive opinion on the film-maker's first two films in the last chapter of his four-volume history of Italian cinema, dedicated to1980s new cinema (1998: 558). Although he lists Archibugi among the film-makers of the minimalist current (which subsumes the *carino* genre), he notes that her début film *Mignon è partita* is 'one of the few authentic revelations of the 1980s' (1998: 558, my translation).[13] He specifies:

> [...] the story is part of the minimalist current, yet has the capacity of being able to show the dynamics of life's decisive phases with the security of an established author [...]. What is most striking about her work is the neatness with which she chooses the shots without any complacency; the elegance with which she subordinates her cinematographic culture to the necessity of grasping the moments of truths in the look of her characters; her assuredness in narrating the difficulties of the relationship between different generations, the unease connected with aging and fully living one's feelings; the delicateness with which she shows strong feelings at their emergence. (Ibid.: 558, my translation)[14]

Vito Zagarrio echoes Levantesi and Brunetta's comments in his survey of 1990s Italian cinema (1998b). He includes Archibugi in a group of film-makers (along with Giuseppe Tornatore, Gabriele Salvatores, Carlo Mazzacurati, Silvio Soldini, Alessandro D'Alatri, and the team of Daniele Ciprí and Franco Maresco) who, according to him, form ' a generation of new authors who have neatly taken the place of the old masters' (1998: 10, my translation).[15]

The reception of Archibugi's films generally insists on their cultural and sociological value and have also been the subject of scholarly publications. Although her films have limited international circulation, they are regularly presented at film festivals and commented on in auteur-informed film magazines. Archibugi has also received scholarly attention by specialists on Italian cinema outside of Italy, especially in English-speaking academic and publishing areas. Àine O'Healy, for instance, offers an authorial reading of Archibugi's work, highlighting 'distinctive preoccupations and carefully considered stylistic choices, striking consistencies of vision and expression that invite an assessment of her work as that of an emerging *autore*' (1999: 122).[16] Flavia Laviosa, an Italian film scholar based in the United States who has published extensively on Archibugi, is more careful about approaching Archibugi's work from an authorial perspective. She appropriately acknowledges that the film-maker's intention is 'to reach many, diverse spectators, as well as achieve a wide commercial distribution' and notes that '[t]hese are the reasons why she develops a personal style that adheres to a conventional cinematic realism based on popular narrative' (Laviosa 2003b). Additionally, Laviosa maintains Archibugi's unassuming stance about her authorial status. In an interview with Laviosa, Archibugi stated that if she had to be credited as an author, it should be for having produced a 'body of work and not only one isolated film [...] several chapters of a human comedy' (Archibugi 2003). In this respect, Laviosa defines Archibugi's work as 'a fresco of urban middle-class family life, painted with the strokes of her heart' (2003b).

Gender is a blind spot in the critical reception of Archibugi, especially in Italy, and does not appear on the film-maker's agenda. Talking to Laviosa, Archibugi strongly rejected 'the principle that stylistic or thematic markers reveal a female presence behind the camera' and stated:

> While I feel very strongly the female side in my life, I also feel that I could not be anything else than a woman. However, I think that art, in some ways, is genderless. The directors I like the most are not women. I think that in cinema there are a few explosive and strong personalities, while there are more explosive and strong personalities in literature throughout the centuries. Except for some directors like Jane Campion, Helma Sanders-Brahms, a German director and a few others, I do not think that there is a female Scorsese or a female Truffaut, even though Varda is a great director, in other words I do not think that there is a female Ozu. [...] when someone is a narrator is a narrator. (Archibugi 2003)

A central issue in feminist discussions of authorship is that the category of the author is founded on western and male-centred models of subjectivity and aesthetic representation (Gaines 2002; Mayne 1990). For this reason, feminist critics have theorized women's film authorship mainly in relation to cinematic practices that propound a feminist agenda or are radically alternative to those found in dominant or classical cinemas (de Lauretis 1987; Kuhn 1990). Feminist scholars have also considered female authorship in terms of feminine enunciation or *écriture*, especially in the work of female film-makers established in dominant contexts of film production and reception (Flitterman-Lewis 1996; Johnston 1988; Mayne 1990 and 1994). The latter approach has often raised questions of essentialism, since the idea of a feminine aesthetic or subjective specificity implies an assumption of a feminine essence and tradition, conceived in opposition and in reference to dominant male paradigms (Mayne 1990: 89–98).

In discussing Archibugi's authorship from a gender-specific perspective, the purpose here is not to suggest that her work reveals more or less conscious marks of enunciation or formal solutions foregrounding a gender-specific or counter-conformist alternative to the tradition of male aesthetics in which she belongs. Archibugi's relation to female authorship is seen from a from feminist point of view that highlights the discursive tensions underlying her film practice within a sociocultural context informed by a male-dominant ideology.[17]

'Everybody, All Go Home!': The reconfiguration of women in the Italian family

Francesca Archibugi has set many of her films in the framework of the family and scrutinized interpersonal relations and generational contrasts among characters related to this important institution in Italian society. As Flavia Laviosa appropriately synthesizes, the film-maker:

> explores themes of friendship and love, with their concomitant emotions, and examines a spectrum of sociological issues relating to the Italian *familyscape*. The changes in the structure and in the educational role of the family have inspired her to narrate a variety of life trajectories, and to chronicle the metamorphosis of the family when individuals are confronted with existential crises and challenged by ethical doubts (2004: 201).

In her representation of the family, Archibugi tends to position women within the private sphere. But in doing so she does not reinstate traditional gender roles or feminine stereotypes; instead, she calls attention to the family as an institution and an area of social and cultural life that has undergone profound changes over the past three decades, linked to Italy's socio-economic development and the Women's Movement. In this respect, for Archibugi the family constitutes a rich terrain to explore the micro-political debates and confrontations that characterize Italian contemporary society.

The family is a constant motif in Italian cinema. In *Italian Film* (2000) Marcia Landy devotes a chapter to the representation of the family ('*La famiglia*: The Cinematic Family and the Nation.' In Landy 2000: 205–33). In Italian cinema, argues Landy, the representation of the family involves a variety of social phenomena, including patriarchal traditions, cultural stereotypes, religious and political oppression, regional and sub-national identities (ibid.: 205). Landy examines the manifestation of these social elements in different filmic forms, genres, and periods of Italian cinema (ibid.: 205–33). With regard to Archibugi's generation, she contends:

> Films produced in Italy in the 1980s and 1990s focused more and more on the family as an index of political, cultural, and aesthetic changes seeing these transformations as connected to emerging gender and class differences in the social positions of men and women, to new conceptions of sexuality that are not always salubrious, and to generational conflicts between parents and children that betoken profound differences and misunderstandings. These changes are indicative as well of the dissolution of conceptions of the family as the basis of the Italian nation, its history and its representations of citizenship, continuity, and morality. (Ibid.: 233)

Landy's characterization of the new representation of the family in 1980s and 1990s Italian cinema perfectly applies to Archibugi's films depicting the contemporary Italian family in *Mignon è partita*, *Verso sera*, *Il grande cocomero*, and *L'albero delle pere*, all of which are set in her native city, Rome. In these films, female characters are, for various reasons, confined within the household; they are housewives and mothers who do not have outside jobs (the mothers in *Mignon è partita* and *Il grande cocomero*); they are employed in the house (the female housekeeper in *Verso sera*); they are young women or girls who live under the tutelage of their parents (the female children in all these films) or else adult females who refuse to work out of ideological principles (Stella in *Verso sera* and Silvia in *L'albero delle pere*). Male characters instead live primarily in the public sphere, either because of their jobs (Giorgio's father in *Mignon è partita*, the psychiatrist and Pippi's father in *Il grande cocomero*, and the two fathers in *L'albero delle pere*), political commitments (Prof. Bruschi in *Verso sera*), or cultural interests (Prof. Bruschi in *Verso sera*, and Giorgio in *Mignon è partita*).

The juxtaposition between a feminine/domestic pole and a masculine/social pole in Archibugi's films does not necessarily coincide with the reinstatement of patriarchal divisions of gender roles within the family with respect to the sociocultural context to which it refers. From this perspective, Archibugi's reconfiguration of female characters within the domestic sphere needs to be considered in light of two phenomena: on the one hand, the social, political, and cultural transformation of the Italian family during the past century; on the other hand, the particular development of the feminist movement in Italy.

In Italian cinema, and before it in Italian literature, the family and the private sphere have been typically associated with feminine issues and popular artistic forms focused on female characters predominantly addressing women. These connections refer back to the emergence of a narrative strand and an aesthetic mode parallel to the nineteenth century's development of the nuclear family and capitalist economy, which Peter Brooks refers to as the 'melodramatic field' (1976). Feminist film theorists have examined the development of the melodramatic form in cinema especially in relation to the classical period of Hollywood and national cinemas (Gledhill 1987; Doane 1990 and 1991).[18] In their analyses, these scholars argue that film genres such as the woman's film or the maternal melodrama serve the purpose of reinforcing ideological consensus over gender roles in society by means of configuring women's place within the domestic and private spheres (Gledhill 1987; Doane 1987 and 1991).

In Italian cinema, the identification of the feminine with the private sphere has different genealogies and manifestations than those identified by the feminist scholarship cited above, and reflects the country's historical specificity and multi-regional culture (Landy 2000: 205–07). More importantly, in Italy, the link between femininity and domesticity has been reinforced by the Catholic Church's influence and the Italian state's conservative legislation on marriage and parental responsibility up to the 1970s, as well as by the fascist regime's representation of the mother as the family's stronghold (ibid.: 205–18). Furthermore, the generic models to which Archibugi's films make reference, the post-war Italian comedy and the realist drama, are quite distinct from those examined in the feminist literature on femininity and domesticity, and propose a different view of women's role within the private sphere. In Italy, a more complex treatment of women's roles in the family (against the fascist ideal of motherhood as symbol of the family's unity and values) begins with the neo-realist film and is subsequently picked up by the *commedia all'italiana* (ibid.: 211–23).

Marcia Landy deems *Ladri di biciclette/The Bicycle Thief* (Vittorio De Sica, 1948) the film that 'opens a window onto changing concepts of family in the cinema, and, more broadly, the character of cinematic representation' (ibid.: 215). She describes the film's innovative take on the family as follows:

> First of all [...] its emphasis is affective, displaying a concern not only with economic issues but with the quality of familial relationships implicated in and threatened by social forces [...] Second, though the film maintains a continuity with the emphasis on the importance of the family as nurturance and mutual support, *The Bicycle Thief* has shifted from a prescriptive and formulaic mode to one that is interrogative. (Ibid.: 215)

As for the post-war comedy, as Peter Bondanella notes, 'the *commedia all'italiana* lays bare an undercurrent of social malaise and the painful contradictions of a culture in rapid transformation' (1993: 144). With regard to the representation of the family, Landy observes that this subgenre touched upon sexual, social, economic, and legislative issues, developing satirical views of patriarchy and machismo (2000: 222–23).

Archibugi's representation of the family mixes the affective tone and inquiring mode of the neo-realist drama with the ironic and cynical criticism of the post-war comedy, while avoiding the mannerisms and the gender biases found in each of these two types of film. Hence, her stories show no trace of the neo-realist drama's sentimental and redeeming humanism and commitment to social change. By the same token, her films do not foreground a prototypically male anti-hero nor reinstate the concept of feminine 'naturalness' predominant in the popular strand of the 1950s neo-realist drama (Grignaffini 1988: 120–23).[19] Similarly, her character treatment bears no trace of the *commedia all'italiana*'s exhausted use of social and cultural stereotypes, including those related to femininity (Landy 2000: 218–23).

Flavia Laviosa has exemplarily contextualized Archibugi's 'family films' in relation to the situation of contemporary Italian families (2004: 202–04). Basing her overview on Italian sociologist Anna Laura Zanatta's *Le nuove famiglie* (1997), Laviosa identifies the conditions that have led to the advent of the 'postmodern family' in Italy in the mid-1960s. The postmodern family, she contends, is the product of 'socio-economic and cultural transmutations [...], advanced industrialization, urban civilization, and the mass entrance of women in the work force' and 'an erosion of Christian values, a greater acceptance of pluralism of ideas, and [...] an emphasis on the ideal of romantic love' (ibid.: 202–04). The postmodern family subsumes various typologies, depending on its composition and of the relations established among its members (ibid.: 203). Regarding Archibugi's depiction of the postmodern family, Laviosa apropos suggests:

The central theme of Archibugi's work is the family's connectedness and interdependence, with a consistent focus on the duties of parenting and the pains of growing up. She traces a psychological and anthropological study of the Italian family, and vividly represents new parental figures in recently evolved family units. While the family has generally been perceived to be a unit that has been structurally stable and unchanging for centuries, Archibugi depicts its constant evolution with its inherent socio-psychological changes. (Ibid.: 203–04)

Another important element to consider concerning the roles of female characters within the family in Archibugi's films is the film-maker's attitude vis-à-vis the feminist movement and the consequences of feminism on the transformation of women's positions in Italian society and in the private sphere.

As chapter 7 illustrates, Italian feminism involved a strong rejection of traditional values and a re-conceptualization of women's identity outside of social systems and institutions. Unlike their North American or French counterparts, Italian feminists firmly rejected the principle of women's equality, which for them entailed recognizing universal, albeit de facto male-informed, norms and institutions (Bono and Kemp 1991: 14–20). Accordingly, they refashioned gender roles first and foremost on the level of private contexts and interpersonal relations. This type of politics was condensed in the slogan 'the personal is the political' (Bono and Kemp 1991: 20–23; Passerini 1993: 179). Paola Bono and Sandra Kemp note in their introduction to their 1991 anthology of Italian feminist writings and documents:

> The way in which the social and economic conditions and problems of women's lives are perceived and dealt with by Italian feminists represents their own version of 'the personal is the political.' What is characteristically Italian here is the uneasy, conflictual but nevertheless sustained relationship between separatist speculation, the effort to analyse and create an autonomous subject-woman, and practical political activities. (Bono and Kemp 1991: 20)

This uneasiness translated into a removal of the Women's Movement from official institutions and political parties and subsequently caused feminism to have very little impact on Italian culture, as is demonstrated in the conspicuous absence of gender-related concerns in Italy's artistic milieus, as well as in academic and intellectual circles. Archibugi's position vis-à-vis gender is common among many women of her generation who, like her, embraced feminism and were active in leftist movements during the 1970s and early 1980s but subsequently abandoned both forms of activism and reintegrated themselves into the social system (Laviosa 2003b). In distancing herself from feminist discourse and notions of sexual difference, Archibugi indeed typifies a problematic phenomenon in contemporary society: the relinquishing of feminism as a political praxis in the name of an alleged equality. Yet her position needs to be set apart from what several feminist film scholars have recently identified as post-feminism.

Sarah Projansky argues that the various forms of post-feminism currently in place in contemporary society and culture place feminism within a historical trajectory and reflect the hegemonic repositioning of a western, white, middle-class élite of women, who benefit from the rights and privileges feminists once fought for (Projansky 2001: 68–70). Tania Modleski, in her book *Feminism Without Women: Culture and Criticism in a "Postfeminist" Age* (1991), provides a very similar definition of post-feminism. In her opinion, post-feminism dislocates femininity from the notion of difference with the purpose of reducing feminism to a theoretical approach connoted as 'gender studies' (Modleski 1991: 1–3). From this perspective, Modleski warns that postmodern culture's proposal of a universalistic subject actually reinstates male subjectivity as a normative model (ibid.: 6–7).

In many ways, Archibugi's attitude vis-à-vis feminism seems to coincide with Projansky and Modelski's definitions of post-feminism. However, Archibugi's work does not propound a linear view of feminism nor does it develop a revisionist discourse on feminism, based on the belief that women's equality has been achieved, sexual difference erased, and men have internalized the basic tenets of feminism. Quite the opposite, her films leave the issue of gender roles and identity politics open by featuring characters in a constant process of becoming, whose quests or problems do not find narrative closure. This is the case with most female characters in her films and, especially, with Stella, the protagonist of *Verso sera*, and Silvia, the mother in *L'albero delle pere*. These characters represent women of Archibugi's generation and, in particular, women who refuse to comply with societal rules. Although the ways in which Stella and Silvia express their resistance to established rules and systems lack political motivation and are based on problematic lifestyle choices, they nevertheless signal a refusal of social or ideological conformity.

On the outside, Stella's opinionated and self-assured attitude is a defence mechanism, one that she developed when she was young. Stella, in fact, comes from a working-class background and was raised by her mother in a desolate neighbourhood. Stella's father left her mother for another woman and chose to raise the children from his second marriage. In this respect, she is – as her father-in-law tells her during a conciliatory moment – a hard, rather than a strong person. During her brief cohabitation with Bruschi, Stella comes to appreciate the advantages of a more disciplined life yet ultimately rejects it and leaves. As she explains to her father-in-law, unlike him, she does not think that the world is confined within a house. Her gesture epitomizes that of many Italian women during the 1970s who refused to be confined within their domestic roles as wives and mothers. On her part, Silvia in *L'albero delle pere* is the epitome of a bad mother. A drug addict, she leaves her fourteen-year-old son, Siddhartha, alone most of the time and lets him take care of the house, causing innumerable problems with her family. Yet, as we infer from the film, her immature behaviour stems from an idealistic search for the freedom she was denied as a child. Like Stella, Silvia is a hopeless idealist who cannot adapt to a regular life and prefers to remain in an eternal state of childhood.

Another element that complicates connections between Archibugi's vision of the Italian family and post-feminist discourse is the fact that in Italy the private sphere and the family are intricately related to feminist discourse. As chapter 7 stresses, the Women's Movement in Italy developed through private networks and organizations (collectives, cultural associations, social centres, bookstores) that found a common denominator in psychoanalytically informed consciousness-raising groups, the *gruppi dell'inconscio* ('unconsciousness groups') (Bruno and Nadotti 1988: 10). Italian feminists' focus on the private translated into an ideological schism among feminist militants who partook in the 1968 protest or were involved in political parties and associations based on the double commitment to Marxism and feminism. This so-called 'dual militancy' formed an anti-institutional, separate type of political discourse and knowledge:

> Therein lies the peculiarity of the Italian situation. In Italy, the Women's Movement, just like the mode of discourse it has produced, has not engaged in a struggle to carve out a space for itself in the given institutions of knowledge [...] in the subtle play between power and knowledge, Italian feminism was strengthened by the force of inventiveness of its deviant, oppositional discourse, which seemed to make separation preferable to confrontation, negotiation with the institution, and possible compromise. By the same token, it was weakened by its own constant self-questioning. The preoccupation with self-analysis which characterised feminist process and strategy, and which was the strength of its form of discourse, was also the locus of its weakness. A political discourse underlined by a desire to break into the unconscious was found to disperse, leaving behind only the most solitary, secret, and individual traces. (Bruno and Nadotti 1988: 8)

The private dimension and the low impact on the public sphere was a constant feature in Italian feminism and formed the basis of its political platform and theory, the *'pensiero della differenza'* ('difference thought'). As Lucía Gómez Sánchez explains, the difference thought was a strand of Italian feminism that during the 1980s began to argue that women's 'failure to achieve in social life' was 'not a representation, or an ideology either,' but rather 'a real experience, anchored in women's bodies' (2006: 345). Since the 1980s, a decade that marks the end of the activist phase in the Women's Movement, Italian feminism further enhances its propensity for a personal and local approach to the social. Italian feminists' retreat into an inter-personal, domestic, and everyday dimension is also superseded by the tendency to withdraw into the private sphere dominant in the 1980s, what has been historically referred to as the *riflusso* ('reflux'). In this respect, women's return to the private sphere during the 1980s is linked both with feminist and post-feminist positions and involves a vast spectrum of gender relations.

The place of women in the family in Archibugi's films reflects this convergence of feminist and post-feminist politics in the private sphere: the female characters in the four films examined here exemplify the various ways in which old and new, traditional and modern, feminist and pre- or post-feminist notions of femininity coexist in the postmodern Italian family and reveal the tensions and the confrontations that ideological or generational differences underline with regard to women's positions in society. Archibugi's films propose personal, albeit never autobiographical, anti-judgmental views of the Italian family. This perspective is an outgrowth of Archibugi's own generation and even in the films set in the past, the characters' psychologies and problems recall those of the present moment.[20] In the predominantly heterosexual, domestic contexts of her films, men and women live in the aftermath of social movements and revolutionary processes (including the Women's Movement) that left many unresolved issues and unanswered questions.

In Archibugi's films, the position of women within the family is closely tied to class. A case in point is Mignon's relation to Giorgio Forbicioni's family in *Mignon è partita*. From the outset, Archibugi carefully delineates the social status of the Forbicionis. The film opens with a zoom into a magnified map of Rome closing in on an area that Giorgio's voice-over identifies as the Flaminio, the neighbourhood where the Forbicionis live. As Alessandra Levantesi specifies, the Flaminio is a 'once petty-bourgeois, now middle class' neighbourhood (Levantesi 1998: 107, my translation).[21] Archibugi contrasts the Forbicionis' social standing with that of Mignon, whose elegance and snooty attitude is a constant provocation, especially for Giorgio's sister, the down-to-earth and casually dressed Chiara.

From the point of view of class designation, one of the most interesting characters is Elvira, Bruschi's housekeeper in *Verso sera* (a role for which the actress, Zoe Incrocci, won David di Donatello and Nastro d'Argento awards). Elvira is an analphabetic woman in her sixties. She is a native of a rural area (probably from the countryside near Rome) and has been employed at Bruschi's house from a very young age and has never had a family of her own. She speaks a pidgin form of Italian, mixed with her native dialect and full of mistakes and neologisms, in part because she has never gone to school, in part because nobody has ever bothered correcting her (young Papere is the first to teach her to pronounce words properly). Elvira represents the subordinate condition of Italian women within the patriarchal family, an institution predominant until the end of World War II. These women would serve the male members of the family and take care of the house and children. More importantly, Elvira exemplifies the female condition typical of women in rural and underdeveloped areas of Italy, who would either be servants within their own houses, or be sent very young to work as servants for bourgeois and aristocratic families, where they would typically spend their whole lives.

Elvira seems to be happy at Bruschi's house; she not only takes the professor's side against the disrespectful Stella, but she is even more severe with the young woman than he is. Yet her contentment is only superficial. When she suspects that Stella is having an affair with her father-in-law, she becomes ill and has to lie in bed. In the scene that follows, one of the most comical and emblematic moments in the film, Stella visits Elvira in her room with Papere to clarify the misunderstanding. The three women start talking and, for the first time, Elvira complains about her subordinate condition and tells the story of her life as an exploited woman. When the professor finds them there and asks what's going on, Papere slyly explains that they are engaging in 'collective consciousness,' a humorous reference to the term connoting women's discussions in feminist collectives during the 1970s.

A crucial issue in Archibugi's treatment of women's roles within the family is the different meaning attached to the figure of the working mother. As the Italian sociologist Franca Bimbi stresses in a survey conducted on three generations of women during the twentieth century, the patriarchal model of the agrarian family was progressively supplanted by the urban model of the mononuclear family (1993: 149–65). This passage, notes Bimbi, raised questions about women's roles within the public and private spheres. Up until the 1970s, explains Bimbi, women working outside the family felt they had a 'dual role' (ibid.: 156). She explains:

They have in common their refusal to consider themselves 'family' women, their awareness of the necessity and the limits of emancipation through work, and their striving to reconcile various needs while maintaining their self-image as 'complete' and fulfilled women, at affective, professional, and public levels. (Ibid.: 156)

For Bimbi, one of the most significant achievements of feminism was the development of 'a different attitude towards work and familial authority' (ibid.: 160). On the one hand, work assumed a different meaning for women, in the sense that it helped improve the emotional climate in the family (ibid.: 161). On the other hand, with feminism, the family became a 'yardstick' for gender equality and inequality, where women would measure their position in society (ibid.: 161).[22]

In the four films here considered, women's self-realization outside the family through work seems to have no impact on the quality of their relationships with their relatives and bears no consequences on power relations within the house. Furthermore, the fact that these women don't work seems to be a choice, rather than an imposition, whether it stems from ideological convictions (Stella and possibly Silvia) or is a consequence of economic position (Pippi's mother and Silvia).

Women's decision to put family before work, without, however, abandoning their personal ideals, returns as a narrative motif in Archibugi's latest film, *Lezioni di volo*. In the film, Chiara (Giovanna Mezzogiorno), the protagonist, is an Italian doctor who works for a non-profit international organization, *Medecins sans Frontières*, devoting her time and energy to curing poor people in a remote village in India. Her total dedication to her work is at the origin of a crisis with her husband, a British man who works in Sri Lanka and would like her to go back to Europe with him and start a family. Chiara's reluctance provokes a marital crisis, during which she has a pressure-releasing fling with one of the two Italian teenagers who are visiting the region. In the end, Chiara opts for her family role: in the final scene, a visibly pregnant Chiara, now happily re-located in Scotland with her husband, sends a letter to the boy, in which she illustrates her new life.

The scarce importance attributed to women's professional achievements in Archibugi's films finds explanation in the film-maker's view of the family. Archibugi has often stressed that the changes in women's roles and responsibilities in the domestic and professional spheres are at the basis of her representation of the family. Flavia Laviosa once asked her about a declaration made in a previous interview, in which she had stated that feminism has eroded the family (Laviosa 2003a). In her reply, the film-maker broadened the scope of the issue, bringing in observations about the socio-anthropological modification of the Italian family since the beginning of the twentieth century:

Let's say that not only feminism, but the entire women's revolution in the 1900s, even before the feminist movement, has affected the family, starting when women came out of their homes and entered the work force. Some believe that this was the greatest anthropological revolution in the century, more important than the October Revolution, to give you an idea. It was a real change in life and in the social structure, I think. Let's say that the family, as an institution without love, as it still was in the 1800s, when people lived together, raised children and continued to live their lives without communicating, gradually lost reason to exist, thank heavens! (Archibugi 2003)

Archibugi's view of the family as a private institution, based first and foremost on two people's commitment to one another and to their children, explains the emphasis in her films on the emotional dimension of her characters, leaving sociological and political questions in the background.

Laviosa views Archibugi's rejection of gender-specific labels or positions in her work as the result of the film-maker's disillusionment with the political experience of the 1970s. She opines:

> Archibugi's cinema can be viewed as a critical reading of her experience as a political activist in both the feminist movement and the communist party. As a daughter of a generation involved in the women's movement and inheritor of the achievements of its battles, she uses her films to distance herself from political militancy, and avoid any associations with an overtly leftist ideology [...] Archibugi's political disillusionment makes her embrace a more civic and social militancy, as expressed in *Il grande cocomero* and *Domani*. (Laviosa 2003b)

Laviosa's reading is in accordance with Archibugi's personal standpoint and offers a valid interpretation of the post-ideological underpinnings of her films. However, this interpretation eschews the political dimension implicit in Archibugi's films, especially those representing the family. From this perspective, Archibugi's family films mark the film-maker's ideological repositioning vis-à-vis the social reality of her time, as well as her aesthetic and cultural alignment with the realist tradition of Italian cinema informing both her authorial approach to film-making and her authorial status. These films cast a different look into the microcosm and micro-politics of the family, bringing forward a private dimension of women's configuration in Italian society. With these films, Archibugi has demonstrated that family matters not only matter, they offer a critical alternative to dominant ideology reinforced by television sitcoms or *carino* films by attempting to establish new connections with film audiences, outside of mainstream circuits.

Patriarchal legacies, feminine appropriations

As Gian Piero Brunetta notes at the end of his aforementioned history of Italian cinema, starting from the second half of the 1980s, a small group of film-makers and screenwriters (among whom he includes Archibugi) restored a connection that had been long lost with the Italian film audience as well as the realist tradition of Italian cinema by reviving the art of storytelling and its ethical implications (1998: 519–24).

Some of Archibugi's films are strictly connected with literary and cinematic forms and texts generally associated with male-specific forms, namely the *bildungsroman*, the realist novel, and Italy's post-war realist cinema, which Flavia Laviosa identifies as follows:

Archibugi has developed her own formal model: a balance between the best literary tradition of the 1800s, and the great cinematic heritage of Neo-realism and the commedia all'italiana. She expresses her strong sense of belonging to the family of the Italian cinema by stating 'I see myself as the great-granddaughter of Neo-realism, the granddaughter of the commedia all'italiana, and the daughter of the new 1970s'. (Laviosa 2003b)

With regard to the bildungsroman, Archibugi's link with realist aesthetics will be examined in relation to Mignon è partita. Il grande cocomero, Verso sera, and Con gli occhi chiusi, which the film-maker adapted from a bildungsroman novel by the same title written by Federigo Tozzi and published in 1919. In relation to Italy's realist tradition, two films produced for Italian television networks will be discussed; Domani, a social drama produced by one of Italy's national television networks about the life of a small community that survived the devastating earthquake in the central region of Umbria in 1997; and the TV movie produced by the Berlusconian television network Canale 5, Renzo e Lucia, an adaptation of I promessi sposi, by Alessandro Manzoni, published in its final version in 1842.[23] The purpose is to demonstrate that these films by Archibugi pay homage to the aesthetic tradition from which they take inspiration yet also depart from it in ways that point to narrative and stylistic elements generally identified with women's cinema, namely the specific attention put on female characters, the focus on domestic settings, and the consideration of feminine agency and desire. These elements, not prominent in Archibugi's films, do not constitute intentional markers of gender-specific expression repressed by a dominant context of film production, but are instead self-reflexive representations of the fluctuating roles that women play both in the aesthetic tradition to which Archibugi claims allegiance and in the culture in which she partakes.

Alessandra Levantesi (1995, 1996 and 1998) and Flavia Laviosa (2003b and 2004), among others, have associated many of Archibugi's films with the 'bildungsroman,' also known as the coming-of-age novel. Alessandra Levantesi describes Archibugi's films as a 'neobildungsroman,' a term she coins to describe the re-emergence of a literary form that, according to Franco Moretti (1986), has been dead since the advent of modernism. Authors such as Joseph Conrad, Heinrich Mann, Robert Musil, Rainer Maria Rilke, Franz Kafka, and James Joyce all wrote coming-of-age novels in which 'the gap between individual and collective destiny becomes absolute' and no formation occurs in the end (Levantesi 1998: 108–09, my translation).[24] Quite the opposite, suggests Levantesi, in Archibugi's neobildungsroman narratives:

[the] characters are exactly committed to recovering within the devalued reality which surrounds them the models in which they are reflected and to re-create the premises upon which they can found their own maturation. And there's one thing to add: in this end-of-the-century glimpse at the fall of ideology and the subsequent refolding into private favour the flourishing of an artistic convention like the novel of formation, whose elected setting is the plane of everyday practice (ibid.: 109, my translation)[25]

Flavia Laviosa also places Archibugi within the tradition of the bildungsroman (2003b and 2004). In an article titled 'Francesca Archibugi: Families and Life Apprenticeship' (Laviosa

2004), she describes the films that Archibugi sets in family contexts as 'films of formation pedagogical films, or films charting an apprenticeship to life, in which young characters learn to grow' (ibid.: 224). She adds:

> The moment of a character's awakening always coincides with a form of separation, Archibugi signals these moments with symbolic and figuratively poetics scenes that round off a key phase in an individual's life and which also conclude her films. (Ibid.: 224)

The most obvious way in which the films by Archibugi based on *bildungsroman* narratives reveal gender-specific concerns is the prominent presence of female characters. Although only one of Archibugi's films structured according to the *bildungsroman* form features a female protagonist (*Il grande cocomero*), most of the films' female characters are not just represented (as in the classical *bildungsroman* literature) as part of the male protagonist's social milieu, but they live their own trajectories towards maturity. This is true of Silvia, who nevertheless remains fixed in the formative phase and dies before her coming-of-age process is completed, and is especially the case with the female protagonists of *Mignon è partita* and *Verso sera*.

As Levantesi notes, in *Mignon è partita*, both Giorgio and Mignon are figures derived from the *bildungsroman* tradition and both undergo a transformational experience (1998: 108–110). In the end, the same shadows are cast on the future of the two young protagonists (ibid.). In this respect, Levantesi concludes, the film's ending stands between those of the two intertextual *bildungsromans* embedded in the film: Charles Dickens's optimistic *Great Expectations*, a novel which both Giorgio and Mignon are, coincidentally, reading at the same time, and Roberto Rossellini's tragic film *Germania, anno zero/Germany, Year Zero* (1948), which Giorgio watches in a cine-club, taking inspiration from the young protagonist's suicide attempt to stage his own attempted suicide by ingesting some mothballs (ibid.: 109). Levantesi finds the same suspension in the ending of *Verso sera*, a film narrated in the form of a flashback through the voice-over of Professor Bruschi, who is the film's protagonist. In the beginning of the film, we see Bruschi writing a letter, in which he gives his opinion on events he has recently experienced and which are subsequently illustrated through flashbacks. The letter, written in 1977, is addressed to his granddaughter Papere, for her to open when she turns eighteen, that is, roughly at the time the film was made (1989). As Bruschi's voice-over repeats at the end of the film (set in an undetermined future) over the images of his abandoned house in front of which stands a 'for sale' sign, Bruschi has written the letter in the hope that Papere may understand things that neither he nor the girl's mother, Stella, were able to understand back in 1977. Levantesi argues that this ending implicitly interpellates the judgment of an omniscient spectator, aware of the ideological inadequacies and political defeats of both Bruschi and Stella's generations (1998: 111). Laviosa agrees with Levantesi's opinion that in *Verso sera* the 'achievement of maturity is seemingly less obvious' and that the film is unclear about whose formation is in question, whether it is Papere, Stella, or Bruschi's (Laviosa 2004: 224). From a gendered perspective, the indeterminacy about who is the subject of the coming-of-age narrative also displaces Bruschi's role as narrator and multiplies the film's narrative focus, ultimately delegating to an adult Papere the task of drawing conclusions about his and Stella's differing world-views. *Il grande cocomero* is the only film by Archibugi that places a female character at the centre of the *bildungsroman* story. As in *Mignon è partita* and *Verso sera*, the narrative is developed through two characters' parallel trajectories towards maturity, one female and one male. The film explores a typical motif in the film-maker's oeuvre, also present in *Mignon è partita* and *Verso sera*: the generational conflict between children and adults. Yet this film shifts the focus from the domestic to the public sphere, presenting the family as the place from which the two protagonists have moved away.

As mentioned in the previous section, film critics saluted Archibugi's abandonment of the family as a privileged setting and her treatment of a controversial topic in Italian society as signs of her transition to a more committed type of cinema. Indeed, many film reviews gave prominence to the discussion of the real person on whom Archibugi had based the character of the psychiatrist, Marco Lombardo Radice, a well-known figure in Italy's intellectual discourse, whose experiences with alternative mental treatments for children, published in a book in 1991, was a sensation in Italian public opinion.[26] Lietta Tornabuoni, an authoritative film critic who expressed many reservations about Archibugi's previous films, began her enthusiastic review of *Il grande cocomero* on the following note:

> It's still a barely emerging phenomenon, limited to few; some film-makers are reacting to the criminal degradation of the Italian reality, to the vulgar and melodramatic excitement of the media, to cinema's cynicism, by portraying as protagonists of a New Resistance (with the risk of falling into edification) ordinary people, honest and good, who, among endless difficulties, try to maintain respect for themselves, and respect for others. These film directors are Scola, Gianni Amelio, Ferreri, in his own way, and now Francesca Archibugi, with this beautiful, serious, moving, and amusing film; a true revelation (Tornabuoni 1993, my translation.)[27]

The emphasis that Tornabuoni and other film critics put on the film's social discourse undermines its continuity with Archibugi's ongoing discourse on the family and, in overlooking the *bildungsroman*-informed structure, downplays the gender politics implicit in the formative trajectory of the two protagonists. The film features twelve-year-old Pippi, who suffers from self-induced epileptic crises, and the middle-aged child psychiatrist, Arturo. Pippi and Arturo establish an unconventional relationship that defies typical professional relationships between patients and doctors. Pippi refuses to be treated as a patient yet finds in the hospital a substitute family, which enables her to become more social. Conversely, Arturo has no private life and spends long days and nights at the hospital, where he occasionally sleeps, even when not on shift duty. From this perspective, the trajectories that Arturo and Pippi take outside their professional and private homes, respectively, also free them from their respective problems with societal roles and expectations.

Another peculiar element in the relationship between Arturo and Pippi is that it does not conform to the age and gender roles with which they are both invested. Arturo is divorced from his wife, who is now happily remarried. When he gets a letter from her announcing that she has become a mother, we also learn the reason for their separation: Arturo had asked her to abort their baby years before because he was too worried about his career. He now bitterly regrets this decision, yet his rejection of fatherhood in the past as much as his present refusal of a love relationship indicate his fear of accepting his age and his masculinity and the responsibilities involved with both. From this perspective, Arturo's attachment to his work and his patients is compensation for his inability to assume another identity. Pippi also fits uncomfortably within her age group; mature and precocious, she often poses as a grown-up woman, with attitudes that disconcert Arturo. Pippi talks to him on an adult basis and even flirts with him. Although their relationship does not have any sexual implications, it certainly involves Freudian undertones and the process of Pippi's recovery epitomizes the psychological process characteristic of a girl undergoing sexual maturity, including an unresolved fascination with the father figure.

As previously illustrated, Italian film critics glossed over these themes, which further develop issues at the core of Archibugi's family-focused films. Instead, they concentrated on the social and extra-textual dimensions of *Il grande cocomero* – i.e. the problems in Italy's public health system and debates about the psychiatric treatment of children. The emphasis on the socio-political dimension of *Il grande cocomero* also helped situate Archibugi within the tradition of Italy's realist cinema.

In many ways, the enthusiastic reception of *Il grande cocomero* is in stark contrast with the negative attention that *Con gli occhi chiusi* received. *Con gli occhi chiusi* was Archibugi's adaptation of Tozzi's *bildungsroman* by the same title. Film audiences drastically rejected the film as being too difficult and austere, and film critics gave mixed reviews; some were perplexed by Archibugi's character development, judged to be too cerebral and detached (Levantesi 1998: 113; Adagio 1995: 119). Critics generally appreciated Archibugi's careful reconstruction of late-nineteenth-century/early-twentieth- century peasant life, inspired by painters of the period and vividly capturing the natural landscape of the Tuscany region (Adagio 1995: 119; Kezich 1994). Yet many of them perceived a strident contradiction between the modernist and the realist registers of the film (Adagio 1995: 119). In this respect, some reviewers put the blame less on Archibugi than on the difficult text she had chosen to bring to the screen (Kezich 1994; Levantesi 1998: 113). Critics struck a parallel between Archibugi's hybrid style and the novel's ambivalent status in Italian literature, which also reflects a more general misunderstanding of Tozzi's work. Tozzi's pre-modernist style and psychological character treatment were, in fact, overlooked for a long time because of the folkloric setting of his narratives, and for many years a conservative strand of Italian film critics erroneously identified him as an epigone of the nineteenth-century's *Verismo* ('realist') tradition (Adagio 1995: 118–19). Speculating on Archibugi's adaptation of *Con gli occhi chiusi*, Levantesi traces a series of elements that would make the novel 'congenial' to the film-maker's world, including the *bildungsroman* structure, its setting nearby Archibugi's home, and the relations among the characters. In the end, Levantesi can only suggest, 'Personally I believe that Archibugi has clashed with the obstacle of a text that, like all great texts, let itself be bent only up to a certain point, then it offers resistance' (1998: 113, my translation).[28]

In this respect, Archibugi's painstaking and unrewarding effort to stay faithful to Tozzi's novel (she wrote seven drafts of the screenplay) stands in striking contrast to her very loose approach to Manzoni's *I promessi sposi*, from which Archibugi adapted *Renzo e Lucia*. In the film of *Con gli occhi chiusi*, the female characters retain the same symbolic function as in Tozzi's novel; in *Renzo e Lucia*, the women lose the emblematic dimension they had in Manzoni's novel. The different ways in which Archibugi dealt with the adaptation of *Con gli occhi chiusi* and *I promessi sposi* bear important consequences for the gender politics underlying these two projects in terms of Archibugi's professional and authorial status in Italian cinema. Lurking beneath these different treatments are the different stakes involved in the making of the two films: on the one hand, a feature film meant for theatrical distribution and to establish a still young film-maker (Archibugi was barely 34 when she made *Con gli occhi chiusi*) within the male tradition of Italian realist cinema and modern literature; on the other hand, a TV film made by a consummate film-maker, meant for a vast mainstream audience yet with total artistic freedom on the part of the film-maker (the filming was completed before the contract with Canale 5 was signed).

With her treatment of *I promessi sposi*, Archibugi prevents any possible comparison with a previous TV adaptation of the same novel produced by the national television network RAI and directed by Sandro Bolchi in 1967. In this respect, she stands in opposition not only to Bolchi's faithful adaptation of Manzoni's masterpiece, but also to the anti-realistic, theatrical style and didactic approach to literature typical of Italian national television's adaptations of the 1960s, best exemplified by Bolchi's serial. About the liberties that she and her two co-writers took in their reading of *I promessi sposi*, Archibugi told journalists at a press conference for the TV movie:

> From such a deep and complex novel anybody could derive a film, foregrounding either the historical or the religious dimension. Our film is about interpersonal relations among the characters; evidently, we of course have not taken pages out from Manzoni's text, we have simply drawn our story from the novel, giving back their emotions to two eighteen-year-olds, Renzo and Lucia, and to the young aristocrat Don Rodrigo. (Archibugi 2004, my translation)[29]

Archibugi distanced her own adaptation from this canon of Italian literature by presenting intimate, psychologically realistic portrayals of interpersonal relations, one of the defining characteristics of her cinema. Indeed, many film critics viewed her take on the novel as a psychoanalytic interpretation of the main character's drives. As mentioned in the first part of this chapter, another much-praised aspect of *Renzo e Lucia* was the accurate and realistic reconstruction of seventeenth-century life, as evidenced particularly in the countryside scenes.

Yet, Archibugi exerted the most authorial control in the treatment of the female characters, especially the two female protagonists of *I promessi sposi*: Lucia, the betrothed, and the sinful Monaca di Monza (the nun from Monza). Archibugi's development of these two characters constitutes the most striking changes that she and her co-writers made to the original text. Archibugi gives amplitude to the story of Monaca di Monza (who in her film is impersonated with great efficacy by one of the most talented actresses of Italy's new cinema, Laura Morante) in a way very similar to the first version of the Manzoni novel, titled *Fermo e Lucia*. In that version, the account of the nun's tragic destiny took the dimensions of a novel-within-the-novel.

Her role was considerably reduced in the two subsequent versions of Manzoni's work. Virginia, the Monaca di Monza, is a beautiful and passionate woman forced to take orders because she is the cadet daughter of an aristocratic family and, like many women in her position, is obliged to join a cloistered order to assure a better dowry to her elder sister. Once in the convent, the nun starts an illicit relationship with her neighbour, a nobleman who lives next door to the convent. In Archibugi's TV movie (whose title recalls *Fermo e Lucia*), the screenwriter-director not only restored this character to its original importance, but developed elements that were not in Manzoni's final draft of the novel (e.g. the child the nun has with her lover, her final punishment). Most importantly, Archibugi enhanced the sensual and passionate aspects of the nun's personality.

Archibugi most drastically departed from Manzoni's work in her treatment of Lucia. To select Lucia, Archibugi went through a very long casting process and finally chose a sixteen-year-old high school girl who had never acted before (reminiscent of the casting of the adolescent Archibugi in the part of Ottilie for a TV movie version of Goethe's *Elective Affinities*). As Archibugi herself explained at a presentation of the film in a Roman high school:

> Lucia is a young girl who, vis-à-vis the attentions of this rich and powerful man, is obliged to ask herself some questions. On the one hand she has a handsome, charming and crazy man; on the other hand she has Renzo, who is capable of loving her and giving her emotional balance. Of the Manzonian Lucia I took out the divine side, linked with the concept of Providence. (Archibugi 2002, my translation)[30]

In Manzoni's novel, Lucia is the symbol of feminine virtuosity and Catholic faith; in Archibugi's TV movie, she is a young peasant with a strong personality and a righteous sense of duty. Whereas *I promessi sposi*'s Lucia is an instrument of God, a creature whose faith allows her to overcome all obstacles, in the TV movie she is a pragmatic and resourceful person. In *Renzo e Lucia*, Lucia is attached to her people and her community: she prefers the humble and honest Renzo because he gives her stability, to the beautiful and tormented aristocrat Rodrigo, because the latter does not belong in her world. The most striking discrepancy between the modest character in Manzoni's novel and the Lucia in Archibugi's TV movie is the latter's assertiveness and desire. A shy, virginal creature in the novel, terrified by the attentions of the bully Don Rodrigo, in Archibugi's film she is an adolescent who is discovering her sensuality and her effect on men. Flattered by Rodrigo's courtship, she is not indifferent to his good looks; as she confesses to her spiritual mentor, Fra' Cristoforo, when Rodrigo first started looking at her, she 'looked back.' Rather than being frightened, she is intrigued by Rodrigo's twisted personality and wants to help him become a better person. At the same time, she is capable of using his weakness for her mission to save some fellow peasants from being hanged for having hidden produce on his property to survive the famine.

In his discussion of the 'fifth generation' of Italian film-makers (which coincides with Archibugi's generation), Pierre Sorlin argues that many of them drew inspiration from television's forms and styles, characterized by factuality and immediacy (1996: 156). He identifies a prototype for this aesthetic in two films made through Italy's national television: Michelangelo Antonioni's

Identificazione di una donna/Identification of a Woman (1982) and Ermanno Olmi's *L'albero degli zoccoli/The Tree of the Wooden Clogs* (1978), although both film-makers' styles are considered to be antithetical to the realist tradition(ibid.: 156–57). According to Sorlin, the informality of the first film and the documentary quality of the second 'help delineate the main characteristics of television-style films' (ibid.: 157). These elements include a weak narrative structure focusing on community rather than the individual, documentary-like treatment of peoples' concerns and activities, and a preference for episodic, scattered narratives that do not require strong involvement or participation on the part of the film spectator (ibid.: 157–59). This comment well applies to Archibugi's films, including those made for television.

With *Domani*, Archibugi tackles the social drama. Using a choral narrative structure, the film is about a rural community devastated by the earthquake that took place in Umbria in 1997. With this film, she confronts an important strand in Italy's post-war realist cinema: the socio-political film based on contemporary historical events. Many Italian film-makers classified within the category of post-neo-realist cinema specialized in this type of film, including the Taviani brothers, Francesco Rosi, Ermanno Olmi (Archibugi's mentor), and Gianni Amelio to name a few. Significantly, since the 1970s, Italy's national television networks produced many of their films, as was the case with *Domani*. *Domani* exhibits many of the television-inspired characteristics that Sorlin recognizes in films made during the 1980s by, among others, Gianni Amelio, Nanni Moretti, and Ettore Scola (ibid.). The documentary-style film intertwines the stories of people whose domestic routines and social relations are altered by the earthquake. Yet in this film, Archibugi also develops a more intimate and personal approach to the individual characters, once again putting family and interpersonal relations at the centre of the narrative.

Three main sub-plots compose *Domani*'s narrative. The first is related to the vice-deputy mayor's family, whose apparent unity is put to the test by the arrival of two interlopers, a young gay man and his elderly, sick mother, who descend upon the family's small trailer, causing friction in the household. Husband and wife grow more and more distant from each other while their two adolescent sons begin to misbehave and disrespect them. The wife becomes friendly with the young man, sympathizing with his worries about his terminally ill mother. Suspecting that their mother is having an extra-marital affair, her youngest son becomes more and more hostile towards her. The second sub-plot focuses on the town's schoolteacher, a woman disillusioned by love after a series of failed relationships. However, her faith is restored when she falls for an art restorer, an Englishman hired on to repair the damages to an important fresco by Beato Angelico. Incidentally, upon his arrival, the art restorer grows increasingly distant from his wife, whose sole purpose in the marriage is to have a baby, causing them to eventually separate. The third narrative strand in *Domani* follows the deterioration of a friendship between two young girls from different social classes. Vale is the only daughter of an industrialist whose sausage factory has provided work for the community for generations; Tina comes from a working-class family whose reality is very different from that of her friend's. The earthquake serves to draw out their class differences but without any resolution. At the end of the film, Vale will be relocated to the city with her wealthy family, while Tina must remain in the destroyed village. Significantly, Archibugi ends the film with an epilogue set a year after the event in which Tina's voice-over comments on the situation. The fact that she and her family are still living in the same housing project is a bitter commentary on the Italian government's chronic delays in natural disaster intervention.

In *Domani*, Archibugi filters the socio-political discourse through the experiences of individual characters whose points of view serve to condemn and expose the government's inadequacy in handling crisis situations. An exemplary scene in this respect is the villagers' protest against the minister's visit (played by Paolo Taviani), whose presence is primarily motivated by his concern over the restoration of the fresco by Beato Angelico instead of housing reconstruction. About this episode and the film's discreet approach to social and political issues, Flavia Laviosa comments:

> *Domani* is never rhetorical and it is animated by a moderate polemic spirit. For example, in the episode where the minister visits the town, he seems to be more concerned with the restoration of damaged art works than with people's living conditions, but Archibugi never overdoes it. Both in *Il grande cocomero* and *Domani*, her tone is not over critical towards the state run infrastructures and public administrators, because she prefers to address political issues as an integral part of family relationships and community problems. (Laviosa 2003b)

In this respect, *Domani* is another remarkable contribution to Archibugi's oeuvre. The film-maker appropriately describes the film as a 'human comedy' that finds its natural milieu in families and small communities.

The authorial tradition to which Archibugi and the 1980s generation of film-makers belong is configured within a realist tradition encompassing literary and cinematic models. Indeed, although Archibugi does not consider her work from a traditionally auteur-oriented point of view, she does identify herself within the tradition of world narrative cinema and literature, which she mainly identifies with male authors. This book suggests that film authorship in post-war European national cinemas is over determined by nationally specific modes of film production and reception. In Italy, the concept of film authorship presents some similarities with the model proposed by the *politique des auteurs*, that of a film director with a unique world-view and an original style. Yet the figure of the film author in contemporary cinema has multifarious connotations and a complex genealogy, which includes Italy's romantic and idealistic currents in aesthetic and literary theory as well as the radical shift to Marxist-oriented aesthetics in the 1950s, influenced by Antonio Gramsci's writings about the role of intellectuals in society ([1949] 1971). These discussions conveyed the polemics around the popular development of neo-realism and re-emerged in the 1970s re-conceptualization of neo-realism in Italian film discourse, which prompted film theorists to consider the traditional opposition between Gramscian theory and neo-realist cinema's practice and theory in a new light.[31]

In Italian film discourse, the figure of the author is associated with different film modes and aesthetics, from neo-realist cinema (Roberto Rossellini) to the post-neo-realist art film-makers (Luchino Visconti, Michelangelo Antonioni, Federico Fellini) and post-neo-realist film directors (Ermanno Olmi, the Taviani brothers, Liliana Cavani), to the 1960s political film-maker (Franco

Rosi).[32] The neo-realist film-maker is the blueprint for the new authorial film practices emerging in Italian cinema since the 1980s. The film historian Gian Piero Brunetta situates a strand of the film-makers who made their débuts in feature film-making during the 1980s within this tradition. In his aforementioned chapter on the 1980s generation which closes his four-volume history of Italian cinema, he divides the decade into two phases, one which he connotes as 'chaotic, transitional, dissipating energy' and one (in which he also places Archibugi) which he views a growth, a move towards 'a (partially successful) attempt to conquer the sense of a new generational identity' (1998: 521, my translation).[33] In the second phase, he explains:

> While the early 1980s was characterised by a sort of amnesic state vis-à-vis the cinema of the past, one of the most conspicuous novelties of the recent débuts is the effort to suture ties with the tradition of our cinema, assuming precise points of reference and re-elaborating a series of linguistic, thematic and contextual elements that belong to that patrimony. (Brunetta 1998: 521, my translation)[34]

Brunetta's commentary subsumes his view of neo-realism as an underlying thread in Italy's authorial cinema since the end of World War II, a perspective that also informs Millicent Marcus' *Italian Film in the Light of Neo-realism* (1986). He first locates the neo-realist legacy in a cinematic '*coiné*' (lingua franca) used by a group of film authors (Pier Paolo Pasolini, Marco Ferreri, Elio Petri, Ermanno Olmi, Vittorio De Seta, Damiano Damiani, Gianfranco De Bosio, Lina Wertmüller, Paolo and Vittorio Taviani) who emerged during the 1960s (Brunetta 1998: 177). Since the 1960s, he argues, the neo-realist patrimony has been dispersed and three generations of film authors have been claiming its legacy, to varying degrees (ibid.: 198). He recognizes as the 'legitimate beneficiaries' of this patrimony, besides the film-makers mentioned above, Francesco Rosi, Florestano Vancini, and Valerio Zurlini (ibid.).

Realist literature and cinema constitute the models in which Archibugi inserts herself and which has informed the critical reception of her work from an authorial perspective. Most of the commentaries on Archibugi's work by Italian and international film critics (some of which appear in previous sections of this chapter) identify her ability in handling characters and situations with realistic and precise strokes. They praise her capacity to render the vividness of everyday situations, achieved, on the one hand, through a meticulous work on the script, trying to create round-off characters and situations; on the other hand, through an inconspicuous use of the camera and a subordination of technical and formal bravura to the circumstances of the *mise-en-scène* on the set. Italian and often foreign film critics attribute these skills to Archibugi's formation.

Arguably, Archibugi has a stronghold in this authorial patrimony: she excels in a storytelling that gives prominence to situations and characters close to people's daily reality and adopts a filming style that adheres to this type of narrative, enhancing spontaneity on the part of the actors. Furthermore, her authorship is certified by her apprenticeship at the school of the great masters of realist cinema, including Olmi, Scarpelli and her teachers at the Centro Sperimentale di Cinematografia.

Francesca Archibugi's alignment with a national tradition of realist cinema and literature sets the premises for the film-maker's recognition as a film author within national and international contexts of film reception. Her pre-established association with this tradition establishes discursive and aesthetic parameters that overlook the gender-relevant aspects of her work. This type of reception confirms the gender-blind orientation of auteur-informed film discourse. Yet Archibugi's alignment with this tradition also points to an assertive strategy of self-positioning by a film-maker for whom feminism is less a political stance than an over-determined element of everyday reality.

Notes

1. The Age-Scarpelli team (Age is a pseudonym for Agenore Incrocci) wrote, among others, several scripts for the famous comic Totó, including *Il vedovo allegro* (1949) and *Totò sceicco* (1950), both directed by Mario Mattoli. The team worked with the most important film directors specializing in the *commedia all'italiana* such as Mario Monicelli, Dino Risi, Ettore Scola, Alberto Lattuada, Pietro Germi, and Luigi Comencini. Some of the films they wrote include *I soliti ignoti/Big Deal on Madonna Street* (Mario Monicelli, 1958) and La grande guerra/*The Great War* (Mario Monicelli, 1959), *La marcia su Roma/ The March on Rome* (Dino Risi, 1962) and *I mostri /Opiate '67* (Dino Risi, 1963), *C'eravamo tanto amati/We All Loved Each Other So Much* (Ettore Scola, 1974) and *La terrazza/The Terrace* (Ettore Scola, 1980), *Tutti a casa/Everybody Go Home* (Luigi Comencini, 1960), *Mafioso* (Alberto Lattuada, 1962), and *Sedotta e abbandonata/Seduced and Abandoned* (Pietro Germi, 1963).

2. This is the case, for example, with Alessia Fugardi, Lara Pranzoni, and Niccoló Senni, who each featured in two films by Archibugi.

3. Papere is a nickname, which translates as 'goslings.' Papere refers to herself in the plural, including her imaginary friend. The little girl's real name is Mescalina, inspired by a poisonous mushroom near which she was conceived.

4. Some of the most authoritative Italian film critics published negative reviews of the film in Italian newspapers. Lietta Tornabuoni (1993) in *La Stampa* opines that the film is too talkative and the characters too schematic, not allowing for identification on the part of the viewer. Gian Luigi Rondi in *Il Tempo* echoes her, judging the film as too verbose and the structure as uneven. Only Giovanni Grazzini in *Il Messaggero* is more positive about the film, praising its ability to move the spectator, although he finds the second part of the film fragmented (both excerpts are available at: http://it. movies.yahoo.com/v/verso-sera/recensioni-128608.html).

5. See, for instance, the reviews written by some of Italy's most prominent critics, including Tullio Kezich (*Corriere della Sera*, 23 December 1994), Morando Morandini (*Il Giorno*, 23 December 1994), and Lietta Tornabuoni (*La Stampa*, 23 December 1994).

6. Laviosa derives Magrelli's comment on the 'carino' cinema from Vito Zagarrio's report in *Cinema italiano anni novanta* (1998). She also cites article by Antonio Vitti titled 'Un profilo dell'identità del nuovo cinema italiano tra crisi, televisione e omologazione culturale' (literally 'A profile of new Italian cinema's identity between crisis, television, and cultural homologation') (Vitti 2003).

7. The talk is quoted in Vito Zagarrio's book on 1990s Italian cinema (Zagarrio 1998: 12–13). As I illustrate in chapter 4, with regard to Gabriele Salvatores's relation to Italy's new cinema, Magrelli's negative take on 1980s Italian cinema was quite widespread among Italian film critics at the time.

8. '[…] un' «estetica ombelicale», una forma degradata di «esistenzialismo». The punctuation is the same as in the original text.

9. '[...] la «carineria» degli anni ottanta nasconde l'afasia, piú che storie si vedono tante Polaroid, dei video familiari, delle foto scolastiche in cui una generazione si mette in posa.' The punctuation is the same as in the original text.

10. 'Si colgono frammenti di commedia all'italiana metabolizzati da Moretti, Archibugi, Mazzacurati, Piccioni, Luchetti, ecc.'

11. Levantesi's articles on Archibugi here cited are listed in the bibliography. The book mentioned in the body of the text is A. Levantesi (ed.), *Francesca Archibugi*, Roma, Alphabet, 1996.

12. 'In un cinema nuovo italiano che oscillava fra narcisismo e confusione, astrazioni intellettualistiche e velleitarismo, una cosí concreta e puntuale dichiarazione d'intenti appariva inusuale [...] La sconosciuta cineasta si permetteva il gesto trasgressivo di presentare due ex sassantottini, ovvero la generazione degli "eterni figli", nelle inedite vesti di genitori trasmigrati dall'ideologia a un crepuscolarismo esistenziale piccolo borghese: lui libraio, scrittore fallito e dongiovanni da strapazzo, lei moglie e mamma rassegnata all'infelicitá matrimoniale come le nonne.'

13. '[...] una delle poche autentiche rivelazioni degli anni ottanta [...].'

14. '[...] la storia rientra nella corrente minimalista, ma ha la capacitá di saper mostrare le dinamiche delle fasi decisive dell'esistenza, con la sicurezza di un autore affermato [...] Colpisce la nettezza con cui la regista sceglie le inquadrature senza compiacimenti, l'eleganza con cui subordina la sua cultura cinematografia all'esigenza di cogliere dei momenti di veritá negli sguardi dei suoi personaggi, la sua sicurezza nel raccontare le difficoltá nel rapporto tra generazioni diverse.'

15. '[...] una leva di nuovi autori che hanno preso nettamente il posto dei vecchi maestri.'

16. Laviosa quotes O'Healy's comment in her aforementioned article (O'Healy 1999).

17. I am referring to the feminist reading of Dorothy Arzner's oeuvre, including Cook (1988), Johnston (1988), and Mayne (1990 and 1994), as well as Bruno's examination of Elvira Notari, the Naples-based film-maker/producer from the 1920s (Bruno 1993). For more discussions on female film authorship, see Bean and Negra (2002: 15-16; 27-138), Maule (2005: 9-20), and Rabinovitz (2005: 21-34).

18. A comprehensive list of references on this literature is too long to be included here. Essential readings include, besides those mentioned in the bibliography about the woman's film and the melodrama: Doane, M. A., *The Desire to Desire: The Woman's Film of the 1940s.* (Bloomington, In.: Indiana University, 1987); Byars, J., *All that Hollywood Allows: Re-reading Gender in 1950s Melodrama.* (Chapel Hill, NC: University of North Carolina Press, 1991). About maternal melodrama, see the debate between E. Ann Kaplan and Linda Williams on King Vidor's *Stella Dallas* (1937), reprinted in many feminist anthologies: E. A. Kaplan, 'The Case of the Missing Mother: Maternal Issues in Vidor's *Stella Dallas*' and L. Williams, '"Something Else Besides a Mother" *Stella Dallas* and Maternal Melodrama,' both in Erens, P. (ed.), *Issues in Feminist Film Criticism.* (Bloomington, Ill. and Indianapolis, In.: Indiana University Press, 1990, pp. 126-36; 137-62); and E. A. Kaplan, *Motherhood and Representation: The Mother in Popular Culture and Melodrama.* (New York: Routledge, 1992).

19. I will return to this point further on in this chapter.

20. I'll further discuss this point in relation to her two literary adaptations, *Con gli occhi chiusi* and *Renzo e Lucia*, the former set at the turn of the twentieth century, and the latter in the seventeenth century.

21. '[...] un tempo piccolob orghese ora medio agiato' (the typo is in the original text).

22. Bimbi bases her article on two research studies in which she participated: 1) an oral history project developed with other scholars in the rural town of Conegliano, in the province of Treviso, situated in

the north-eastern region of Veneto; and 2) a survey conducted among four hundred women between the ages of twenty and fifty in two provinces of Veneto (Verona and Padua) in the mid-1980s (Bimbi 1993: 150–51). On changes in the Italian family, see also the aforementioned Zanatta (1997).

23. The TV movie's title recalls the first version of the novel, published in 1821, as *Fermo e Lucia*.

24. '[...] la discrepanza fra destino individuale e collettivo si fa assoluta.'

25. '[i] personaggi siano impegnati proprio a ritrovare nella realtá svalorizzata che li cicrconda modelli in cui potersi rispecchiare, e ricreare le premesse su cui fondare la propria maturazione. C'è da aggiungere una cosa: in questo scorcio di secolo la caduta dell'ideologia e il conseguente ripiegamento nel privato favoriscono il rifiorire di una convenzione artistica come il romanzo di formazione che ha per luogo elettivo il piano della pratica quotidiana.' Levantesi also wrote an earlier article about the use of the *bildungsroman* in Francesca Archibugi's films (1995).

26. The book's title is *Una concretissima utopia* (1991), which translated, *A very concrete Utopia*. Lombardo Radice, who died in 1989, only thirty-nine years old, when he was young had written, in collaboration with a friend, the feminist journalist Lidia Ravera, another scandalous book, *Porci con le ali* (1977), an autobiographical account of two adolescsents' sexual experiences in the years of the student protests.

27. 'È un fenomeno ancora appena accennato, limitato a pochi: alla degradazione delinquenziale della realtà italiana, all'eccitazione melodrammatica e volgare dei media, al cinismo dello scherno, alcuni registi reagiscono raccontando come protagonisti d'una Nuova Resistenza (e con tutti i rischi dell'edificazione) gente comune onesta, brava, che tra infinite difficoltà cerca testardamente di far bene il proprio lavoro, di conservare il rispetto di sé e l'affetto per gli altri. Sono Scola, Gianni Amelio, Ferreri alla sua maniera, a esso Francesca Archibugi con questo film bello e serio, commovente e divertente: un'autentica rivelazione.'

28. 'Personalmente penso che l'Archibugi si sia scontrata contro l'ostacolo di un testo che, come tutti i grandi testi, si fa piegare fino a un certo punto, poi oppone resistenza.'

29. 'Da un romanzo così profondo e complesso chiunque potrebbe trarne un film, mettendo in evidenza il lato storico piuttosto che il lato religioso. Il nostro è un film di relazioni interpersonali tra i personaggi; resta inteso che ovviamente non abbiamo strappato le pagine del testo di Manzoni, noi abbiamo semplicemente desunto dal romanzo la nostra storia, restituendo ai due diciottenni, Renzo e Lucia, e al giovane signorotto don Rodrigo, le loro emozioni.'

30. 'Lucia è una ragazzina che di fronte alle attenzioni di questo signore ricco e potente è costretta a porsi degli interrogativi. Da una parte ha un uomo bello, affascinante e pazzo e dall'altra Renzo, capace di amare e di darle un equilibrio sentimentale.

31. The literature on this topic is too vast to be considered here. For an essential overview of the relation between Italian cinema and Italian aesthetic theory, see Dalle Vacche (1992) and Brunetta (1998). On the relations between Italian aesthetics and neo-realism, see Miccichè (1975); Cannella (1973); Marcus (1986: 3–29); specifically in the relation between Gramscian theories and neo-realism, see Abruzzese (1975) and Chemotti (1975).

32. On the various typologies of Italian authors in Italian cinema, see also Gieri (1995).

33. 'caotica, di transizione, di dissipazione di forze [...] tentativo (in parte riuscito) di conquista del senso di una nuova identità generazionale.'

34. 'Mentre i primi anni ottanta erano caratterizzati da una sorta di stato amnesico nei confronti del cinema del passato «una delle novità piú vistose degli esordi recenti è data dallo sforzo di riannodare i legami con la tradizione del nostro cinema, assumendo precisi punti di riferimento e rielaborando

una serie di elementi linguistici, tematici e ambientali che appartengono a tale patrimonio.' The punctuation is the same as in the original text. The quoted passage comes from an article by the Italian film scholar Leonardo Quaresima (1992: 35).

References

Abruzzese, A. 1975. Per una nuova definizione del rapporto politica-cultura. (In Micciché, L., (ed.). Il neo-realismo cinematografico italiano. Venezia: Marsilio, pp. 31–60.)

Adagio, C. 1995. Con gli occhi chiusi. Cinema nuovo, XLIV, 1–2: 118–120, gennaio-aprile.

Archibugi, F. 2002. Francesca Archibugi. Renzo e Lucia in chiave illuminista. Nano, C (interviewer). Cinecittà News. [Online.] Available: http://news.cinecitta.com/people/intervista.asp?id=503.

—. 2003. Conversations: Italian Director Francesca Archibugi Talks to Flavia Laviosa. Kinema. [Online.] Available: http://www.kinema.uwaterloo.ca/lavi2-032.htm.

—. 2004. Renzo e Lucia nuova versione. La Archibugi rilegge Manzoni, Interview. La Repubblica. [Online.] Available: http://www.repubblica.it/2004/a/sezioni/spettacoli_e_cultura/renzoelucia/renzoelucia/renzoelucia.html.

Bean, J., Negra, D. (eds). 2002. A Feminist Reader in Early Cinema. Durham: Duke University Press.

Bimbi, F. 1993. Three Generations of Women: Transformations of Female Identity Models in Italy. (In Cicioni, M. and Prinster, N. (eds). Visions and Revisions: Women in Italian Culture. Providence, RI/Oxford, UK: Berg, pp. 149–165.)

Bondanella, P. 1993. Italian Cinema: From Neo-realism to the Present. New York: Frederick Ungar-Continuum.

Brooks, P. 1976. The Melodramatic Imagination: Balzac, Henry James, Melodrama and the Mode of Excess. New Haven: Yale University Press.

Brunetta, G. P. 1998. Storia del cinema italiano. Dal miracolo economico agli anni novanta. 1963–1993. Roma: Editori Riuniti.

—. 2004b. Gli intellettuali e il cinema. Milano: Bruno Mondadori.

Bruno, G. and Nadotti, M. (eds). 1988. Women and Film in Italy. New York and London: Routledge.

Bruno, G. 1993. Streetwalking on a Ruined Map: Cultural Theory and the City Films of Elvira Notari. Princeton, NJ: Princeton University Press.

Cannella, M. 1973. Ideology and Aesthetic Hypotheses in the Criticism of Neo-Realism. Screen, 73–74: 5–60.

Chemotti, S. 1975. La problematica gramsciana e la questione del neo-realismo. (In Micciché, L. (ed.). Il neo-realismo cinematografico italiano. Venezia: Marsilio, pp. 61–66.)

Cook, P. 1988. Approaching the Work of Dorothy Arzner. (In Penley, C. (ed.). Feminism and Film Theory. New York, NY and London, UK: Routledge, pp. 46–56.)

De Lauretis, T. 1987. Technologies of Gender: Essays on Theory, Film, and Fiction. Bloomington and Indianapolis: Indiana University Press.

Dalle Vacche, A. 1992. The Body in the Mirror: Shapes of History in Italian Cinema. Princeton, NJ: Princeton University Press.

Doane, M. A. 1987. The 'Woman's Film': Possession and Address. (In Gledhill, C. (ed.). Home is Where the Heart Is: Studies in Melodrama and the Woman's Film. London: BFI, pp. 283–98.)

—. 1990. Film and the Masquerade: Theorising the Female Spectator. (In Erens, P. (ed.). Issues in Feminist Film Criticism. Bloomington, Ill. and Indianapolis, In.: Indiana University Press, pp. 41–57.)

—. 1991. Masquerade Reconsidered: Further Thoughts on the Female Spectator. (*In* Doane, M. A. *Femmes Fatales: Feminism, Film Theory, Psychoanalysis*. New York and London: Routledge, pp. 33–43.)

Flitterman-Lewis, S. 1996. *To Desire Differently: Feminism and the French Cinema*. Urbana and Chicago: University of Illinois Press.

Gaines, J.M. 2002. Of Cabbages and Authors. (*In* Bean, J.M. and Negra, D. (eds). *A Feminist Reader in Early Cinema*. Durham: Duke University Press, pp. 88–118.)

Gieri, M. 1995. *Contemporary Italian Film-making: Strategies of Subversion. Pirandello, Fellini, Scola and the Directors of the New Generation*. Toronto,/Buffalo,/London: University of Toronto Press.

Gledhill, C. (ed.). 1987. *Home is Where the Heart Is: Studies in Melodrama and the Woman's Film*. London: BFI.

Gomez Sanchez, L. 2006. Redefining the Boundaries between Body and Discourse: Experience, Subjectivity and Politics in the Italian Feminist Movement. *European Journal of Women's Studies*. [Online.] Available: http://ejw.sagepub.com DOI: 10.1177/1350506806068653.

Gramsci, A. 1971. The Intellectuals. (*In* Q. Hoare, Q. and G. Nowell-Smith, G. (trans. and eds). *Selections from the Prison Notebooks*. New York: International Publishers, pp. 3–23.)

Grignaffini, G. 1988. Female Identity and Italian Cinema of the 1950s. (*In* Bruno, G. and Nadotti, M., (eds). *Women and Film in Italy*. New York and London: Routledge, pp. 11–123.)

Johnston, C. 1988. Critical Strategies. (*In* Penley, C., (ed.). *Feminism and Film Theory*. New York/London: Routledge/BFI, pp. 36–56.)

Kuhn, A. 1982. *Women's Pictures: Feminism and Cinema*. New York and London: Routledge and Kegan Paul.

—. 1990. Textual Politics. (*In* Erens, P. (ed.). *Issues in Feminist Film Criticism*. Bloomington, Ill. and Indianapolis, In.: University of Indiana Press, pp. 250–67.)

Landy, M. 2000. *Italian Film*. Cambridge, Mass.: Cambridge University Press.

Laviosa, F. 2003a. Intervista con Francesca Archibugi. La famiglia post-moderna nella sua firma d'autore. (*In* Vitti, A., (ed.). *Incontri con il cinema italiano*. Caltanisetta: Sciascia Editore, pp. 375–386.)

—. 2003b. Themes and Motifs in the Cinema of Francesca Archibugi. *Kinema*. [Online.] Available: http://www.kinema.uwaterloo.ca/lavi2-032.htm.

—. 2004. Life Apprenticeship in Francesca Archibugi's Cinema. (*In* Everett W., Hope W. and Goodbody A., (eds). *Italian Cinema: New Directions*. Oxford-Bern: Peter Lang, pp. 201–27.)

Levantesi, A. 1995. Il neo-bildungsroman di Francesca Archibugi. (*In* Brugiamolini, F., Gabelli, S. and Capelli, L. (eds). *Le donne riprendono l'infanzia ovvero regie al femminile e maternitá da Jane Campion a Francesca Archibugi*. Roma: Dino Audino Editore, pp. 29–45.)

—, (ed.). 1996. *Francesca Archibugi*, Roma: Alphabet.

—. 1998. Padri, figli e nipoti: il cinema di Francesca Archibugi. (*In* Miccichè, L. (ed.). *Schermi opachi. Il cinema italiano degli anni '80*. Venezia: Marsilio, pp. 107–15.)

Marcus, M. 1986. *Italian Film in the Light of Neo-Realism*. Princeton, NJ: Princeton University Press.

Marrone, G. 1999a. Il nuovo cinema italiano: pregiudizi, realtá e promesse. (In Marrone, G. (ed.). *New Landscapes in Contemporary Italian Cinema*. 17: 7–13).

—. 1999b. *New Landscapes in Contemporary Italian Cinema*. 17.

Maule, R. 2005b. Présentation. *Femmes et cinéma muet: nouvelles problématiques, nouvelles methodologies*. Spec. issue of *Cinémas*. 16(1): 9–20, Fall.

Mayne, J. 1990. *The Woman at the Keyhole: Feminism and Women's Cinema*. Bloomington: Indiana University Press.

—. 1994. *Directed By Dorothy Arzner*. Bloomington, Ill. and Indiana, In.: Indiana University Press.

Mellencamp, P. 1995a. *A Fine Romance...: Five Ages of Film Feminism*. Philadelphia, PA: Temple University Press.

—. 1995b. Il neo-bildungsroman di Francesca Archibugi. (*In* Brugiamolini, F. Gabelli, S. and Capelli, L., (eds). *Le donne riprendono l'infanzia ovvero regie al femminile e maternitá da Jane Campion a Francesca Archibugi*. Roma: Dino Audino Editore, pp. 29-45.)

Modleski, T. 1991. *Feminism Without Women: Culture and Criticism in a "Postfeminist" Age*. New York: Routledge.

Moretti, F. 1994. *Opere mondo*. Torino: Einaudi.

Mulvey, L. 2000. Visual Pleasure and Narrative Cinema. (*In* Kaplan, E. A. (ed.). *Feminism and Film*. Oxford, UK: Oxford University Press, pp. 34-47.)

O'healy, À. 1999. Are the Children Watching Us? The Roman Films of Francesca Archibugi. (*In* Marrone, G. (ed.). *New Landscapes in Contemporary Italian Cinema*. Annali d'Italianistica 17, pp. 121-36.)

Passerini, L. 1993. The Women's Movement in Italy and the Events of 1968. (*In* Cicioni, M. and Prinster, N. (eds). *Visions and Revisions: Women in Italian Culture*. Providence, RI/Oxford, UK: Berg, pp. 167-82.)

Quaresima, L. 1992. Non è carino. *Cinema & Cinema*, Spec. Issue, XVIII(62): 32-35, settembre-dicembre.

Rabinovitz, L. 2005 Past Imperfect: Feminism and Social Histories of Silent Film. *Femmes et cinéma muet: nouvelles problématiques, nouvelles methodologies*. Spec. issue of *Cinémas* 16(1): 21-34, Fall.

Sesti, M. (ed.). 1994. *Nuovo cinema italiano. Gli autori I film e le idee*. Roma and Napoli: Theoria.

—. 1995. Non sono bambini, sono persone di pochi anni. (*In* Proto, C. (ed.). *Francesca Archibugi*. Roma: Dino Audino, pp. 10-14.)

Sorlin, P. 1996. *Italian National Cinema, 1896-1996*. London and New York: Routledge.

Tornabuoni, L. 1993. Il grande cocomero, Review. *La Stampa*. [Online.] Available: http://www.mymovies.it/dizionario/critica.asp?id=5244.

Vitti, A. 2003. Un profilo dell'identità del nuovo cinema italiano tra crisi, televisione e omologazione culturale. (*In* Morosini, R. and Vitti, A. (eds). *In Search of Italia*. Pesaro: Metauro Edizioni, pp. 235-56.)

Zagarrio, V. 1998b. *Cinema italiano anni novanta*. Venezia: Marsilio Editori.

Zanatta, A. L. 1997. *Le nuove famiglie*. Bologna: Il Mulino.

CONCLUSION

The purpose of this book was to delineate the notion of authorship in relation to the multifaceted components and different players of the contemporary audio-visual system and culture, as well as with respect to some of the theoretical directions that have emerged in film discourse during the past twenty years. As stressed in the Introduction, the geo-political delimitations are justified by the premise that the figure of the author is mainly the expression of nationally over-determined film practices and discourses. However, in highlighting the sociocultural specificity of author cinema in the three national contexts here considered, this study does not intend to gloss over the global dimension of cinema. Quite the opposite, the relative and provisional nature of this perspective is inherent in the book's central contention: that since the 1980s the practices and discourses associated with author cinema in Western European countries represent different strategies for addressing the global development of the audio-visual industry. By this token, while in examining the reception and discursive frames related to the concept of film authorship, emphasis was put on national film traditions and sociocultural contexts, significant attention was given to the international circuits of film reception in which the notion of authorship circulates.

The historical delimitation underlying this work is based on the belief that the film author is still operative as a film mode and as a promotional strategy for a median and fluctuant sector of the film market. A study on the author as a sociology-of-production in specific contexts illuminates the ideological, economic, and aesthetic parameters and interests that maintain this category in place. The overall purpose is to suggest that although the concept of the film author might not constitute a viable theoretical or critical methodology, it remains a crucial standpoint from which to address some phenomena and issues at the core of cinema today.

BIBLIOGRAPHY

A new golden age of Spanish cinema is in the works. [Online.] Available: http://www.filmfestivals.com/cannes_2000/market/europe_worldwide.htm.

Inchiesta: il cinema italiano e gli anni '90. 1990/1991. *Cinecritica*, XIV(19–20): 56–74, ottobre /marzo. Historia del feminismo en España. [Online.] Available: http://www.fmujeresprogresistas.org/feminismo4.htm.

1989. *Per una nuova critica: i convegni pesaresi 1965–1967*. Venezia: Marsilio Editori. Pratica economica e pratica politica. Questionario. 1984. *Filmcritica*, 343–344: 136–58.

ABRUZZESE, A. 1975. Per una nuova definizione del rapporto politica-cultura. (*In* Micciché, L. (ed.). *Il neorealismo cinematografico italiano*. Venezia: Marsilio, pp. 31–60.)

ADAGIO, C. 1995. Con gli occhi chiusi. *Cinema Nuovo*, XLIV, 1–2: 118–120, gennaio-aprile.

ALEMANNO, R. 1993. Segnali di fumo. Per una verifica della crisi. Teoria e prassi di politica cinematografica. Roma: Edizioni Associate.

ALEXANDER, M. 1994. A Gaul in Hollywood. *Variety*, 356.10: 10, October.

ANDREW, D. 1993. The Unauthorized Auteur Today. (*In* Collins, J., Radner, H. and Preacher Collins, A. (eds). *Film Theory Goes to the Movies*. New York-London: Routledge, pp. 77–85.)

AMELIO, G. 1994. Autoritratto. (*In* Sesti, M. (ed.). *Nuovo cinema italiano. Gli autori, i film, le idee*. Roma-Napoli: Teoria, pp. 37–43.)

AMENÁBAR, A. 1996. Entrevista. *Plano Corto*, 11: 3–7.

——. 2001. *The Others: Guióon cinematográfico original*. Madrid: Punto de lectura.

AMIEL, M. and RABOUDIN, D. 1979. Entretien avec Maurice Pialat. *Cinéma*, 250: 60–64.

AMITRANO, A. 1998. *El cortometraje en España: Una larga historia de ficciones breves*. Valencia: Filmoteca Generalitat Valenciana.

ANCIAN, A. 2002. Claire Denis: An Interview. Pruks, I. (trans.). *Senses of Cinema*. [Online.] Available: http://www.sensesofcinema.com/contents/02/23/denis_interview.html.

ANDREW, D. [1978] 1990. *André Bazin*. New York and Oxford: Columbia University Press.

——. 1993. The Unauthorized Auteur Today. (*In* Collins, J., Radner, H. and Preacher Collins, A. (eds). *Film Theory Goes to the Movies*. New York-London: Routledge, pp. 77–85.)

APRÁ, A. and TURIGLIATTO, R. (eds). 1996. *Giovinezza del cinema francese*. Venezia : Marsilio.

ARCHIBUGI, F. 2002. Francesca Archibugi. Renzo e Lucia in chiave illuminista. Nano, C. (interviewer). *Cinecittà News*. [Online.] Available: http://news.cinecitta.com/people/intervista.asp?id=503.

——. 2003. Conversations: Italian Director Francesca Archibugi Talks to Flavia Laviosa. *Kinema*. [Online.] Available: http://www.kinema.uwaterloo.ca/lavi2-032.htm.

——. 2004. *Renzo e Lucia* nuova versione. La Archibugi rilegge Manzoni, Interview. *La Repubblica*. [Online.] Available:

http://www.repubblica.it/2004/a/sezioni/spettacoli_e_cultura/renzoelucia/renzoelucia/renzoelucia.html.

ARGENTIERI, M. 1995. Cinema italiano: una grave crisi strutturale. *Cinemasessanta*, 1: 4–8, gennaio/febbraio.

AROCENA, C. 1996. *Víctor Erice*. Madrid: Cátedra.

ASSAYAS, O. 1980a. SPFX news (1ère partie): ou situation du cinéma de science-fiction envisagé en tant que secteur de pointe. *Cahiers du Cinéma*, 315: 19–27, septembre.

—. 1980b. SPFX news (2ème partie): ou situation du cinéma de science-fiction envisagé en tant que secteur de pointe. *Cahiers du Cinéma*, 316: 36–40, octobre.

—. 1980c. SPFX news (3ème partie): ou situation du cinéma de science-fiction envisagé en tant que secteur de pointe. *Cahiers du Cinéma*, 317: 22–33, novembre.

—. 1980d. SPFX news (suite et fin): ou situation du cinéma de science-fiction envisagé en tant que secteur de pointe. *Cahiers du Cinéma*, 318: 34–40, décembre.

—. 1981a. Jean-Pierre Mocky: le malentendu. *Cahiers du Cinéma. Situation du cinéma français I*, 323–324: 95, mai.

—. 1981b. George Lucas: un cinéma conceptuel. *Cahiers du Cinéma*, 328: 24–26, octobre. ó et al. 1982a. *Cahiers du CinÈma. Made in USA*, 334–335: avril.

—. 1982b. Un auteur-artisan. *Cahiers du Cinéma*, 336: 30;32, mai.

—. 1982c. Entretien avec Jean-Pierre Mocky. *Cahiers du Cinéma*, 336: 31;33, mai.

—. LE PÉRON, S. and TOUBIANA, S. 1982d. Entretien avec John Carpenter. *Cahiers du cinéma*, 339: 15–23, septembre.

—. 1983a. Sur une politique. *Cahiers du Cinéma. Cinéma d'auteur: la côte d'alerte*, 353: 22–25, novembre.

—. 1983b. Eastwood in the country. *Cahiers du Cinéma. Cinéma d'auteur: la côte d'alerte*, 353: 56–57, novembre.

— and TESSON, C. 1984. Hong Kong Cinema. Paris: *Cahiers du Cinéma*, 360–361, septembre.

— and TESSON, C. 1985. Le sourire "off": entretien avec Clint Eastwood. *Cahiers du Cinéma*, 368: 22–29, février.

—. 1985. Du scénario achevé au scénario ouvert. *Cahiers du Cinéma*, 371–2: 7–8, mai.

—. 1986. L'émotion pure: entretien avec Olivier Assayas. *Cahiers du Cinéma*, 389: 8–11, novembre.

— and BJÖRKMAN, S. 1990. *Conversations avec Bergman*. Paris: Cahiers du cinéma.

—. 1999a. Le passé devait trouver sa place au coeur de ma vision du cinéma. Entretien avec Olivier Assayas. *Cahiers du Cinéma*, 548: 35–41.

—. 1999b. *Fin août, début septembre*. Paris: Petite bibliothèque des Cahiers du cinéma.

—. 1999c. *Kenneth Anger: vraie et fausse magie au cinéma*. Paris: Cahiers du cinéma, Collection Auteurs.

— and FIESCHI, J. 2000. *Les destinées sentimentales*. Scénario d'après le roman de Jacques Chardonne. Paris: Petite bibliothèque des Cahiers du cinéma.

—. 2001. Cassavetes, Posthumously. (*In* Charity, T. (ed.). *John Cassavetes: Lifeworks*. London: Omnibus Press, pp. 199–203.)

—. 2003. Préface. (*In* JOUSSE, T. *Pendant les travaux, le cinéma reste ouvert*. Paris: Cahiers du cinéma.)

—. 2004. Personal interview. Paris: 20 and 29 December.

—. 2005a. 'Pour moi, la vérité est dans le geste.' Interview with Olivier Assayas by Thomas Sotinel. *Le Monde*. [Online.] Available: http://www.lemonde.fr/cgibin/ACHATS/acheter.cgi?offre=ARCHIVES&type_item=ART_ARCH_30J&objet_id=911806.

—. 2005b. *Une adolescence dans l'après-mai. Lettre à Alice Debord*. Paris: Cahiers du cinéma.

AUBERT, J-P. 2002. Quand le cinéma espagnol assume sa promotion. Étude de la page web d'Abre los ojos. (*In* Berthier, N. (ed.). *Penser le cinéma espagnol (1975–2000)*. Lyon: GRIMH/GRIMIA, Université Lumière-Lyon 2, pp. 131–42.)

AUBRON, H. 2006. Angel-A. *Cahiers du Cinéma*, 608: 42, January.

AUDÉ, F. 1981. *Ciné-modèles cinéma d'elles: situations de femmes dans le cinéma francais 1965–1979*. Paris: L'Âge d'Homme.

—. 1987. 'Werther.' Rev. of *Werther*, dir. Pilar Miró. *Positif*, 322: 78, décembre.

—. 1990. S'en fout la vie (S'en fout la mort). *Positif*, 356: 70–72, octobre.

AUMONT, J. and MARIE, M. 1988. *L'analyse des films*. Paris: Nathan.

AUMONT, J. 1989. *L'oeil interminable. Cinéma et peinture*. Paris: Librairie Séguier.

AUSTIN, G. 1996. *Contemporary French Cinema: An Introduction*. Manchester and London: Manchester University Press.

BALIO, T. 1998. The art film market in the new Hollywood. (*In* Nowell-Smith G. and Ricci, S. (eds). *Hollywood and Europe: Economics, Culture, National Identity: 1945–95*. London: BFI, pp. 63–73.)

BAZIN, A. 1971. *What is Cinema?* Gray, H. (trans. and ed.). Berkeley, Los Angeles and London: University of California Press.

BEAN, J., and NEGRA, D. (eds). 2002. *A Feminist Reader in Early Cinema*. Durham: Duke University Press: 14–16; 27–138.

BECK, J. 2000. Mediating the Transnational in Contemporary Spanish Cinema: Pedro Almodóvar and Julio Medem. *Lugares Sin Limites: Cinema of the 80s and 90s in Latin America, Spain, and Portugal*. (*In* Guízar Álvarez, E. and Brígido Corachán, A. (eds). *Torre de Papel*, Spec. Issue 10.1: 134–69, Spring.)

BENAVENT, F. M. 2000. *Cine español de los noventa*. Bilbao: Ediciones Mensajero.

BENVENISTE, É. 1980. *Le vocabulaire des institutions indo-éuropéennes: Pouvoir, droit, religion*. Paris: Édition de Minuit.

BERGALA, A., NARBONI, J. and TOUBIANA, S. 1983. Le chaudron de la création: Entretien avec Maurice Pialat. *Cahiers du Cinéma*, 354: 11–18, décembre.

BERGALA, A. 1983. Maurice Pialat, le marginal du centre. *Cahiers du Cinéma*, 354: 20–21, décembre.

—. 2006. Erice-Kiarostami: The Pathways of Creation. Hammond, P. (trans.). *Rouge*. [Online.] Available: http://www.rouge.coom.au/9/erice-kiarostami.html.

BERTHIER, N. 2002. Voir ou ne pas voir: la fonction du hors-champ dans Tesis (Alejandro Amenábar). (*In* Berthier, N., (ed.). *Penser le cinéma espagnol (1975–2000)*. Lyon: GRIMH/GRIMIA, Université Lumière-Lyon 2: 119–30.)

BESSON, L. 2001. Le plus grand défi de Luc Besson: entretien avec Jean-Pierre Lavoignant et Christophe d'Yvoire. *Studio Magazine*, 169: 72–83.

—. 2002. Je n'ai plus peur: entretien avec Lionel Cartégini et Olivier de Bruyin. *Première*, 300: 92–7.

—. 2003. Le système B: entretien avec Aurélien Ferenczi. *Télérama*, 2781: 32–6, 30 April.

—. 2006. Interview Luc Besson. *Première*. [Online.] Available: http://www.premiere.fr/premiere/magazine-et-exclus/interviews/interview-lucbesson/(affichage)/interviewPage/(interview_id)/410269/(interviewPage_question)/9.

—. 2007. Press Conference. Montreal: Hotel Sofitel, 5 January.

BEUGNET, M. 2004. *Claire Denis*. Manchester and New York: Manchester University Press.

BIMBI, F. 1993. Three Generations of Women: Transformations of Female Identity Models in Italy. (*In* Cicioni, M. and Prinster, N. (eds). *Visions and Revisions: Women in Italian Culture*. Providence, RI/Oxford, UK: Berg, pp. 149–165.)

BOLLAÍN, I. 2003. Cine con tetas. *Duoda*, 24: 83–88.

BONDANELLA, P. 1993. *Italian Cinema: From Neorealism to the Present*. New York: Frederick Ungar-Continuum.

BONDY, J-A. 1997. Le cinquième élément. *Première*, 244: 35, juin.

BONITZER, P. 1983. C'est vous qui êtes tristes. *Cahiers du Cinéma*, 354: 6–10, décembre.

BONO, P. and KEMP, S. (eds). 1991. *Italian Feminist Thought: A Reader*. Cambridge, Mass.: Basil Blackwell.

BORAU, J. L. 1999. Prologue: The Long March of the Spanish Cinema towards Itself. (*In* Evans, P. W. (ed.). *Spanish Cinema: The Auteurist Tradition*. Oxford and New York: Oxford University Press, pp. xvii–xxii.)

BORDWELL, D. 1985. *Narration in the Fiction Film*. Madison, WI: University of Wisconsin Press.

BOSCHI, A. and MANZOLI, G. (eds). 1995. *Oltre l'autore I*. Fotogenia, 2.

BOUQUET, S. 1999. Les Temps modernes. *Cahiers du Cinéma*, 548: 32–34.

—. 2000. La hiérarchie des anges. *Cahiers du Cinéma*, 545: 48–49, avril.

BROOKS, P. 1976. *The Melodramatic Imagination: Balzac, Henry James, Melodrama and the Mode of Excess*. New Haven: Yale University Press.

BRUNETTA, G. P. 1998. *Storia del cinema italiano. Dal miracolo economico agli anni novanta. 1963–1993*. Roma: Editori Riuniti.

—. 2004a. *Cent'anni di cinema italiano.* Bari-Roma: Laterza.

—. 2004b. *Gli intellettuali e il cinema.* Milano: Bruno Mondadori.

BRUNO, G. and NADOTTI, M. (eds). 1988. *Women and Film in Italy.* New York and London: Routledge.

BRUNO, G. 1993. *Streetwalking on a Ruined Map: Cultural Theory and the City Films of Elvira Notari.* Princeton: Princeton University Press.

BUCKLEY, C. 2002. Alejandro Amenábar's Tesis: Art, Commerce and Renewal in Spanish Cinema. *Post Script,* 21(2): 12–25, Winter-Spring.

BURKE, S. 1992. *Death and Return of the Author: Criticism and Subjectivity in Barthes, Foucault and Derrida.* Edinburgh: Edinburgh University Press.

BUTLER, A. 1994. The Politics of Location as Transnational Feminist Practice. (In Grewal I. and Kaplan, C. (eds). *Scattered Hegemonies. Postmodernity and Transnational Feminist Practices.* Minneapolis, MN: University of Minnesota Press, pp. 137–52.)

—. 2000. *Women's Cinema: The Contested Screen.* London and New York: Wallflower Press.

CANNELLA, M. 1973. Ideology and Aesthetic Hypotheses in the Criticism of Neo-Realism. *Screen,* 73–74: 5–60.

CANOVA, G. 1996. *Sulle tracce del cinema di Gabriele Salvatores.* Milano: Zelig.

CARRÈRE, E. and SINEUX, M. 1984. Entretien avec Maurice Pialat. *Positif,* 275: 4–11, janvier.

CASETTI, F. 1998. Gabriele Salvatores, o del cinema impuro. (In Micciché, L. (ed.). *Schermi opachi: il cinema italiano degli anni '80.* Venezia: Marsilo, pp. 156–63.)

CAUGHIE, J. (ed.). 1981. *Theories of Authorship.* London and New York: Routledge and Kegan Paul.

CAVANI, L. 1999. Piccoli e grandi schermi: il cinema in televisione. Intervista a cura di Gaetana Marrone. (In: MARRONE, G. (ed.). *New Landscapes in Contemporary Italian Cinema.* 17, pp. 247–52.)

CÉLESTIN, R., DALMOLIN, E. and DE COURTIVRON, I. 2003. *Beyond French Feminisms: Debates on Women, Politics, and Culture in France, 1981–2001.* New York, NY: Palgrave Macmillan.

CHEMOTTI, S. 1975. La problematica gramsciana e la questione del neo-realismo. (In Micciché, L. (ed.). *Il neo-realismo cinematografico italiano.* Venezia: Marsilio, pp. 61–66.)

CHOLLET, L. 2004. *Les situationnistes: l'utopie incarnée.* Paris: Gallimard.

CLOVER, C. J. 1992. *Men, Women, and Chain Saw.* Princeton, N.J.: Princeton University Press.

COB, A. A. 2002. Contracampo y el cine español, Otrocampo. [Online.] Available: http://www.otrocampo.com.

COOK, P. 1988. Approaching the Work of Dorothy Arzner. (In Penley, C. (ed.). *Feminism and Film Theory.* New York, NY and London, UK: Routledge, pp. 46–56.)

CORRIGAN, T. 1991. *A Cinema without Walls: Movies and Culture after Vietnam.* New Brunswick, New Jersey: Rutgers University Press, pp. 101–36.

CROFTS, S. 1993. Reconceptualizing national cinemas. *Quarterly Review of Film and Video,* 14(3): 49–68.

—. 1998a. Authorship and Hollywood. (In Hill, J. and Church Gibson P. (eds). *The Oxford Guide to Film Studies.* Oxford: Oxford University Press, pp. 310–24.)

—. 1998b. Concepts of National Cinema. (In Hill, J. and Church Gibson P. (eds). *The Oxford Guide to Film Studies.* Oxford: Oxford University Press, pp. 385–94.)

DALLE VACCHE, A. 1992. *The Body in the Mirror: Shapes of History in Italian Cinema.* Princeton, NJ: Princeton University Press.

DARKE, C. 1993. Rupture, Continuity and Diversification: Cahiers du Cinéma in the 1980s. *Screen,* 34.4: 362–79.

—. 2000. Desire Is Violence. *Sight and Sound,* 10(7): 16–18, July.

DE BAECQUE, A. 1991. *Histoire d'une revue. Tome 1: Les Cahiers à l'assaut du cinéma: 1951–1959.* Paris: Cahiers du cinéma.

—. 1998. *La nouvelle vague: portrait d'une jeunesse.* Paris: Flammarion.

—. 2003. *La Cinéphilie: Invention d'un regard, histoire d'une culture. 1944–1968.* Paris: Fayard.

DEBORD, G. 1992. *La société du spectacle.* Paris: Gallimard.

DE GRAZIA, V. 1998. European cinema and the idea of Europe: 1925–95. (In Nowell-Smith G. and Ricci, S. (eds). *Hollywood and Europe: Economics, Culture, National Identity: 1945–95.* London: BFI, pp. 19–33.)

DE LAURETIS, T. 1987. *Technologies of Gender: Essays on Theory, Film, and Fiction.* Bloomington and Indianapolis: Indiana University Press.

DELEUZE, G. 1981. *Francis Bacon: logique de la sensation* (2 vols.). Paris: Editions du Seuil.

—. 1986. *Cinema 1: The Movement-Image*. [1983] Tomlinson, H. and Galeta, R. (trans). Minneapolis: University of Minnesota Press.

— and Guattari, F. 1987. *A Thousand Plateaus: Capitalism and Schizophrenia*. [1980] Massumi, B. (trans. and forewords). Minneapolis, MN and London: University of Minnesota Press.

—. 1989. *Cinema 2: The Time Image*. [1985]. Tomlinson, H. and Galeta, R. (trans). Minneapolis: University of Minnesota Press.

— and Guattari, F. 1994. *What Is Philosophy?* [1991] Tomlinson, H. and Graham Burchell, G. (trans). New York: Columbia UP.

DENIS, C. 1994. J'ai pas sommeil. Entretien aven Claire Denis. Jousse, T and Strauss, F. (interviewers). *Cahiers du Cinéma*, 479–80: 25–30, mai.

—. 2000a. Je me reconnais dans le cinéma qui fait confiance à la narration

plastique: Entretien avec Claire Denis. Lalanne, J-M. and Larcher, J. (interviewers). *Cahiers du Cinéma*, 545: 50–53, avril.

—. 2000b. Claire Denis Interviewed by Jonathan Romney. *Guardian Unlimited*. [Online.] Available: http://film.guardian.co.uk/interview/interviewpages/0,,338784,00.html.

— and K. Jones. 2003. Audio commentary. *Friday Night*, DVD, Wellspring.

DEL RIO, E. 2003. Performing the Narrative of Seduction: Claire Denis' *Beau travail* (*Good Work*, 1999). *Kinoeye: New Perspectives on European Film*, 3(7). [Online.] Available: http://www.kinoeye.org/03/07/delrio07.php.

DIBIE, J-N. 1993. *Aid for Cinematographic and Audio-visual Production in Europe*. London: John Libbey.

D'LUGO, M. 1991a. Catalan Cinema: Historical Experience and Cinematic Practice. *Quarterly Review of Film and Video*, 13 (1–3): 131–46.

—. 1991b. Almodóvar's City of Desire. *Quarterly Review of Film and Video* 13.4: 47–66.

DOANE, M. A. 1987. The 'Woman's Film': Possession and Address. (*In* Gledhill, C. (ed.) *Home is Where the Heart Is: Studies in Melodrama and the Woman's Film*. London: BFI, pp. 283–98.)

—. 1990. Film and the Masquerade: Theorising the Female Spectator. (*In* Erens, P. (ed.). *Issues in Feminist Film Criticism*. Bloomington, Ill. and Indianapolis, In.: Indiana University Press, pp. 41–57.)

—. 1991. Masquerade Reconsidered: Further Thoughts on the Female Spectator. (*In* Doane, M. A. *Femmes Fatales: Feminism, Film Theory, Psychoanalysis*. New York and London: Routledge, pp. 33–43.)

DUFRENNE, M. and FORMAGGIO, D. 1981. *Trattato di estetica. Volume 1*. Milano: Mondadori.

DUROVICOVÁ, N. 1994. Some Thoughts at an Intersection. *Velvet Light Trap*, 34: 3–9.

EHRLICH, L. C. 2000. *An Open Window: The cinema of Víctor Erice*. Lanham, MD: Scarecrow Press.

—. 2006. Letters to the World. Erice-Kiarostami: Correspondences. Curated by Alain Bergala and Jordi Balló. *Senses of cinema*, 41. [Online.] Available: http://www.sensesofcinema.com/contents/06/41/erice-kiarostami-correspondences.html#3.

ELSAESSER, T. 1989. *New German Cinema: A History*. New Brunswick, NJ: Rutgers University Press.

— and HOFFMAN, K. (eds). 1998. *Cinema Futures: Cain, Abel, or Cable?* Amsterdam: Amsterdam University Press.

ESPINOSA, J. G. 2000. Por un cine imperfecto. (*In* Stam, R. and Miller, T. (eds) *Film Theory: An Anthology*. Malden Mass.: Blackwell Publishing, pp. 287–97.)

ESQUENAZI, J.-P. (ed.). 2002. *Politique des auteurs et théories du cinéma*. Paris: L'Harmattan.

EVANS, P. W. (ed.). 1999. *Spanish Cinema: The Auteurist Tradition*. Oxford: Oxford University Press.

FACCHINARO D. 1997. *Territori di fuga. Il cinema di Gabriele Salvatores*. Alessandria: Falsopiano.

FANON, F. 1961. *Les damnés de la terre*. Paris: François Maspero.

FERENCZI, A. 2003. Sa petite entreprise ne connaît pas la crise. *Télérama*, 2781: 36–9, 30 April.

FERNANDEZ-SANTOS, A. 1983. Treinta y tres preguntas eruditas sobre "El Sur." *Casablanca*, 31–32: 55–58, julio/agosto.

FIDDIAN, R. W. and EVANS, P. W. (eds). 1988. *Challenges to Authority: Fiction and Film in Contemporary Spain*. London: Tamesis Books Limited.

FIESCHI, J. 1983. Tourner avec Pialat. *Cinématographe*, 94: 188–89, novembre.

FINNEY, Angus. *The State of European Cinema: A New Dose of Reality*. London: Cassel, 1996.

FLITTERMAN-LEWIS, S. 1996. *To Desire Differently: Feminism and the French Cinema*. Urbana: University of Illinois Press.

FOFI, G. 1994. *Amelio secondo il cinema: conversazione con Goffredo Fofi*. Roma: Donzelli.

FORMISANO, D. 1996. Il grande imbroglio. Produzione e finanziamento nel cinema italiano degli anni Novanta. (In Sesti, M. (ed.). *La 'scuola' italiana: storia, strutture e immaginario di un altro cinema (1988–1996)*. Venezia: Marsilio, pp. 203–11.)

FORNARA, B. and SIGNORELLI, A. (eds). 1995. *Olivier Assayas*. Bergamo Film Meeting '95 (exhibition catalogue).

FOUCAULT, M. 1981. What Is an Author? [1969] (In CAUGHIE, J. (ed.). *Theories of Authorship*. London and New York: Routledge, pp. 282–91.)

FRODON, J.-M. 2001. Il s'agit de s'aventurer au-devant d'une forme. *Le Monde*: 3, 11 July.

—. 2004. Où vas-tu, Emily? *Cahiers du Cinéma*, 593 (septembre): 22–24.

GAINES, J. M. 2002. Of Cabbages and Authors. (In Bean, J. M. and Negra, D. (eds). *A Feminist Reader in Early Cinema*. Durham: Duke University Press, pp. 88–118.)

GARBARZ, F. 1997. *Nénette et Boni*: Mère, pouquoi nous as-tu abandonnés ? *Positif*, 432: 38–39, février.

—. 2001. Alejandro Amenábar: jouer avec les projections mentales du spectateur. *Positif*, 491: 15–20, janvier.

GAUT, B. 1997. Film Authorship and Collaboration. (In Allen, R. and Smith, M. (eds), *Film Theory and Philosophy*, Oxford: Oxford UP, pp. 149–72).

GENZLINGER, N. 2007. The Human and the Animated, Shrunk to Size. *The New York Times*. (January 12). [Online.] Available:
http://movies2.nytimes.com/2007/01/12/movies/12art.html.

GERSTNER, D. and STAIGER, J. (eds). 2003. *Authorship and Film*. New York: Routledge.

GIERI, M. 1995. *Contemporary Italian Film-making: Strategies of Subversion. Pirandello, Fellini, Scola, and the Directors of the New Generation*. Toronto: University of Toronto Press.

GILI, J. A. 1988. Entretien avec Claire Denis sur *Chocolat*. *Positif*, 328: 14–16, juin.

GIRARD, R. 1977. *Violence and the Sacred*. [1972] Trans. P. Gregory, Baltimore, MD and London, Johns Hopkins University Press.

GLEDHILL, C. (ed.). 1987. *Home is Where the Heart Is: Studies in Melodrama and the Woman's Film*. London: BFI.

GOLDSCHMIDT, D. and TONNETERRE, J. 1983. Entretien avec Maurice Pialat. *Cinématographe*, 94: 3–7, novembre.

GOMEZ SANCHEZ, L. 2006. Redefining the Boundaries between Body and Discourse: Experience, Subjectivity and Politics in the Italian Feminist Movement. *European Journal of Women's Studies*. [Online.] Available: http://ejw.sagepub.com DOI : 10.1177/1350506806068653.

GOODRIDGE, M. and WILSON, V. 2005. In a White Room. *Sight and Sound*, 15(3): 6, March.

GRAMSCI, A. 1971. The Intellectuals. (In Q. Hoare, Q. and G. Nowell-Smith, G. (trans and eds). *Selections from the Prison Notebooks*. New York: International Publishers, pp. 3–23.)

GRANT, C. 2002. Recognizing Billy Budd in Beau Travail: Epistemology and Hermeneutics of an Auteurist 'Free' Adaptation. *Screen*, 43(1): 57–73.

GREWAL, I. and KAPLAN, C. (eds). 1994. *Scattered Hegemonies. Postmodernity and Transnational Feminist Practices*. Minneapolis, MN: University of Minnesota Press.

GRIGNAFFINI, G. 1988. Female Identity and Italian Cinema of the 1950s. (In Bruno, G. and Nadotti, M. (eds). *Women and Film in Italy*. New York and London: Routledge, pp. 11–123.)

GROSSBERG, L. 1988. Putting the Pop Back into Postmodernism. (In ROSS, A. (ed.). *Universal Abandon?: The Politics of Postmodernism*. Minneapolis: University of Minnesota Press: 167–190).

GUERIN, M-A. 2001. Catho hanté: *Les Autres* d'Alejandro Amenábar. *Cahiers du Cinéma*, 563: 81–82, décembre.

GUICHARD, L. 2004. Besson un peu débouté. *Télérama*, 2857: 26 October.

HALIMI, G. 2004. A Deceptive Universalism. (In Oliver, K. and Walsh, L. (eds). *Contemporary French Feminism*. Oxford and New York: Oxford University Press, pp. 31–39.)

HAWKINS, J. 1999. Sleaze Mania, Euro-trash, and High Art: The Place of European Art Films in American Low Culture. *Film Quarterly*, 53(2): 14–29, Winter 1999–2000.

HAYWARD, S. 1993a. *French National Cinema*. London and New York: Routledge.

—. 1993b. State, Culture, and the Cinema: Jack Lang's Strategies for the French Film Industry. *Screen*, 34(4): 380-91.

— and VINCENDEAU, G. (eds). 1990. *French Film: Texts and Contexts*. London: Routledge.

—. 1998. *Luc Besson*. Manchester: Manchester University Press.

—. 2001. Claire Denis' Films and the Post-colonial Body – with special

reference to *Beau travail* (1999). *Studies in French Cinema*, 1(3): 159-65.

HELLER, S. 2000. Playing Soldier. *American Prospect*, 7(14): 42-43. June 5.

HENNEBELLE, G. and PRÉDAL, R. (eds). 1987. L'influence de la télévision sur le cinéma. *CinémAction*, 44.

HEREDERO, C. F. 1999. Cine español: nueva generacion. *Dirigido*: 49-67, abril.

HEWITT, N. (ed.). 1989. *The Culture of Reconstruction: European Literature, Thought, and Film, 1945-50*. New York: St. Martin's Press.

HIGGINBOTHAM, V. 1988. *Spanish Film Under Franco*. Austin: University of Texas Press.

HILLIER, J. (ed.). 1985. *Cahiers du Cinéma. Volume 1: The 1950s, Neorealism, Hollywood, the New Wave*. London: RKP/BFI.

HOPEWELL, J. 1986. *Out of the Past: Spanish Cinema after Franco*. London: BFI.

—. 1991. Art and a Lack of Money: The Crises of the Spanish Film Industry: 1977-1990.

Quarterly Review of Film and Video, 14 (4): 113-122.

HUTCHEON, L. 1989. *The Politics of Postmodernism*. London and New York: Routledge.

ILOTT, T. 1996. *Budgets and Markets: A Study of the Budgeting of European Film*. London and New York: Routledge.

JÄCKEL, A. 1996. European co-production strategies: the case of France and Britain. (*In* Moran A. (ed.). *Film Policy: International, National, and Regional Perspectives*. London and New York: Routledge, pp. 85-100.)

—. 2003. *European Film Industries*, London, BFI.

JACKSON, P. and PENROSE, J. (eds). 1993. *Construction of Race, Place, and Nation:*

Postmodernity and Transnational Feminist Practices. Minneapolis: University of Minnesota Press.

—. 1994. *Construction of Race, Place, and Nation. Postmodernity and Transnational Feminist Practices*. Minneapolis, IN: University of Minnesota Press.

JOHNSTON, C. 1973. *Notes on Women's Cinema*. London: BFI.

—. 1988. Critical Strategies. (*In* Penley, C. (ed.). *Feminism and Film Theory*. New York/London: Routledge/BFI, pp. 36-56.)

JONES, K. 1996. Tangled Up in Blue: The Cinema of Olivier Assayas-French Film Director. *Film Comment*, 32.1 (January): 50-58.

JORDAN, B. and MORGAN-TAMOSUNAS, R. (eds). 1998. *Contemporary Spanish Cinema*. Manchester and New York: Manchester University Press.

JOUSSE, T. 2003. *Pendant les travaux, le cinéma reste ouvert*. Paris: Cahiers du cinéma.

KEMP, P. 2004. I'm Not Scared. *Sight and Sound*, 14 (3): 46-47.

KENNEDY, B. 2002. *Deleuze and Cinema: The Aesthetics of Sensation*. Edinburgh, UK: Edinburgh University Press.

KINDER, M. 1993. *Blood Cinema: The Reconstruction of National Identity in Spain*. Berkeley: University of California Press.

—, (ed.). 1997. *Refiguring Spain: Cinema/Media/Representation*. Durham and London: Duke University Press.

KOEHLER, R. 2006. Arthur and the Invisibles. Arthur et les minimoys. *Variety*. (21 December). [Online.] Available:

http://www.variety.com/review/VE1117932356.html?categoryid=31&cs=1&p=.

KOVÁCS, K. 1991. The Plain in Spain. *Quarterly Review of Film and Video*, 14(3): 17-46.

KRUGER, A. 1994. Léon. *Première*, 211: 40, novembre.

KUHN, A. 1982. *Women's Pictures: Feminism and Cinema*. New York and London: Routledge and Kegan Paul.

—. 1990. Textual Politics. (*In* Erens, P. (ed.). *Issues in Feminist Film Criticism*. Bloomington and Indianapolis: University of Indiana Press, pp. 250-67.)

LAGNY, M., ROPARS, M-C. and Pierre, SORLIN, P. (eds). 1990. *L'état d'auteur* Spec. issue of *Hors Cadre* 8: printemps.

LANDY, M. 2000. *Italian Film*. Cambridge, Mass.: Cambridge University Press.

LAVIOSA, F. 2003a. Intervista con Francesca Archibugi. La famiglia post-moderna nella sua firma d'autore. (*In* Vitti, A. (ed.). *Incontri con il cinema italiano*. Caltanisetta: Sciascia Editore, pp. 375–386.)

—. 2003b. Themes and Motifs in the Cinema of Francesca Archibugi. *Kinema*. [Online.] Available: http://www.kinema.uwaterloo.ca/lavi2-032.htm.

—. 2004. Life Apprenticeship in Francesca Archibugi's Cinema. (*In* Everett, W., Hope, W. and Goodbody, A. (eds). *Italian Cinema: New Directions*. Oxford-Bern: Peter Lang, pp. 201–27.)

LEBLANC, G. 1969. La notion de production: producteurs/produits. *Cinéthique*, 4: 1.

—. 1987. Le clip et le clap ou l'esthétique publicitaire. (*In* Hennebelle, G. and Prédal, R. (eds). L'influence de la télévision sur le cinéma. *CinémAction*, 44: 98–103.)

LEQUERET, É. 2002. Les inconnues de l'après-Canal+ (dossier). *Cahiers du Cinéma*, 570: 68–71, juillet-août.

LEV, P. 1993. *The Euro-American Cinema*. Austin: University of Texas Press.

LEVANTESI, A. 1995. Il neo-bildungsroman di Francesca Archibugi. (*In* Brugiamolini, F., Gabelli, S. and Capelli, L. (eds). *Le donne riprendono l'infanzia ovvero regie al femminile e maternitá da Jane Campion a Francesca Archibugi*. Roma: Dino Audino Editore, pp. 29–45.)

—, (ed.). 1996. *Francesca Archibugi*, Roma: Alphabet.

—. 1998. Padri, figli e nipoti: il cinema di Francesca Archibugi. (*In* Micciché, L. (ed.). *Schermi opachi. Il cinema italiano degli anni '80*. Venezia: Marsilio, pp. 107–15.)

LEYDON, Joe. 1998. Rev. of *Abre los ojos*, dir. Alejandro Amenábar. *Variety*, CCCLXIXX/9: 64, January 12.

—. Rev. of *Thesis* (*Tesis*), dir. Alejandro Amenábar. *Variety*, CCCLXII/4: 73–74.

LOUSTALOT, G. 2006. Angel-A. *Première*, 348: 44, février.

LYOTARD, J-F. 1971. *Discours, figure*. Paris: Klincksieck.

MALAVASI, L. 2002. Amnésia. *Cineforum*, 414: 68–69.

—, (ed.). 2005. *Gabriele Salvatores*. Milano: Il Castoro.

MALRAUX, A. 1978. *The Voices of Silence*. Princeton: Princeton University Press.

MANZOLI, G. 2001. Riportando a casa i cari estinti. *Cineforum*, XLI (409): 19–21, October.

MARCHANTE, O. R. 2002. *Amenábar, vocación de intriga*. Madrid: Paginas de Espuma.

MARCUS, M. 1986. *Italian Film in the Light of Neorealism*. Princeton, NJ: Princeton University Press.

MARGOLICK, D. 2002. Vivendi's Mr. Universe. *Vanity Fair*, 500: 240–77.

MARÍAS, M. and VEGA, F. 1983. En el camino del Sur. Una conversación con Víctor Erice. *Papeles de Cine Casablanca*, 31–32: 59–70, julio-agosto.

MARIE, M. 1998. *La Nouvelle Vague: une école artistique*. Paris: Nathan Université.

MARKER, C. 1999. Sleepless in Paris: J'ai pas sommeil (Denis, 1993). (*In* Powrie, P. (ed.). *French Cinema in the 1990s: Continuity and Difference*. Oxford, UK, Oxford University Press, pp. 137–47.)

MARRONE, G. 1999a. Il nuovo cinema italiano: pregiudizi, realtá e promesse. (In Marrone, G. (ed.). *New Landscapes in Contemporary Italian Cinema*. 17: 7–13.)

—. 1999b. *New Landscapes in Contemporary Italian Cinema*. 17.

MARTINEZ, D. 2005. Mar adentro: l'évasion du poète. *Positif*, 528: 43–44, février.

MARTIN-MÁRQUEZ, S. 1999. *Feminist Discourse and Spanish Cinema: Sight Unseen*. Oxford: Oxford University Press.

MASSARA, D. 2006. Storia delle donne nella storia del cinema delle registe. *Donne e conoscenza storica*. [Online.] Available:
http://www.url.it/donnestoria/film/storia/immstorsimposio06.htm.

MAULE, R. 2000. Death and Cinematic Reflexivity in Alejandro Amenábar's Tesis. (*In* Guízar Álvarez, E. and Brígido Corachán, A. (eds). *Lugares Sin Limites: Cinema of the 80s and 90s in Latin America, Spain, and Portugal*. Torre de Papel Spec. Issue 10: 65–76, Spring.)

—. 1998. De-authorizing the Auteur: Postmodern Politics of Interpellation in Contemporary European Cinema. *Postmodernism in the Cinema*. (*In* DEGLI-ESPOSTI, C. (ed.). Oxford: Berghahn Books, pp. 140–62).

—. 2003. The Multiple Commitments of the Film Author. (*In* ANTONINI, A. (ed.). *Il film e i suoi multipli/Film and its Multiples*. Udine: Forum, pp. 241–50.)

—. 2005a. *Une histoire sans noms: les femmes et le concept d'auteur au cinéma des premiers temps.* (*In* Maule, R. (ed.). *Femmes et cinéma muet: nouvelles problématiques, nouvelles methodologies. Cinémas*, Spec. issue 16(1): 35–58, Fall.)

—. 2005b. Présentation. *Femmes et cinéma muet: nouvelles problématiques, nouvelles methodologies.* Spec. issue of *Cinémas.* 16(1): 9–20, Fall.

—. 2006. The Dialectics of Trans-national Identity and Female Desire in the Films of Claire Denis. (*In* Dennison, S. & Lim, S. H. (eds). *Remapping World Cinema: Identity, Culture and Politics in Film.* London and New York: Wallflower Press, pp. 73–85.)

MAYNE, J. 1990. *The Woman at the Keyhole.* Bloomington and Indianapolis: Indiana University Press.

—. 1994. *Directed By Dorothy Arzner.* Bloomington, Ill. and Indianapolis, In.: Indiana University Press.

—. 2005. *Claire Denis.* Urbana and Chicago, Ill.: University of Illinois Press.

MAZDON, L. (ed.). 2001. *France on Film: Reflections on Popular French Cinema.* London: Wallflower.

MCCABE, C. 1985. *Theoretical Essays: Film, Linguistics, Literature.* Manchester: Manchester University Press.

MELLENCAMP, P. 1994. *Indiscretions: Avant Garde Film, Video, and Feminism.* Bloomington and Indianapolis: Indiana University Press.

—. 1995a. *A Fine Romance...: Five Ages of Film Feminism.* Philadelphia, PA: Temple University Press.

—. 1995b. Il neo-bildungsroman di Francesca Archibugi. (*In* Brugiamolini, F. Gabelli, S. and Capelli, L. (eds). *Le donne riprendono l'infanzia ovvero regie al femminile e maternitá da Jane Campion a Francesca Archibugi.* Roma: Dino Audino Editore, pp. 29–45.)

MERKEL, F. 1992. *Il cinema di Gabriele Salvatores.* Roma: Dino Audino.

MERLEAU-PONTY, M. 1964. *L'oeil et l'esprit.* Paris: Gallimard.

MET, P. 2003. Looking for Trouble: The Dialectics of Lack and Excess. Claire Denis, Trouble Every Day (2001). *Kinoeye: New Perspectives on European Film.* [Online.] Available: http://www.kinoeye.org/03/07/delrio07.php.

MICCICHÉ, L. 1998. Il lungo decennio grigio. (*In* Miccichè, L. (ed.). *Schermi opachi: il cinema italiano degli anni '80* . Venezia: Marsilo, pp. 3–16.)

MILLER, T. 1998. Hollywood and the World. (*In* Hill, J. & Church Gibson P. (eds). *The Oxford Guide to Film Studies.* Oxford: Oxford University Press, pp. 371–381.)

MINH-HA, T. T. 1989. *Woman, Native, Other: Writing Postcoloniality and Feminism.* Bloomington and Indianapolis: Indiana University Press.

—. 1991. *When the Moon Waxes Red: Representation, Gender, and Cultural Politics.* New York and London, Routledge.

MODLESKI, T. 1991. *Feminism Without Women: Culture and Criticism in a "Postfeminist" Age.* New York: Routledge.

MOHANRAM, R. 1999. *Black Body: Women, Colonialism, and Space.* Minneapolis, MN: University of Minnesota Press.

MOLINA-FOX, V. 1977. *New Cinema in Spain.* London: British Film Institute.

MONTINI, F. (ed.). 1988a. *Una generazione in cinema: esordi ed esordienti italiani.1976–1988.* Venezia: Marsilio Editori.

—. 1988b. *I novissimi, gli esordienti nel cinema italiano degli anni '80.* Torino: Nuova Eri.

— and SPILA, P. 1990. Il cinema di Gianni Amelio. Intervista. *Cinecritica*, 19–20: 7–12, ottobre1990/marzo 1991.

MORAN, A. (ed.). 1996. *Film Policy: International, National, and Regional Perspectives.* London and New York: Routledge.

MORETTI, F. 1994. *Opere mondo.* Torino: Einaudi.

MORICE, J. 1997. *Nénette et Boni. Télérama.* [Online.] Available: http://www.telerama.fr/cine/film.php?id=42008.

MOUNT, J. 2001. Dread Again. *Sight and Sound*, 53: 18–19, 53, November.

MULVEY, L. 2000. Visual Pleasure and Narrative Cinema. (*In* Kaplan, E. A. (ed.). *Feminism and Film.* Oxford, UK: Oxford University Press, pp. 34–47.)

MURPHY, K. 1992. The Color of Home. *Film Comment*, 28: 62–63. September-October.

NANCY, J-L. 2005. *L'Intrus selon Claire Denis.* [Online.] Available: http://remue.net/spip.php?article679.

NESSELSON, L. 2006. Angel-A. *Variety.* 23, 28. 26 December.

NOWELL-SMITH, G., RICCI, S. (eds). 1998. *Hollywood and Europe: Economics, Culture, National Identity: 1945–95*. London: British Film Institute.

O'HEALY, À. 1999. Are the Children Watching Us? The Roman Films of Francesca Archibugi. (*In* Marrone, G. (ed.). *New Landscapes in Contemporary Italian Cinema. Annali d'Italianistica*, pp. 121–36.)

OLIVER, K. and WALSH, L. 2004. *Contemporary French Feminism*. Oxford; New York: Oxford University Press.

PASSERINI, L. 1993. The Women's Movement in Italy and the Events of 1968. (*In* Cicioni, M. and Prunster, N. (eds). *Visions and Revisions: Women in Italian Culture*. Oxford: Berg, pp. 167–82.)

PAYÁN, M. J. 2001. *Cine español actual*. Madrid: Ediciones JC.

PENLEY, C. (ed.). 1988. *Feminism and Film Theory*. New York: Routledge, 1988.

PERANSON, M. 2003. Reattaching the Broken Thread: Olivier Assayas on Film-making and Film Theory. *Cinema Scope*, 14 (Spring): 30–39.

PEREIRA PRATA, A. 2003. Women's Political Organizations in the Transition to Democracy: An assessment of the Spanish and Italian Cases. *Journal of Women's History*, 15(3): 143–47, Autumn.

PESCATORE, G. 2006. *L'ombra dell'autore: teoria e storia dell'autore cinematografico*. Roma: Carrocci.

PETRIE, D. 1991. *Creativity and Constraint in the British Film Industry*. London: MacMillan.

—, (ed.). 1992. *Screening Europe: Image and Identity in Contemporary European Cinema*. London: BFI.

PETROCCHI, F. 1996. *Il cinema della televisione italiana: La produzione cinematografica di RAI e Fininvest (1976/1994)*. Roma: RAI ERI.

PIALAT, M. 1987. La ligne droite. Entretien avec Maurice Pialat. *Cahiers du Cinéma*, 399: 6–7; 60–62, septembre.

PINTO, F., BARZOLETTI, G. and SALIZZATO, C. (eds). 1988. *La televisione presenta: la produzione cinematografica della RAI 1965–1975*. Venezia: Marsilio Editori.

POLAN, D. 2001. Auteur Desire. *Screening the Past*. [Online.] Available: http://www.latrobe.edu.au/screeningthepast/firstrelease/fr0301/dpfr12a.htm.

PORTUGES, C. 1996. Le Colonial Féminin: Women Directors Interrogate French Cinema. (*In* Sherzner, D. (ed.). *Cinema, Colonialism, Postcolonialism: Perspectives from the French and Francophone World*. Austin, TX: University of Texas Press, pp. 30–102.)

POWRIE, P. 1990. *Contemporary French Fiction by Women: Feminist Perspectives*. Manchester: Manchester University Press.

—, (ed.). 1997. *French Cinema in the 1980s: Nostalgia and the Crisis of Masculinity*. Oxford: Clarendon Press.

—. 1999. *French Cinema in the 1990s: Continuity and Difference*. Oxford: Oxford University Press.

—. 2001. *Jean-Jacques Beineix*. Manchester: Manchester University Press.

PRÉDAL, R. 1988. *900 cinéastes français d'aujourd'hui*. Paris: Cerf.

PROJANSKY, S. 2001. *Watching Rape: Film and Television in Postfeminist Culture*. New York and London: New York University Press.

PUTTNAM, D. 1997. *The Undeclared War: The Struggle of the World's Film Industry*. London: Harper Collins.

QUARESIMA, L. 1992. Non è carino. *Cinema & Cinema*, Spec. Issue, XVIII(62): 32–35, settembre-dicembre.

—. 1994. Gabriele Salvatores. (*In* Costa, A. (ed.). Dossier: Cinema italiano anni novanta. *Lettera dall'Italia*, 9 (36), pp. 27–43.)

RABINOVITZ, L. 1991. *Points of Resistance: Women, Power and Politics in the New York Avant-garde Cinema, 1943–71*. Urbana and Chicago: University of Illinois Press.

—. 2005. Past Imperfect: Feminism and Social Histories of Silent Film. (*In* Maule, R., (ed.). *Femmes et cinéma muet: nouvelles problématiques, nouvelles methodologies. Cinémas*, Spec. issue 16(1): 21–34, Fall.)

RABINOW, P. (ed.). 1984. *The Foucault Reader*. New York: Pantheon Books.

REID, M. 1996. Colonial Observation: Interview with Claire Denis. *Jump Cut*, 40: 67–73.

RICOEUR, P. 1977. *The Rule of Metaphor: Multi-disciplinary Studies of the Creation of Meaning in Language*. [1975]. Czerny, R., McLaughlin, K. and Costello, J. (trans.). Toronto and Buffalo: University of Toronto Press.

RODOWICK, D. N. 1997. *Gilles Deleuze's Time Machine*. Durham and London: Duke University Press.

—. 2000. Unthinkable Sex: Conceptual Personae and the Time-Image. *Invisible Culture: An Electronic Journal for Visual Studies*. [Online.] Available:
http://www.rochester.edu/in_visible_culture/issue3/rodowick.htm.

—. 2001. *Reading the Figural, or, Philosophy after the New Media*. Durham & London: Duke University Press.

RODRIGUEZ-ORTEGA, V. 2005. 'Snuffing' Hollywood: Transmedia Horror in *Tesis*. *Senses of Cinema*, 36. [Online.] Available:
http://www.sensesofcinema.com/contents/05/36/tesis.html.

ROLLET, B. 1998. *Coline Serreau*. Manchester, UK: Manchester University Press.

ROMNEY, J. 2000. Claire Denis Interviewed by Jonathan Romney. *The Guardian Unlimited*. [Online.] Available:
http://film.guardian.co.uk/interview/interviewpages/0,,338784,00.html.

—. 2004. Stop Making Sense. *Sight & Sound*. [Online]. Available:
http://www.bfi.org.uk/sightandsound/feature/238/.

RONDOLINO, G. 1995. A Film History without Authors? (*In* Boschi, A. and Manzoli, G. (eds). Oltre l'autore I. *Fotogenia*, 2.)

ROSENBAUM, J. 2001. The Hit Parade: Rosenbaum's Top 40 Films of 2000. *Chicago Reader*. [Online.] Available: http://www.chicagoreader.com/movies/archives/2001/0101/010105_3.html.

RUSSELL, C. 1995. *Narrative Mortality: Death, Closure, and New Wave Cinemas*. Minneapolis: University of Minnesota Press.

SALVATORES, G. 2005. Interview with the author on 20 September 2005. Montréal. [Cassette recording in possession of author.]

SARRIS, A. 1991. Sarris' film column. *New York Observer*, 1 April.

SAURA, A. 1997. El nuevo cine español. *Viridiana*, 15: 103–17, March.

SCHATZ, T. 2003. The Whole equation of Pictures. (*In* Wright Wexman, V. (ed.). *Film and Authorship*. New Brunswick: Rutgers University Press, pp. 89–95.)

SCHWARTZ, R. 1986. *Spanish Film Directors (1950-1985): 21 Profiles*. Metuchenm N.J. and London: Scarecrow Press.

SEMPERE, A. 2000. *Alejandro Amenábar: Cine en las venas*. Madrid: Nuer Ediciones.

SERCEAU, D. 1987. Tourner pour la Télé ou pour le cinéma: des réalisateurs parlent. (*In* Hennebelle, G. and Prédal, R. (eds). L'influence de la télévision sur le cinéma. *CinémAction*, 44: 106–11.)

SESTI, M. (ed.). 1994. *Nuovo Cinema Italiano: gli autori, i film, le idee*. Roma-Napoli: Theoria.

—. 1995. Non sono bambini, sono persone di pochi anni. (*In* Proto, C. (ed.). *Francesca Archibugi*. Roma: Dino Audino, pp. 10–14.)

—, (ed.). 1996. *La « scuola » italiana. Storia, strutture e immaginario di un altro cinema (1988–1996)*. Venezia: Marsilio Editori.

SHERZNER, D. (ed.). 1996. *Cinema, Colonialism, Postcolonialism: Perspectives from the French and Francophone World*. Austin, TX: University of Texas Press.

SHOHAT, E. and STAM, R. 1994. *Unthinking Eurocrentrism: Multiculturalism and the Media*. London and New York: Routledge.

SIMON, J.-P. 1983. Énonciation et narration. *Communications*, 38: 155–91.

SISKA, W. 1979. Metacinema: A Modern Necessity. *Film Quarterly*, 7(1): 285–89.

SKLAR, R. 2005. The Sea Inside. *Cineaste*, XXX(2): 52–53, Spring.

SMITH, D. 2005. *L'Intrus*: an Interview with Claire Denis. [Online.] Available: www.sensesofcinema.com/contents/ 05/35/claire_denis_interview.html.

SMITH, P. J. 2001. The Others. *Sight and Sound*, 53: 53–54, November.

SORLIN, P. 1996. *Italian National Cinema, 1896-1996*. London and New York: Routledge.

STAIGER, J. 2004. Authorship Studies and Gus Van Sant. *Film Criticism* 29.1: 1–22 (Fall).

—. 2003a. Synthesizing Feminism, Theory, and History. Symposium Review. 2003–2004 Oberman Humanities Symposium. 101 Becker Communication Building, University of Iowa, Iowa City, IA, USA, 7 November 2003.

—. 2003b. Authorship Approaches. (*In* Staiger, J. and Gerstner, D. A. (eds). *Authorship and Film*. New York: Routledge, pp. 27–57.)

STRAUSS, F. 1990. Mémoires d'exil. Féminin colonial. *Cahiers du Cinéma*, 434: 28–33.

TALENS J. and ZUNZUNEGUI, S. 1998. *Modes of Representation in Spanish Cinema*. Minneapolis, MN: University of Minnesota Press.

TARR, C. and ROLLET, B. 2001. *Cinema and the Second Sex: Women's Film-making in France in the 1980s and 1990s*. New York and London: Continuum.

TERRASA, J. 2002. Les écrans noirs d'Alejandro Amenábar: des voix en quête d'images. (*In* Berthier, N. (ed.). *Penser le cinéma espagnol (1975–2000)*. Lyon: GRIMH/GRIMIA, Université Lumière-Lyon 2, pp. 161–71.)

TESSON, C. and TOUBIANA, S. 1998. Quelques vagues plus tard: table ronde avec Olivier Assayas, Claire Denis, Cédric Kahn et Noémie Lvovsky. *Cahiers du Cinéma. Nouvelle Vague: une légende en question*, spec. issue: 70–75, décembre.

TESSON, C., PAQUOT, C. and Roger GARCIA, R. (eds). 2001. *L'Asie à Hollywood*. Paris: Cahiers du cinema/ Festival International du Film de Locarno.

THIBAUDEAU, P. 2002. Réalités virtuelles et destines manipulés à travers Abre los ojos de Alejandro Amenábar et Nadie conoce a nadie de Mateo Gil. *In* Berthier, N. (ed.). *Penser le cinéma espagnol (1975–2000)*. Lyon: GRIMH/GRIMIA, Université Lumière-Lyon 2, pp. 143–60.)

TOFFETTI, S., and TASSONE, A. (eds). 1992. *Maurice Pialat. L'enfant sauvage*. Torino: Lindau.

TUORNABUOI, L. 1993. Il grande cocomero, Review. *La Stampa*. [Online.] Available: http://www.mymovies. it/dizionario/critica.asp?id=5244.

TORRI, B. 1996. Un po' di luce. Limiti e prospettive dell'intervento dello stato nella produzione e nella distribuzione. (*In* Sesti, M. (ed.) *La « scuola » italiana. Storia, strutture e immaginario di un altro cinema (1988–1996)*. Venezia: Marsilio Editori, pp. 213–17.)

TOUBIANA, S. 1991. Trajectoire en 20 points. *Cahiers du Cinéma*, 443–444: 43–48.

——. 1999. Beau travail! *Cahiers du Cinéma*, 539: 28–31, octobre.

TRUFFAUT, F. 1954. Une certaine tendance du cinéma français. *Cahiers du Cinéma*, 31: 15–28, janvier.

TRUONG, N. 2003. Claire Denis: 'je suis une être séparé'. *Le Monde de l'éducation*, 316: 72–77, juillet-août.

TUBAU, I. 1983. *Crítica cinematográfica española: Bazin contra Aristarco, la gran controversia de los años sesenta*. Barcelona: Edicions Universitat de Barcelona.

VERNON, K. 1997. Reading Hollywood in/and Spanish Cinema: From Trade Wars to Transculturation. (*In* Kinder, M. (ed.). *Refiguring Spain: Cinema/Media/Representation*. Durham and London: Duke University Press, pp. 35–64.)

VINCENDEAU, G. 1986. Women as Auteur-e-s: Notes from Créteil. *Screen*, 27(3–4): 156–62, May-August.

——. 1987. Women's Cinema, Film Theory, and Feminism in France. *Screen*, 28(4): 4–18.

——. 1990. Therapeutic Realism: Maurice Pialat's A nos amours (1983). (*In* Hayward, S. and Vincendeau, G. (eds). *French Film: Texts and Contexts*. London and New York: Routledge, pp. 257–68.)

——, (ed.). 1995. *Encyclopedia of European Cinema*. New York: Facts on Life.

——. 1996. *The Companion to French Cinema*. London: Cassell.

——. 1998. Issues in European Cinema. (*In* Hill, J. and Church Gibson P. (eds). *The Oxford Guide to Film Studies*. Oxford: Oxford University Press, pp. 440–48.)

VITTI, A. 2003. Un profilo dell'identità del nuovo cinema italiano tra crisi, televisione e omologazione culturale. (*In* Morosini, R. and Vitti, A. (eds) *In Search of Italia*. Pesaro: Metauro Edizioni, pp. 235–56.)

WILLIAMS, A. 1992. *Republic of Images: A History of French Film-making*. Harvard: Harvard University Press.

WILLIAMS, M. 1999. French Filmmaker of the Year. *Variety*, 373: 105, January 11–17.

WILSON, E. 1999. *French Cinema Since 1950: Personal Histories*

ZANCHI, C. 1996. La lenta eutanasia di un articolo. Archeologia e disavventure del '28'. (*In* Sesti, M. (ed.) *La «scuola» italiana. Storia, strutture e immaginario di un altro cinema (1988–1996)*. Venezia: Marsilio Editori, pp. 219–37.)

INDEX